Radio:
The Resilient Medium

Papers from the
third conference of the
ECREA Radio Research Section

Published by the
Centre for Research in Media and Cultural Studies,
University of Sunderland,
Sunderland,
United Kingdom SR1 3SD

A catalogue record for this book is available from the British Library.

Typeset at the Centre for Research in Media and Cultural Studies.

Cover design by John Bullar, bpd, Tynemouth, UK.

Printed in the United Kingdom by
Copytech (UK) Limited, Peterborough.

ISBN 978-0-9929805-0-4

Radio:
The Resilient Medium

Papers from the
third conference of the
ECREA Radio Research Section

Edited by
Madalena Oliveira, Grażyna Stachyra and Guy Starkey

Contents

Part One: Technologies

Part Two: Geographies

Part Three: Histories

Introduction
Madalena Oliveira, Grażyna Stachyra and Guy Starkey

Radio is undoubtedly a resilient medium. This assertion can be evidenced in a number of ways, any of which may be contested, but many of which demonstrate a robustness that lends a good deal of credibility to such a claim. That its history as a medium spans more than a hundred years is incontestable, as it is generally accepted that the Canadian inventor Reginald Fessenden made an experimental broadcast of audio content alternating between music and speech in 1906. We are also fast approaching the centenaries of the inauguration of 'wireless' broadcasting services, experimental at first, in the 1920s that are very well documented and evidenced. The technology demonstrated around the turn of the nineteenth century by the Italian inventor Guglielmo Marconi and others as suitable for point-to-point transmission of coded messages is used today not only for radio broadcasting, but also for the distribution of newer media, some of which combine visual content with sound and often using point-to-point principles very similar to Marconi's. Some electronic content-distribution technology is even commonly referred to today as being 'wireless', a term which once referred only to what we now usually call 'radio', then became old-fashioned and yet is once again a widely-recognised signifier of modernity.

As newer media have appeared and challenged radio's once dominant position as a means of simultaneous communication with large and unseen audiences, it has adapted to those challenges - firstly by becoming portable, thanks to the development of the transistor, and secondly by becoming interactive through its readiness to embrace many of the opportunities to engage with its audiences offered by such newer phenomena as web sites, social networking and digital broadcasting. The medium may now be heard through many more platforms than the original, bulky wireless receiver and even the once modern transistor radio might earlier have suggested might become possible. We carry about with us the technological capacity to tune in to radio stations via our mobile phones and other 'connected' devices, whether using an app we have downloaded or a built-in FM receiver. Furthermore, there are few regions of the world where radio has not established itself and where it does not remain a popular means of accessing audio content that is at various times informative, entertaining and educational.

This collection of academic papers from a number of leading scholars of radio studies is organised in three sections: technologies, geographies and histories. It presents further and far more detailed evidence in support of of our bold assertion that radio is a resilient medium. It is a durable outcome of the third conference of the Radio Research Section of the European Communication Research and Education Association (ECREA), held at the University of Sunderland London Campus in September 2013, at which more than a hundered scholars and practitioners shared their research and practice. Of course, not every word, idea, perspective, research finding or networking opportunity encountered at a conference can be preserved in book form, but nonetheless this selection of papers has been subjected to a two-stage process of double-blind peer review in order to ensure academic rigour, and it does represent some of the best academic work presented among the eclectic surroundings of the curious mix of old and new architecture that is London Docklands. Neither is this is an uncritical account of the history or the nature of radio, and many of the chapters problematise the medium in new and challenging ways, presenting original research data and analyses that allow readers to draw their own conclusions about the resilience of radio.

Technologies

Technology of various kinds enables radio producers to communicate with radio audiences, be it through production, dissemination or interaction. Most production technology used in radio is now digital in nature, although it is only in a handful of countries that digital transmission has become popular. Interactivity, though, in all its various forms, is now almost ubiquitous - even in the radio industries of the developing world. Radio is, however, not *defined* by the technology it exploits for its various purposes, but rather by its forms, genres and essential characteristics, to which we return later in this volume. Technological development has, however, contributed to the evolution of radio in many ways which will become apparent.

Predicting the future is notoriously problematic, and especially so when the subject is technology, but the first section of the book opens with a well-argued and evidenced suggestion by Richard Berry that the synergies already developed between radio and the internet are here to stay. He recognises its potential as a platform for distribution, but says the strength of broadcasting technology means radio will mainly use the internet for interaction. Stanisław Jędrzejewski provides a road map through the various developmental stages of digital transmission technology, examining along the way a range of digital platforms and forms found in radio. Then Joanna Bachura-Wojtasik considers some of the effects of the technological transformation of the audio sphere, particularly on audiences and programming for them that can be described as 'cultural'. In the fourth chapter, Ana Isabel Reis focuses on radio news, drawing on a case study in Portugal to ask whether sound is still dominant or whether the development of radio websites has led to a greater focus on text and image. In turn, Paulina Czarnek's focus is on entertainment on commercial radio in Poland in an obviously convergent world of mediatisation. In a comparative study involving both Italy and Spain, Toni Sellas and Tiziano Bonini examine the practices of the content producers working on the social networking of eight public and private radio stations in those countries. Susana Herrera Damas and José Luis Requejo Alemán drill down through the chatter of social networking in Spain to explore the use of Twitter by three prominent music stations and find it is predominently used by them for promoting their own brand, rather than to really engage with their listeners. Finally, in reminding us that the steady 'progress' radio transmission technology has made into the digital domain is a relatively recent phenomenon, Evangelia Karathanasopoulou asks if something intrinsic to the medium has been lost in the process, because of the progressive elimination of interference.

Geographies

In our second section we present nine chapters we have characterised as 'geographies', either of particular lands or of radio landscapes. Each one relates the medium of radio to political, social or cultural phenomena in a specific place - and, in each place, radio has a significant role to play. We visit Africa, Europe, Australasia and Latin America.

The section opens with Esther Dorn-Fellerman's exploration of community radio in South Africa and the nature of interaction with and participation in radio stations in places where access to other media can be limited. Mirosława Wielopolska-Szymura examines issues around identity, comparing traditional analogue broadcasters with internet-only radio stations, asking whether the latter might play as significant a role in community building in Poland and elsewhere. Grażyna Stachyra considers why that country's radio stations still need listeners to express their emotions when most of them have marginalised conversation on air because of rigorous formatting and trivialisation of content to the extent that the game show is one of the last genres to include it. Paradoxically, she concludes, it is not the prize on which the game show is focused, but the dialogue involved in winning it. In considering the motivations of community radio volunteers in Western Australia, Simon Order applies a theoretical framework of value to three stations in Perth. He finds active participation to be motivated more by selfishness than altruism, although it does bring benefits to wider audiences. Journalists working in public broadcasting for minority language communities in Scotland and the Basque Country are investigated by Irati Agirreazkuenaga, Ainara Larrondo and Koldo Meso, who observe the effects of convergence on their daily routines, professionalism and job satisfaction. Then Emma Rodero, Lluís Mas, Olatz Larrea and María Blanco visit the fictitious English village of Ambridge to explore the soundscape occupied by *The Archers* and the ways in which traditional radio soap opera can be transformed online and in podcasting. The origins, the evolution and the current status of the third sector of free and community radio in Spain are explained by Carmen Peñafiel, who identifies a range of collaborative initiatives as a response to challenges to the very existence of the sector. An historical and sociological perspective is then adopted by Carlos Eduardo Esch and Nélia R. Del Bianco, who use original survey data to propose solutions to very low levels of satisfaction with public service broadcasting among Brazilian citizens. Finally in this section, Urszula Doliwa examines religious radio broadcasting in Poland and visits a community station to ask whether engaging with faith-based audiences risks alienating others.

Histories

The third section of the book unites a collection of chapters dedicated to specific histories of the medium, be they of individual genres or of particular radio stations. Madalena Oliveira investigates the development of radio comedy as a genre which in Portugal is particularly inspired by news and current affairs stories as well as the formats in which such content is normally reported. As such, she suggests, comedy on radio represents an aural barometer of society and a critical voice of some significance in wider democratic discourse. Then, Ania Mauruschat explains the development of *avant-garde* experimentation with noise in radio art in Germany, as exemplified in the *Hörspiel* and 'extended' radio before and after the rise of the Nazis, and which actions contributed to the 'liberation' of noise research. Karolina Albińska focuses on visualisation. Reconsidering the concepts of 'theatre of the imagination' and of 'theatre of the mind', she analyses some examples of 'visualised' audio theatre and advocates the further visualisation of radio drama as a consequence of radio's role in media convergence. Monika Białek also investigates convergence, with an emphasis on the radio documentary, as she traces the blurring of boundaries between different narrative genres through the appropriation of creative production practices where once only genuine actuality would suffice. Then, Elżbieta Pleszkun-Olejniczakowa compares past with present and further examines the relationship between artistic radio, reportage and technology in the evolution of culture. Our attention to radio drama is sustained by Aleksandra Pawlik, who explores the development of radio series in Poland and the likelihood that only public radio can preserve the genre, because of the responsibility it has for maintaining high standards in broadcasting. Finally, Rogério Santos examines the contribution of Rádio Clube Português after the splitting of its AM and FM frequencies to the cultural and political life of Portugal, mainly during the 1950s and 1960s, and the station's relationship with the Salazar government.

At the end of the book you will find biographies of the authors, written by the authors.

Acknowledgements

The editors wish to thank the authors for their thoughtful and well-researched contributions to the book, and their tolerance of any stylistic alterations made to their work in the editing process. The support and encouragement of the former and current directors of the Centre for Research in Media and Cultural Studies, Professors John Storey and Julia Knight, for the hosting of the ECREA Radio Research Section conference at our London Campus in 2013 and for this first book to be published by CRMCS, has been invaluable. We also wish to thank the management and staff of the London Campus of the University of Sunderland, whose support and generous hospitality helped make the conference such a success, as well as the Scientific Committee for their peer reviewing of submissions and the enthusiastic team of Jay, Lianne and Tiffany, for working tirelessly over the three days. Full credits are to be found on the conference website, which remains online as a permanent record of the event at http://radioresearch2013.sunderland.ac.uk. Finally, we wish to thank in advance our colleagues in the Department of Media office in the David Puttnam Media Centre on the St Peter's Campus in Sunderland - currently Amy, Ashleigh, Lianne and Simon - upon whose collective shoulders now falls the additional task of distibuting the book.

Part One
Technologies

Chapter 1

The future of radio is the internet, not *on* the internet
Richard Berry

Abstract

The internet, we were told, was the future of radio. The internet was going to remove the need for broadcast platforms and at a single stroke allow listeners to consume content on an open platform, free of national boundaries and complicated licences. The development of 3G, and now 4G, mobile broadband seemed to add fuel to the argument, with promises of audiences consuming radio via smartphones on the move. There is no doubt that listening online is a growing element of radio's future but it is not *the* future, at least not in isolation. More listeners are consuming radio online, via computers and mobile devices, and this raises an added dilemma, because in the online world the more listeners you have, the more it costs to provide the service, and when you add in the problems of data capping policies the argument forecasting the end of broadcasting begins to unravel.

This chapter argues that while the internet is an important platform for content distribution it is not solely where our future lies; it will be an integral part of the ecosystem but it will not replace FM or digital broadcast technologies, or at least not within our lifetimes. We should, therefore, see the internet not as a platform through which to push content but as a place to engage listeners in conversations and with added content, metadata, visuals and branded experiences.

Keywords: online, internet, multiplatform, social media, interaction, United Kingdom

Introduction

This chapter is about radio and the internet and my choice of words is deliberate. The future for radio has a lot to do with the internet but my argument here is that the future of radio is not the internet as a means of sending programmes to the audience but as a wider tool creating a hybridity in the programme-making process and the listening experience. Great radio content, made by passionate and creative minds will still be at the heart of what radio does, but hybridity offers previously unavailable opportunities that we should consider within the context of programme production and distribution. In the month that followed the Radio: the Resilient Medium conference in London, the BBC's Head of Radio, Helen Boaden, addressed some of the challenges that radio faces. 'Digital technologies,' she warned, 'have disrupted our listeners' habits, our business models and many of our approaches to broadcasting. And we could easily be put off our stride. Now more than ever it seems important to face the world as it is, understand and marshal our strengths, understand our vulnerabilities and begin to adapt for a changing future. Because, in amongst the disruption and challenge, lie great potential opportunities' (2013).

It is these challenges and opportunities that I intend to explore. While the internet has created a platform for new and current broadcasters to reach global audiences, often at low cost, to assume that this alone is the future misses the real opportunities that are there. The future is not simply being online; it is using online tools to change the relationship between listener and broadcaster. This is about convergence in an environment where radio stations make content, not just radio shows, and it reflects changes within the industry where the managers once known as Programme Controllers now have the new title of Content Controller, managing content generated at their radio station on both analogue and digital platforms. This is what Paula Cordeiro called 'r@dio', an environment where a 'combination of online and offline contexts results in a hybridisation of practices' (2011: 157). When it comes to convergence in the radio industry, it is not convergence with television that we should be concerned with, but rather it is 'the relationship between radio and the internet that is more important' (Chignell 2009: 124).

The internet is indeed a valuable tool for creative programme makers, acting as it does as an opportunity for radio listeners to hear programmes they would have otherwise missed, using 'listen-again' services or downloading them as podcasts. However, it is the aim of this chapter to look elsewhere for ways in which the internet helps radio build a survival plan for the digital age, rather than to focus on the internet as a solution to our distributive needs.

The myth of the internet as platform panacea

Since the first stations discovered web streaming in the 1990s, a natural assumption developed that a radio station should be broadcasting simultaneously online. The rise of the smartphone during the first part of the next century meant similarly that radio stations also felt compelled to have an 'app' to allow the audience to listen via their mobile phone. While some mobile applications are excellent, many miss the benefits of being on a visually-orientated device that never leaves their owner's side, and this is the crux of this chapter. The internet is more than just a platform through which to push audio streams. Similar debates also suggest that the internet will replace platforms such as DAB, DAB+, HD Radio and even FM. Radio futurologist James Cridland talks frequently about the problems of this binary debate. 'I don't believe it's the right argument to have,' he said, 'because a binary argument like this only works if the correct answer is one or the other... for audiences broadcast is still an attractive option, even when you have internet on the same device' (2013). Hallet (2012) and Anderson (2012) agreed, suggesting that analogue radio will be around for some time to come, despite the promises of a single-platform digital future. When the debate centres on separating radio listening on broadcast platforms and radio listening on internet-based platforms, then the debate leads us down the wrong path.

When radio first appeared on the web, listeners, practitioners and academics agreed that the internet gave fresh opportunities to broadcasters, acknowledging that, for example: 'The possibilities the internet offers a broadcaster with vision and foresight are vast. This new medium's most effective utilisers will be those who approach it with a new way of thinking, rather than relying on an existing mind-set' (Lind & Medoff 1999: 220). Writing a year later, Chris Priestman noted: 'The internet brings a whole range of supplementary benefits... This is a time for radio practitioners and fans to pause for reflection' (2001: 27). A debate then began as to whether the online nature of radio via internet meant that it suddenly became something we could no longer call 'radio'. Some academics, such as David Black (2001) and Jo Tacchi (2000), argued that radio on the internet had as much right to use the name radio, as radio by more traditional means. Tacchi noted that: 'Radio can be said to have certain characteristics, but the evidence suggests that radio is what history says it is: it has no essence since it has already taken, and continues to take, different forms' (2000: 292). David Hendy (2000) also argued that while economic factors could hinder digital developments, (as I will outline later,) increased interactivity was inevitable, and in 2008 the international group of academics behind the DRACE project noted that: 'There are good reasons to believe that the next 10 years will be very important... for radio' (Ala-Fossi *et al* 2008: 7).

In this framework we can consider the developments discussed in this chapter as radio; not necessarily as radio in the conventional sense but as elements that contribute to the radio experience, in the same way that content in an interactive iPad or Android tablet app can now be part of the experience of a watching television programme. The problem here is that debate often centres on the auditory aspects of internet radio, rather than a holistic view of the benefits of radio being on the internet. Just as movie studios and TV networks consider the wider opportunities available outside of their media (Jenkins *et al* 2013) so radio networks and producers should consider what the internet can offer them by being on devices capable of delivering pictures as well as sound. This is a point echoed by Chignell, who suggested that when video and audio share a platform, such as a computer or a mobile device, '...the distinctions between the conventional categories of radio, film and television start to break down completely' (2009: 124). This creates an opportunity to consider how the internet can benefit the radio programme maker.

The presence of the internet radio on the kitchen worktop at home and on apps, means that global radio is at our fingertips. It is as easy to listen to Triple J, CBC Radio 3 or KCRW, as it is to listen to local stations on FM or DAB. That said, in the UK online listening only accounts for around 6 per cent of listening (RAJAR 2013), a figure which is statistically the same as the number of people who weren't able to fully identify how they had listened. The company TuneIn, (the most prolific directory of internet radio streams,) claims to list over 70,000 radio streams attracting 40 million active monthly users (2013). These numbers make some commentators wonder if there is any need to persist with the broadcast model we have had since the 1920s. However, we should realise that, just as technology made the internet seem like a viable proposition for broadcasters, economic and regulatory factors intervened and suddenly broadcasting online became more complicated and more expensive. In July 2013, the UK royalty collection agency PPL (Phonographic Performance Limited) wrote to several US broadcast groups informing them they needed to pay royalties for music heard by listeners in the UK (*Radio Today* 2013). These are not listeners a radio station has asked for, needs or can monetise, yet because they hear the programmes, (and the music within those programmes,) then royalty payments are legally due. This is a reality many stations face, even if it doesn't represent the best solution (Van Den Bulck & Hermans 2011; Wall 2004).

When we consider the success of radio, we often refer to the fact that is a highly portable medium that we can consume anywhere. This was one factor which seemed to hinder the development of internet radio (MacFarland 1997). The arrival of 3G and 4G mobile internet connections seemed then to offer some solution, allowing listeners to consume radio online on mobile devices. However, in the same way in which the political economy of rights restricts development, so does the cost of using the internet on the move for radio listening. If we use typical UK radio listening hours, (as identifed by RAJAR,) of around 21 hours a month as a guide, then in radio listening alone we could consume somewhere between 300 and 600 MB of data. This is before we add in emails, social media, gaming or visiting websites. This might be fine at home, but it represents a problem for mobile listeners. Helen Boaden also referred to this challenge in her speech to the Radio Festival, confirming that: 'Mobile phones are a critical part of our connected future and radio is well suited to listening on-the-go. Yet, as you know, buffering, data charges, bill-shock and poor design are all too common problems when listening on mobile phones. In fact, an average data package of 1GB allows listeners to stream radio for barely an hour a day and then not use their phones at all for Facebook, YouTube, email... ' (2013). It is clear that despite increased speeds and coverage the mobile web is not yet ready to replace broadcast platforms as our primary source of radio listening (Johnson 2012).

In a blog, the Norwegian technologist Gunnars Garfors goes further, noting that when it comes to listening via a mobile telephone, broadcast radio on FM, AM or DAB is also seven times greener than streaming, as it uses less battery power. He refuted political claims that the internet would be a better solution than DAB, saying: 'For a political party to even suggest, on environmental grounds, that radio should be distributed via mobile internet instead of broadcasting, is beyond any reasonable logic' (2013). The problem here is two-fold. Online costs more to deliver and consume, and over reliance on this as a future misses the real power of the internet. Barboutis and Baltzis noted that: 'The economics of webcasting radio and the requirements of its use and operation suggest that the realisation of its promises is more complicated than it looked like at its inception in the mid-nineties' (2012: 120). In this context, we can see that while online listening in isolation can add benefit for some broadcasters, it is by no means a solution to ensuring radio defends its position against radio-like rivals such as Rdio (rdio.com) or iTunes Radio. The solution is, it seems, an amalgam of practices coming together. The arrival of the RadioPlayer in the UK was an indication that this is being understood, and its Managing Director, Micheal Hill, wrote: 'The future of radio isn't FM or DAB or internet – it's all of them, working together seamlessly' (2012).

The arrival of the immersive listener

In 1932, the German dramatist Bertolt Brecht famously suggested that radio ought to be a network of pipes, where listeners had a voice. He suggested that radio imitated the previous forms of media, such as newspapers or theatre, silencing rather than enabling the voices of the audience. The internet, however, might offer radio that much needed backchannel, not only as a means for communication but also as a place to share that communication beyond the studio. Stations such as Now Radio in Edmonton, Canada, actively encourage the audience to engage with them in online spaces, sharing that content on the air and posting it all in a live stream on their website (1023nowradio.com). Presenters make frequent reference to the incoming messages and constantly encourage the audience to 'join the conversation ', by using the website, the app or by sending a text message. This is a station that looks and feels very different and became the most listened-to station in the city within 90 days of launch (Giger 2012). In this setting, the internet is both a means for distributing the programmes globally but also a key tool in the programming-making process, where the audience becomes a constantly engaging source of content in a dialogue between equals.

Just as in television, social media have become a second screen for radio where social exchanges online can be as important as those heard more widely on the radio. If the music played by radio is the same music offered on Spotify, how does the listener choose? Cost might be a factor, as might the ability of radio to curate music but we could also consider how the listening experience makes the listener feel. Could it be that the opportunity to share thoughts and ideas with a community changes the relationship we have with the radio? In his analysis of the use of Facebook in Italy, Tiziano Bonini suggested that it does, saying: 'While until recently the audience was invisible to radio and was confined to its private sphere…today listeners linked to the online profile of a radio programme are no longer invisible or private, and the same goes for the opinions and emotions' (2012: 18). Bonini described social media as an 'umbilical cord' (*ibid*: 24) linking listeners and producers even when the radio is turned off - or even when the programme has ended. In their review of Facebook and radio in the US, Germany and Singapore, Freeman, Klapczynski and Wood noted that while there appeared to be no clear pattern to how radio was using social media it was a trend that was gaining traction. Radio, they concluded, 'is always exploring ways to add value while keeping costs down… [and] continues to look for creative and rewarding ways to connect to their listeners' (2012). Others such as Rooke and Odame (2013) have also examined the ways in which tools such as social media and blogs enhance, develop and influence radio programmes as never before.

In *The Art of Immersion*, Frank Rose talks extensively about how corporate television and film in the United States struggled with how the internet added a new dimension to their industries (2012: 87). Viewers, he noted, were on a journey of control that started with the remote control and ended, via the VCR, with the internet. The funnel, which used to shovel the audience from show to show, is he says, 'irretrievably busted'. Through shows such as *Lost* and *The Office* the studios began to engage with the audience. At the Edinburgh TV Festival in 2013, the actor Kevin Spacey spoke eloquently about the shifting sands of the television audience, noting that audiences no longer seem to care where their stories came from. Platforms are not important; stories are. The audience, Spacey said, are 'hungry for stories and they will talk about it… engage with it with a passion and an intimacy that a blockbuster movie could only dream of' (Spacey 2013). Cordeiro suggested that: 'People and content are in the centre of conversation, using media as part of the process, since web 2.0 tools have allowed them to improve their media experience' (2011: 158).

In this setting listeners contribute to, comment on and share radio content, because if listeners are involved in our stories (Bonini 2012), or if radio can tell a better story than a streaming music service by using this interaction, then the internet can help to differentiate immersive radio programming from music streams which sound like or claim to be radio. Spotify cannot tell a story but radio can and does. Social media can place radio in the role of an aggregating filter, 'delving into niches and re-emerging with a little treasure trove that can be used productively' (Bonini 2011: 18). The listeners provide the stories and the ideas and the radio producer frames them, shares them and uses them to direct further interaction. The impact of social media on the nationally-syndicated NPR programme *Weekend Edition* was anaysed in detail, with the researchers concluding that 'the longer listeners follow *Weekend Edition* on Facebook and/or Twitter, the more engaged with NPR they become' (Robins & Lazano 2010). This has to be good news for programme makers, as it shows how internet-based technologies offer a useful supporting role in engaging with and building audiences. We can also see these trends illustrated very well by Schmidt (2012: 28) in her examination of interactivity in French radio. She considered that: 'Interactivity is very attractive to radio professionals because it ensures dynamism on air while establishing a relationship of proximity with the listener. This can build up a loyal audience'. Just as social media allow the listeners to immerse themselves in the production of speech content, so software systems such as Jelli (jelli.com) and Listener Driven Radio (ldrinteractive.com) allow listeners to influence the music radio stations play. Where stations use these systems, listeners can rate tracks on the radio station site, which then directly influences output. In the case of LDR, the website tells the studio computer which of a number of preselected songs, (from a certain type,) to play. Across the media industry we see movement away from what David Gauntlett has described as the 'sit back and be told' culture that we have been used to (2011: 8).

The ability to then gain further insights into artists played on the radio (Nyre & Ala-Fossi 2008) and then to share this information with friends is becoming part of radio's future. We can see such features as a key part of newer platforms such as the UK RadioPlayer, where listeners can easily tweet about what song they are hearing, a message that may even solicit a reply from the station, thus offering opportunities to recognise listener loyalty, something which may be key to building and maintaining audiences. This is a cross-industry supported venture that developed a common web player for all UK radio stations. All subscribing stations share the same platform, making stations and programmes searchable on web players and the Radioplayer app.

This works very much in the same way as the Electronic Programme Guide does for television. It offers an easy way to find content, without the need to visit each website individually or know their streaming addresses. The company is also working to develop a radio powered by the same technology. In 2013, the BBC announced its Playlister service, which, (much like other tagging services,) would allow listeners to capture the details of songs they like on the radio and then export them to such other platforms as Spotify or YouTube. Tools like these mean that listening to radio via the internet becomes a social experience or one which aids musical discovery and curation. While online listening alone is not a solution to the future, software enhancements make it useful to understanding the audience. Innovations such as InStream by Absolute Radio means logged-in listeners online hear fewer but better-targeted commercials which can be illustrated by graphics or video that, when clicked, take the listener to the client's website. Here we see the radio experience enhanced when using the radio station's mobile application, not simply by offering audio but by adding value as well. Audiences are being asked to be more involved, either by making choices on what to listen to and when via websites (Jackson-Pitts & Harms 2003; Belanger 2012) or engaging with programmes and presenters via social media (Bonini 2012). Indeed, it is often this power to interact that streaming services highlight as their point of differentiation with radio (Friere 2007), but if radio also moves into this space this may cease to be the case, proving that radio is, once again, an adaptable medium, capable of finding a place for itself both through, and in spite of, new technologies.

Radio and screens

The internet not only offers radio programmes an opportunity to interact with the audience, it also allows broadcasters to offer images, video and graphics. In contemporary media, there is a noticeable move towards visualising radio programming; not through the old-fashioned webcam on the wall but through more complex and considered processes of live HD cameras, recorded events and enhanced radio experiences. While this application of the visual may feel contrary to the fundamental principles of what we know radio to be, it is a recognition that contemporary radio listening may be via devices with screens - such as digital televisions, connected radio sets, smartphones or laptops. As Michelle Hilmes said: 'Today radio is a screen medium: we access it through screens both mobile and static, using tactile visual and textual interfaces… Radio crosses platforms' (2013: 44).

The use of screen-based imagery in radio is diverse: encompassing everything from scrolling text, known as DLS (Dynamic Segment Labelling), to on-screen images of artists and the ability to tag songs through services such as iTunes tagging or the BBC Playlister service, much like the ideas outlined by Dubber and Wall (2009). The open source system Radio DNS is also a good example of the how the internet adds value to broadcast radio. A server at the radio station adds a simple code to FM or DAB broadcasts, which, when received by an appropriately equipped device, will instruct the radio (or smartphone) to download images and text from the internet. This is not radio to be looked at all the time, but one with visual opportunities to enhance the experience for '10 per cent of the listeners, 10 per cent of the time' (Piggott 2010).

Since the mid-2000s producers and managers have been experimenting with 'visualised' radio, where listeners can see programmes, as well as hearing them. In the UK, the national BBC radio networks for young people are Radio 1 and Radio 1Xtra. The two services recently moved into new studios at New Broadcasting House in Central London, designed with the desire to visualise more in mind. As well as radio studios and production spaces, there are also cameras, lights and a control room to allow content to be shot, edited and streamed live online with ease. In essence, Radio 1 uses the internet to become a broader brand, which broadcasts radio shows and offers additional content in visual spaces. In October 2013 the BBC announced that Radio 1 will now also appear as a visual channel on the BBC's iPlayer service for television, meaning that any videos recorded or broadcast by the radio station will be available to view on-demand via the BBC website or the iPlayer applications for mobile telephones, tablets, laptops or internet-connected television sets (BBC 2013).

The controller of BBC Radio 1 and 1Xtra, Ben Cooper, has been a passionate advocate of approaches to make radio sit more comfortably in visual spaces, such as digital television, or to allow the audience to see funny things or star guests that they hear on the radio. In 2008, he told the industry magazine *Broadcast* '...if there is a funny moment in the studio just listening to it means you can't appreciate it in the same way. I want listeners to be able to see it' (Shepherd 2012). The station recently hired two new presenters, not from another radio station, but from YouTube, and the indications are that this has had a positive impact. The network has a team of producers developing visual content, led in part by Head of Visualisation, Joe Harland, who wrote: 'Radio needs a visual if it's going to reach young people on their second-favourite search engine, YouTube. Views of Radio 1's live lounge performances frequently outstrip the numbers that listened live' (2012). As well as welcoming these changes, Helen Boaden also warns of the risks. She said: 'In the UK the national BBC radio channels for the demographic most likely to want to experience radio this way are BBC Radio 1 and BBC Radio 1Xtra... I am delighted by this innovation. But it's important not to be seduced into thinking "visualisation" is the panacea to all radio's challenges' (2013). This is radio for a generation who grew up online (McMillan & Morrison 2006; Albarran *et al* 2007), for whom one screen is no longer enough (Ofcom 2013), created by a radio station with an awareness that they need to consider what radio looks like on screen-centric devices like phones and tablets. From *Tiny Desk Concerts* on NPR (National Public Radio) in the United States, to song parodies on Nova FM in Australia, the use of video to complement radio is growing and is part of radio's hybrid future. Elsewhere radio stations such RTL 102.5 (www.rtl.it) in Italy broadcast their entire radio output as a television channel, showing music videos and visually attractive studios. While the motivations here may differ from broadcaster to broadcaster, there is evidence that the nature of radio as a purely auditory medium is shifting.

We are moving towards a new paradigm for radio; one where radio stations are recognising the internet not as a threat or as a new means of audio distribution, but as a platform to do more and create new opportunities to tell stories and interact with the audience. Radio no longer lives solely in the kitchen; it is becoming a mix of websites, social media interactions, podcasts, customisable experiences, videos and hybrid radios. Evans and Smethers highlight these benefits as 'the flexibility of Web technology to provide visual information with audio features [which] presents new opportunities to offer services for listeners that were previously unimaginable' (2001: 17).

Conclusion

At the start of the digital revolution, David MacFarland posed the question, what business is radio in? (1997: 9) and while he could not have predicted what followed, the question remains valid, because radio stations are now increasingly in the business of creating and distributing 'content', and not just 'radio'. It is a change that does require additional skills to be learnt or talent found (Damome: 2011), but it seems we are now reaching a key point in the future of our media. Social media platforms such as Facebook are becoming more widely used as tools to engage with the listeners and draw them into radio programmes (Bonini 2012; Freeman *et al* 2012). Websites also provide useful opportunities to offer additional content, such as pictures, videos or live streams from the studio, that augment the radio programme and so build loyalty (Geller 2011). The internet has provided radio with the means to *enhance* programmes, (where programmes are supported by images and text,) and to *extend* programmes, (where content is expanded into new spaces, to allow for deeper engagement even after the show has ended,) in ways which far exceed the benefits of an audio stream or simple webpage. Loyal listeners will follow radio into these new spaces, relishing the opportunity to interact with, or become immersed in, content from programmes they enjoy. New audiences may also discover radio through this digital content.

Listeners will continue to seek out radio stations from beyond their localities because they prefer the music, the format or the presenters, or they find the programmes more fascinating. Online listening is likely to continue to grow, but, for the reasons explored in this chapter, it is unlikely that broadcasters will view this future with relish. However, if we consider the stream as part of a wider approach, that includes features to make the listening experience more immersive or more interactive, then the additional costs incurred by both parties could prove worthwhile. The changes radio is making augment and enhance current content without being expensive or complicated (Shaw 2010), because, as Stephen Lax explained, '...rather than replacing existing media, new media is as much about the augmentation of existing media' (2009: 176). Despite technological shifts, the product at the centre of the experience will still be the live presenter sequence, the drama or the documentary. The wrapping around of other practices in this hybrid future presents producers and managers with fresh opportunities and places to maintain and build audiences. Adam Bowie, Head of Strategy at Absolute Radio (UK) wrote: 'Radio's way of fighting back is to quickly adopt a hybrid model. Of course there's fairly broad consensus that this is something we need to do' (2012). Helen Boaden appears to agree, as she concluded: 'The trick for all of us will be to keep playing to those inherent strengths whilst not being afraid to embrace the whole spectrum of digital opportunities. Opportunities which could help us create a passionate new generation of radio lovers who instinctively expect access to content on its own terms, multimedia experiences and the ability to interact with and help shape the content' (2013).

In this chapter, I have addressed a range of trends, technologies and approaches that see the internet not as a rival to radio or as a new platform through which to distribute existing content, but as a tool to extend and enhance radio experiences. The developments discussed here will not affect every listener. Neither do they change the close relationship between listener and presenter or the need for creative or engaging content, both of which are essential to the future of the medium. It is, though, an acknowledgment that just as the arrival of television was a catalyst for change in radio, so the arrival of visually-driven or socially-interactive content online should signal fresh challenges and opportunities for radio.

References

Albarran, A *et al* (2007) 'What happened to our audience? Radio and new technology uses and gratifications among young adult users', *Journal of Radio and Audio Media*, volume 14, issue 2.

Ala-Fossi, M, Lax, S, O'Neil, B, Jauert, P & Shaw, H (2008) 'The future of radio is still digital – but which one? Expert perspectives and future scenarios for radio media in 2015', *Journal of Radio & Audio Media*, volume 15, issue 1.

Anderson, J N (2012) 'Radio's broadcasting digital dilemma', *Convergence*, Volume 19, Issue 2.

Barboutis, C & Baltzis, A (2012) 'Casting doubts on web media: can internet radio make a difference in the Greek case?' in Oliveira, M, Portela P & Santos, L (eds), *Radio evolution: Conference Proceedings*, Braga: University of Minho.

BBC (2013) 'Radio 1 to have own channel on BBC iplayer', 7 October. http://www.bbc.co.uk/mediacentre/latestnews/2013/radio-1-channel.html

Belanger, P (2012) 'The net-amorphosis of radio as a survival strategy', in *Radio and Society,* Newcastle-Upon-Tyne: Cambridge Scholars Publishing.

Black, D (2001) 'Internet radio: a case study in medium specificity', *Media, Culture & Society,* volume 23, issue 3.

Boaden, H (2013) Speech to the Radio Festival, 15 October. http://www.bbc.co.uk/mediacentre/speeches/2013/helen-boaden-radio-festival.html

Bonini, T (2012) 'Doing radio in the age of Facebook', in Oliveira, M, Portela P & Santos, L (eds), *Radio evolution: Conference Proceedings*, Braga: University of Minho.

Bowie, A (2012) 'A radio future'. http://www.adambowie.com/weblog/archive/003306.html

Brecht, B (1932) 'Radio as a means of communication: A talk on the function of radio'. http://www.nyklewicz.com/brecht.html

Chignell, H (2009) *Key Concepts in Radio Studies*, London: Sage.

Cordeiro, P (2011) 'From Radio to R@dio: Broadcasting in the 21st century', in Oliveira, M, Portela P & Santos, L (eds), *Radio evolution: Conference Proceedings*, Braga: University of Minho.

Cridland, J (2013) 'Internet vs. Broadcast', a video version of a paper for the IBC conference. http://www.youtube.com/watch?v=xKwg1bA-FVI

Dubber, A & Wall, T (2009) 'Specialist music, public service and the BBC in the internet age', *The Radio Journal*, volume 7, issue 1.

Darwine, F, Douglas A & Greer, C (2011) 'Local radio and microblogging: How radio stations in the US are using Twitter', *Journal of Radio and Audio Media*', volume 18, issue 1.

Evans, C & Smethers, S (2001) 'Streaming into the future: A delphic study of broadcasters' attitudes toward cyber radio stations' *Journal of Radio Studies*, volume 8, issue 1.

Freeman, B, Klapczynski, J & Wood, E (2012) 'Radio and Facebook: The relationship between broadcast and social media software in the US, Germany and Singapore', *First Monday*, volume 17, issue 4.

Friere, A (2007) 'Remediating radio: Audio streaming, music recommendation and the discourse of radioness', *The Radio Journal*, volume 5, issue 2 & 3.

Garfors, G (2013) 'Broadcasting 7 times greener than streaming', 23 August. http://www.garfors.com/2013/08/media-broadcasting-7-times-greener-than.html

Gauntlett, D (2011) *Making is Connecting*, Cambridge: Polity.

Geller, V (2011) *Beyond Powerful Radio: A Communicator's Guide to the Internet Age'* Oxford: Focal Press.

Giger, T (2012) http://www.radioiloveit.com/radio-programming-radio-formats/social-media-run-the-radio-show

Hallet, L (2012) 'How new technologies impact community radio', in Oliveira, M, Portela P & Santos, L (eds), *Radio evolution: Conference Proceedings*, Braga: University of Minho.

Harland, J (2012): 'The vision of Radio 1's official chart with Reggie Yates gets bigger', *Huffington Post*, 24 February. http://www.huffingtonpost.co.uk/joe-harland/the-vision-for-radio-1_b_1296617.html

Hendy, D (2000) 'A political economy of radio in the digital age', *Journal of Radio Studies*, volume 1, number 1.

Hill, M (2012) 'Radioplayer on a radio – updated', blog post, 9 November. http://www.radioplayer.co.uk/radioplayer-on-a-radio/

Hilmes, M (2013) 'Listening in the Digital Age', in Lovilglio & Hilmes (eds), *Radio's New Wave*, New York: Routledge.

Jackson-Pitts, M & Harms, R (2003) 'Radio websites as a promotional tool', *Journal of Radio Studies*, volume 10, issue 2.

Jenkins, H, Ford S & Green, J (2013) *Spreadable Media: Creating Value and Meaning in a Networked Culture*, New York: NYU Press.

Johnson, K (2012) 'Audience use of new media technologies on NPR.org', *Journal of Radio and Audio Media,* volume 19, issue 1.

Lax, S (2009) *Media and Communication Technologies*, Basingstoke: Palgrave.

Lind, R & Medoff, N (1999) 'Radio stations and the World Wide Web', *Journal of Radio Studies*, volume 6, issue 2.

MacFarland, D (1997) *Future Radio Programming Strategies*, New York: Routledge/Lawrence Erlbaum.

Meikle, G & Young, S (2012) *Media Convergence*, New York: Palgrave Macmillan.

McMillan, S & Morrison, M (2006) 'Coming of age with the internet: A qualitative exploration of how the internet has become an integral part of young people's lives' *New Media and Society*, volume 9, issue 1.

Nyre, L & Ala-Fossi, M (2008) 'The next generation platform: comparing audience registration and participation in digital sound media', *Journal of Radio & Audio Media*, volume 15, issue 1.

Ofcom (2013) '2013 Market Report, Key Points', London: Office for Communications. http://stakeholders.ofcom.org.uk/binaries/research/cmr/cmr13/UK_Key_Points.pdf

Penafiel Saiz, C (2011) 'Radio and web 2.0: Direct feedback', in Starkey, G, Gazi, A & Jedrzejewski, S (eds), *Radio Content in the Digital Age*. Bristol: Intellect.

Piggott, N (2010) 'Hybrid radio: How does it work listeners?' paper at the Radio Days Conference 2010.
http://www.radiodayseurope.com/sites/default/files/mediafiles/Nick_Piggott_-_Hybrid_Radio.pdf

Plunkett, J (2012) 'Interview: Ben Cooper, controller of Radio 1, on getting younger' *The Guardian*, 5 February. http://www.guardian.co.uk/media/2012/feb/05/ben-cooper-controller-radio-1?INTCMP=SRCH

Priestman, C (2001) *Web Radio: Radio Production for Internet Streaming*, London: Focal Press.

Radio Today (2013) 'UK's PPL wants US radio to pay royalties', 26 July.
http://radiotoday.co.uk/2013/07/uks-ppl-wants-us-radio-to-pay-royalties/

RAJAR (2013) 'All digital radio listening, third quarter', 1 August.
http://www.rajar.co.uk/content.php?page=listen_market_trends

Robins, B & Lozarno, S (2010) 'How social media can complement radio listening: 'A *Weekend Edition* case study at npr.org', 30 March.
http://www.npr.org/templates/story/story.php?storyId=125345149

Rooke, B & Odame, H (2013) 'I have to blog a blog too?' Radio jocks and online blogging', *Journal of Radio and Audio Media*, volume 20, issue1.

Rose, F (2012) *The Art of Immersion: How the Digital Generation is Remaking Hollywood, Madison Avenue and the way we tell stories*, New York: W Norton & Co.

Schmidt, B (2012) 'Interactivity on radio in the internet age: A case study from France', in Gazi, A, Starkey, G and Jedrzejewski, S (eds) *Radio Content in the Digital Age*, Bristol: Intellect.

Shepherd, R (2012) 'Interview: radio content must become more visual, says BBC radio boss', *Broadcast*, 30 August. http://www.broadcastnow.co.uk/interview-radio-content-must-become-more-visual-says-bbc-radio-boss/1310315.article

Spacey, K (2013) Speech to the Edinburgh Television Festival, http://www.theguardian.com/media/interactive/2013/aug/22/kevin-spacey-mactaggart-lecture-full-text

Shaw, H (2010) 'The online transformation: How the internet is challenging and changing radio', in O'Neill, B, Ala-Fossi, M, Jauert, P, Lax, N, & Shaw, N (eds) *Digital Radio in Europe: Technologies, Industries and Cultures*, Bristol: Intellect.

Tacchi, J (2000) 'The need for radio theory in the digital age', *International Journal of Cultural Studies*, volume 3, issue 2.

TuneIn (2013) 'What's TuneIn', fact sheet, 8 October. http://d11im0xz45jykv.cloudfront.net/press/TuneIn_FactSheet_May_2013.pdf

Van Den Bulk, H & Hermans B (2011) 'The future of local radio in the digital era: Opportunity or threat? The case of small local, community radio in the Flemish community' in Gazi, A, Starkey, G & Jedrzejewski, S, *Radio Content in the Digital Age*, Bristol: Intellect.

Wall, T (2004) 'The political economy of internet music radio', *The Radio Journal*, volume 2, issue 1.

Chapter 2

Radio in the new media environment

Stanisław Jędrzejewski

Abstract

Today, two mediamorphoses are occurring simultaneously: a transition to digital and a transition to information technology (IT). This applies to all aspects of broadcasting: collection and storage, processing and distribution. All now use digital technology in the context of convergence of traditional radio and television, telecommunications and IT. Radio, television, phones and computing all share a number of common characteristics. This technological revolution is so profound that we are talking today about the twilight of the 'old' print and electronic media and the emergence of the 'new'. The critical point in the evolution of the newer media and dissemination via the internet was in the 1990s, because it is the internet - a medium, yet also a powerful information resource – that lies at the heart of the new realities of media and the technologies underpinning them.

For radio broadcasting there is no unique and inevitable future which can be predicted in advance. We can, however, identify trends and tendencies, as a snapshot of the development dynamic. Currently, technology is one of the most important determinants of the development of radio. This chapter considers the possibilities available to radio broadcasters in these evolving circumstances.

Keywords: radio, technology, digital radio, web radio, new media, Poland

Developments in radio

Advances in technology have been accelerating as the digital environment has been evolving. As the European Broadcasting Union Digital Strategy Group II said (EBU 2006:15), ' Digital technology makes possible new ways to produce and deliver media, and brings a wider use of ever more sophisticated multimedia, interactivity, the option of multi-channel services, on-demand services, and the availability of different picture and sound quality options'. The group identified trends in the development of radio as:

- *From analogue to digital*
Digital audio takes less frequency space and transmitter power, and allows for a wider choice of offer within the same bandwidth.

- *From flow to demand (from linear to non-linear services)*
Traditional flow radio, formatted for specific programme genres or target groups will be supplanted by a series of on-demand or near-on-demand services, where the listeners can pick and choose the desired programmes when it suits them.

- *From broadcasting to narrowcasting*
In order to meet the listeners' demands for free choice round the clock, broadcasters must provide a wide range of formats. The same content might be shared or versioned for different channels and outlets – or even automatically repeated in order to serve different listeners in different time slots.

- *From one-platform to multi-platform*
The radio of the future is a multiplatform phenomenon. Radio will be available on a wide range of technical devices, from racks and hifi's through stand-alones and portables to handheld and pocket receivers. Everything digital – from television and computers to cell phones, mobiles and PDAs - will be able to carry sound, and thus carry radio, too.

- *From one-standard to many-standard*
There will be no single, winning standard for digital radio. DAB/DMB, DAB+, DRM, DVB - they all have their strengths and weaknesses, which will mean they need to co-exist. Manufactures will make dual, triple and eventually multi-standard radio sets for the consumers. And the consumers will not have to navigate through a jungle of frequencies or abbreviations, as the tuners will have easy-to-navigate browsers on displays with station brands.

- *From passive listening to active choosing*
With a broader range of programme and channel offer, and hundreds of thousands of internet radio stations, listeners will be able to pick and choose their favourite programmes or channels, possibly aided by electronic program guides or intelligent 'radio agents'.

(EBU 2006: 29-30)

The context for developments in radio and other media

The new communications landscape, including the media, can be described as moving from a more vertical, authoritarian, paternalistic model to models involving participation and horizontal dialogue. A new communication landscape, with a much wider choice of content created by an increasing number of sources is not limited by monopolies but has an impact on established national channels, both television and radio, because customers can seek out niche channels - diminishing the importance of large media corporations that own big media brands. However, this contemporary media landscape, with the ability of audiences to navigate around it, has created a tendency to downplay the traditional media, which continue to play an important role in the lives of a large part of the public. The diversification of the content needs of individuals and communities alike has led to the abandonment of an asymmetrical relationship between broadcasters and audiences. The hierarchical system characterised by the traditional, unilateral, 'top-down' flow of information has been replaced by a horizontal structure which respects the subjectivity of participants in the communication process, and assumes some interchangeability of their roles. While in the traditional media, the message was delivered to mass audiences without their participation, in the case of newer media the most important element has become interactivity and active participation in the community of consumers, creating a 'creative efficacy' (or agency) and this has developed consumers' sense of their own citizenship.

Members of the new 'involved and independent media culture' have introduced such neologisms as 'prosumers' (Toffler 1980). They are needed here for two reasons. Firstly, the mass audience is not as passive as it is assumed to be in the theory of 'a mass society'. Secondly, in the context of new media, any statements about audience involvement, interactivity and their consequences must be considered in the context of the fundamentally changing 'real' user experience. Increasingly, ordinary consumers of media have changed from 'buyers-only' into content providers, publishers and broadcasters, such as bloggers, participants in forums and discussion groups, members of online communities, and even radio broadcasters, publishers and video presenters. Note, however, that such a model does not accomodate the importance of the so-called media institutions. Mainstream media organisations, with the professional experience of their staff and their professional skills, as opposed to those in alternative media, have little in common with participatory media communities, so some very optimistic assumptions about the extent to which participatory processes occur in the media exaggerate reality. Social networking does, however, in many of its forms, represent a clear challenge to the conventional representation of audiences as masses, creating communities and fundamental social groups.

In general terms, new technologies have the following properties: the use of digital recording and data processing, the integration of different networks of communication, and interactivity between users or between the user and the content producer. This means that the broadcaster and receiver roles have become interchangeable, and interactivity can give a consumer complete control over the pace, structure and content of communication. The integration of the communication network involves all content elements, such as video and audio data and metadata. This complexity has significantly disrupted the routines of analogue technology and traditional vertical, linear relationships between content production and distribution. Now, development, transfer and distribution of content using new technologies and associated software are decentralised and individualised, having created both multimedia and hypermedia, and the space opened up is a cyberspace defined as a communication space, open to operation on a global scale, integrating media content production and distribution with computing and data transmission. In addition to established telecommunication services, such as telephony and fax, the widespread use of digital technology with broadband and high-capacity distribution networks using various transmission media and signal processing techniques, allows content to be conveyed repeatedly in megabits, including the transmission of visual information, such as video conferencing, multimedia, e-mail and file-sharing. Now commonplace on the media landscape are increasingly individualised interactive multimedia, such as video and audio on demand, pay TV and radio, computer games, teleshopping, banking, ticket booking, educational services, medical consultations and many others, the provision of which has become possible thanks to technological convergence, the development of broadband internet access and the standardisation of network devices using IP (Internet Protocol).

However, according to the authors of *From Public Service Broadcasting to Public Media Service*, while television and the internet are often experienced as mutually competing platforms, radio and the internet are complementary by their very nature. Among young internet users aged 25-34, 36 per cent listen to radio while searching the internet (EIAA 2008). FGI research conducted for Danmarks Radio (DR) found that young people do not always conform to the audience groups as defined by radio producers, because they are more individualistic. DR has experimented with a personalised internet radio platform, a mix of radio on-demand and podcasting, on which listeners can create their own radio stream by picking and mixing different kinds of content (Heiden 2009). Another example is combining multiplatform and mobile radio - so-called Pod Radio - where mp3-browser and player combine to play podcast content from Swedish public radio through Wi-Fi or 3G (Torberg 2009).

Concerning the much-discussed distribution platforms and technical standards of radio, many platforms and standards do and will continue to co-exist. Practically every radio broadcaster has had an online presence for a number of years, offering simulcast services of their broadcasts, enabling listeners to access their stations via a computer. However, new devices such as smartphones or other mobile devices and Wi-Fi enabled radios are giving broadcasters new ways of reaching listeners as well as enabling new market entrants to offer services other than traditional radio.

An analysis of digital and online radio consumption in five countries, France, Germany, Sweden, the UK and the USA, revealed the following trends:

- In general, radio listening via broadcast AM or FM networks is declining and the average listening time per listener is decreasing. The decline in the number of radio listeners and the time spent listening is most marked among younger generations.
- Online audio streaming is growing in most countries, driven in particular by personalised interactive music services such as Pandora, Spotify, Last.fm etc.
- The advent of the smartphone, bringing with it rapid growth in the availability of radio apps and the increase in popularity of interactive music services, is driving growth in radio listening on the mobile phone.
- Mobile apps are making radio more interactive and personal.
- The impact of social media networks is growing. Listeners, particularly younger generations, are increasingly accessing radio via social network sites such as Facebook and Twitter.

- Video viewing and targeted advertising are becoming increasingly common for online radio services.

(EBU 2011: 11)

Radio and pararadio technologies

Digital radio In the mid-1990s it seemed that the only digital standard for the development of radio transmission would be the DAB standard Eureka 147. DAB would be a natural successor to FM, as well as a proven technology with solid foundations to ensure its widespread adoption. Now DAB is no longer the only such audio transmission technology, as other digital audio distribution standards have emerged, and those which can be used by radio can categorised in four groups:

- terrestrial radio (DAB audio, DAB +, DRM, IBOC)
- terrestrial TV (DVB-T)
- mobile multimedia (DVB-H, DMB)
- systems not dedicated to radio broadcasting (satellite radio, web radio, advanced mobile systems, broadband, podcasting, hybrid systems)

Today, none of these standards are dominant. Some of them will probably disappear, while others will in future be subject to a process of convergence, creating the next generation of digital standards. The growing number of standards is tending to outpace the ability of national regulators and broadcasters to thoroughly evaluate them and the implications for their national digitisation plans.

Web 2.0 The second wave of technological change has enabled the creation of social networking websites and big projects shaped by users and based on content created by them. This phenomenon is socially beneficial in the sense that it encourages involvement and cooperation. Some even consider this can become a challenge to mainstream media producers in terms of the production, packaging and distribution of cultural heritage. This has advantages and disadvantages. While on the one hand content created and distributed by users can be a challenge to the mainstream media, on the other hand, these established media producers have learned to exploit this phenomenon for their own benefit, as a source of free content. In this context, there are broader questions related to intellectual property and protection of the creators of the web content, as media corporations try to control the content and its distribution. Therefore, internet users have an interest in preventing the appropriation of the internet, such as through the development of the concept of free software licensing termed Creative Commons. Broadly, this concept allows consumers free transfer, copying and use of derivative works in non-commercial ways, while respecting the author of the original work, in order 'to develop mechanisms that can operate a global repository of knowledge - ideas published under protection. Creative Commons licenses are available to all and thus can become a leaven of new knowledge' (Gawrysiak 2010: 99). The most significant characteristics of Web 2.0 are interactivity and user involvement, the sharing of data and content, the common platform, the potential for innovative development through exchange within the network community and support for using the software. Examples are blogs, forums, tools, wikis, other open source projects and the release of source code. API (Application Programming Interface) allows the creation of hybrid applications known as mashups. This was the second developmental stage of the internet, encouraging rapidly-developing social networking sites like MySpace, Facebook, Bebo and other easy ways to receive individualised content online.

Blogs The dynamic growth and the popularity of blogs and social networking sites is one aspect of the social use of Web 2.0 that emerged through the development of infrastructure, faster access to the network and the ever increasing number of computers and other equipment to facilitate direct contact, such as mobile devices. Blogs emerged in the late 1990s. Soon, software was created to facilitate blog creation and the form has evolved, giving rise to such formats as the photoblog, video blog (vlog), mobile blog and the microblog with very short entries, such as Twitter. Another feature of blogs is that they tend to foster interaction and stimulate a sense of belonging to a community. As the *Why it Works* EBU project research showed, listeners appear to be spending more time on the social media profiles of their favourite programmes than on the official websites. The blogs with a strong focus on the presenters were seen to be the most popular. When blogs are personal, informal in tone and frequently updated, they seem to gain (and retain) audiences, as in the case of the Spanish programme *Asuntos Propios*, whose presenter, Toni Garrido, is able to generate a sense of intimacy among his listener-readers. Along with photos and videos, blogs are the best 'Trojan horse' to attract listeners from social media profiles and guide them back into the official website of the radio channel. All eight programmes with blogs used them to publish the links to fresh blog posts on their Facebook walls and Twitter profiles, to draw fans from social media to them. Social media are based on so called 'push'-technology, while blogs are based on 'pull-technologies'. A good strategy for broadcasters is to use these two different models in a hybridised manner (EBU 2011a).

Social media These have experienced a similarly rapid increase in popularity to blogs and social networking sites. The largest number of users of these services are young people – the 'digital natives', according to Prensky (2001). In June 2011 two stations of Jelli Radio in Las Vegas (KHIJ-FM, KVBE-FM) were the first ever social terrestrial radio stations completely powered by the social web (Jelli 2011). The listeners could choose, in real time, any song on air via Jelli's website or Jelli's free iPhone app. The listeners (users) could vote for songs, share songs on Twitter and Facebook, discuss with the other community members content being broadcast and use two unique Jelli 'power-ups', a Rocket and a Bomb, to further influence the content to be aired next. In addition, users were able to access a much broader selection of music than is typical of radio, and connect with other music fans during special night sequences. Even if social media use has only entered into the production routines of public radio broadcasters over the last few years, they have become a crucial, but also frequently misunderstood and underestimated, tool. In recent programme case studies, a number of similar social media practices, both effective and innovative, were identified. On the one hand, in general the social media strategies used by the analysed programmes showed that most of them had finally understood the importance of social media in nurturing the relationship with their audiences, using social media like an umbilical cord connecting listeners to producers when the radio is off. On the other hand, not all the programmes fully exploit their potential audience reach. Many differences in levels of interaction can be observed from one programme to another, due to their different target audiences and genres, or, sometimes, even due to a simple underestimation of the potential of the tool.

Podcasting Podcasting is a form of audio content distribution, periodically received by the consumer's computer on a subscription basis for a fee or free of charge. Since its first phase around 2004, podcasting has become popular among many radio stations in order to provide users with some time-shifted radio content. They are non-linear services, going beyond the limited scope of the traditional broadcast and schedule. In this way, podcasting is a means of extending the coverage and the impact of the station and strengthening the commitment and loyalty of its listeners. It also allows listeners to mix genres and receive them on mobile devices. Podcasting can offer the ultimate mode of consumption of radio, according to the EBU (2007). In the autumn of 2006, in Europe approximately 12 per cent of internet users had downloaded podcasts in order to listen to them in the future. But only one per cent downloaded them on a typical day. In the period 2004-5, many European broadcasters began podcasting. In 2007, Radio France reported 350,000 downloads in a week, and in Italy RAI reported 200,000. This activity concerns largely young listeners who are also active users of mp3 players. Most podcasts are offered by public stations for free, yet they focus on speech content.

This initially posed a number of questions. Is podcasting the future of radio? Is there a missing element in the relationship between radio and the network which the internet radio stations cannot provide? Is the technology really revolutionary or is it just a passing trend, culture-wise? Finally, is podcasting a more democratic system or just another tool to be used by the international music industry? On the basis of just a few years of experience and observation we may now attempt to give at least a cautious response to the last two questions. Currently, podcasting is not yet an effective means of developing media democracy. However, it is valued and used by the record industry, by radio stations and by political and cultural organisations, and it is an important element in promoting and strengthening ties with listeners, supporters and consumers, partly because of its element of active subscription.

Visual radio Radio, in the digital world, can now use new technologies and techniques to add a visual dimension to its content. In its simplest form, this consists of the radio station displaying simple graphics on digital televisions, in various applications on smartphones and networking players, (such as the UK RadioPlayer,) and in social media content. Such projects as RadioDNS and dDAB indicate that radio listeners use the screen in order to see information that may be omitted from the audio narrative, such as song titles. However, the RadioDNS system goes one step further and allowed, for example, the London radio station Capital FM to display on-screen information about delays on the Underground and other local information. Trying to visualise entire radio programmes on multiple platforms, in January 2009 BBC Radio 1 experimented with a visual version of two radio programmes, providing live footage of the presenter of the radio programme simultaneously with text messages sent in by listeners via the internet (Spencer & Torberg 2009). Visibility is increasingly being made use of by the BBC - on Radio 1, Radio 2 and Radio 5 Live, for example, but crucially, the technology and its relationship with the audience has evolved to the point where the radio can visualise content without reducing the impact of the audio. It does not need to significantly change the nature of the radio content, as happened in the case of the Polish station PR 4 Czwórka, when the visual element began to dominate the audio.

Conclusion

Today, radio is being consumed in new and different ways across a variety of platforms and devices, yet the traditional strengths of radio are undiminished: mobility, ease of access, real-time broadcasting, integration with the community, personalities, entertainment, established journalistic standards and creative audio programming. The challenge is to transpose these strengths and unique attributes into the new media environment. Meanwhile, the threat to radio is that other media and new devices could potentially become substitutes for it in some of these areas. The threat may not be immediate - for example, in Europe radio consumption through mobile phones remains marginal and the rise in internet radio listening has not been shown to significantly diminish broadcast radio consumption. On the other hand, many listeners first experience digital-only radio channels through digital television platforms. Consumers are satisfying their needs in different ways and they naturally seek the easiest and cheapest ways to do so. Few doubt that radio will persist as a medium. Certainly, other media have become more like radio in some respects, as some newspapers now produce audio - and it is also inevitable that radio will exhibit characteristics of other media with its visualisation. Yet, the distinct and defining features of radio will most likely remain.

Radio's digital and internet strategies have been driven by a culture of innovation and technical progress. The environment for media delivery is still changing, and radio broadcasters need to understand, adapt and respond to the changes. Technology today offers a large range of options. Radio broadcasters must grasp those which will best serve their listeners and users. The success of radio in the competitive digital environment depends on whether it is able to provide the content people want on convenient platforms in accessible, customisable and easy-to-navigate ways.

The challenges for radio broadcasters in the future were summed up by the EBU as to: 'support open standards, secure provision of adequate spectrum, secure the free access to digital platforms, secure digital content rights including music rights, provide distinct and competitive content on all platforms, increase availability of programmes in a convenient form, and create new forms of intriguing, innovative, involving and interactive radio formats' (2007: 196).

References

EBU (2002) *Media with Purpose*, Geneva: European Broadcasting Union.

EBU (2006) *Public Service Media for the Digital Age*, Geneva: European Broadcasting Union.

EBU (2007) *Public Radio in Europe*, Geneva: European Broadcasting Union.

EBU (2011) *Public Radio and New Media Platforms*, Geneva: European Broadcasting Union.

EBU (2011a) *Why It Works*, Geneva: European Broadcasting Union.

EIAA (2008) *Digital Generation Report*, London: European Interactive Advertising Association.

Gawrysiak, P (2010) 'Wolne idee kontra "świat copyright"', in Jedrzejewski, S & Francuz, P (eds) *Nowe media i komunikowanie wizualne*, Lublin: Wydawnictwo KUL.

Gorman, L & McLean, D (2009) *Media and Society into the 21st Century*, London: Wiley-Blackwell.

Heiden, H (2009) 'Delivering innovative services', presentation at *Multimedia Meets Radio* conference, Prague, 5-6 April.

Jenkins, H (2007) *Kultura konwergencji: zderzenie starych i nowych mediów*, Warszawa: Wydawnictwa Akademickie i Profesjonalne.

Krzysztofek, K (2010) 'Internet uspołeczniony: Web 2.0 jako zmiana kulturowa', in Jedrzejewski, S & Francuz, P (eds) *Nowe media i komunikowanie wizualne*, Lublin: Wyd. KUL.

O'Reilly, T (2005) 'What is Web 2.0?Design patterns and business models for the next generation of software'.
http://www.oreilly.com/pub/a/oreilly/tim/news/2005/09/30/what-is-web-20.html

Prensky, M (2001) 'Digital Natives, Digital Immigrants', in *On the Horizon*, Bradford: MCB University Press, October, volume 9, issue 5.

Radio Nederland (2011) '"First-ever" social radio stations to launch in US', Amsterdam: Radio Nederland Worldwide Newsletter.

Spencer, B & Torberg, H (2009) 'Thinking multiplatform', presentation at the *Multimedia Meets Radio* conference, Prague, 5-6 April.

Toffler, A (1980*) The Third Wave*, New York: Bantam Books.

Torberg, H (2009) 'Delivering innovative services', presentation at *Multimedia Meets Radio* conference, Prague 5-6 April.

Trappel, J, Meier, WE, D'Haenens, L, Steemers, J, Thomas, B (eds) (2011) *Media in Europe Today*, Bristol: Intellect.

Chapter 3

Radio days (are now). The radio marketplace of innovation in the context of audio-visual culture

Joanna Bachura-Wojtasik

Abstract

In recent years the technological transformation of the audiosphere has taken place in the context of modern audio-visual culture. However, a discussion of issues concerning the modern audiosphere cannot be limited to technology alone. This chapter considers the impact of this technological transformation on the arts, artists and audiences. Since the 1980s, Maryla Hopfinger has been emphasising that the revolutions taking place in contemporary culture, especially in the area of art and social communication, have affected audiences, who are described as active participants in culture. In this digital age the participation of the audience in the creation of many cultural texts is undeniable.

This chapter examines several cultural audio texts produced by European radio broadcasters which bring together tradition and modernism at the level of content or form. These include the radio drama series *One Minute Short* (The Netherlands), which won the festival Prix Europe 2012, the *Possible Conversation* radio-play series, (Sweden) which featured imaginary discussions between ordinary people and grand politics about global issues, *Narrenturm* (Poland), an audiobook produced as a radio play and the show *Formiddagen med Rebecca og Johanne* (Denmark), a radio novelty directed at a particular audience group, children aged three to six. Online audio projects such as *Hackney Hear* (UK), *Radioortung* (Germany) and Docusound (Italy) provide additional examples of the convergence of different forms of communication.

The strength of radio in today's media-dominated world will become evident, as will the continuing interest of audiences, who can be seen as active participants in culture. Today radio exists alongside other modern media which can function online with images and text. In spite of this, however, radio will never become television, although we already see examples of 'enhanced radio', 'resilient radio', or 'radio beyond radio'.

Keywords: artistic radio, radio drama, radio innovations, technology, Poland

Introduction: Cultural context

Characteristics of contemporary culture include its mediatisation and its relationship with an increasingly progressive technologisation. Mediatisation is not just about providing information, but is also a carrier of meaning. According to Andrzej Gwóźdź, the medium is considered 'not in a theoretical and informational way – as a means of transferring information – but rather as a form of cultural output tightly fused with a specific technology, subject to social institutions and acting as a compass for orienteering, and thus an apparatus for social perception' (2001: 8). Taking the cultural background into account helps us to see the relationship between radio as a medium and the latest means and technologies for communication, and, above all, that in the face of technological transformations and changes in communication, the genres specific to radio, and radio itself, have now become a field of experimentation and searching for new means of expression. Audience contact with the medium has become interactive in nature, while still being influenced by an ongoing convergence (Jenkins 2007: 9). The process of convergence and its various consequences are behind the transformation that the media and the media market are undergoing today. It is also a key concept for understanding the essence of the phenomena occurring in media systems, specifying the technical lineage of these phenomena and acting as a metaphor for the wider process of change to which this phenomenon contributes (Jakubowicz 2011: 27). In this chapter, selected cultural texts taken from European radio broadcasting are analysed. These examples combine tradition and modernity, both in terms of form and content, which undoubtedly makes them part of the landscape of cultural convergence. They demonstrate radio's strong position in today's mediatised world and the extent of interest it enjoys from general audiences. The popularity of radio, as well as the interest of academics in this medium, is supported by several recently published books, including *Radio Content in the Digital Age: The Evolution of a Sound Medium* (Gazi, Starkey & Jędrzejewski 2011), *Radio Evolution: Conference Proceedings* (Oliveira, Portela & Santos 2012), *Radio and Society: New Thinking for an Old Medium* (Mollgaard 2012) and *Radio in Context, Second Edition* (Starkey 2014).

The development of the media and, consequently, the development of specific media genre forms has been considered an integral part of the generation and formation of modern societies. The cultural transformations of the twentieth century, a shift from a verbal culture to an audiovisual one, as Maryla Hopfinger, among others, has emphasised (Hopfinger 1997: 75-97), resulted in the particularisation of the concept of 'intermediality', which highlights mutual dialogue amongst various media. Contemporary culture is not 'homogeneous'. That is, the texts that contribute to it cannot be reduced to categories controlled by clearly fixed rules. Instead it resembles a conglomerate comprised of different qualities. Texts tend to cross genre boundaries and therefore become hybrid forms, having, in essence, a process-based character. They consist of many heterogeneous elements; they are a kind of collage, and their semantics are often disclosed only in the context of other cultural texts. Since intertextual connections are characteristic of these cultural texts, they take shape and operate in social space in a permanent process of birth and discovery of cultural contexts and connections (Miczka 2001: 20-21). Cultural texts correspond with the experiences of their audience/participants (Pleszkun-Olejniczak 2012: 262-63), and the latter are increasingly becoming active co-creators of these texts. This is the essence of reception, to quicken the activity on the part of the recipient. The texts 'require the recipient to be cognitively active, knowledgeable and culturally competent' (Ogonowska 2004a: 12). Gradually, we are beginning to talk more often about strategies of reception. Agnieszka Ogonowska pointed out that linear forms give way to 'hypertextual' forms. Reading is being displaced by a journey through the intricacies of the text and other texts, (including extra-textual reality,) that form the plane of cultural references necessary for semantic activation in the process of sense-making (2004a: 12; Miczka 2001: 12-16).

The development of audiovisual culture and, following this, the invasion of computers into cultural life have led to changes in communication behaviors that apply to all cultural texts, and thus to artistic audio texts (Miczka 1999: 445-54). The concept of 'communication shifts' is an essential one because it is integrally connected with the phenomena of the hypertext (Fiołek-Lubczyńska 2004: 182-83; Levinson 2006: 233-51; Lichański 2009: 59-66; Suszczyński 2002: 521-36) and interactivity. These concepts, in turn, relate to instances in which the reception of audio texts takes place not in the traditional way, using a radio receiver, but via the internet (Jędrzejewski 2003: 193-222; Siwak 2002: 170-71). Computers have given birth to a new type of textuality, as evidenced by internet radio or even the websites of traditional radio stations. These websites adopt a heterogeneous structure, since they mix audio transmission, the opportunity to listen to podcasts and discover written text, photographs and video. Another issue raised here is the hypertextual structure of files. Maryla Hopfinger in her discussion of cultural communication in the twentieth century identified audio-visuality as a unique quality it possesses (2003; 1985; 1976; 1974). However, she emphasises the fact that 'contemporary culture has not become a culture of the image, though images are what its critics perceive, above all else. Contemporary culture integrates verbal and non-verbal, visual and aural, verbal and pictorial information into an audiovisual manifestation' (2002a: 9). These changes in the field of communication have become permanent, and they are closely related to new technologies for storage and transmission. They enable the creation of a new, previously unknown paradigm of expression, as in the past the field of communication did not have at its disposal the possibilities it possesses today. The quality that distinguishes contemporary media from traditional ones is their inherent connection with technology. The authors of the introduction to the book *Radio Content in the Digital Age* accurately noted that: 'Technology is one of the most important factors in the development of radio' (Gazi, Starkey & Jędrzejewski 2011: 10). In the seventies, Michał Kaziów claimed that: 'Specific radio broadcasts are always listened to at the same time and the information contained in these broadcasts is received simultaneously by numerous audiences' (1973: 21). Meanwhile, contemporary media enable the recipient to overcome the barriers of time and space. The twenty-first century is characterised by a convergence of media, 'where the old and new media come into more and more complex interactions...' (Jenkins 2007: 7).

Contemporary radio is changing, especially in terms of the shift from analogue to digital technology. As early as 1932, Bertolt Brecht pointed out the potential of radio: 'Radio must change from a means of distribution to a means of communication. Radio could become ... a great interconnected system... that allows the recipient to not only listen but also speak; not isolating him but allowing him to make contact' (Filiciak 2008: 264). As a result of the internet, radio, once understood as a linear service with a traditional programme format is now becoming a non-linear service. This means that listeners consciously choose the broadcast or show that interests them from a wide-ranging set of choices. The computer can thus be 'understood' as a form of technology that defines contemporary culture (Bolter 2002: 357-65) and a technology that defines a new area in contemporary culture, one of social communication (Hopfinger 2002b: 448-60). There are two theoretical concepts that best describe contemporary culture in its most recent terms: firstly Lev Manovich's definition of new media (2006) and secondly Henry Jenkins' notion of participatory culture. The reason for this choice is these authors' emphasis on the continuity of media development. According to Bauer, 'Manovich wants the techniques and technologies of the new media to reveal to us the old forms of culture and that these old forms of culture light up in front of us that which is created in the world of the new media' (2006: 24).

Mirosław Filiciak, who supports the idea that the user is simultaneously a producer, claimed: 'The media do not operate in a vacuum they are an important part of a modern world and as such are involved in an infinite number of relations. For this reason, they constantly evolve and never reach the final form' (2008: 269). In order to treat audio texts as an example of implementing the idea of media joining at various levels and interacting more deeply, it is necessary to look at the mass media in general and not just at radio. This also supports the principle of convergence as cultural change, involving, among other things, a combination of the content and form of communication, (audio, video, text,) specific to each traditional medium. It demands a shift from content being associated with a particular medium in the direction of 'cooperation' between different media, taking into account the opinions and expectations of the recipients. Convergence applies to all layers of the audio piece: the subject, its means of implementation, the shape of the sound, and its presence on the internet, examples of which will be provided later in this chapter.

Contemporary culture is based on the allegory of 'remix' (Manovich 2006: 14-15), in which a particular cultural text is no longer an unalterable whole but becomes a potential element of subsequent texts (Filiciak 2008: 263). Aleksandra Pawlik, in a study of the premiere of a multimedia drama by Marcin Libera, which was a form of adaptation of the radio drama *Rekonstrukcja poety* (Reconstruction of the Poet) by Zbigniew Herbert, pointed out the beginnings of a highly organised form of coexistence involving media texts of diverse origins in a single work of art (Pawlik 2010: 84-94). This modern, meaning multimedia, method (Pleszkun-Olejniczakowa 2008) of adaptation used audiovisual material recorded in the studio by actors from Teatr Nowy (The New Theater) in Warsaw, as well as interactive animations presented 'live' on three screens. Pawlik further claimed that it is difficult to identify 'to what extent this kind of genre fits into the aesthetics of a radio art, to what extent it is still an adaptation, and to what extent it is a new and hard to clearly define art phenomenon yet. It is, however, a definite sign of convergent co-creation of the work belonging to the audial art by means of texts of various origin expressed through different media' (Pawlik 2010: 90). Therefore, the previously cited words of H. Jenkins about cooperation between what is old and what is new in the newfangled paradigm of culture also refer to the audio medium.

Innovations in radio

Technology is used to explore various aspects of the world (Heidegger 1977; Gołębiewska 2003: 33-44). It has become an integral part of modern culture. Meeting the expectations of the audience, creators of audio constantly strive to modernise techniques of production and search for unusual formal solutions, trying create content that will engage the demanding participants of a new type of society – the participants of the information society. In order to interpret and understand the importance of radio and of other audio texts today, it is essential to change the cultural and communication context. These audio texts exist in radio as a traditional medium, but also live outside of it – on the internet, on CD, in the MP3 audio format or in the form of audiobooks. Technology has played a major role in creating sound and the space it has occupied from its inception. Maryla Hopfinger provided a rather laconic summation of what has occurred in the world of sound: 'Recording studios with multi-track recording technology, cutting tables and mixer desks, other devices for electro-acoustic and electronic sound processing became the standard place of creation and production of audio-texts. Also, the effects of the digital revolution joined this. The development of synthesisers controlling analogue sound synthesis, taking sound samples and their processing using samplers as well as other computer techniques of the audio-reality simulation significantly expanded the existing spectrum of sound and music. The internet brought innovative solutions for a way of social functioning of the audiosphere and has given rise to a new era in audio technology' (2010: 142-43). The strictly technical aspect of sound evolution is not the main focus of this article, and consequently the links between technology, radio and art present in this medium are our main concern here. These links are studied from the perspective of aesthetics and in connection with the consequences of that which technology bringsw to the meaning of audio texts, especially artistic ones. Wojciech Siwak deals in his work with technological transformations and the directions of sound's development from the 1920s to the present (2002: 153-177). It should also be noted that Elżbieta Pleszkun-Olejniczakowa claimed technology has a huge impact on the shape of the medium and its content, but that it is not acceptable to blindly believe in technological determinism of digital technologies, as cultural factors and social context determine to a large extent the adaptability of radio (2012: 181-239).

Hackney Hear Radio, as a traditional medium, appears to exhibit some resilience and fits well into new platforms, which certainly casts doubt on apocalyptic claims about the death of the medium. According to Mollgaard: 'Radio is now developing synergies with visual aspects of the media, creating hybrid forms of practice and content previously unimaginable. This is another way that radio offers incredibly rich ways to interrogate media forms and how we make and use them' (2012: 9). A new innovative technology was used by the creators of the *Hackney Hear* i-Phone App, the winner of the Prix Europe 2012 festival in the 'Radio Market Place of Innovation' category. It is an application somewhat like a guidebook, focused on the London Fields and Hackney areas of the city. It triggers audio related to the user's current location, because the iPhone knows where it is and plays stories automatically, (including interviews, archive audio, field recordings, music and performances). The way the app works is that users plug in headphones and load the app, then explore the area with their phone in their pocket because there is no need to press any other buttons. The narrative journey is non-linear, as the locations to which the users walk decide the order of what they hear. In this way, walking anywhere within range will create its own narrative, and on walking out of the zone, the phone will say to turn around. With Tri-Sound technology, at any given time users can hear three layers of sound: speech, binaural field recordings and music, creating a rich and immersive soundscape. The binaural field recordings play with the boundaries of reality and fiction, creating audio 'ghosts', with cyclists spinning past or pub crowds spilling into the street. The ideas and technology used in this project show enormous potential of sound in terms of its creative and aesthetic power. Similarly, Lance Dann expressed his excitement about the audio drama project *The Flickerman*, claiming that: 'The internet and its associated digital and mobile technologies offer so many other creative opportunities that there is no need to feel that any particular project should be locked into one form' (2012: 354).

Radioortung A very similar technology was applied in developing *Radioortung*, a collection of projects in radio format designed for mobile phones and produced by Deutschlandradio Kultur. Since the plays can be experienced within the city, not only by using a free app, but also online on an interactive map, the options for enjoying the project are multipled. The stories are site-specific and non-linear, as well as reflecting the latest mobile technologies. In contrast to *Hackney Hear*, this format refers to the history and culture of specific sites. One of the projects is *50 Aktenkilometer: Ein begehbares Stasi-Hörspiel* (50 kilometres of files: A walk-in Stasi Radio Drama), audio acquired from 50 km of stored Stasi files made by the former Ministry for State Security in the German Democratic Republic and interviews with the victims or subjects of surveillance. Users can check out how the surveillance protocols sound at the sites where they were recorded, and sometimes find themselves located within the stories. A total of 10 hours of audio material were distributed across Berlin, and were later made available as an audible and highly subjective archive.

Formiddagen med Rebecca og Johanne In 2011, the Danish Broadcasting Corporation (DR) launched a new radio channel targeted specifically at children. The first programme on air each day, from 08:00-12:00, was *Formiddagen med Rebecca og Johanne* (Mornings with Rebecca and Johanne). The authors proved that children could not only use radio as a background or as a source of music, but could learn from an early age how to listen in a world almost totally dominated by images. The situation was new in many ways because DR had no prior experience with the target group of three to six-year-old children, or the way they perceived and interacted with the radio medium, and they acknowledged that almost every child within the target group would be attending kindergarten at the time the show is broadcast. Thus, the resulting show was built on findings from a focus group with professional educators. Realizing that educators were 'gatekeepers' between the target group and the radio, DR had to build a show they would find useful, one which could match their day-to-day activities in kindergarten. Specifically, three factors were taken into consideration as being particularly important: firstly pedagogical – the show must be built on pedagogical principles matching those of the kindergartens; secondly inspirational – the show must provide children, as well as educators, with inspiration; and thirdly structural – the show must follow the structure of the everyday activities in the kindergartens. The result was a show about the imaginary country of Ramasjang, where Rebecca and Johanne dream up funny stories that children can relate to, for example, how to dance like a cat, speak like a Japanese person, or sing like a bird, all triggering the imagination of a three to six year-old child. Just as the day evolves in kindergarten, the show evolves in a similar way. In the mornings, it is *Hyggetimen* (Cosy Hour) and the tempo is relaxed with good music and stories that inspire the imagination. Later on in the day when things are more lively, it is time for *Gang I stuen* (Lively Living Room), and the show revolves around physical activities, such as animal-gymnastics or dancing.

Studies showed that the introduction of the show changed the way children and professional educators thought about radio. The findings were extraordinary because educators reported that Ramasjang Radio became the most popular radio channel, and the main source of musical entertainment instead of CDs, which had previously been more popular than the radio set. They described it as instructive, inspiring and innovative radio, which made them think about the role and potential of radio, as well as accept it as child-friendly because there are no bad surprises or scary news bulletins, and it was no longer just background noise. They also revealed that the children loved the music and characters it presented. The show set a new standard for children's radio, since it helped to bring the medium of radio to an entirely new audience of very young children. Certainly, this programme provided a cultural education of the youngest. It familiarised young listeners with the radio and made them sensitive to sound. It should be noted that the need to show them how to listen was demonstrated in research by Titti Forsslund, who claimed that: '…radio not only provides opportunities for listeners to create their own images, but also requires special imagination skills' (2012: 331). Thus, there is a good chance that young people who are taught how to listen to the radio, to love the medium and recognise the benefits it brings, will also listen later in life.

Docusound As a society, we are over-exposed to images; audiences are so used to seeing that almost every fact becomes a show, everything is before our eyes and yet we do not seem to be able to actually see it and make sense of it. This was the conclusion of the Docusound project, a cross-media platform for the production and distribution of creative audio documentaries, run by the Doc in Progress group in Italy. Docusound went back to sound in order to rediscover the essence of communication, and to open the world of documentaries to the blind and partially-sighted, and to invite the sighted to close their eyes and imagine reality with their ears wide open. The producers tried to argue for the importance of sound and its ability to influence audiences, which was previously emphasised by some theorists (Oliveira 2013: 177-88; Street 2012). They also believed that, in reality, storytelling without images would bring the audience back to the essence of the story, allowing them to be inspired by it. The world told through sounds, noises, words and music could be a reality as never before heard. As a result of this philosophy, Docusound presented a collection of radio stories as an ever-expanding radio journal, with each month new tales from the real world, audio portraits and audio postcards by authors taking 'pictures' with a microphone. The producers showed the many advantages of audio: compared to video, audio is cheaper and lighter, and so easier to collect, edit, store and exchange online and through mobile devices; a sound recorder is less invasive then a camera, so it gains access where a camera would not be allowed. Sound is also easier to handle by non-professionals and the audience involvement was crucial for the Docusound project workshop, which taught how to record and tell extraordinary everyday stories. Docusound Lab may be the first workshop where sighted and non-sighted people joined forces to learn how to share their own stories through a microphone. Working on participants' ideas and projects with the support of a tutor and an audio expert, short radio stories were produced and published on a website. Participants were also invited to join a more focused training in production and postproduction techniques, and the whole project was developed in association with the Italian association for the blind and partially-sighted.

Innovations in artistic radio

The technical origin of an audio production is often considered to be non-negotiable and therefore not discussed. Audio works all owe their existence to a particular technology, and without this technology their creation would not be possible. Walter Benjamin's thesis concerning 'technical reproduction', concerning the purpose of technique in the work of art (1972), has been adapted specifically to the audio medium by Jerzy Tuszewski, who emphasised that 'the basis for any transformations in art and culture is the development of technical means' (1979: 15). Technology serves aesthetics, which can be clearly seen from the example of radio plays. The radio play is considered to be the result of one of the first experiences of cooperation between literature and technology. Initially, radio theatre was treated as a kind of technological curiosity, until it eventually gained the rank of an independent artistic form. The above statement indicates the priority of the concept of 'technicalism' before artistry, which means that the imagination and the creativity of the creator give way to technology. However, it should be noted the technique does not determine the action of the artist, but that the artist, inspired by a variety of outside factors, produces his creative idea using technology. Accordingly, progress and evolving 'surround sound techniques' are the source of everything in the audiosphere that is considered art (Hopfinger 2010: 141-7; Misiak 2009; Ong 2002: 178-86; Siwak 2002: 153-77). Technical and artistic components are inseparably mixed in radio drama, and technical capabilities can revolutionise the act of creation or at least give it new aesthetic values. Michał Libera's interpretation shows that this discussion does not concern the tools for producing radio plays, but the technology employed and its operation (2008: 293), where these modes, skillfully exploited by the artist, 'give birth' to any subsequent radio play.

However, it is not only recording an artistic vision and structure that is important to a specific audio work; there is also the matter of technical quality. A radio drama, like a movie, cannot be isolated from technology. Furthermore, the possibilities and even limitations of the technology strongly influence the development of audio art. Innovation and technical improvement very often resolve the shape and form of radio drama. The link between artistry and 'technicism' allows the former to keep pace with the development of the audio industry, which is, undoubtedly, beneficial to audio art. Jerzy Tuszewski claimed: 'The radio work, being a kind of contamination of an audio text, equipment and the overcoming of a sphere (action at a distance), and thus an artefact of technical reproduction, is a reflection of things and occurrences, or a structure comprised of different audio forms, or an expression of thoughts and experiences or, finally, all of these at the same time. However, only such a reflection, such a structure, or such an expression, individually or together, and realised at a specific time and acoustic space, as well as in conditions of intimacy and individual directness, are able – along with informing – to induce an admiration or a thrill, and to shake or raise specific intellectual attitude' (1979: 10).

One Minute Short Radiomakers Desmet from Holland produced a series of one-minute audio stories for children between eight and 12 years old, called *1-Minuutjes* (One Minute Short), which won the Grand Prix of Prix Europe festival in 2012 in the radio series category. Some of the stories were documentaries, others were fiction, and some challenged or stretched the boundaries between fact and fiction. The stories can be played on the internet children's radio station Kinderwebradio, and on the website of the daily educational TV programme *Klokhuis*. Every week a new story was added. The stories were produced by independent radio producers in cooperation with artists and, consequently, people from other disciplines, including photographers, composers, and writers, are regularly involved in the medium that is radio. Moreover, in this way, radio producers were inspired by outside ideas. The stories, commissioned by NTR, an independent public service broadcaster, were meant to surprise children and make them familiar with the medium of radio. It is of great significance that this project was sponsored by subsidies from Mediafonds, the Dutch cultural media fund.

Possible Conversation As part of a search for new forms of expression in fiction radio, the broadcast *Possible Conversation* was created in Sweden. These were fictional conversations between two specific people, public or private, living or dead, who, according to the authors, might talk to one another at a particular point in time. Local and personal issues collide with grand politics and global problems. The conversations created, usually 10 minutes long, have generated many discussions and debates elsewhere in the media and among listeners. The origin of the series was a search for more than just two possible alternatives resulting from two specific people finding themselves face to face and forced to try to understand each other instead of fighting or doing nothing. The head of the drama department of Swedish Radio, Stina Oscarson, was afraid that this belief could be radically naïve, but she always had great faith in the concept of people talking to one another, which is why she chose to work in theatre. One very interesting conversation was Bin Laden's daughter Safyiah standing face to face with the American soldier who had come to kill her father. This was of course an improvised conversation, based on extensive research into the characters and context.

Narrenturm Creative dialogue between art and technology has also been developed by Polish Radio. In 2009 a three-CD album was released of *Narrenturm*, the first part of the Hussite trilogy by Andrzej Sapkowski. An audiobook delivered as a radio play, emphasis was placed on the acoustic dimension and changes in the place and time of the plot. However, it is not just a novel being read into a microphone. This was an elaborate super-production because it combined elements of novel reading and radio drama. In fact, it could not be called a classic audiobook because a number of sound effects were added, original music was composed and songs were written specifically for the project. As many as 112 actors took part, playing 176 roles. The recording was directed by Janusz Kukuła, a famous director at Polish Radio and the winner of many prestigious awards given to authors of theater and radio. The recording, enhanced with a booklet with photos and interviews with filmmakers and artists, was released in mp3 audio format with a total recording length of approximately 1,500 minutes. Kukuła said: 'I've never had to deal with such a major undertaking. It was not just an artistic challenge, but also an intellectual one. Sapkowski's trilogy is a perfect guide through the history of Lower Silesia, and it requires a lot of preparation, one of the reasons being the different languages the characters speak.'

Conclusion

Modern radio is part of evolving contemporary culture, which was initiated in the twentieth century based on continuing advances in technology. Technological development is contributing to changes in thinking and our perception of the world. It helps to change people's thinking and expectations. Radio will remain an attractive form of culture for the listener and will 'raise up' faithful new listeners only if it is a constantly growing art form, allowing for the development of ever newer forms of expression, and if there is sufficient space in the medium for everything that is inspiring in terms of both art and mass culture. To be mutually inspiring means to have a dialogue, to 'talk to' and complement each other. In this chapter, we have discussed examples from different parts of European to demonstrate ways in which today radio is still a medium with potential for the creation and development of new audio forms of great value, but which also has a connection to everyday life, and above all, courageously corresponds to changes in communication, technology and the status of the audience. The direction of the evolution of our culture, as well as the organisation of social communication, which now uses the internet every day, certainly implies the continued presence of audio content in new media (Hopfinger 2002b: 456). This occurrence supports the thesis that in the twenty-first century sound art still occupies a very important place despite pessimistic forecasts predicting the twilight of 'real' art and culture or the transformation of our culture into a culture of icons or images.

A fitting summary of the situation of radio in the context of contemporary culture is that of Wolfgang Welsch, reflecting on the audiosphere, or human sound environment: 'Our culture, so far determined primarily by vision, is just now able to become a culture of hearing. This is desirable and necessary. After two thousand years of the domination of sight, hearing should acquire an independent or even privileged position, and not only because of the right to equal treatment. A human being who hears is a better human being – he is in fact able to engage in something else, to respect something, rather than just controlling it… the domination of viewing in our technology-dominated modern times is leading us straight to disaster, which we can only be kept from by a receptive, communicative, and symbiotic relationship with the world of hearing' (2001: 56).

References

Bauer, Z (2006) 'Między stuleciami', in Manowich, L, *Język nowych mediów*, translated into Polish by Cypryański, P, Warszawa: Wydawnictwa Akademickie i Profesjonalne.

Benjamin, W (1972) 'Dzieło sztuki w epoce możliwości jego technicznej reprodukcji', in Helman, A (ed), *Estetyka i film*, translated into Polish by Krzemień, K, Warszawa: Wydawnictwa Artystyczne i Filmowe.

Bolter, JD (2002) 'Komputer: maszyna i narzędzie', in Hopfinger, Maryla (ed.), *Nowe media w komunikacji społecznej w XX wieku. Antologia*, Warszawa: Oficyna Naukowa.

Dann, L (2012) 'One half of the Story: Radio drama, online audio and transmedia storytelling', in Oliveira, M, Portela P & Santos, L (eds), *Radio evolution: Conference Proceedings*, Braga: University of Minho.

Filiciak, M (2008) 'Użytkownik jako producent. Ku genealogii nowych mediów', in Wilk, Eugeniusz, Kolasińska-Pasterczyk, Iwona (eds.), *Nowa audiowizualność - nowy paradygmat kultury?*, Kraków: Wydawnictwo Uniwersytetu Jagiellońskiego.

Fiołek-Lubczyńska B (2004) *Film, telewizja i komputery w edukacji humanistycznej: o audiowizualnych tekstach kultury*, Kraków: Wydawnictwo Impuls.

Forsslund, T (2012) 'Radio – the forgotten medium for user's creative mental interaction and co-production', in Oliveira, M, Portela P & Santos, L (eds), *Radio evolution: Conference Proceedings*, Braga: University of Minho.

Gazi, A, Starkey, G & Jędrzejewski, S (eds.) (2011) *Radio Content in the Digital Age: The Evolution of a Sound Medium*, Bristol: Intellect.

Gołębiewska, M (2003) 'Człowiek w technologii. Benjamina szkic do portretu', in Gołębiewska, M, *Demontaż atrakcji*, Gdańsk: słowo/obraz terytoria.

Gwóźdź, A (2001) 'Przez okno technologii. Wprowadzenie', in Gwóźdź, A (ed), *Widzieć. Myśleć. Być. Technologie mediów*, Kraków: Universitas.

Heidegger, M (1977) 'Pytanie o technikę', in Heidegger, M, *Budować, mieszkać, myśleć. Eseje wybrane*, compilated by Michalski, K, Warszawa: Czytelnik.

Hopfinger, M (1974) 'Kultura audiowizualna a rozumienie literatury', *Pamiętnik Literacki*, volume LXV, issue 4.

Hopfinger, M (1976) 'Audiowizualny kontekst kultury współczesnej', in Żółkiewski, S & Hopfinger, M (eds), *Kultura - komunikacja - literatura. Studia nad XX wiekiem*, Wrocław - Warszawa - Kraków – Gdańsk: Zakład Narodowy im. Ossolińskich.

Hopfinger, M (1985) *Kultura współczesna – audiowizualność*, Warszawa: Państwowy Instytut Wydawniczy.

Hopfinger, M (1997) *Kultura audiowizualna u progu XXI wieku*, Warszawa: Instytut Badań Literackich.

Hopfinger, M (2002a) 'Wprowadzenie', in Hopfinger, M (ed), *Nowe media w komunikacji społecznej w XX wieku. Antologia*, Warszawa: Oficyna Naukowa.

Hopfinger, M (2002b) 'Sztuka i komunikacja: sygnały zmian całej kultury' in Hopfinger, Maryla (ed.), *Nowe media w komunikacji społecznej w XX wieku. Antologia*, Warszawa: Oficyna Naukowa.

Hopfinger, M (2003) *Doświadczenia audiowizualne. O mediach w kulturze współczesnej*, Warszawa: Wydawnictwo Sic!

Hopfinger, M (2010) 'Literatura audialna', in Hopfinger, M, *Literatura i media. Po 1989 roku*, Warszawa: Oficyna Naukowa.

Jakubowicz, K (2011) *Nowa ekologia mediów. Konwergencja a metamorfoza*, Warszawa: Wydawnictwo Poltext.

Jenkins, H (2007) *Kultura konwergencji. Zderzenie starych i nowych mediów*, translated into Polish by Bernatowicz, M and Filiciak, M, Warszawa: Wydawnictwa Akademickie i Profesjonalne.

Jędrzejewski, S (2003) *Radio w komunikacji społecznej. Rola i tendencje rozwojowe*, Warszawa: Wydawca Profi-Press Sp. z o.o.

Kaziów, M (1973) *O dziele radiowym. Z zagadnień estetyki oryginalnego słuchowiska*, Wrocław - Warszawa - Kraków – Gdańsk: Zakład Narodowy im. Ossolińskich.

Levinson, P (2006) 'Hipertekst i odwrócenie ról autora i czytelnika', in Levinson, P (ed), *Miękkie ostrze, czyli historia i przyszłość rewolucji informacji*, translated into Polish by Jankowska, H, Warszawa: Wydawnictwo Muza.

Libera, M (2008) 'Studio nagrań - techniki uprzestrzenniania dźwięku', in Wilk, E & Kolasińska-Pasterczyk, I (eds), *Nowa audiowizualność - nowy paradygmat kultury?*, Kraków: Wydawnictwo Uniwersytetu Jagiellońskiego.

Lichański, J (2009) 'Retoryka - hiperteksty - cyberprzestrzeń. Wyjaśnienie pewnych nieporozumień', in Ulicka, D (ed), *Tekst (w) sieci 1. Tekst, język, gatunki*, Warszawa: Wydawnictwa Akademickie i Profesjonalne.

Manovich, L (2006) *Język nowych mediów*, translated into Polish by Cypryański, P, Warszawa: Wydawnictwa Akademickie i Profesjonalne.

Miczka, T (1999) 'O zmianie zachowań komunikacyjnych we współczesnej kulturze audiowizualnej', in Gwóźdź, A (ed), *Panoramy i zbliżenia. Problemy wiedzy o filmie. Antologia prac śląskich filmoznawców*, Katowice: Wydawnictwo Naukowe Śląsk.

Miczka, T (2001) 'Multimedia - „multi' w mediach. O nowych formach i wymiarach pluralizacji kultury', in Borkowski, I & Woźny, A (eds), *Nowe media. Nowe w mediach*, Wrocław: Oficyna Wydawnicza Arboretum.

Misiak, T (2009) *Estetyczne konteksty audiosfery*, Poznań: Wyższa Szkoła Nauk Humanistycznych i Dziennikarstwa.

Mollgaard, M (ed) (2012) *Radio and Society: New Thinking for an Old Medium*, Newcastle upon Tyne: Cambridge Scholars Publishing.

Ogonowska, A (2004a) 'Kilka uwag o współczesnych zjawiskach kulturowych', in Ogonowska, A, *Tekst filmowy we współczesnym pejzażu kulturowym*, Kraków: Wydawnictwo Naukowe Akademii Pedagogicznej.

Ogonowska, A (2004b) 'Czy kryzys współczesnej kultury audiowizualnej?', in Ogonowska, A, *Tekst filmowy we współczesnym pejzażu kulturowym*, Kraków: Wydawnictwo Naukowe Akademii Pedagogicznej.

Oliveira, M (2013) 'Sounds and Identity: The role of radio in community building', in Stachyra, G (ed) *Radio: Community, Challenges, Aesthetics*, Lublin: Maria Curie-Skłodowska Univeristy Press.

Oliveira, M, Portela P & Santos, L (eds) (2012) *Radio evolution: Conference Proceedings*, Braga: University of Minho.

Ong, W (2002) 'Wtórna oralność', in Hopfinger, M (ed), *Nowe media w komunikacji społecznej w XX wieku. Antologia*, Warszawa: Oficyna Naukowa.

Pawlik [Mucha], A (2010) 'Współczesne tendencje rozwojowe adaptacji słuchowiskowych na tle uwarunkowań komunikacyjno-kulturowych', in Wolny-Zmorzyński, Kazimierz, Furman, Wojciech Nierenberg, Bogusław, Marszałek-Kawa J (eds), *Radio i gazety. Transformacja polskich mediów regionalnych po 1989 roku*, Toruń: Wydawnictwo Adam Marszałek.

Pleszkun-Olejniczakowa, E (2008) ''Dwa Teatry' - czyli o Teatrze wyobraźni i Teatrze Polskiego Radia', in Bogołębska, B & Kudra, A (eds) *Wypowiedź dziennikarska. Teoria i praktyka. Skrypt dla studentów Dziennikarstwa*, Łódź: Wydawnictwo Uniwersytetu Łódzkiego.

Pleszkun-Olejniczakowa, E (2012) *Muzy rzadko się do radia przyznają. Szkice o słuchowiskach i reportażach radiowych*, Łódź: Wydawnictwo Primum Verbum.

Siwak, W (2002) 'Audiosfera na przełomie stuleci', in Hopfinger, M (ed), *Nowe media w komunikacji społecznej w XX wieku. Antologia*, Warszawa: Oficyna Naukowa.

Starkey, G (2014) *Radio in Context: Second edition*, Basingstoke: Palgrave Macmillan.

Street, S (2012) *The Poetry of Radio. The Colour of Sound*, London: Routledge.

Suszczyński, Z (2002) 'Hipertekst a „galaktyka Gutenberga'', in Hopfinger, M (ed), *Nowe media w komunikacji społecznej w XX wieku. Antologia*, Warszawa: Oficyna Naukowa.

Thompson, JB (2006) *Media i nowoczesność. Społeczna teoria mediów*, translated into Polish by Mielnik, I, Wrocław 2006: Wydawnictwo Astrum.

Tuszewski, J (1979) 'Istota sztuki słuchowej', *Zeszyty Prasoznawcze*, volume 20, issue 3.

Tuszewski, J (2002) *Paradoks o słowie i dźwięku. Rozważania o sztuce radiowej*, Toruń: Wydawnictwo Adam Marszałek.

Welsch, W (2001) 'Na drodze do kultury słyszenia?', in Wilk, E (ed), *Przemoc ikoniczna czy „Nowa widzialność"?*, Katowice: Wydawnictwo Uniwersytetu Śląskiego.

Chapter 4

Radio news on the internet: is sound still dominant?

Ana Isabel Reis

Abstract

Radio on the internet is no longer just something to be listened to. It has become part of a hypermedium, where diverse elements of multimedia communication found in other genres and contrasting modes of address are brought together in an interactive and non-linear narrative. It is often now more of a production for the eyes than for the ear. Nonetheless, sound still seems to be the dominant element in news on national radio station websites in Portugal. This chapter examines the journalistic content of three such Portuguese radio station websites, examining the use of sound and other multimedia elements within them. It explores over a period of five years the evolution of the use of audio, video, still images and infographics on the news pages of the three websites.

The research underpinning the chapter is part of the externally-funded Portuguese project Net Station: Shaping Radio for the Web Environment. A major concern of the project is to identify convergence of media elements and genres where it exists and to determine to what extent these elements are interrelated. Moreover, the chapter will consider whether radio stations are effectively enhancing the multimedia narrative and diversifying the resources at its disposal or missing an opportunity.

Keywords: news, internet, websites, multimedia, journalism, Portugal

Introduction: From sound medium to hypermedia

For almost a century radio consisted only of sound, but today we ask whether sound is still dominant in radio news on the internet. Scholars long claimed the only connection that radio established with its audiences is through its codes, which are purely auditory (Crisell 1994: 5), that radio interprets the universe from a sound perspective (Herreros, 1995: 313), it represents the world to the ear (Arnheim 1980: 27), that it is an 'acoustic experience' (Lazarsfeld 1946: 38) and that 'radio speaks to us' (Adorno 2006: 77). Live or recorded sound is an essential journalistic element in the discourse of radio news, and the most important in broadcast radio, because we can only listen to the news on radio. We let sound transport us to the scene of an event or bring us face-to-face with the people in the news. On the internet, however, there is a form of radio journalism that consists of more than just sound. If we take as a reference point the notion of journalism as a map from which to view the world (Kovach & Rosentiel 2001), the potential for hypertextual, interactive and multimedia navigation of the internet multiplies this concept, irrespective of the nature of the core medium presenting itself on the web.

In radio we conceptualise sound journalism, while on the internet we can refer to hypermedia journalism. If radio is expression through sound, internet radio is simultaneously sound, multimedia and interactive expression (Herreros 2008: 63). It encompasses not only one form of expression but several, one which is intrinsic to radio - that is, sound - and now others which are intrinsic to the new medium or platform. It is the radio of our time, being both multimedia and multiplatform, because radio is not an island, as stated by Herreros (2011: 69), but it implies a permanently evolving communication ecosystem. Haye (2011:19) brought it closer to the concept of transmedia, as regards the confluences and intersections of media technologies and industries in which the content is interwoven through the actions of the audience - that is to say, when they interact with narratives with 'multiple entry points' that develop engaging narratives, thus generating an 'immersive experience'.

Digitisation and its consequences

From the analogue domain, radio has evolved through digitisation to something new, making the recording, editing, broadcasting and distribution of sound faster and more efficient in professional newsroom workflows. It was a second industrial or technological revolution, as suggested by Hendy (2004:48), that paved the way for digitisation, convergence and interactivity on this adaptable and still relatively new platform, the internet. If, on the one hand, digital technology favours diversification of content and the emergence of new narratives, on the other hand the ease in transferring content from one medium to another makes it more prone to the risk of simply replicating content (Starkey & Crisell 2009:125-6), which is aggravated in the context of concentration of media ownership, ultimately at a global level. These two authors highlight another impact of digitisation to which they attribute greater importance, 'a convergence of previously separate media', where everyone can see, read and listen to the news from a mobile device. Although some radio content can be displayed as text or images on a screen, some researchers continue to argue that it is still the sound that distinguishes it from other media. That is, sound still remains as its essence (Starkey & Crisell 2009; Herreros 2011). Sound is the essence of radio's identity, irrespective of the means, platform or device through which audiences accesses its content. In particular, it is the predominance of sound that distinguishes web radio from other online media forms, as all are multimedia and interactive, but only radio has the resources to offer new auditory experiences, as well as other sound creations born from the fusion of the radio with the web. In fact, sound is a secondary element in online media that normally emphasises the primacy of the image at the expense of audio recording. Sound may even be the predominant resource in some radio websites, but now it is just an option and not all radio websites or web radio stations privilege it in the design of their homepage or graphically highlight the presence of audio alongside to the text. Radio has reached the screens, where the first contact is now visual. It can be seen, read and eventually listened to, but listening is only an option here, unlike with broadcast radio.

In online editing manuals, audio seems more like an extra that accompanies, illustrates or complements the text. Despite the theories of hypermedia interconnection, in practice, sound does not come in a logic of integration, but instead of separation as, indeed, happens with other audio-visual components. In a multimedia context, radio (and its journalistic content,) absorbs and enhances the characteristics attributed to the internet as a means of communication and transmission: hypertext, multimediality and interactivity - features that interconnect or combine to create a new language and a new discourse. Radio unites sound with new resources, becoming a hypermedia product. That is, hypermedia is the result of applying interactivity to multimedia systems that are interconnected in a network. Of the internet, we rarely talk, in the pure sense, about newspapers, radio or television but instead we conceptualise a new means of communication with a narrative and a language of its own. The internet enabled the possibility of combining in a single message text, images and sounds, all in a dynamic interconnection and integration of various expressive resources. Therefore, we rarely speak of each individually or consider them in isolation. The journalistic product on the web is a result of their articulation together, and their evolution and exploitation by users, through the proliferation of interactive tools and features often called Web 2.0. Radio, more than any other medium, identifies and strengthens itself with new means of dissemination, communication and expression. It is through these new electronic channels that it transforms itself, ceasing now to be an exclusively auditory means of communication and expression. Radio websites try to be more appealing, not through sound, but through the diversification of content and resources used, through design, colour and image, and by offering more than just that which is broadcast. Nevertheless, sound content does not often include much more than that which was already broadcast. In particular, there are few signs of new sound narratives, even at an embryonic stage.

Newspapers, radio stations and television channels adopt similar strategies and offer similar content, using multimedia resources to capture and secure the user's attention. Image and video are often referred to as key elements in the launching or relaunching of websites, even those published by radio stations. The internet continues to stimulate competition among media to attract and maintain the public's attention, just as early on in this revolution Priestman raised a very pertinent question, asking what given pictures really add to the radio (2002: 48). Radio has found its place in the evolution of media, and the multimedia challenge that the internet has initiated focuses more on the behaviour of audiences and how they appropriate the new media. Radio's evolution on the internet is more than a visual phenomenon, so we must take into account how it is used and 'the challenges multimedia structures represent' (Oliveira *et al* 2012: 4).

In Portugal, radio ventured onto the internet in the mid-1990s, and despite digital production and distribution allowing quick processing and then distribution of sound on the web without changing too many routines in the newsrooms, only more recently have large numbers of radio stations truly begin to invest in production for the platform. Studies of the relationship between radio and the internet show that there are differences compared with other media. 'In fact, it can be complementary since radio is the one medium that easily adapts itself to Web 2.0 and, furthermore, amplifies the social networks' (Cardoso *et al* 2009). Throughout its history, radio has survived new challenges and has been able to adapt to new technologies by integrating them - a resilience already dubbed Radiomorphosis (Fidler 1997). Even so, in the internet age it is well known that radio is still not able to take advantage of all the potential of the web (Bastos *et al* 2012: 104), nor of the characteristics they share. Journalists were until now only concerned with sound as contributing to news values, but now they must take care to narrate events using more than just sound. A new professional role is that of 'interactive multimedia journalist' (Garrand 2006: 23) or even a 'net handler' (Saíz Olmo 2005). A study of Portuguese radio reporters and their relationship with the internet concluded that most agree that the multimedia component is very important in the presentation of news on the websites of their respective radio stations (Bastos *et al* 2012: 108). Nevertheless, multimedia elements apparently have a limited role on radio websites; sound remains the most common resource, although it is losing ground.

The Portuguese radio sector

For this study we selected three national radio stations: the public broadcaster RDP Antena 1, the Catholic broadcaster Rádio Renascença and the private broadcaster TSF with its all-news format. RDP Antena 1 is the heiress of the National Radio created in the 1930s. It is a public radio station, and part of the public media group Rádio e Televisão de Portugal, along with the public television service RTP. The state-owned group runs various free-to-air (FTA) and cable TV channels, as well as the radio stations Antena 1, Antena 2, Antena 3, RDP Africa, RDP International, RDP Madeira and RDP Açores, as well as several web radio stations. They can all be found on a single website, RTP, meaning radio and television of Portugal. The site uses the address of the television service, through which one accesses the radio pages that do not have their own URLs. Rádio Renascença (RR) was born in the 1930s, and it is owned by the Portuguese Catholic Church, being also part of 'r/com', which groups other radio stations in the group, namely RFM, Mega Hits and Radio Sim. On the internet, each station has its own page, being separate but linked to the others. On its website, RR distributes a newspaper in .pdf format, *Página 1*, and it also has a WebTV called V+. TSF Rádio Jornal was born as a pirate radio station in the 1980s in Lisbon. It is a private radio station with an all-news format, the only of its kind in Portugal. TSF is part of one of the largest national media groups, Controlinveste, which owns some of the daily newspapers with the largest national circulations, *Jornal de Notícias* and *Diário de Notícias*, and the sport television channels of Sport TV which is distributed on cable. Despite not having a national radio frequency, it broadcasts to the entire country using a network of enough local and regional stations and frequencies to provide coverage. The three radio stations built their websites in the second half of the 1990s.

Methodology and results

The goal we set ourselves was to establish whether there is a predominance of sound in relation to other multimedia elements on the news websites of the Portuguese radio stations. Therefore, the analysis focused on the frequency and evolution of various items posted online. The sample consisted of the top stories on the opening page of the websites. A week was randomly chosen in the years 2008 2010 and 2013, and data collection was performed from Monday to Sunday, with three daily census points that corresponded to major periods of web access according to the Netpanel of Marktest, a Portuguese company that measures audiences. These were 09:00 to 10:00, 15:00 to 16:00 and 22:00 to 23:00. We selected the websites of the three radio stations, RDP Antena 1, Rádio Renascença and TSF because they emphasised news content either on air or online. Given the impportance of these criteria, we excluded music-oriented radio stations, local radio stations and stations that exclusively distributed on the web. In all, 1,127 news items were analysed.

In the period analysed, it was clear that audio was still the most frequently-used element of the news websites of the three stations. Text with audio and audio with still images amounted to 76.9 per cent in 2008, 45.5 per cent in 2010 and 47.9 per cent in 2013. Audio was still a predominant element, not only because alone it still had a high occurance, but also because news with video or infographics usually had one or more audio elements. Excluding text-only and video-only news, the items with audio, even if combined with other elements, result in high percentages: 82.8 per cent in 2008, 68.8 per cent in 2010 and 51.6 per cent in 2013. Noticeably, sound was present in most of the news items over the three years, although it was losing ground to video and text-only news. Two factors contributed to this result: RDP only featured news with audio, (a single clip,) and only in 2010 did it add still images or the radio station's logo to news items. On all the sites the audio uploaded to the news page had been broadcast or edited from what was recorded for the radio, so it required little additional production outside the usual routines of the newsroom, which posted it on the website soon afterwards.

However, the percentage of text-only news was still high: in 2008 and 2010 it remained at 17 per cent, but it rose to 21.8 per cent in 2013. This increase is significant as it indicates a tendency to not include any multimedia elements in some stories, which may have different interpretations that only time can clarify. Some are last minute text-only stories which may explain in part the lack of audio or other multimedia elements that only emerge after an update. Another explanation may lie in the nature of the stories, (politics and the economy,) and in the sources used, which are often official documents, reports, newspapers and other written sources, so the first iteration of the story is often text-only news, with other multimedia elements being added only later. This scenario was especially common in the week in 2013, when most of the news content was related to the political and economic crisis that Portugal was experiencing. There is another factor to take into account, which can only be confirmed in the long term. On the one hand, we saw the urgency to publish news that impacts upon people's daily lives, but on the other, there is evidence that internet users may want to quickly access information and move on to the next item without wasting much time, grasping the title and headline and skimming the body of the text. In particular, one option is to just read the text, which can lead the radio stations to under-invest in the multimedia elements which require longer and costlier production time. Regarding the use of audio-visual resources, the overall percentage indicates a significant increase from 5.9 per cent in 2008 to 37.1 per cent in 2010, but in 2013 it recorded a decrease to 30.3 per cent. In other words, we have seen an increase in text-only news, (or text and still images,) and news with audio, (or audio and still images), and although there was significant growth of multimedia elements in news at first, there was a decrease in the last year being studied.

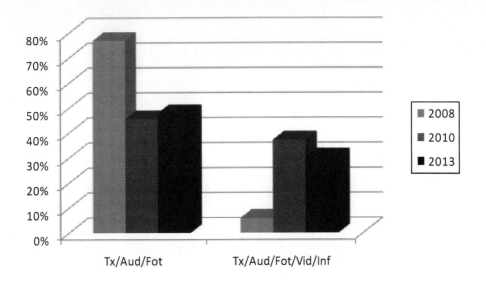

Figure 4.1: Use of different elements in the sample, with and without moving images per year

Video was present on only two of the websites analysed, Rádio Renascença (RR) and TSF. In 2008 RR did not post videos, in 2010 it started to offer three videos in a highlighted section, and by 2013 it had already begun streaming *V+*, the video channel that on its homepage had a box with five videos. On RR videos were from the news of the day, and since 2012 there has been a daily news video. They are either RR-produced videos or from a news agency in the case of international news, for which the station has no reporter or correspondent on site. *V+* has a page where videos of news, programmes and sport intentionally appear in different channels. Initially, on TSF, most videos were reports of issues that were not current. They were almost always 'best of' news reports with audio and video versions, news in brief, programmes or columns of station editorials. Only after 2010 did TSF start to include videos of the news of the day, although they were not RR-produced, but videos from the Portuguese news agency LUSA or SportTV, which belong to the same group as the radio station. There were even videos of great interviews previously broadcast on the radio and published in newspapers of the group. Most of these videos are not in the Highlights of TSF's homepage, but in other sections. In the final sample, videos from non-journalistic programmes, posted with greater emphasis on the homepage, were not included.

The audio news page of RDP has no video, but video is the main element on the website of the group Radio and Television of Portugal, which is dominated by the video content of RTP, the public television station, within whose site the radio pages are integrated. However, there is no interconnection on the website between the content of the radio station and of the television service. Both are displayed on the homepage of the website, but then each brand is accessed from its own page, RTP or RDP. These features contribute to the results obtained against each parameter analysed, and simultaneously reflect the brand and the editorial line of each radio station on their respective websites. The use of all elements was changed over the period surveyed, due to the renewal or modification of the websites or the integration of new elements, sections or features, greater or lesser investment in online staff, and consequently in the presence of radio on the internet. The infrequent use of infographics or other non-text-based elements, such as audio, video, and the still image was very noticeable. Regarding the results, in 2008 news with infographics represented 1.1 per cent of the total, in 2010 it was 3.1 per cent and in 2013 no examples were found in the week analysed. In 2008 'multimedia news' that would integrate various elements amounted to 1.1 per cent, but in 2010 and in 2013 not a single one was recorded in the highlighted sections of the three radio station websites. In other words, the so-called multimedia narrative is not a significant feature of the radio stations' websites, and in two of them, (not RDP due to the nature of the website,) the different elements do not appear integrated into the text, as there is no real hypertext nor hypermedia narrative. The elements appear in juxtaposition, flanking the text, in isolated boxes for audio, video and so on, as if they were different versions of a news story. In short, there is not a hypermedia narrative with its own language, but instead, the sum of separate items of sound and image.

The top stories are usually more immediate current news, hence the lack of infographics or images, since the time needed to produce them would mean delaying posting the story. This may also be one of the reasons for the predominance of audio, because it has already been broadcast, and so can be rapidly posted on the website. The production and post-production of a video is also slower than producing just sound or text. It is also necessary to take into account that the diversity of multimedia elements requires equipment and staff with specific skills other than those in the traditional radio newsroom. In addition, there is another factor that should not be overlooked: now, the radio journalist has to not only keep in mind news values relating to sound, but also to consider whether there is any visual perspective to stories. All these factors may contribute to a still cautious use of audio-visual elements. Infographics were the least used element in the period analysed, and among highlighted stories they only appear on a single website, RR. TSF also posts some infographics or photo galleries, but usually elsewhere on the page, often for feature stories that integrate themes or special reports involving some advance planning, which is more consistent with the production time for infographics.

In the three years analysed, there has been a gradual evolution of the use of multimedia tools, especially in integrating video. As shown in Figure 4.2, video is the element that most evolved over the period analysed. With none recorded in 2008, it rose to 13.8 per cent in 2010 and to 26.6 per cent in 2013. In 2008 there was no instance of news with text, audio and video, but in 2010 18.2 per cent was recorded, yet in 2013 that figure decreased to 1.8 per cent. This was due to many videos being posted without other associated elements. That is, they were just video reports, which is largely due to the appearance of the Web TV channel of one of the websites and the football section of another that sometimes publishes videos of goals or summaries of matches, adding just the audio later. Text-only news with audio declined over the period analysed, from 38.5 per cent in 2008 to 23.3 per cent in 2010, and 14 per cent in 2013. This corresponds almost entirely with the RDP public station that initially had only text and audio, beginning by 2013 to post, although not always, a still image relating to the event. For this reason, text-only news with audio and still image fell in 2010 but returned by 2013 to identical values to those in 2008. Still images are often used only among the Highlights of the homepage, so the news page does not always have images.

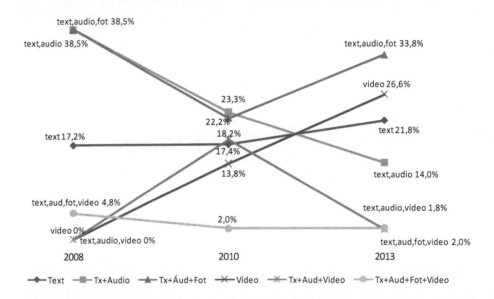

Figure 4.2: Change in the use of different multimedia news elements in news stories on radio station websites

Photo galleries with or without sound or slideshows are not very common on the three websites, either in the highlights or elsewhere. There are some examples on blogs associated with dossiers or special programmes, but not on a daily basis. Radio creates images through sound, but it is not used to dealing with the physical image, and although there are newsrooms with video journalists, there are no photojournalists. This will be one of the reasons leading to a new cyberjournalistic genre not often used, because the production time needed does not synchronise well with the more immediate present. Of the few examples found, we noted two findings: the photographs were from radio journalists or from news agencies. On one of the websites, especially for news of accidents or natural disasters, photographs are posted by journalists sent to the location, who first photograph with the phone and then record the sound - a clear reversal of the priorities of the radio journalist, who is now becoming multimedia in nature and where image has become a news value, just like sound. The priority is to tell the news by using the tools they have at their disposal, depending on the platform which first breaks the news to the audience. However, many stations still choose to broadcast breaking news in the traditional way and only then post it on the internet, but sometimes websites published some aspects of running stories and only later added them to the newscast. For some news stories it is common for one of the websites to appeal to their listeners and internet users to send photos of a blizzard, a flood or a fire. Photographs are published after being checked by an editor or another journalist who selects them. A curious result is the increase in text-only news, as discussed previously. In 2008 and 2010 it remained at around 17 per cent but by 2013 it had risen to 21.8 per cent. The percentage of stories which included various multimedia elements fell, which could mean that the stations' investment in hypermedia narratives with new languages is losing ground, from 4.8 per cent in 2008 to only 2 per cent in both 2010 and 2013. In other words, there is now more text and less multimedia.

Conclusion

Sound is still the most widely-used multimedia element on the websites of the three Portuguese radio stations analysed, extending to the web the main raw material of traditional radio. There is a predominance of sound, but there has been a gradual convergence of approaches and languages, albeit juxtaposed but with the various elements separate from each other, and not in a truly convergent hypermedia narrative or any kind of narrative or language with its own and distinctive characteristics. Furthermore, there is no evidence that leads us to identify the existence of new sound or hypermedia narratives, on any of the three sites analysed. We simply found three different ways to present the news that reflect the editorial line of the radio station and its brand. There is also the extension to the internet of the original broadcast audio, without a real distinction being made between the different distribution platforms. Sound predominates, although increasingly less so, as video has gained ground, but there is more and more text-only news and less news that uses a range of multimedia elements. There is clearly an underusage of the potential of the internet, which can be due to multiple interconnected scenarios, including a lack of human resources or technical staff and specific training, a lack of investment, insufficient advertising revenue, radio professionals' resistance to or difficulty in adapting to the new environment, the absence of a long-term strategy for online content, and the recent crisis in the media sector in Portugal, which has led to substantial cutbacks in newsrooms.

After more than 15 years, we can say that in Portugal radio on the internet is still in an 'experimental' phase in which each radio station chooses its own path. The sample represents three stations with three different websites, with structures, usability options, design, content presentation and elements that reflect different visions of what may be the website of a radio station. Each website follows a path and then tries and tests possibilities which it abandons, adopts or transforms. What we see, read and listen to from radio stations on the web does not necessarily result in consciously outlined strategies and options for the digital domain, but is the result of newsroom routines, the technical, human and logistical possibilities of each station, the challenge of faster information delivery, and how the internet is still seen in the radio sector. That is, as a complement to traditional broadcasting that continues to be the most important platform. Despite the trend towards greater use of multimedia elements, more so in some websites than in others, the truth is that a decade and a half after the entry of Portuguese radios onto the internet, their hypermedia possibilities are still underused.

References

Adorno, T (2006) *Current Music. Elements of a Radio Theory Suhrkamp*, Frankfurt: Suhrkamp.

Arnheim, R (1980). *Estética radiofónica*. Barcelona: Editorial Gustavo Gili.

Bastos, H, Lima, H, Moutinho, N & Reis, A (2012) 'Radio journalists and the internet: a study of perceptions', in Oliveira, M, Portela P & Santos, L (eds), *Radio evolution: Conference Proceedings*, Braga: University of Minho.

Cardoso, G, Espanha, R & Araújo, V (2009) *Da Comunicação de Massa à Comunicação em Rede*, Porto: Porto Editora.

Caridad, M & Moscoso, P (1992) 'Una introdución a los sistemas de hipermedios', *Revista General de Información e Documentación*, volume 2, issue 1, Madrid: Edit. Complutense.

Crisell, A (1994) *Understanding Radio*, London: Routledge.

Fidler, R (1997) *Mediamorphosis: Understanding New Media*, California: Pine Forge Press.

Haye, R (2011). *La radio que viene. Rádio-Leituras*.
http://radioleituras.files.wordpress.com/2011/08/3-haye_port1.pdf

Garrand, T (2006) *Writing for multimedia and the web*, Burlington: Focal Press.

Hendy, D (2004) *Radio in the Global Age*, Cambridge: Polity Press.

Herreros, C (1995) *Información Radiofónica. Mediación técnica, tratamiento y programación*, Madrid: Editorial Síntesis.

Herreros, C (2001) *La radio en la convergencia multimedia*, Barcelona: Editoial Gedisa.

Herreros, C (2008) *La radio en internet*. Buenos Aires: La Cruíja.

Herreros, C (2011) 'La radio en el entorno de las multiplataformas de comunicaciones', *Rádio-Leituras*.   http://radioleituras.files.wordpress.com/2012/04/3-cebrian-herreros-pt.pdf

Kovach, B & Rosenstiel, T (2001) *The Elements of Journalism: What Newspeople Should Know and the Public Should Expect*. New York: Three Rivers Press.

Landow, G (2006) *Hypertext 3.0*, Maryland: The John Hopkins University Press.

Lazarsfeld, P & Field, H (1946) *The People Look at Radio*.

http://www.archive.org/search.php?query=radio%20research%20AND%20collection%3Aamericana

Merayo Perez, A (2001) 'Formación, nuevos contenidos y creatividad sonora: apuestas para un tiempo de incertidumbre tecnológica', in *Reinventar la radio*, *Actas de las XV Jornadas Internacionales de la Comunicación*, Pamplona: Universidad de Navarra.

Nielsen, J (1995) *Multimedia and Hypertext: The Internet Beyond*, San Diego: Academic Press.

Oliveira, M, Portela, P & Santos, L (2012) Preface to *Radio evolution: Conference Proceedings*, Braga: University of Minho.

Priestman, C (2002) *Webradio. Radio Production for Internet Streaming*, Oxford: Focal Press.

Saíz Olmo, J (2005) *Periodismo de Radio*, Valencia: Universidad Cardenal Herrera.

Starkey, G & Crisell, A (2009) *Radio Journalism*, London: Sage Publications.

Chapter 5

Radio entertainment from the perspective of convergence: Case studies of Polish commercial radio stations

Paulina Czarnek

Abstract

Convergence is a complex phenomenon which can not be ignored when talking about the nature of contemporary media. It is a significant influence on the Polish radio industry, including its commercial sector. This chapter presents two case studies of modern commercial radio from the perspective of convergence.

Competition in the Polish radio market has led commercial radio stations to use many different approaches and to create increasingly diverse content in order to reach their audiences. These include exploiting the possibilities offered by the phenomenon of convergence, which allows radio stations to gain from the experience of other media, as well as to influence and exploit them. Of course, it is difficult to predict how developments in state-of-the-art technologies might change radio in the future, but it seems unlikely that they will bring about its demise.

The chapter concentrates on the evolution of radio in the field of entertainment, looking briefly at some early examples of the genre and examining in detail two more recent initiatives which exploit the possibilities of convergence on Polish commercial radio, where entertainment is a significant part of the content. This raises a number of questions. Does entertainment radio benefit from user-generated content? How does it interact with the audience using the internet, social media and mobile applications? How do radio broadcasters combine their radio and new media content? What are the implications of the answers to these questions for the resilience of entertainment genres on radio?

Keywords: commercial radio, entertainment, convergence, visuality, Poland

Introduction: towards visuality

'Despite predictions about having reached the end, we are merely at the beginning of the path to understanding (very far from the end) the changes in modern society, an effect and driving force of which are new media and new technologies', wrote Karol Jakubowicz (2011: 273). The process of convergence is a many-sided phenomenon, and its future is very difficult to predict. What is certain, however, is that the development of new technologies is significantly influencing the shape of social media today, as well as the work of those involved in them. This is also true in the case of audio media. Stanisław Jędrzejewski has stressed: 'Without a doubt all radio broadcasters nowadays, including public ones, have to make use of the possibilities offered by new technologies' (2010: 251). The functioning of the mass media is not only based on a relay, but also on the participants in the act of communication, especially the receivers. Aleksandra Pawlik has focused on this issue when writing about radio series: 'The question if radio will become a modern medium depends on the effect of the process of convergence and media listeners having sufficient media competence to allow them to create a coherent perception of sound, picture and words' (2012: 384).

The entertainment offered by commercial radio stations has often taken the form of precisely-planned campaigns which combine different functional aspects of today's audio media. That is, those connected with being on-air, on the internet, and in social media, as well as those outside the radio studio and involving interaction with the audience. An example of this kind of campaign is a competition organised by radio RMF FM, entitled *Ja Cię kręcę!* The title of the competition is quite equivocal, and can be explained on two different levels – literally as 'make a film with somebody' or as an expression of excitement and astonishment. It premiered on 24 June 2013 at the beginning of the summer holidays in Poland. The idea of the competition was to encourage listeners to send short films with their own interpretations of well-known songs to the station. The main aim of this campaign was to promote the music played in radio RMF FM and music compatible with the format of the station.

It seems intentional that the radio broadcaster organised this competition at the beginning of the summer holidays. The campaign was supposed to be a pleasant form of light entertainment accompanying listeners during their summer trips. From the listeners' point of view, a very important aspect was the mercantile character of this competition, which harmonised with its entertainment character. The best recordings were selected by the audience and rewarded. One hundred people whose films were posted at www.rmf.fm received a guaranteed prize, a CD entitled *RMF FM The Best Music Under The Sun 2013*. In the next stage of the competition, smartphones were awarded each week to the winner in an online listener competition. The main winner, also chosen by the audience, received a special award: a performance during the Top of the Top Sopot Festival, organised in Opera Leśna by Polsat, a commercial television station, in which Polish and foreign artists participate. This event was linked to a series of well-known music festivals held in Sopot, previously produced by a Polish public broadcaster, (and later TVN,) in which such performers as Whitney Houston, Elton John and Annie Lennox had performed. The winner of the *Ja Cię kręcę!* competition, Natalia Walczak, (who, in her recording, covered the Jennifer Paige song *Crush*,) sang with the music group Enej on the second day of the festival (Saturday 24 August 2013) in a concert featuring summer hits. Interestingly, this band first entered Poland's show-business in a similar way, by winning a talent show called *Tylko muzyka* ('Must be the music'). It would seem that the producers consciously chose this musical duet because both partners in it shared similar experiences and had followed comparable musical paths. They sang *Skrzydlate ręce*, the song that had been used in the advertising campaign promoting the competition. Enej was also among a group of artists who travelled through Poland singing with radio listeners. Their performance at the Top of the Top Sopot Festival became a topic in radio programmes and on the news website www.rmf24.pl. An article about it was published on 24 August (Łuczkowska 2013). On the radio station website 653 recordings sent by listeners were posted. Most of them showed people having great fun while performing popular songs. Only a small group displayed concrete musical and aesthetic values. Twelve films qualified for the final. Those taking part in the competition were adults, children, soloists, duets and even larger groups composed of friends and family members.

These kinds of media initiatives are connected with creating the image of the station, as well as connecting with its community of listeners. Radio RMF FM has given a very clear signal that it wants to make listeners active on-air, on its website and on profiles in social media. An element of creating the station's image through this competition was an advertising campaign that allowed the broadcaster to reach its audience through other forms of mass media. On television they used TVP 1, TVP 2, TVP Info, Polsat, TV 4, TVN and thematic channels from the Polsat portfolio, Atmedia and Discovery, as well as newspapers and on the internet YouTube, Ipla and sites run by AtMax. In terms of entertainment, the amusing character of the advert should be noted. It presented radio journalists Przemysław Skowron, Darek Maciborek, Daniel Dyk, Iwona Bołdak-Kołyszko, Jacek Tomkowicz, Adrianna Byszewska, Radosław Terlecki, Marek Rusinek and Balbina Maciejewska travelling by car and singing hits that are well-known from radio RMF FM. This kind of promotional material showed that taking part in the competition would let listeners experience happy times and the same emotions as those seen in the advertisement. This raises an important aspect of this campaign, identification with the station. This can be achieved or strengthened through entertainment initiatives. Using well-known and popular presenters in this campaign intensified the attractiveness of its message and made it self-referential. It also showed journalists as 'ordinary' people who, like listeners, love listening to the radio while driving a car and humming the melodies they hear. Of course, the whole advertisement is clearly staged and was created especially for this campaign, but it was entertaining and impressive. Listeners may delight in watching their favourite journalists in completely new circumstances, usually singing badly and out of tune.

In the advertising campaign two different spots were used. One was set to a song made by the group Enej entitled *Skrzydlate ręce* and the other was a hit by Maciek Malenczuk and Yugopolis, *Ostatnia nocka*. Additionally, on the radio website two short 30-second films were posted. The first one was a 'making-of' production. The second was satirical in character and showed a journalist disguised as Little Red Riding Hood and images of two very important Polish politicians who are rivals on the Polish political scene – the chairman of Prawo i Sprawiedliwość (Law and Justice), former Prime Minister Jarosław Kaczyński and the chairman of Platforma Obywatelska (Civic Platform) and the then Prime Minister, Donald Tusk. This spot was confined to the internet because of concerns about its political correctness and possible consequences. Its aim should be acknowledged as purely entertainment. The recording was supposed to show that RMF FM can play with different conventions and sometimes even engage in spheres characteristic of a completely different kind of message, such as stand-up comedy.

The competition was accompanied by an event called the Hit Tour in which artists connected with radio RMF FM participated. The schedule was as follows:

> 3 July: Pectus (Nowy Dwór Mazowiecki – Piaseczno)
>
> 9 July: Ania Wyszkoni (Wrocław – Brzeg)
>
> 15 July: Enej (Kazimierz Dolny nad Wisłą – Radom)
>
> 24 July: Bracia (Lublin – Łuków)
>
> 31 July: Rafał Brzozowski (Grodzisk Mazowiecki – Łowicz)
>
> 6 August: LemON (Hel – Władysławowo)
>
> 13 August: Andrzej Piaseczny (Kielce – Kraków)
>
> 21 August: Sylwia Grzeszczak (Poznań – Września).

Musicians travelled in characteristic yellow and blue cars bearing the logo of RMF FM, inside which cameras were installed. During each trip, artists were supported by listeners who performed popular songs with them. Films and photos from the Hit Tour were published on www.rmf.fm. Artists reached numerous regions of Poland such as Pomorze, Dolny Śląsk, Mazowsze and Małopolska. Information about all the events taking place on the tour could be found in radio programmes, on the radio website, and in local media. Many special events were organised involving the musicians, such as Pectus visiting a car wash in Wołomin, Ania Wyszkoni tasting delicious sweets in one of the cafés in Oleśnica, Enej singing with fire fighters from Zwoleń and a shop assistant from Wólka Łagowska, Bracia taking part in the technical servicing of their car and meeting a group of motorcyclists. Rafał Brzozowski impersonated a conductor, a riding instructor, an excavator operator, a beekeeper and a member of a traditional folk band. LemON spent a pleasant time on a beach on the Baltic Sea, Andrzej Piaseczny visited an open-air museum in Chęciny and the ruins of the castle in Sobkowo, and Sylwia Grzeszczak made candies and a lollipop with her own hands in Poznań.

All of these events seemed spontaneous, but the truth is that they were precisely planned. We became convinced of this while attentively watching the numerous films from the Hit Tour and, for example, seeing musicians and their guests singing songs from a printed text. What is more, artists had the possibility of choosing these from a list prepared by the producers. Despite this, everything looked very good and was funny, like the best entertainment. Listeners who wanted to take part in this tour had to fill in a special questionnaire and justify their choices. The creators of the 25 most interesting ideas were invited to participate in the artist tours. One of them, Sebastian Dudka, a paramedic from Września, who appeared in the episode with Sylwia Grzeszczak, said of the benefits he derived from taking part in the Hit Tour: 'I thought that my entry would get lost among the thousands of others. But this didn't happen, and

I'm very happy about this, especially because I'm the last participant on the whole tour. It will be a great adventure that I will remember for a long time' (Dai 2013).

Tomasz Szlendak and Tomasz Kozłowski in a book entitled *Naked Monkey in Front of TV: Pop Culture in the Light of Evolutionary Psychology*, stressed that the influence of watching television was causing a shift away from a culture of reflection towards a culture of addiction: 'The culture of text or print was at the same time a culture of reflection in which the strength and legitimacy of argumentation was essential' (2008: 146). They wrote that a culture of addiction does not support or require all of the cognitive instruments that we possess, which in consequence, leads to the substitution of a hierarchy of rules and values with a hierarchy of prizes and punishments. This is also caused by an entertainment offer. These mechanics are skilfully used by television producers who are able to arouse emotions in numerous episodes of a series, so viewers will not leave it even for a moment. This concerns television series, talent and reality shows, morning shows and even the news. The *Ja Cię kręcę!* competition also tried to benefit from this culture of addiction. Over two months, listeners were being kept posted about the course of the on-air campaign, via radio website or social media, taking part in the numerous stages of the Hit Tour, voting for their favourite recordings, commenting on them and consistently waiting for a final decision and the climax, which was the performance at the Top of the Top Sopot Festival. At this moment the winner of the competition changed significantly from a dowdy Cinderella into a princess. This could be seen at a very basic level, taking into consideration the image of women. In the recording she sent to the station she looked quite natural and casual, while in Sopot she was appropriately prepared by stylists, hairdressers and make-up artists. But what will the future of the winner look like? Will she benefit from her success? At this moment it is surely too early to know unambiguously but it seems like participation in this competition was only an interesting summer adventure - an experience which won't lead to anything more. The first prize was limited to a single performance, which potentially might interest somebody from show-business but success wasn't guaranteed.

The *Ja Cię kręcę!* competition can be described as a campaign presenting multiplied, multilayered amusement. The entertainment goal is fulfilled in different ways that complement each other. Firstly, listeners work on their recordings and have fun while doing it. This is an extraordinary form of entertainment which provides an opportunity for personal involvement in the mass media. The next level of entertainment occurs when the recordings get through to radio producers who verify and publish them on the website. Potentially they can take pleasure in the act of seeing this content. This also occurs at the next stage of the entertainment process – listeners who watch films on the radio website join in the feeling of amusement. In this way, radio fulfils the hypertrophy of the entertainment function that relates to each stage of the competition.

Radio talent shows

The course of the *Ja Cię kręcę!* competition is in some aspects quite similar to that of the television talent shows that dominate the programme offer of public and commercial broadcasters all over the world. The origin of such shows is connected to radio. The history of radio talent shows starts early in the medium's existence, as evidenced by some examples from American and British radio stations. One of these was *the Major Bowes Amateur Hour*, broadcast from April 1934 by WHN and moving to other stations until September 1952, when ABC decided to end production. Its author was Edward Bowes – a visionary radio personality who searched for talented people and had a keen marketing sense. This allowed him create what would become one of the most popular television programme formats. Bowes looked for people with different abilities, which were then presented during special show tours. In the 1940s the programme moved to television, initiating the audiovisual era in the history of talent shows. A similar transition took place in British radio. In September 1949 the BBC Light Programme started broadcasting a programme called *Opportunity Knocks*, (from 1950 it was on Radio Luxembourg,) which moved to television in 1956. It was based on a postal vote by the audience, who decided the final results in the competition.

How did the *Ja Cię kręcę!* competition compare to the typical features of talent show productions? Let us consider this question according to a number of common criteria:

Contestants In talent show programmes the people competing are usually unknown to wider audiences. Their aim is to become visible in the media and show their extraordinary abilities. In the case of some contestants, the most important reason is simply to become famous. In *Ja Cię kręcę!*, the competitors were radio listeners who decided to share their vocal attempts with other people. Contrary to the participants of television programmes, they did not have to give live shows in front of an audience. They could calmly prepare their recordings, edit them properly, and sometimes even direct them. What is more, nobody wanted to get into their private lives, which is quite typical of television programmes. Showing the history of each contestant creates an emotional performance and is familiar in character, such as thanking the local communities they come from. In the case of *Ja Cię kręcę!* this aspect was significantly limited, although there were some initiatives supporting contestants organised in their local communities, on blogs or regional websites and so on.

Mercantile character The aim of people taking part in this kind of rivalry is to win a prize defined in the competition regulations. In music talent show productions, this is usually a considerable amount of money or a contract for recording debut material. In the case of the competition analysed in this paper, the producers decided to prepare a system of prizes appropriate for the each stage of the competition. In the first, there were CDs (all contestants), then smartphones (the winners of the finals each week), and finally, the first prize which was a performance at the Top of the Top Sopot Festival. Furthermore, television talent show programmes are a great source of income for their producers. Profits can be earned from text messages sent as a form of voting or advertisements shown during a programme. Radio RMF FM decided to move voting, as well as a significant part of the competition, to the internet. Listeners chose their favourite performances on the radio website. On the one hand, this form of voting was not a source of substantial profit, but on the other, it contributed to increasing the number of people visiting the radio station's website, which may result in some positive benefit in the future.

Multiple-stage structure Talent show programmes consist of many different levels, in order to build the drama of the events. They usually begin with precastings, then have castings with famous judges and experts and the next stages of eliminations, and finally live programmes in which the audience decides about the future of each competitor. Radio RMF FM also offered a multiple-stage competition – listeners first sent their recordings to the station, then the twelve best videos were selected, from which the winner was chosen. The main difference is that the contestants of television talent shows have to prove their abilities numerous times and complete different tasks, while in *Ja Cie kręcę!* the number of performances was limited to just one.

Judges Judges are an essential part of talent show programmes, deciding about the professionalism of the production as well as influencing its emotional potential. They create their image through their opinions about contestants, but also through interactions with other members of jury. Viewers also play the role of judge when they express their opinions about each performance in their voting. Radio RMF FM decided to cede the responsibility for the final results to the audience. Listeners voted online and commented via social media, which could be seen as the equivalent of the judges' opinions on television talent shows.

Promotional campaigns In terms of the way a successful talent show is produced, we cannot forget about advertising and a substantial promotional campaign to arouse and maintain the interest of listeners and viewers. In the radio RMF FM competition such elements were also apparent. Firstly, adverts were published in different types of media. The aim of these was to encourage listeners to participate in the competition. Secondly, there were self-advertising operations that included the radio station's on-air content, its website and profiles in social media. The Hit Tour, which visited different pats of Poland, also helped promote the competition. Shows given by special guests at each stage of the tour can be compared to mini-recitals performed by music stars in television talent shows as a kind of special attraction. A lot is said in the media about talent shows and their contestants in order to keep viewers' attention. In the case of *Ja Cię kręcę!*, information about it was mostly in media connected with the owner of RMF FM, such as the Interia.pl and Rmf24.pl websites, the trade press and some local media.

Radio RMF FM has experience in talent show productions because of its work on six seasons of a television programme it co-created, *Tylko muzyka* ('Must be the music'), broadcast on Polsat. In the *Ja Cię kręcę!* competition, they also cooperated – the first prize was a performance at a festival organised and broadcast by Polsat. Between the audio and audiovisual type of talent show there were many similarities and differences, as noted in this analysis. The RMF FM production was supposed to give so-called 'ordinary' people the chance to exist in the media, which is typical of programmes searching for talent. The *Ja Cię kręcę!* competition had also most of the features characteristic of talent shows, but they were carried out on a different level, without such a spectacular flourish as in television productions. Radio RMF FM did not appeal to emotions as strongly as television, and its entertainment was thus less expressive. Promotional campaigns were quite intensive but they did not attack the audience as intensely as in television. Listeners made decisions about whether to take part in this competition by preparing their own recording or by voting independently. The radio talent show gave them much more freedom and did not overwhelm people as strongly as in the very spectacular and difficult-to-avoid confrontations in television productions.

Value network The Radio RMF FM campaign can be also considered according to the idea of a value network (Kowalski 2008: 86), which is quite popular in the theory of management, including that of the media. It consists of carrying out a series of campaigns at the levels of content creation, distribution and promotion, which complement each other and make a network of strong relationships. According to this rule, each stage of a campaign results in specific consequences, and should be analysed from the point of view of the elements that constitute the project. In the process of working on a concrete product, such as in radio, there are some basic stages which lead to the final results. They are:

Stage 1: creation of content

Stage 2: placing a product in a group of other products, (such as on radio or online)

Stage 3: placing the product on the market through an appropriate advertising campaign

Stage 4: distribution – the product is put before an audience, whose reactions are observed

Stage 5: maintaining the interest of the target audience (Kowalski 2008: 65-81).

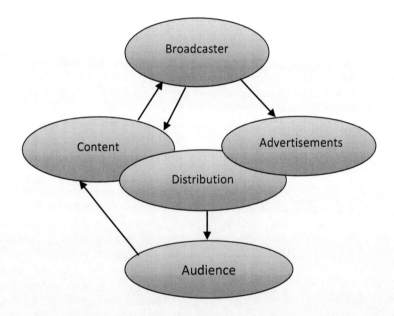

Figure 5.1: The value network of the RMF FM *Ja Cię kręcę!* competition

All of these elements can be found in the process of creating the *Ja Cię kręcę!* competition. At the first stage, the broadcaster had to work out the concept and content of this event. Then it made the decision to place it among a group of products, which was the radio series for the summer holidays in 2013. At the next stage, the producer initiated the advertising and promotional campaign in order to inform listeners about the competition and the benefits connected with it. In this way, listeners found out about the product not only from radio but also from other mass media, especially the internet, which became a place of rivalry. Thanks to the possibilities offered by the internet, the broadcaster was able to observe listeners' reactions through the films sent to the station, as well as through opinions expressed on the radio website and in social media. This is a significant example of how media producers can use the phenomenon of convergence to strengthen their market position and obtain a very important tool for communicating with their audiences. A significant aspect was also the necessity of maintaining listeners' interest in the campaign over a two-month period. The Hit Tour helped to fulfil this goal because of its attractiveness and its cyclical character. This is the next important element of the value network of this radio product. Listeners had the opportunity for permanent participation in the campaign and having a great time while meeting their favourite pop stars. Thanks to this element, radio RMF FM showed that it is open to its listeners and wants to provide them with entertainment.

Tadeusz Kowalski thinks that in the case of radio, 'from a management point of view the challenge is... to enrich the number of functions and utilities, but also to strengthen key competences at the same time' (2008: 254). In my opinion, this kind of situation took place in this instance. Radio RMF FM created a product in the guise of a game which connected numerous elements essential for audio media today, namely a radio programme, the internet, social media, events, advertisements and interaction with listeners. At the same time, it stressed its basic competences and abilities, which are delivering music content. In fact, music was the most important element in this campaign. Listeners sent films with songs known from the radio which were compatible with the station's music format, adult contemporary, and in this way these songs became fixed in listeners' minds. The Hit Tour also contributed to this process.

Radio as a virtual concert studio

The tradition of live radio concerts, the genre of our second case study, dates back to the very beginning of the medium's existence. As Paul Levinson wrote, maintaining it was one of the priorities for the first radio broadcasters, and avoiding broadcasting 'second-hand' music was a source of satisfaction (2006: 165). However, nowadays most radio programmes are based mainly on previously-recorded pieces of work, which are then replayed numerous times. Organising concerts in a radio studio, especially in the case of commercial stations, is not now very common practice. This situation is caused by the characteristics of radio content today – as a rule, it is divided into many different segments that alternate dynamically, such as music, station promotions, advertisements and news, which does not favour organising large concerts or even small recitals. In the first half of 2013, the commercial broadcaster Radio ZET decided to implement an idea connected to the tradition of radio concerts. It was called *Bliskie ZETknięcia III-go stopnia* ('Third-degree close contacts'). However, it had a completely different character from traditional radio gigs, as a result of the new media forms used in the production and distribution of the programme. The idea of the project consisted of organising encounters with Polish music stars, especially those known from Radio ZET, during which they performed their songs and talked with listeners. The moderator of these conversations was a music radio journalist and member of the Radio ZET team, Marcin Wojciechowski. The programme was broadcast at 20:00 each Saturday between 16 February and 6 April, after the Radio ZET music chart show. On 22 April, the formula was changed significantly. They were limited to video chats, and they continued in this form until the beginning of the summer holiday, and the last episode was broadcast on 17 June. During this period, the programme was presented on-air on Mondays, from 20:00. In creating *Bliskie ZETknięcia III-go stopnia*, Radio ZET cooperated with the record label EMI Music Poland, using both a radio studio and the Google+ platform. The musicians who took part in this programme included Beata Kozidrak and Bajm, T.Love, LemON, Myslovitz, Sylwia Grzeszczak, Patrycja Markowska, Liber and Natalia Szroeder, Justyna Steczkowska, Rafał Brzozowski, Ania Wyszkoni, Robert Kupicha from Feel, Tomasz Szczepanik from Pectus, Margaret, Robert Gawliński, Urszula and Dawid Podsiadło. Interestingly, most of these artists were, or are still are, connected with EMI Music Poland.

What exactly did these encounters look like? Hangouts were taking place via the EMI Music Poland site at Google+ (www.google.com/+emimusicpoland). They could be viewed by internet users at www.radiozet.pl or the EMI Music Poland channel on You Tube. Some parts of the conversations were broadcast on-air. People who wanted to become actively involved in *Bliskie ZETknięcia III-go stopnia* had to register on Google+ and suggest a question for a specific musician or complete a special questionnaire on the Radio ZET website. Those submitting the best ideas, a maximum of 10 due to the constraints of the platform, were invited to take part in the programme and talk to their favourite musicians. In the opinion of Rafał Olejniczak, the chief editor of Radio ZET, this solution gave the station a marvellous opportunity to interact with listeners: 'We have now a new way to be closer to our listeners. It's fantastic that thanks to new technology we can organise live video chats. Every day we talk with our listeners on-air, on our website, on Facebook, and now we are offering something new' (LR 2013). Kinga Siennicka, director of marketing and promotion at EMI Music Poland stressed how innovative the idea was: 'The series of live Google+ hangouts is an example of innovative internet use in contacts between stars and their fans. They can take part in a cosy concert and engage in small talk with their favourite artists. Not long ago this kind of direct form of interaction between an artist and a listener was impossible' (LR 2013). The participants in the video chat could get special surprises, which were CDs by the musicians involved. Winners, (the contributors of the best questions,) were chosen by the artists. Listeners could also comment during the course of the encounters, which lasted approximately 40-50 minutes.

Bliskie ZETknięcia III-go stopnia took place on the internet, although small extracts of each programme, especially the live shows, were broadcast on Radio ZET. Despite this fact, the new media possibilities were essential for the characteristics of this production. Why? First of all, the means of distribution was a internet platform: Google+ Hangouts. What is more, participation in each meeting was possible only in virtual reality, using special software. Because of that, this kind of message differs from a traditional radio programme, in that it became visual. Marcin Wojciechowski, who chaired the hangouts, stressed that from his point of view it was a completely new communication situation, as he wasn't used to working with cameras and 'being visible'. Encounters also had a quite different atmosphere, being more informal and unpredictable because they were not as strongly limited by time as is usual in radio. Hangouts sometimes completely changed during their duration, with, for example, stars performing more songs than planned, which happened in the case of Natalia Szroeder and Liber. It seems that the musical aspect of *Bliskie ZETknięcia III-go stopnia* was the strongest point of this idea because this kind of radio initiative does not happen very often. In this case, radio listeners received an interesting opportunity not only to talk to their idols, which, in fact, is not very original, as well as to listen to and watch live acoustic concerts by them. The musicians presented their biggest hits, but did so in completely new circumstances, which might have been a real find for their fans.

So, why after two months did Radio ZET decide to change the idea of the programme? No official reasons were given by the broadcaster, but some probable answers can be found. On the one hand, we have to consider the economic aspects of time and money. Preparing a live show requires the involvement of a group of specialists responsible for sound, picture and internet transmission in the process of its production. Video chats do not require so many people, and can be easily operated by a single journalist. It is also probable that the decision was influenced by the results of audience research made by the Radio Research Committee. Hangouts were broadcasts mainly on the internet, so it is likely they did not result in an increase in the number of people listening to the radio on Saturday evenings. Radio ZET was not the first station in the Polish radio market to decide to use hangouts. Radio ESKA, with a CHR music format and a young audience, came up with the idea of video chats with musicians and celebrities via Google+ in 2012. They were slightly different from those organised by Radio ZET in that they took place solely online, artists did not perform during hangouts, listeners were not able to talk to them, they could only write their questions via a chat utility, and sometimes these questions were used by a journalist during a conversation. Listeners' influence was not as significant as in *Bliskie ZETknięcia III-go stopnia* on Radio ZET.

Conclusion

Mark Ramsey, in an essay about the potential benefits derived from using tools offered by Google+, claimed that 'the future of radio is beyond radio' (2013). I think that this opinion can be considered not only in the context of this platform, but also in terms of the whole relationship between radio and new or 'new new' media, as Paul Levinson said (2006). On the one hand, programme solutions presented in this analysis show that radio broadcasters try to benefit from the phenomenon of the convergence of mass media and create projects which include different aspects of radio's essence. On the other hand, in this kind of attitude to radio production, it is important not to lose the essence of the audio medium and let it become an advantage. The future of radio lies in radio itself, and a key for market success, including when talking about entertainment, is to establish a skilful connection between tradition and modernity which would meet audiences' needs.

References

Dai (2013) *Września miastem szalonych fanów*.
http://wrzesnia.info.pl/tematyczne/kultura/item/3356-wrze%C5%9Bnia-miastem-szalonych-fan%C3%B3w-galeria

Jakubowicz, K (2011) *Nowa ekologia mediów. Konwergencja a metamofroza*, Warszawa: Wydawnictwo Poltext.

Jędrzejewski, S (2010) *Radiofonia publiczna w Europie w erze cyfrowej*, Kraków: Universitas.

Kowalski, T (2008) *Między twórczością a biznesem. Wprowadzenie do zarządzania w mediach i rozrywce*, Warszawa: Wydawnictwa Akademickie i Profesjonalne.

Levinson, P (2006) *The Soft Edge: A natural history and future of the information revolution*, Warszawa: Warszawskie Wydawnictwo Literackie MUZA.

LR (2013) *Hangouty z gwiazdami w Radiu ZET*. http://lubieradio.pl/zet/213-hangouty-z-gwiazdami-w-radiu-zet

Łuczkowska, A (2013) *Drugi dzień Top of the Top. Na scenie zwyciężczyni Ja Cię kręcę!*   http://www.rmf24.pl/kultura/news-drugi-dzien-top-of-the-top-na-scenie-zwyciezczyni-ja-cie-kre,nId,1015845

Pawlik, A (2012) 'Seriale radiowe w Internecie. Sztuka audialna w procesie konwergencji' in Oniszczuk & Wielopolska-Szymura, M (eds), *Konwergencja mediów masowych i jej skutki dla współczesnego dziennikarstwa*, Katowice: Wydawnictwo Uniwersytetu Śląskiego.

Ramsey, M (2013) *What Google+ and Hangouts can do for Radio Broadcasters*. http://www.markramseymedia.com/2013/08/what-google-and-hangouts-can-do-for-radio-broadcasters

Szledak, T & Kołowski, T (2008) *Naga małpa przed telewizorem*, Warszawa: Wydawnictwa Akademickie i Profesjonalne.

Chapter 6

Masters of brand: A study of social media workers in the Italian and Spanish radio industries

Toni Sellas and Tiziano Bonini

Abstract

In the era of networked publics, social media (SM) and social network sites (SNS) transform the communicative attitudes of citizens and their interaction with mass media. Radio broadcasters have adopted social media as a means by which to interact with listeners, but they are using them basically as a promotional tool. This chapter analyses how structural factors determine the use of social media, focusing on daily production routines, professional cultures and material and organisational contexts. The methodology used is based on a qualitative approach, combining a questionnaire with in-depth interviews with the social media managers of eight public and private broadcasters from Italy and Spain. The results show that they do seem to have understood the value of engaging with listeners. However, it doesn't seem that the radio industry, at least in the Italian and Spanish stations that we analysed, have completely grasped the value of the social media managers' job. In addition, structural factors such as the dynamics of production and the lack of a consolidated professional culture for social media make the professional management of these channels in the daily routines of the stations difficult.

Keywords: social network sites, social media management, network culture, Italy, Spain

Introduction

The digitisation and evolution of the internet have led to a paradigm shift in communicative and cultural uses that breaks with the verticality characterising the relationship between the media and their publics (Castells 2010). In this era of networked publics (Boyd 2010), social network sites (SNS) transform the communicative attitudes of citizens and their interaction with the mass media. These platforms may be seen as an evolution of the public sphere, where users change the dynamics of publishing and distributing content. The result is a new media context in which the logic of the mass media converges with the new communication practices of consumers who, via technology, intervene in the flow of information and interact with professionals and other citizens (Jenkins 2006). The internet and social networks compete with the mainstream media for users' media consumption time. They also act as a filter for the flow of content that citizens select according to their interests. Social recommendation becomes a key element for users and the mainstream media have to deal with the challenge of being part of their publics' trusted networks and the fact that their content forms part of the latter's media consumption time. SNS represent an opportunity for them to engage with their audience and social networking therefore makes sense as part of a media strategy of anywhere, anytime and on any platform. It is within this context that the radio industry is understood to have incorporated social networks into its communication strategies.

This study is based on previous research regarding the use of Twitter by two European public broadcasters, RAI (Italy) and RNE (Spain), which showed that Twitter could be, but in fact is not, used as a public service medium (Bonini & Sellas 2014). In this chapter, we aim to analyse how structural factors determine the use of SNS, focusing on daily production routines, professional cultures and material and organisational contexts. Our purpose is to determine not just what broadcasters are doing on social network sites but also how and why.

Radio and social network sites

Radio broadcasters have adopted social network sites as a channel for interacting with listeners, but this use is still in its nascent stage. Research has revealed that the media are using SNS to promote their content, rather than exploring a new relationship with users (Armstrong & Gao 2010). In the field of radio, Bonini and Sellas (2014) showed how Spanish and Italian public radio services fail to use Twitter as a public service medium, only focusing on promoting their content and raising web traffic figures, without connecting with the audience. Herrera and Requejo (2010) showed how Spanish talk radio stations primarily use Twitter to disseminate information, despite timid attempts to establish a dialogue with their followers. In the United States, Ferguson and Greer concluded, based on the analysis of a hundred stations on Twitter, that messages from music channels are mostly promotional, while talk radio stations focus on news content, but their tone is more personal (2011).

Other studies have compared corporate and personal accounts and shown that the human factor is an important element in social networking (Blasingame 2011). Social networks foster a relationship whereby the audience is more involved in the dissemination and discussion of information, with real-time feedback and an interaction in which both amateurs and professionals take part (Hermida 2010). This is especially true with regard to breaking news, emergency situations, and major or important events (Palser 2009).

In the radio sector, social networks are one of the keys to the future of the medium, along with multiplatform distribution and applications for tablets and smartphones (EBU 2011). Social media expand the possibilities of audience participation, while also being a way of caring for the relationship with the audience and maintaining the bond when the programme finishes or the radio is turned off. SNS are especially relevant for public broadcasters, who may use new technologies to achieve their public service remit obligations in a multiplatform scenario (Bonet, Fernández-Quijada & Ribes 2011). Social networking sites represent a step further when it comes to audience participation. Throughout history, technological innovations have expanded the options available for listeners to contribute to the radio and its programmes, to the extent that the evolution of the medium can be seen as a path on which broadcasters and audience have come gradually closer together (Bonini 2014b). The audience is now more visible due to profiles being connected to broadcasters' social media channels, giving the latter the opportunity to understand what users want and what they expect from the medium (Gazi, Starkey & Jedrzejewski 2011; Sellas 2012). As Ala-Fossi (2010) has pointed out, above and beyond how radio evolves, its future will ultimately depend on the will of listeners.

A constructivist perspective of SM management

Research into the use of social networks in the radio sector has mainly focused on the content disseminated by broadcasters on these channels and the purposes broadcasters use them for. However, studying media strategies with regard to social media and SNS also requires focusing on the structural and ethnographic factors that may condition them. A constructivist perspective understands innovation as a dynamic process which results from the sum of decisions taken by certain actors, the use of a particular technology and the production dynamics characteristic of the setting (Schmitz Weiss & Domingo 2010). With the growth of social media comes the return of some of the promises that accompanied the advent of the internet, often as a result of technological determinism that leaves economic growth and transformation of the media ecosystem exclusively in the hands of technology (Boczkowski 2002). However, research has shown that many of these expectations have either not been met or only met in part, largely as a consequence of structural factors (Lewis, Kaufhold & Lasorsa 2010). In the face of deterministic discourse, other perspectives arise that are more critical of linear models of technological innovation and place an emphasis on the social dimension (Fernández-Quijada 2011).

Incorporating social media affects the logic of the media, understood as the set of institutional, organisational, technological and cultural factors that determine how to work in a medium and the outcome of this process (Deuze 2008). Traditionally, this logic has also led to a controlled socialisation of new professionals, who acquire conventions, norms and limits through their progressive incorporation into production dynamics and daily contact with the hierarchies, customs and assumptions that characterise the medium (Sivek 2010). Social networks alter these conventions, which are often overwhelmed by the dynamics of the social web, affecting the content creation chain and professionals' routines (Podger 2009).

Production studies have focused on the logic of the processes by means of which mass communication takes place and how work is organised in each medium. In this sense, the professionals' relationship with sources is one of the factors that condition how material is collected (McQuail 2000). Moreover, the role of gatekeeper comes into play in the selection process; that is, the person who decides how messages are explained to the public, how much time is devoted to different content and what tone the story has (Shoemaker *et al* 2001). Other structural and systemic factors also influence selection, such as the professional culture or how work is organised and the dynamics and mechanisms of production (Wolf 1987). With regards to production, a constructivist approach allows us to analyse the internal dynamics of the medium as if they were those of a community of practice in which learning and knowledge construction naturally become not an end in themselves but a result of daily practice and via participation (Wenger 1998). Also, research into the tradition of the social shaping of technology describes how technological innovations do not develop autonomously but can only be explained within a given social context (Bijker 1995). If we focus on group members, research from the perspective of the Actor Network Theory shows how the relationships between the different individual actors and the internal balance of power affect innovation processes in the media (Domingo 2008).

This chapter adopts such a constructivist perspective with the aim of developing a holistic approach to the object of study. The introduction of social media into the everyday reality of radio in recent years has generated much academic literature on content, broadcasters' objectives and the relationship with the audience on these channels. But these results cannot be properly understood if we do not take into account the internal reality of broadcasters, both their structural elements and the human factor.

The research methodology

This research studies how structural factors determine the use of SNS, focusing on: 1) daily production routines, 2) professional background, 3) the material and organisational context, and 4) work flow. We began with the following research questions as our starting points:

- What strategy and dynamic for managing social networks have been adopted by the broadcaster?
- What management structure is used for these channels and which professionals are responsible for them?

The proposed research approaches the object of study by means of a combination of various analytical tools used in the field of research into broadcasting and press organisations. An ethnographic perspective is adopted to address production, an area of study whose purpose is to investigate what lies behind the content disseminated by the media. The aim is to study how professionals incorporate social media into their routines and productive mechanisms so as to gain a better understanding of the circumstances and decisions that condition this activity.

The method was based on a qualitative approach that combines in-depth interviews with professionals responsible for the strategic design and/or management of corporate activity in relation to social networks and a closed online questionnaire answered by twenty managers responsible for the profile of radio programmes on the two major social networks, Facebook and Twitter. Using this research method, we also aimed to collect the explanations, motivations, experiences and feelings of interviewees, an important complement to contextualise the information obtained (Wimmer & Dominick 2011). For this research, seven radio stations were analysed, four from Italy and three from Spain. They were:

Radio 3 RAI, a cultural public station (Italy)

Radio 2 RAI, a music and light entertainment public station (Italy)

Radio 24, a news & talk private station (Italy)

Radio 105, a CHR private station (Italy)

RNE, a news & talk public station [RTVE group] (Spain)

Cadena SER, a news & talk private station [PRISA Radio group] (Spain)

Los40, a CHR private station [PRISA Radio group] (Spain).

The in-depth interviews were conducted between May and September 2013, according to the availability of the professionals interviewed. Seven interviews were conducted, involving discussions of, on average, one hour, with the following people:

Cristina Faloci, social media manager for Radio 3 RAI

Marta Pezzino, social media manager for Radio 2 RAI

Katia Marinelli, social media manager for Radio 24

Laura Saldamarco, social media manager for Radio 105

Luís Pinheiro, subdirector of projects for RTVE.es

Izaskun Pérez, social media manager/strategist for Cadena SER

Puerto González, community manager for *Webs Musicales* on PRISA Radio (interviewed by email, at his request).

The in-depth interviews consisted of a first set of questions regarding the strategy, structure and dynamics of using social networks, including some specific questions regarding Facebook and others regarding Twitter, and a second group of questions related to the professional profiles of the people responsible for strategy and management with regard to these social channels. This second part also formed the basis of the online questionnaire that was sent to twenty programmes of the stations studied so as to understand the profiles of the respective social media managers.

Findings

An analysis of the in-depth interviews with the social media managers of the official profiles of the seven Italian and Spanish radio stations we studied allows us to identify a number of common issues in the interviewees' perceptions of social media. Five issues emerged: social media strategies, social media and radio synchronicity, the value of social media for radio, interaction with the networked public and the skills needed to do this work. Every radio station has enacted different strategies, while every SM manager has developed his or her own views, rules and practices, but we can still find many similarities in the ways that social media are perceived by the public service stations analysed, as well as by the private broadcasters. In this case, a comparative analysis of the three Spanish and the four Italian stations tells us that the differences are mostly based on genre (public or private), and not on nationality (Italian or Spanish).

Social media strategies Differences in the aims of public as opposed to private stations can already be found in the definitions of the strategic objectives of the individual radios:

> 'A well-defined policy doesn't exist, although you have to post certain types of images, the text has to be a standard length, you always have to insert the link in order to bring web traffic to the website; but we don't have a policy regarding use by radio employees, although at times we may feel the need for one.' *(Laura, Radio 105, Italy)*

> 'Our SM strategy is to broadcast our content to a different public: the online listeners instead of the FM ones.' *(Puerto, Los40principales, Spain)*

> 'The main strategy is simply to bring traffic to the website, so there aren't big operations for engagement or for communication with users or fans…So our work on the social networks is to publish the content that comes from the programmes, which can be cuts from the news or in-depth information, and when we publish them on the website, we share them on both Twitter and Facebook at the same time. This type of strategy has mainly been decided by the marketing sector.' *(Katia, Radio24, Italy)*

> 'The corporate profiles in SM are basically a tool for promotion and information. In the case of some programmes, we are experimenting with Social media as a production network, searching there for quotes or to discover new stories.' *(Izaskun, SER, Spain)*

> 'The strategy is generally inspired by those used by public services; the challenge is to act like a public service on media that are very emotional and visceral, trying to move towards a way of communicating, drawing on the best and not 'tainting' it. Trying to find a captivating language. Our public is naturally inclined to criticism and reflection, so we try to avoid simplification, even if a means like Twitter sometimes forces you into it.' *(Cristina, Radio3 RAI, Italy)*

> 'As a public medium, our obligation is to be where our listeners are and to get an audience for our content. We try to use the SNS not only as a promotional tool, but also as a new channel for interacting with the audience.' *(Luis, RNE, Spain)*

> 'We try to differentiate what is published on the website from what is proposed on the social networks, in terms of both content and language, in the sense that we try to use a more informal and younger language on the social networks, because social networks target a lower age range than those who visit the website. So beyond

sponsoring content, that is what happens during the broadcasts…I go to take photographs or videos with the iPad during the broadcasts, and I post them directly on Facebook; I also try to include more news that could be of common interest, especially for youth.' *(Marta, RAI Radio2, Italy)*

Social media and radio synchronicity Social media seem to be perceived by all the interviewees as a narrative tool for real-time reporting of what's happening in radio:

'The type of post is different throughout the day, because there are posts that 1) tend to move parallel to what is happening on-air, some posts that 2) tend to promote what is on the website, and others that 3) tend to create an interaction on the page. So these are the three macro-categories that we publish on Facebook.' *(Laura, Radio 105)*

'Posting on Facebook strictly follows the posting of updates on the website.' *(Katia, Radio24, Italy)*

'Twitter is a more ephemeral channel. We use it to publish breaking news or to catch the attention of the audience to what's happening on-air. Facebook has a slower flow of publication. It is a useful space for photo galleries, to debate some topics, to organise a competition or a game show…' *(Luis, RNE, Spain)*

'We usually publish news on Twitter, with a link to the website. But we want it to be closer to the programming, to what's on-air in this moment.' *(Izaskun, SER, Spain)*

SM managers are aware that listeners use social media to comment on what is happening on-air in real time, and one of their main strategies is to use social media to tell what is happening on-air. Social media commenting and chatting about radio broadcasting while listening is a common feature of the relationship between social media and old media. Television viewers also seem to do the same with Twitter and Facebook, as the Pew *Internet and American Life Research* report on 'connected viewers' shows: 52 per cent of all adult cell phone owners now incorporate their mobile devices into their television watching experiences (Smith & Boyles 2012). Similarly, 25 per cent of US Twitter users routinely tweet about their television viewership, generating roughly 300 million television-related tweets per day. In the UK, 40 per cent of all Twitter traffic at peak television viewing time is about television, and 60 per cent of all Twitter users use Twitter while watching television (Carmody 2013). According to industry professionals, this has made Twitter an extension of the television experience, a sort of 'second screen', and has positioned the audience very differently in relation to both programming and advertising content. Social media are the second screen of radio and television, a public sphere where one's feelings about media content may be expressed.

The value of social media How are social media useful for radio? Or rather, what are SM useful for, according to SM managers? Do they believe that they can help build audiences or not?

'The SM are only useful for one thing: they do not increase the FM audience, they help increase the website traffic.' *(Marta, RAI Radio2, Italy)*

'The ultimate aim is to bring traffic to our website. Social media are good for that.' *(Puerto, Los40principales, Spain)*

This obsession for website traffic performance imposed by a marketing mindset could explain the unidirectional, top-down use of SM made by traditional media, from radio to newspapers. Scholars have shown how traditional media corporations only conceive of social media as promotional tools and not as conversational ones. The analysis by García de Torres *et al* (2011) of thirty Spanish media noted that Facebook is basically a channel used for the unidirectional broadcasting of content as less than six per cent are conversation messages, while Twitter is a more interactive platform, with over 25 per cent of the content being conversation. Messner, Linke and Eford (2011) analysed the messages on Twitter from one hundred newspapers and one hundred television broadcasters. Most of them have incorporated this microblogging service, but just for promoting the stories published on their websites. Even the more 'enlightened' SM managers, those who do not only take into account web traffic figures, believe that SM are mostly valuable for engaging with their radio brand:

> 'Social media are tools that have been essential for companies here in the past few years, especially for radio: they increase awareness, control a channel where there are currently two million Italians, so not being on it would mean playing into the others' hands. The main reason is surely brand awareness...' *(Laura, Radio 105, Italy)*

Lazarsfeld (1940) told us that a good frame of reference could help listeners to be prepared and to better understand 'serious' programmes. What we can learn from Ferguson and Greer (2011) is that radio stations don't benefit from Twitter in a quantitative way, (by attracting additional FM listeners,) but their benefits in using it could be qualitative: putting the listeners in the right frame of mind for experiencing, listening to and engaging directly with the show:

> 'Everything about social media is a critical point for media today. It is a window for various uses, both for spreading content and for interacting with the audience. The most important element is what we call the *participation rate*: what kind of feedback we get for each action we propose on SM.' *(Luis, RNE Tres, Spain)*

> 'Basically, social media are a direct way of communicating with the audience. Radio has always been a very participative medium. Now we have another channel for this relationship with our listeners. Social media are just an extension of radio's participatory tradition.' *(Izaskun, SER, Spain)*

> 'Social media could be useful for radio because they could really help shape a new means of communication and dialogue with listeners. They could be used to link broadcasters to listeners, but most of all they could be used as a place where listeners can meet each other, interact and exchange knowledge.' *(Katia, Radio24, Italy)*

> 'Social networks offer an opportunity for reflection, for the discussion of criticism and self-analysis, because Facebook does not only generate compliments or Likes, but sometimes harsh criticism as well.' *(Cristina, Radio3 RAI, Italy)*

SM managers seem to understand the real value of SM for radio: they are tools for managing the relationship with a community of listeners who like to engage with their content and brand. This visible group of people, nodes or links is the most important new feature produced by the hybridisation between radio and SNS. A radio programme's network of friends or fans on SNS could represent its specific social capital (Bourdieu & Wacquant 1992), while the wider (and invisible) radio public, as charted by audience rating companies, still constitutes the programme's economic capital, the more restricted public of social media should be considered the real social capital of a programme - a tangible and visible capital. For radio producers, a wide network of friends or fans is of great importance for their future. Even if the fan network does not generate a tangible economic value, as the radio audience already does, it nevertheless generates great reputational capital. The message of the SNS public of a radio programme is the network itself. The value embedded in the networked public is not yet convertible into economic capital, but the crisis of traditional mass advertising will lead to a future increase in, and refining of, tools for the capitalisation of the wealth of networked publics linked to radio programmes and stations.

Interaction Obviously, all the SM managers interviewed, both private and public, mentioned interaction as the main aim of their everyday efforts. They perceive themselves as a kind of master of interaction with the audiences, as spin doctors of interaction. SM are the spark that can start an interaction between content and the audience.

> 'Interaction is surely what interests me the most. Followers can obviously be a consequence of interaction, but interaction is the litmus test that you have launched a message that has been received; everything that has to do with interaction is, for us, a success.' *(Cristina, SM editor, Radio3 RAI, Italy)*

> 'I'm also interested in the interaction, I'm not interested in having passive users, but users that interact, so for me the number of mentions and retweets is definitely important. For Facebook, the main data that we consider is 'talking about', because it's the only external number, so it's visible to everyone, and it can also be monitored by those who don't access the Insights, and that's the number that allows people, even those who are not specialists in the field, to evaluate the page's progress. The more people that interact with our pages, the more our page is visible, and the more awareness of it increases.' *(Laura, Radio 105, Italy)*

Another dimension of interaction is the way SM managers cope with censorship and free speech. Do they reply to all the requests? Do they simply ban negative comments, or do they engage with listeners and explain their point of view?

> 'I try to reply to all the requests about programming, while I avoid replying to very harsh and negative comments in order to not raise debates that could degenerate. We don't delete anything, except for very obscene off-topic messages.' *(Marta, RAI Radio2, Italy)*

> 'I explain a lot and I censor a lot. We have a series of banned words that self-censor themselves, so a lot of obscene language, profanity, insults, etc. are actually automatically hidden, and I also usually delete them. We also respond to specific questions regarding the radio, but most of the interactions that we register on the page are either completely irrelevant to the content that is posted, for example requests to play one album instead of another, or we often delete all those promotional comments, and also all the spam.' *(Laura, Radio 105, Italy)*

'We answer all the direct or private messages. With public comments, it depends on the reason and on the content. We publish all the opinions and don't reply to them. If there is a massive complaint about the content of any program, we communicate it to the corresponding managers, including the Dircom.' *(Izaskun, SER, Spain)*

Skills The SM managers insisted strongly on the skills needed to do this job. All of them agreed that this is a very experiential job that is learned through experimentation, with no written rules. Public service SM managers pay more attention to listening skills, while commercial radio SM managers are more sensitive to brand management skills:

'I think that, first of all, you need to have a quality of being able to listen and to put yourself in the shoes of those who are outside; you shouldn't put yourself on your high horse. I try to put myself in the shoes of those who follow our profiles, our pages, asking myself what they want to know from us and what they expect: I myself am a passionate listener and fan of Radio3. Style is fundamental for us.' *(Cristina, Radio3 RAI, Italy)*

'You have to be a good observer; you have to know your content, your product and your audience.' *(Puerto, Los40principales, Spain)*

'I would probably end up talking about strategy, that is, being a kind of strategist…Why do you communicate something? Because you have to meet certain goals that you have probably set for yourself, so you have to have a strategic vision. Maybe it's not exactly knowledge, but still…' *(Laura, Radio 105, Italy)*

'You need to be proficient in content and, in our case, to understand the role of a public medium like RNE. Obviously, you must have some knowledge about the dynamics of social networks. Another interesting skill should be your curiosity: every day, be curious in order to continue learning how the SM environment flows.' *(Luis, RNE, Spain)*

'Twitter and Facebook are just tools. We spend a lot of time talking about social networks. But for me, it is more important to have an in-depth knowledge about the content and the brand. In other words, it is more about managing content and managing the brand reputation than managing social networks. And it is obviously necessary to know the characteristics of our audience and how the community works.' *(Izaskun, SER, Spain)*

Even if every SM manager has his or her own idea of the role of social media for radio, we have shown that they share some common beliefs, although there is still a slight difference between public service radio and private radio stations. SM managers who work for public services are more interested in bringing the values of public service media (PSM) to social media. Both seek interaction, but give it a different value: for PSM, more interaction means accomplishing goals with PSM values and connecting with citizens, while for private radio, seeking interaction mostly aims to promote brand awareness. Social media are perceived by public service SM managers as an opportunity to start a dialogue with the listeners, in order to better understand their point of view. Public service managers are more sensitive to the role of social media as listening tools, not only as broadcasting ones. Listening is a good metaphor for understanding social media as well. As Crawford (2009: 525) claimed: 'The metaphor of listening can offer a productive way to analyse the forms of online engagement that have previously been overlooked, while also allowing a deeper consideration of the emerging disciplines of online attention'. For private-sector SM managers they are mostly a tool for promoting their content and increasing web traffic figures. Public services seem to pay more attention to the voice of the listeners online, as shown in table 6.1.

	Public service radio	Private commercial radio
SM strategy	to be where the listeners are to interact with listeners while avoiding simplification to tune in to the listeners' voices to bring traffic to the website	a tool for promoting the radio content to bring traffic to the website
SM and radio synchronicity	as a countermelody to radio to inform listeners about what's on-air to discuss what's on-air (second screen)	to create interaction to inform about what's on-air to discuss what's on-air (second screen)
SM value	an opportunity for reflection, criticism and self-analysis an opportunity for listener participation a tool for broadcasting a tool for listening	a tool for improving brand awareness a tool for increasing the web traffic, not the radio audience a tool for surveillance
Interaction	interaction as a way to be connected with the listeners, for the success of public media values	a way to promote brand awareness SM interaction as a preliminary step towards radio interaction
Skills	being able to listen proficiency in content attention to style curiosity	managing content managing brand reputation strategic vision

Table 6.1: The main issues in social media management for radio.

The cultural profile of social media managers

The seven social media managers interviewed all share the same cultural background: they have all studied humanities, and most of them hold degrees in journalism and communication studies. Even if they dedicate their entire working day to social media management, and although they are in charge of the management of wide communities of networked audiences and responsible for their station's brand awareness, their wages did not seem to reflect the quality and strategic importance of their work. Most of them said that their wages ranged from 800 to 1300 euros per month, and only in two cases (in Spain) did wages range from 1800 to 3000 euros per month, but these employees also had other responsibilities within their companies. All of them are young, between 28 and 40 years old, and highly educated, but the broadcasters, both public and private, still did not perceive social media management to be as valuable as the work of their presenters and journalists. Social media are perceived as necessary tools, but social media management is a job that is still emerging, so it is still struggling to establish itself and earn credibility and economic value.

Radio producers as social media curators that are always wired

The second part of our research examined another type of social media curation: not that done by the managers of the radio stations' official SNS profiles, but the work performed by the curators of the Facebook and Twitter profiles for the individual radio programmes. We investigated who the people who manage these profiles are, and what differences there are between them and the social media managers, who only deal with the management of the communities linked to the radio brands. The results of the questionnaires, which were distributed online, tell us that the curation of the Twitter accounts and Facebook fan pages of the radio programmes is mostly carried out by the programme producers. In fact, 69 per cent of respondents declared being paid by the station as a producer, and that with time they were assigned the job of curating the programme's social media, without receiving a corresponding increase in pay for the increased amount of work to be done. Instead, few journalists and presenters of radio programmes curate their official social media: the producer is the one to curate the management and communication with networked listeners, in both Spain and Italy, for both public and private stations (Bonini 2014a). Radio authors and producers are becoming increasingly like curators, a cultural shift in the role of all kinds of creative labour that was already noted by Brian Eno in 1991, as Reynolds reminded us, saying: 'Curatorship is arguably the big new job of our times: it is the task of re-evaluating, filtering, digesting, and connecting together. In an age saturated with new artifacts and information, it is perhaps the curator, the connection maker, who is the new storyteller, the meta-author' (2011).

We also gathered a large amount of data about the professional profiles of the social media curators and their SM strategies. Of them 93 per cent were between 26 and 40 years old, and 46 per cent were between 36 and 40 years old. Our social media curators were slightly older than the social media managers, because they began working in radio not as experts of new media, but as radio producers or journalists. Of them 69 per cent received internal training from their company in order to learn how to use social media, but after this initial training did not receive any other kind of update. They were highly educated, with 38 per cent holding a higher university degree and 23 per cent even holding a PhD. The most-used social media platforms are Facebook (used by 100 per cent) and Twitter (95 per cent), but YouTube (48 per cent) and Soundcloud (31 per cent) are also well established platforms. Just 15 per cent of them also manage Instagram and five per cent Google+, Vimeo and Tumblr. They also spend a lot of time replying to listeners' comments and mentions. In all, 83 per cent of respondents claimed to reply to most of the messages received from listeners.

Social media curators differ from the SM managers for their greater attention to listeners, with a communication style that is less corporate and more horizontal and bidirectional. Their experience as producers makes them more used to contact with the public. For them, social media represent another way to create opportunities for contact with listeners. The relationship between the public and the radio programmes that is mediated through social media is more intimate than that between audiences and the official radio brands' SNS. While SM managers are the masters of radio brands on social media, the social media curators are the masters of connection with listeners. They contribute to the management of the general radio brand by managing the brand of the single radio programme. This kind of brand management is not based on promotional language, but is built on a close connection with listeners. Most of the SM curators are passionate lovers of their station and their listeners: 'I am not only a producer but also a big listener to Radio24, and I think social media are useful for sparking a conversation with our audience,' claimed Margherita, a producer and social media curator at Radio24, Italy. When they are not at work they schedule social media updates, using software tools for automated publishing, but, as Margherita claimed, 'I also check the SM profile I manage from home, and sometimes I publish tweets or posts when I am at home, even after dinner or at night'. Working as a producer for a radio programme before the era of social media meant going to the radio station, producing the recorded or live programme, then going home, like a worker finishing a shift at a factory. Working as a producer in the era of social media means working constantly, even from home, confusing the boundaries between work and life. The radio programme has a limited duration, a beginning and an end, but the relationship that this content establishes with its public is one that lasts over time. Social media allow the radio programme to continue living, before and after it goes on-air.

Bonini (2014b) studied the strategies of seven European public service radio stations on Facebook, and noted that most of the Facebook posts followed a specific dramaturgy: before, during and after the radio show. Facebook fans and Twitter followers of a radio programme interact with the programme not only during its transmission, but also throughout the rest of the day. Passionate fans go back to the Facebook page of a radio programme several times during the day (Bonini 2014b). Social media profiles need continuous updates of content in order to keep the contact with the public alive. Producing radio today not only means making high quality audio content, it also means taking care of the audience through social media. The SM curators who responded to our survey claimed to spend a lot of time managing social media: 77 per cent dedicate one to four hours per day to social media updates and replies, beyond their own work as producer, journalist or presenter. Some 80 per cent create more than three Facebook posts per day, and 61 per cent write five or more tweets per day.

Taking care of the social media profiles of a radio programme means working more than before, without any increase in terms of pay. Mobile phones allow us to easily access social media platforms wherever we are, and this means that SM curators can also check their SM profiles wherever they are, even during holidays, at night or at a party. Francesco, 37 years old, an Italian host working for Radio2 RAI, admitted to frequently checking the station's Facebook page from home, on Sundays or at night: 'It takes me nothing to jump from my personal Facebook profile to the one of the radio, so I do it frequently. It's work, I know, but we are used to replying to work emails from our phones, we are already used to working from everywhere; this is how things go today. I like it, because I can easily check the feedback from listeners after my radio show, I get the feeling I can better understand my audience' (interviewed 14 October 2013). This is exactly what Australian scholar Melissa Gregg (2011) called 'work intimacy': late capitalism makes no distinction between work and life spaces. It captures the ambition, dedication, and commitment of an aspiring professional class that seeks ultimate fulfillment and passion in creative work. The boundaries between work and life are blurring. Work is creeping into the most intimate spaces of our private life: we respond to an email as we wait for our girlfriend to finish in the bathroom before going out, we update our Facebook profile as we're cooking a dinner for friends. Late capitalism, claimed Jonathan Crary (2013), is stealing our sleep.

Conclusions: from audience surveillance to listeners' listening

Swedish sociologist Adam Arvidsson (2006) stressed the emergent importance of brands as social institutions that mediate social life in the late age of capitalism. Brand value is an intangible asset of institutions and media companies, Arvidsson claimed. Once corporations, political parties and individuals acquire a public image, they all have to cope with personal brand management. Radio companies, be they public or private, have to face the same problem: how to manage their public image. Social media are the latest step in the history of brand management. The purpose of brand management, continued Arvidsson (2006: 82), is 'to transform brands into "popular ideas that people live by"; to create "enduring relations" with customers; to make the brand into one of the many significant others that anchor people to reality... It is supposed that people use brands to build solidarity, meaning, experiences – all the things that are supposedly no longer happening, provided to the same extent by the social context, or in an equally straightforward manner as before.' Brands like commercial and public service radio stations employ social media managers to produce the particular relationship with consumers that the brand embodies. So, the main role of social media managers in the radio industry is to master the radio brands. If we frame their role under this perspective – as brand masters – we understand the delicate and fundamental role they play within the radio industry. Before the age of social media and networked publics (Boyd 2010), the radio industry never had the opportunity to potentially establish such a personal and close relationship with its audience.

While presenters and journalists are the masters of a radio's relationship with its audience, SM managers are the masters of this relationship online. All of them, from the presenters to the SM managers, contribute to the brand management of their radio station, embodying the station's values. But the daily job of SM managers is more delicate than that of the radio personalities. Journalists and deejays, the radio personalities, speak primarily for themselves, they communicate both the values of the radio brand and those of their personal brand: if a host behaves aggressively during a listener's phone call, his personal brand will be the one that is mostly damaged. SM managers only speak for the radio brand. They only embody the brand's values, not their own personal ones. They hide their voice behind the tweets and posts of the official social media account of a radio station or a radio programme. The official SM profiles of a radio company speak through the voice and sensitivity of social media managers. They are aware, as we have shown, that they need more social than technical skills. Social media management for radio means tuning in to listeners' needs, requests and opinions; it means treating the audience fairly and being responsive to their feedback; it means managing the reputational capital of the radio, an important asset of the radio brand, although it is immaterial. SM managers lie in a very difficult position, between the brand values and aims of their radio company and the listeners. They have to be fair with both, and this represents an extremely complex everyday exercise of listening, word-crafting, gauging the right distance/closeness to the public and finding a balance.

For an institution such as radio, born to broadcast content, it could be very difficult to understand that it is now time to listen to its audiences. The SM managers we interviewed seem to have partially understood this value. Those working for public services know that mastering their brand values means engaging with listeners. Those working for commercial companies still adopt more of a broadcasting attitude: they want people to be aware of a radio brand as much as they can, and in order to do so they monitor the listeners' engagement with their brand. But this monitoring activity of how many people like, comment on, talk about or share their content has more to do with surveillance than paying real attention to listeners. Listeners don't want to be under surveillance, they want to listen and to be listened to. Even if the boundary between surveillance and listening is very thin – every listening activity is potentially a surveillance activity – there is a major difference between surveillance and listening: the aim of the first is to track listeners', (or consumers',) behaviour in order to commodify them, while the aim of the latter is to tune in to listeners' thoughts, opinions and comments in order to serve them better quality content that is closer to their needs. This could be an aim of commercial radio too, since more suitable content means more audience. SM managers are the ones in charge of paving the way for this paradigm shift: they have to start to listen to the listeners.

So far it doesn't seem that the radio industry, at least at the Italian and Spanish radio stations that we analysed, have completely grasped the value embedded in the social media managers' role. They pay them modest wages, they think that it is a job for youth, they think they need to colonise social media too, but only as a surveillance tool. We fear they will never grasp the real value of social media until they start listening to the listeners. Mastering media brands in a networked age should mean more listening and less surveillance.

References

Ala-Fossi, M (2010) 'Future scenarios for the radio industry', in O'Neill, B, *et al* (eds), *Digital radio in Europe: technologies, industries and cultures*, Bristol: Intellect.

Armstrong, C & Gao, F (2010) 'Now tweet this: how news organisations use Twitter', *Electronic News*, volume 4, issue 4.

Arvidsson, A (2006) *Brands. Meaning and Value in Media Culture*, London:Routledge.

Bijker, W (1995) 'Sociohistorical technology studies', in Jasanoff, S, Markle, GE, Petersen, JC & Pinch, T (eds) *Handbook of Science and Technology Studies*, London: Sage.

Blasingame, D (2011) 'Twitter first: changing TV news 140 characters at a time' paper at the International Symposium of Online Journalism, University of Austin, Texas, 20-21 April.

Boczkowski, PJ (2002) 'The development and use of online newspapers: What research tells us and what we might want to know', in Lievrouw, L & Livingstone, S (eds) *Handbook of New Media*, London: Sage.

Bonet, M, Fernández-Quijada, D & Ribes, X (2011) 'The changing natures of Public Service Radio: A case study of iCat fm', *Convergence: The International Journal of Research into New Media Technologies*, volume 17, issue 2.

Bonini T (2014a) 'The listener as producer: the rise of the networked listener', in Bonini T & Monclus B (eds), *Radio Audiences and Participation in the Age of Network Society*, London: Routledge.

Bonini, T (2014b) 'Doing Radio in the Age of Facebook', *The Radio Journal: International Studies in Broadcast and Audio Media*.

Bonini T & Sellas T (2014) 'Twitter as a public service medium? A comparative content analysis of the use of Twitter by Radio RAI and RNE', in *Communication & Society*, volume 2, April 2014.

Bourdieu, P and Wacquant, L (1992) *An invitation to Reflexive Sociology*, Chicago: University of Chicago Press.

Boyd, D (2010) 'Social network sites as networked publics. Affordances, dynamics, and implications', in Papacharissi, Z (ed), *A networked self. Identity, community, and culture on social network sites,* New York: Routledge.

Carmody T (2013) 'Better than Nielsen: Twitter breaks down TV behavior by demographics, device, and genre', *The Verge*, 10 January. http://www.theverge.com/2013/1/10/3861954/twitter-uk-study-real-time-television-ads, accessed 13 October 2013.

Castells, M (2010) *Comunicació i poder,* Barcelona: Editorial UOC.

Crary J (2013) *24/7: Late Capitalism and the Ends of Sleep*. London: Verso.

Crawford K (2009) 'Following you. Disciplines of listening in Social Media', *Continuum, Journal of Media & Cultural Studies*, volume 23 , issue 4.

Cregg M (2011) *Work Intimacy*, Cambridge: Polity Press.

Deuze, M (2008) 'Understanding journalism as newswork: how it changes, and how it remains the same', *Westminster Papers in Communication and Culture*, volume 5, issue 2.

Domingo, D (2008) 'Interactivity in the daily routines of online newsrooms: dealing with an uncomfortable myth', *Journal of Computer-Mediated Communication*, volume 13, issue 3.

EBU (2011) *EBU Report. Public Radio and new media Platforms,* Geneva: EBU Press.

Ferguson, D & Greer, C (2011) 'Local radio and microblogging: how radio stations in the U.S. are using Twitter', *Journal of Radio & Audio Media*, volume 18, issue 1.

Fernández-Quijada, D (2012) 'La necessitat d'un estudi sociocèntric de la tecnologia i els mitjans', in Fernández-Quijada, D (ed), *Medi@tic. Anàlisi de casos de tecnologia i mitjans*, Barcelona: UOC.

García de Torres E *et al* (2011) 'See you on Facebook or Twitter? How 30 local news outlets manage social networking tools' paper at the International Symposium of Online Journalism, University of Austin, Texas. http://online.journalism.utexas.edu/2011/papers/Elvira2011.pdf

Gazi, A, Starkey, G & Jedrzejewski, S (2011) (eds.) *Radio Content in the Digital Age: The Evolution of a Sound Medium*, Bristol: Intellect.

Hermida, A (2010) 'Twittering the news', *Journalism Practice*, volume 4, issue 3.

Herrera, S & Requejo, J (2010) 'Uses of Twitter by the main Spanish talk radio stations', paper presented at the ECREA Conference, University of Hamburg, Hamburg, 12-15 October.

Jenkins, H (2006) *Convergence Culture: Where Old and New Media Collide,* New York: New York University Press.

Lazarsfeld P (1940) *Radio and the Printed Page*, New York: Duell, Sloan and Pearce.

Lewis, S, Kaufhold, K & Lasorsa, D (2010) 'Thinking about citizen journalism. The philosophical and practical challenges of user-generated content for community newspapers', *Journalism Practice*, volume 4, issue 2.

McQuail, D (2000) *Introducción a la teoría de la comunicación de masas*, third edition, Barcelona: Paidós.

Messner M, Linke M & Eford A (2011) paper at the International Symposium of Online Journalism, University of Austin, Texas. http://online.journalism.utexas.edu/2011/papers/Messner2011.pdf

Palser, B (2009) 'Hitting the tweet spot', *American Journalism Review*, volume 31, issue 2.

Podger, P (2009) 'The limits of control', *American Journalism Review*, volume 31, issue 4.

Reynolds, S (2011) *Retromania. Pop Culture Addiction to its Own Past*, New York: Faber.

Schmitz Weiss, A & Domingo, D (2010) 'Innovation processes in online newsrooms as actor-networks and communities of practice', *New Media & Society*, volume 12, issue 7.

Sellas, T (2012) 'A two-dimensional approach to the study of podcasting in Spanish talk radio stations', *The Radio Journal: International Studies in Broadcast and Audio Media*, volume 10, issue 1.

Shoemaker, P, Eichholz, M, Kim, E & Wrigley, B (2001) 'Individual and routine forces in gatekeeping', *Journalism & Mass Communication Quarterly*, volume 78, issue 2.

Sivek, S (2010) 'Social media under social control. Regulating social media and the future of socialization', *Electronic News*, volume 4, issue 3.

Smith A, Boyles J (2012) 'The rise of the connected viewer', report, Pew Internet and American Life Project, 22 July. http://www.pewinternet.org/Reports/2012/Connected-viewers.aspx

Wenger, E (1998) *Communities of Practice, Learning, Meaning and Identity*, Cambridge: Cambridge University Press.

Wolf, M (1987) *La investigación de los medios de comunicación de masas. Crítica y perspectivas,* Barcelona: Paidós.

Wimmer, R & Dominick, JR (2011) *Mass Media Research. An Introduction,* ninth edition, Belmont: Wadsworth.

Chapter 7

2.0 in form, yet still 1.0 in purpose: A comparative study of Spanish music radio stations on Twitter

Susana Herrera Damas and José Luis Requejo Alemán

Abstract

Social media tools and platforms have been widely adopted by broadcasters seeking new ways to maintain, reach and attract audiences in a shifting and evolving media environment. The use of Twitter by media organisations has largely followed the pattern of adoption of the internet more than a decade earlier, when newspapers shoveled print copy online. This chapter examines how music radio stations have adopted Twitter. It is based on a comparative study of the official Twitter accounts of three prominent music radio stations in Spain in 2010 and 2013. While radio is considered an interpersonal medium, our analysis shows that the stations are mainly using Twitter as a one-way medium for self promotion, rather than to engage with audiences. The use of Twitter is increasingly 2.0, as far as form is concerned, yet it is still being used for a very 1.0 purpose. The stations in our study are following the same pattern of integration of earlier web technologies by broadcasters using it for promotional purposes, with very few stations using interactive features such as feedback mechanisms.

Keywords: music radio, radio stations, Twitter, Spain

Introduction

Although social media tools and platforms have been widely adopted by broadcasters seeking new ways to maintain, reach and attract audiences in a shifting and evolving media environment, their use of Twitter has largely followed the pattern of adoption of the internet more than a decade earlier, when newspapers simply replicated print copy online, as noted, for example, by Singer (2001). Studies of the institutional accounts of media organisations point to a similar practice on Twitter, with social media used as a free and fast channel to disseminate content (Blasingame 2011; Greer & Ferguson 2011; Messner *et al* 2011). A study of the use of Twitter by 111 US radio stations found differences between the approach of music and news stations (Ferguson & Greer 2011). Tweets from news stations tended to have a human feel, and were far more likely to provide news, whereas music stations favored promotional messages. Ferguson and Greer suggested that radio stations could do more in using social networking tools to connect with listeners, arguing that: 'radio has greater potential to increase its use of Twitter to reach existing and potential audiences that are more mobile than television viewers' (2011: 43). In this context, the aim of this paper is to examine how Spanish music radio stations have adopted Twitter.

Methodology and findings

In our analysis, we looked at the messages themselves, their apparent purpose, the uses of retweets, replies, mentions, the adoption of hashtags and the use of links. The music radio stations were chosen based on the number of listeners (AIMC, 2013). Those selected were Los 40 (@Los40_Spain), Cadena 100 (@CADENA100) and Europa FM (@europa_fm). We analysed the tweets posted by these three stations on their official Twitter accounts between 20 November and 20 December 2010, and we repeated the analysis for the same time period two and a half years later, from 20 April to 20 May 2013 to examine how the use of Twitter had evolved. The 2010 sample included 200 tweets and the 2013 sample contained 1,662. After finishing the coding, we exported the data from Excel to SPSS to extract the frequencies and the crosstabs. Finally, we compared the results and interpreted the most significant findings. Over the two sample periods, the Tweets were distributed very differently across the stations, as in table 7.1.

	2010	**2013**
@Los40_Spain	114	1,337
@CADENA100	11	40
@europa_fm	75	285
Total	**200**	**1,662**

Table 7.1: Number of tweets by the three music radio stations studied, over the periods analysed in 2010 and 2013

The main use of Twitter by all three radio stations was to promote their own content, in line with previous research on the use of Twitter by news organisations in several countries (Rindfuss 2009; García de Torres *et al* 2010; Orihuela 2011; Greer & Ferguson 2011; Holcomb, Gross & Mitchell 2011; Pew Research Center 2011). As shown in figure 7.1, self-promotional messages made up 44.5 per cent of the 2010 tweets, with the number rising in 2013 to 65.9 per cent. The use of Twitter to provide information fell from 41 per cent in 2010 to 25.8 per cent in 2013. We considered a set of variables to discover if the stations were using the interactive functionality of Twitter, such as retweets, mentions or replies. Our results suggest that the stations have yet to grasp the conversational aspect of Twitter. Interactions between institutional accounts and audience members were very rare, with stations failing to reply to messages from the public.

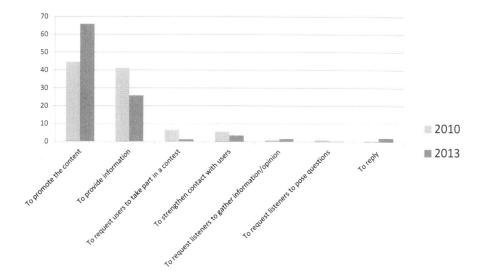

Figure 7.1: Main purposes of sampled radio stations when using Twitter

Self-promotion used different strategies, as follows: saying which song was 'now playing', using the hashtag #NP; saying what was 'coming up'; providing information on the latest audience research; retweeting from presenters' personal accounts; retweeing tweets from listeners on how 'cool' the station was; and links to the station website. The immediate, real-time nature of Twitter served as an ideal channel to publicise interviews or commentary coming up on air.

Taking into account the different approaches of each station, in figure 7.2 we can see how in 2010 Los 40 promoted its content in 28.1 per cent of its tweets. The station also used this platform to provide information (59.6 per cent). Only in a few cases did they request the participation of the audience to take part in a contest (6.1 per cent), to strengthen contact with users (2.6 per cent), to request listeners' opinions (1.8 per cent) or to pose questions to a guest (1.8 per cent). In 2013, Los 40 increased the number of

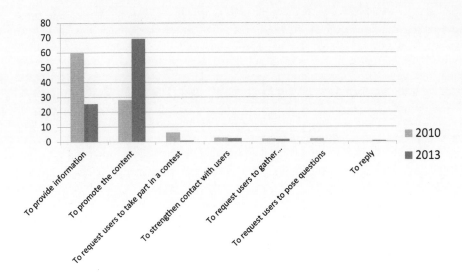

Figure 7.2: Twitter use by Los 40 during the two survey periods

promotional messages to 69.2 per cent and reduced the number of informative messages to 25.4 per cent. Surprisingly, in 2013 Los 40 also reduced other purposes more related to community engagement, although this is one of the eight journalistic potentialities that Twitter provides, as Barnard observed, saying: 'This is not only because competition in the field is greater today than ever before, largely due to the opening up of the field on the web and the excess of information sources available there, but also because the proliferation of new media tools and their leveraging by countless actors increasingly afford the kinds of engagement that both improve the news experience and keep users loyal. Furthermore, increased engagement may also mean increased profit for news institutions in the long run' (2012: 150).

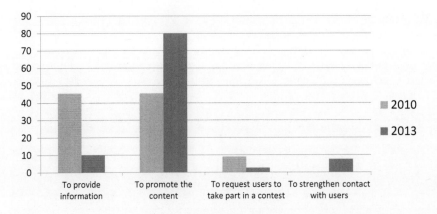

Figure 7.3: Twitter use by Cadena 100 during the survey periods, 2010 and 2013

Figure 7.3 shows how in 2010 the second radio station studied, Cadena 100, used Twitter to provide information (45.5 per cent), to promote content (45.5 per cent) and to request users to take part in a contest (9 per cent). In 2013 promotion remained the main purpose, accounting for 80 per cent of all updates. 10 per cent of the messages aimed to provide information and 7.5 per cent to strengthen contact with users. Only 2.5 per cent requested users to take part in a contest.

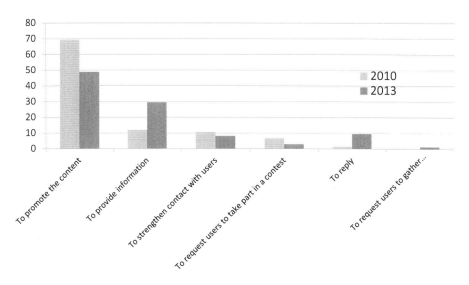

Figure 7.4: Twitter use by Europa FM during the survey periods, 2010 and 2013

In figure 7.4 we see that in 2010 Europa FM mostly used Twitter to promote content (69.3 per cent) and, to a lesser extent, provide information (12 per cent) and strengthen contact with its followers (10.7 per cent). In 2013 promotion fell to 48.8 per cent and providing information rose to 29.5 per cent. One of the best results for this station was the increase in the number of replies to 9.5 per cent of the sample, which demonstrates a more appropriate use of the conversational functionalities that Twitter provides.

Furthermore, our analysis indicated that at times stations used messages for dual purposes. In 2010 half of the messages with a dual purpose also contained an element of self promotion. To a lesser extent, tweets often provided information (12.5 per cent) and requested the participation of the audience to take part in a contest (12.5 per cent). In 2013, self promotion was also the predominant secondary use of Twitter (49.3 per cent). Over the same period, the use of Twitter to strengthen contact with followers rose to 16.8 per cent, as shown in figure 7.5. The use of retweets, mentions or links is considered in a positive light on Twitter as these practices are seen as reinforcing the concept of transparency, one of the most accepted norms in digital journalism (Van der Wurff & Schönbach 2011). Such practices also imply new forms of community engagement through social media, above and beyond the traditional phone-in.

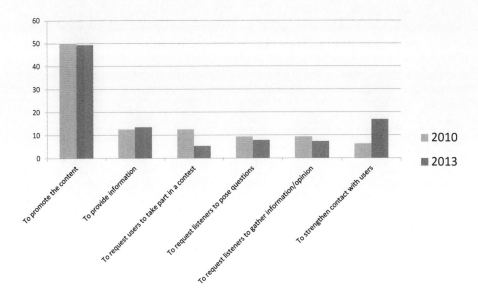

Figure 7.5: Secondary purposes of Twitter use by the three sampled radio stations

According to Lasorsa *et al* (2012: 26), 'retweeting is an indication of a journalist's "opening the gates" to allow others to participate in the news production process'. In this sense, Ingram also advised retweeting others because: 'social media gets very boring if all you do is post links to your own things, or post your own thoughts. Lots of other people have interesting things to say - find some and re-tweet them. Maybe they will return the favour' (2011). In fact, the social media policies of some American news organisations require journalists to clearly attribute the content they source online, since acknowledging the original source is part of the ethos of social media. However, in 2010 this practice was rare among Spanish music radio stations. Figure 7.6 shows how

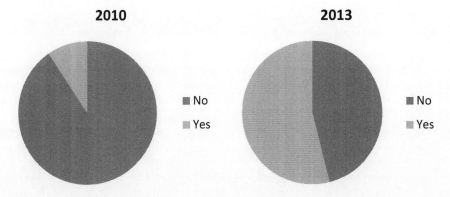

Figure 7.6: Use of retweets by the sampled radio stations during the two survey periods

just 9.4 per cent of our sample were retweets. In 2013, retweets rose to 53.9 per cent, although most of them were originally posted by the station presenters through their personal accounts and also by external users saying how 'cool' the station was. Along with retweets and replies, references to other users through the use of the mention functionality can also be interpreted as a sign of dialogue and conversation. However, as shown in figure 7.7, the use of mentions was very infrequent and only registered in 8.5 per cent of the 2010 sample. In the few occasions when stations mentioned other users, they were internal mentions, referring to presenters' accounts or those of other programmes, or presented in an endogamic fashion. As with retweets, this changed significantly in 2013 with 39.7 per cent of the sample mentioning one account and 27 per cent mentioning two. These mentions referred both to the station and its presenters, as well as to the personal accounts of the artists and groups with songs being played.

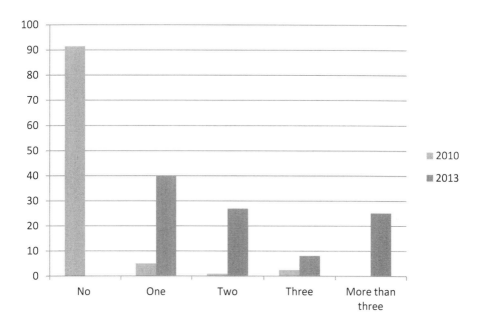

Figure 7.7: Use of mentions of other users by the sampled radio stations during the survey periods

Other findings

In 2010 38.5 per cent of the tweets sampled were used to drive audiences to the station's own website, as shown in figure 7.8. This percentage increased to 47.8 per cent in 2013. Such practices suggest a one-way, broadcast approach to Twitter, rather than a two-way model of interaction.

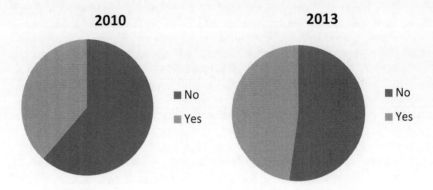

Figure 7.8: Use by the sampled radio stations of tweets linking to their own websites

Very few of the messages in our sample included a link to an external website, as shown in figure 7.9. In 2010, just 9 per cent of the messages directed users to external websites, while the remaining 91 per cent did not link to any site, or solely provided links to their own site. In 2013, this percentage fell to just 0.6 per cent. The virtually non-existent practice of linking to external websites suggests that stations are prioritising their own corporate interests in driving user traffic. It also reflects initial reluctance to use external hyperlinks in websites. The lack of external links suggests that stations are missing out in terms of interactivity, credibility, transparency and diversity (De Maeyer 2012).

Linking to pictures through third-party services such as Twitpic (figure 7.10) increased from 2.5 per cent in 2010 to 3.7 per cent in the 2013 sample, but the practice remained

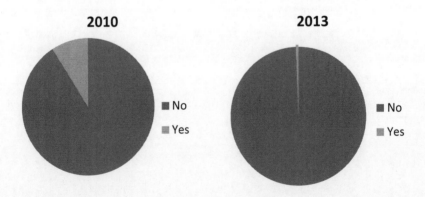

Figure 7.9: Use by the sampled radio stations of tweets linking to external websites

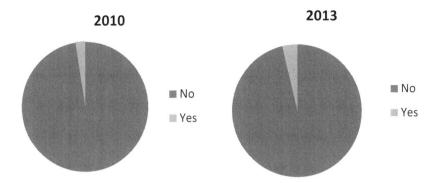

Figure 7.10: Use of links to online pictures by the sampled radio stations

underused if we take into account the many possibilities this resource provides, such as showing the visit of an artist to a studio or the backstage of a concert. However, to avoid missing the opportunity to drive traffic to stations' own websites, pictures were almost always posted on the websites themselves and linked afterwards through Twitter.

A common practice is for a media organisation to link to its other social media accounts on different platforms, such as Facebook, as it has the potential to reinforce the brand, as well as increasing visibility and reach. However, we found little evidence that the stations sampled were taking advantage of the ability to direct audiences to their other social media accounts. The practice of referencing other social media platforms showed a significant drop from 32.5 per cent in 2010 to 0.7 per cent in 2013 (figure 7.11). The results suggest a lack of a coordinated social media approach by the stations sampled.

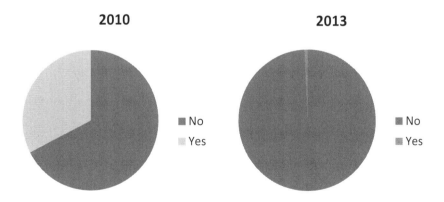

Figure 7.11: Use by the radio stations sampled of links to other social networks

Finally, the hashtag has developed as a means of labeling and highlighting content on Twitter, helping to identify and follow online conversations on specific topics. In 2010 our analysis revealed very limited use of hashtags (just 2 per cent of the sample), despite the value of this mechanism for information retrieval and to extend the reach of a message beyond one's own network (Herrera & Requejo 2012). In 2013, there was a significant increase, up to 32.3 per cent, as shown in figure 7.12.

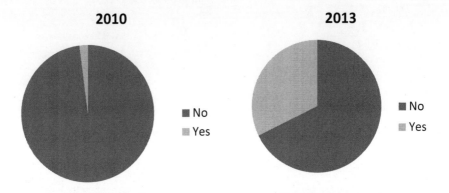

Figure 7.12: Use of hashtags by the radio stations sampled

Conclusions

Our findings on the use of Twitter by the main Spanish music radio stations are at odds with the way music radio operates as a space for interpersonal communication that relies on the participation of a segment of its audience. Tweets were largely used for self promotion, mostly with links back to the home station's website, with virtually no exchanges taking place on the network. Among the most positive indicators were the rise in the number of tweets from 200 to 1662, the increase in the number of replies from 0.5 to 2 per cent and the greater use of the retweet and mention functionalities, from 9.4 to 53.9 per cent and from 8.5 to 100 per cent, respectively. Increases in the use of the reinforcement function as a secondary purpose, from 6.3 to 16.8 per cent, and in the number of hashtags, from 2 to 32.3 per cent, should also be noted. Among the most negative signs are the increase in self-promotional messages from 44.5 to 65.9 per cent, the drop in listeners' requests from 8.5 to 2.9 per cent and the reduction in links to external websites, from 9 to 0.6 per cent, and even to other networks, from 32.5 to 0.7 per cent. In conclusion, we could say that there was a 2.0 use of Twitter, as far as form is concerned, yet it is still being used for a very 1.0 purpose. Radio has a history of adapting to the arrival of new competitive forms of communication, such as the rise of television (Pitts & Harms 2003). Berland (1990) noted how music took over a significant proportion of airtime in the 1950s as television replaced the radio set in the living room. When it comes to Twitter, the stations in our study are following the pattern of assimilation of earlier web technologies by broadcasters. Most sites focused on promotional content, with very few stations using such interactive features as feedback mechanisms (Pitts & Harms 2003; Potter 2002; Ren & Chan-Olmsted 2004). We hope to observe more positive findings in future research.

References

Barnard S (2012) *Twitter and the structural transformation of the journalistic field. How the growth of a new(s) medium is transforming journalism*, PhD thesis presented at the University of Missouri. https://mospace.umsystem.edu/xmlui/bitstream/handle/10355/15860/research.pdf?sequence=2

Berland, J (1990) 'Radio music and space and industrial time: Formats, local narratives technological mediation', *Popular Music*, volume 9, issue 2.

Blasingame, D (2011) 'Gatejumping: Twitter, TV News and the Delivery of Breaking News', *#ISOJ Journal: The Official Journal of the International Symposium on Online Journalism,* volume 1, issue 1. http://online.journalism.utexas.edu/ebook.php

De Maeyer, J (2012) 'The journalistic hyperlink', *Journalism Practice*, volume 6, issues 5-6.

Ferguson, D & Greer, C (2011) 'Local radio and microblogging: How radio stations in the U.S. are using Twitter', *Journal of Radio & Audio Media*, volume 18, issue 1.

García de Torres, E, Yezers'ka, L, Rost, A, Calderín, M, Rojano, M, Edo, C, Sahid, E, Jerónimo, P, Arcila, C, Serrano, A, Badillo, J & Corredoira, L (2011) 'See you on Facebook or Twitter: the use of social media by 27 news outlets from 9 regions in Argentina, Colombia, Mexico, Peru, Portugal, Spain and Venezuela', paper presented at the 12th International Symposium on Online Journalism. http://online.journalism.utexas.edu/2011/papers/Elvira2011.pdf

Greer, C and Ferguson, D (2011) 'Using Twitter for promotion and branding: A content analysis of local television Twitter sites', *Journal of Broadcasting & Electronic Media*. volume 55, issue 2.

Hermida, A (2011) 'Tweet the News: Social Media Streams and the Practice of Journalism', in Stuart, A (ed) *The Routledge Companion to News and Journalism*, second edition, London: Routledge.

Herrera, S, and Requejo, J (2012) '10 good practices for news organizations using Twitter', *Journal of Applied Journalism and Media Studies,* volume 1, issue 1.

Herrera, S, and Hermida, (2014) 'Tweeting but not talking: The missing element in Canadian talk radio's use of Twitter', *Journal of Broadcasting & Electronic Media*, volume 58, issue 4. http://www.tandfonline.com/toc/hbem20/current#.VI7RAqSG_F4

Holcomb, J, Gross, K & Mitchell, A (2011) 'How Mainstream Media Outlets use Twitter', Journalism.org. http://www.journalism.org/analysis_report/how_mainstream_media_outlets_use_twitter

Ingram, M (2011) 'Social media policies: Let's talk about what you *should* do', *Gigaom.* http://gigaom.com/2011/05/03/social-media-policies-lets-talk-about-what-you-should-do/

Lasorsa, D, Lewis, S & Holton, A (2012) 'Normalizing Twitter: Journalism practice in an emerging communication space', *Journalism Studies*, volume 13, issue 1.

Messner, M, Linke, M & Esford, A (2011) 'Shoveling tweets: An analysis of the microblogging engagement of traditional news organizations', *#ISOJ: The Official Research Journal of the International Symposium on Online Journalism*, volume 2, issue 1.

Orihuela, J (2011) 'Los medios deben mejorar su interacción en Twitter', *Digital Media Weblog*. http://www.abc.es/blogs/jose-luis-orihuela/public/post/los-medios-tienen-que-mejorar-su-interaccion-en-twitter

Pew Research Center (2011) 'How mainstream media outlets use Twitter'. http://pewresearch.org/pubs/2130/twitter-news-organizations

Pitts, M & Harms, R (2003) 'Radio websites as a promotional tool', *Journal of Radio Studies*, volume 10, issue 2.

Potter, R (2002) 'Give the people what they want: A content analysis of FM radio station home pages', *Journal of Broadcasting & Electronic Media*, volume 46, issue 3.

Ren, W & Chan-Olmsted, S (2004) 'Radio content on the World Wide Web: Comparing streaming radio stations in the United States', *Journal of Radio Studies*, volume 11, issue 1.

Rindfuss, A (2009) 'The Use of Twitter by America's Newspapers', The bibings report. http://www.bivingsreport.com/2009/the-use-of-twitter-by-americas-newspapers/, consulted on July 5, 2010.

Singer, J (2001) 'The metro wide web: Changes in newspapers' gatekeeping role online', *Journalism and Mass Communication Quarterly*, volume 78.

Van der Wurff, R & Shönbach, K (2011) 'Between profession and audience. Codes of conduct and transparency as quality instruments for off- and online journalism', *Journalism Studies*, volume 12, issue 4.

Chapter 8

Ex-static but not ecstatic: Digital radio and the end of interference

Evangelia Karathanasopoulou

Abstract

Since its beginnings radio has struggled to rid itself of interference, which was regarded as a nuisance and a distraction from its message. Mainstream radio broadcasting, especially, has focused on delivering spotless, studio-quality sound, with digital technology being at the centre of recent developments. This paper argues that it is time to reconceptualise 'interference', to consider it not as an impairment of radio's message but, more inclusively, as an integral part of its special texture. In a curious way, it has contributed to radio's authenticity and its status as a medium of magic and intimacy, and in that sense it performs an aesthetic role.

Drawing upon radio theory as well as wider media and cultural studies, this paper will consider the positive functions and implications of interference as well as its connection with issues of space, both physical and imagined. With digital radio becoming ever more popular and the end of analogue in prospect, this paper argues that such transition involves a degree of loss as well as gain. Will radio ever be the same without the on-air meetings and clashes between broadcast sounds? What will *on air* mean if we can no longer detect broadcasting's interaction with the physical space and objects around it? Is the digital domain a lonely space compared to the analogue radiophonic ether?

Keywords: interference, aesthetics, analogue, digital

The nature of interference

Interference in broadcasting has never been desirable. It is by definition something negative; the prevention of a process from continuing properly. However, when radio communication allowed us to transcend spatial boundaries in order to communicate messages instantly over long distances, it was impossible to completely bypass those things with which broadcasts had to share their space. As radio broadcasting became more and more popular, stations also had to compete with other stations for air-space. The latter was partly addressed with the regulation of the airwaves, but pirate stations have at times operated against these regulations.

The effect of interference is most often annoyance on the part of both listeners and broadcasters. Paddy Scannell wrote:

> Radio listening in its early years was a hit and miss affair: the signal strength fluctuated and its range was limited. Transmissions from other stations on the same or similar wavelength interfered with what listeners had tuned into, and oscillation from other nearby radio sets was a menace in the 1920s... The elimination of interference, the achievement of clear, strong signals and the auditory quality (clarity, tone, timbre etc) of the sound transmitted by the receiving apparatus have been constants from the beginning of the audio industries to now. (Scannell, quoted in O'Neill *et al* 2010: 11)

Scannell's description is indicative of the fact that interference is normally seen as undesirable. It is implicit that 'sterile' or noise-free sound is good sound. However, in this paper I wish to argue that there are positive elements to the disruption of such sterility and I will be relating the concept of interference to the elements of time and space, both crucial to all radio. My analysis will be looking at radio as a medium which, crucially, evokes presence.

In my research for my PhD thesis I considered a wide range of radio theory texts, including work by avant-garde theorists in order to better understand the concept of intimacy in relation to radio. To generalise, it may be argued that it is in what may be termed 'mainstream' theory (and practice) that interference has been seen as purely negative, and to be fair not without good reason. Some representative works of mainstream radio theory, widely used in higher education, are Crisell (1994), Shingler & Wieringa (1998), Hendy (2000), Barnard (2000) and Starkey (2014), amongst others. Their work mostly analyzes mainstream radio practice, audiences and histories and deals with radio as it is in the 'real world' across the range of programme genres.In the non-mainstream (or avant-garde) strand of radio theory, writers such as Allen S. Weiss and Gregory Whitehead seem to argue that interference can be more radiophonic than the clear, programmed, articulate sound of mainstream radio. While I do not wholly share their ideas, I am intrigued by some of their arguments, however vague and open to interpretation these might be. The non-mainstream strand of radio theory is all about disarticulation – literal, in terms of what is heard on the radio, and metaphorical, representing an opposition to mainstream theory - and disengagement of any pre-conceived ideas of what radio is and should be. The position of this paper is by no means so radical, but engagement with such texts allows the radio scholar to look at the functions of interference in a different light. As early as 1990, Whitehead was concerned about digital technology eliminating the rich sound-world of interference. He wrote then: 'Hidden behind the present fetish for fiber optics and laser discs is the powerful desire to eliminate the slightest trace of pneumatic interference' (1990: 62).

If we look at interference through the tension between mainstream and non-mainstream theorisations of radio, we observe a contrast relating to organisation versus disorganisation of sound, articulation versus disarticulation, clarity versus polysemy, linearity versus non-linearity. On the one hand, we have the well orchestrated, well rehearsed, well organised, and very live – or *as*-live - mainstream conceptualisation of a medium which seeks constantly to purge itself of interference; on the other hand, we have the idea of a medium which is naturally chaotic, disarticulate and unregulated. The truth, this paper argues, is somewhere in the middle. Interference would not be meaningful if it were not *interfering* with organised broadcasts. Interference is only a natural by-product of the broadcasting process. The disruption it creates is aesthetically reliant on the random meeting of articulate broadcasts and it is physically determined by the matter through and next to which these broadcasts move.

Even though interference might be more appreciated within the avant-garde, experience of interference in the past has come through the everyday use of the technology. The 'hunt' for the broadcast has traditionally been part of the process of tuning in to a radio station, and so culturally interference has become associated with the very essence of radio. It helps to declare that radio is indeed 'radio'. Sonically, in media production, the sound of interference is often chosen as the means to identify radio sound. The presence of radio sound is often understood through its interruptions and imperfections which aesthetically can help us separate it from other recordings. Moreover, the aesthetics of radio sound are very strongly bound up with the element of the unexpected. For instance, when wishing to convey the sound-effect of radio sound within a radio or television drama, a producer might start with interference which develops into a clearer signal or use continuous interruptions to a primarily music or voice broadcast. The way that radio is represented in media production can tell us a lot about the nature of the medium. Interference presents radio as a medium which travels through long distances and bypasses several obstacles; *material* such as buildings, bodies and so on, and *immaterial* such as other broadcasts.

Radio has been dubbed an intimate medium and it may be argued that this intimacy relies on a particularly intense sense of *presence* that radio possesses. In the case of interference, despite its seemingly disruptive character, the element of presence is, I would argue, retained and expressed in two distinct ways: the presence of matter and the presence of other broadcasts. We may, then, categorise interference into two types:

Interference consisting of one or more broadcasts interfering with another Here the human voice becomes interwoven with others, part of a chorus of voices, songs and sound effects. This means that now the broadcast seems to communicate not only with the listener, but, however unwillingly, with other broadcasts too. For example, while listening to a song, one might suddenly hear the voice of a news presenter. This effect presents the ether as a populated space and a meeting place and, in allowing broadcasts to leak into each other, evokes a sense of fluidity.

Interference coming from physical objects and human bodies In interference of this kind, physical objects as well as the listener's body may acquire a 'voice'. For example, we may often affect the sound of our radio when we walk near the receiver; we create interference and we cause the sound to break up. The materiality of the broadcast then becomes apparent: to intercept its space means to interrupt it, or rather, to change it. This is a rather embodied experience that contrasts somewhat with a common perception of radio sound and the radio voice as disembodied. This kind of interference is really a marker of the objects and bodies which share the same space with the radio transmission. Steven Connor, a professor of English at Cambridge who has written extensively on radio and sound, in his essay 'Atmospherics', argued that with radiophony the air itself was given a voice. 'What came through *on* the air was the sound *of* the air, given voice by being given over to the electromagnetic carriage of voice' (Connor 2006: 3). The 'voice' of a building, a mountain, or a listener's body is indeed a very fragile, fleeting one. Interference is an event that only happens once and cannot be replicated. And considering the absolute power of live sound in radio, (which means often recording 'as live'), then, perhaps paradoxically, interference is very close to the evanescence associated with radio sound. It is a manifestation of radio's materials: sound-waves, air, antennas, bodies, voices and ears.

The technology of interference

The fluidity and fragility of interference evoke a blurriness of boundaries which for most of radio's history was reinforced by the tactile technology of round dials on radio receivers, which allowed for an experience of fluidity rather than the set boundaries that buttons established later on. Aesthetically these buttons often even try to imitate the old circular dials. But they can only turn position by position, the fluidity of the old dial broken into little segments. Digital radio technology has perfected, then, the elimination of what is *in between* broadcasts and has separated them perfectly. On the one hand, the turning of the analogue dial re-enforces the medium's serendipity and perfectly represents the fluidity of the analogue radiophonic ether. On the other, the pressing of a button imposes a *separation*. The latter seems to transform radio signals from broadcasts which are delivered through the ether to broadcasts that are tightly confined within narrow radiophonic spaces.

Interference is a reminder that radio is in fact a form of *tele*communication, that is, of communication over distances. Interference carries with it the 'grain', the dust of the journey of the broadcast through space. The disappearance of this element will, I would argue, constitute a loss for radiophony and its audience. If interference at first glance seems to be a threat to the linearity of articulate, organised single radio broadcasts, it does signify and ensure a broader linearity related to the way that radio as a whole travels. Interference creates a conceptual duality within which 'radio' and 'a radio programme' are somewhat differentiated. If one were to devise a makeshift radiophonic ontology for the purpose of this argument, the medium would not, of course, be 'radio' as we know it without radio *programmes*. Yet, at the same time, radio programmes are born, owe their existence to and move along the constant linearity of what we call 'radio'. Interference is a material manifestation of this ontology and the means by which we place radio within a broader system of space and time. Paradoxically, interference, while continually threatening that second level of linearity at which programmes exist, represents a more fundamental level of linearity which characterises *all* radio. It is a kind of sound-enriching *ison* - that is, a constant which represents and unifies radio, in the way that a drone note is often used in a Byzantine chant to enrich the singing within a harmonised or polyphonic work.

From its beginnings, radio has been a medium that was part of its message. From the early radio enthusiasts, to the radio pirates, to the everyday listener tuning in her different radio sets to her favourite station in order to be able to hear it throughout the house, the technology was always 'hands on', and sometimes, perhaps, even fiddly. Analogue radio technology allows the listener to interact with the signal, to try to fix it by adjusting the aerial or the whole receiver, or to move herself closer or further from the radio set in order to get a better signal. DAB receivers, however, have been marketed as interference-free, but in reality they are not and listeners seem to be less tolerant of digital interference than analogue interference. One obvious reason is that DAB receivers cost considerably more and so consumers want to get what they paid for. But, crucially, the listener does not have the embodied means of the analogue to try to fix the digital interference, which occurs when the signal is too weak. The process could be very complicated and involve trying to find other devices which may be interacting with the digital receiver. Another reason that digital interference is so unwelcome could be sonic. Interference on DAB sounds electronic, disconcerting. Digital interference is more of a loss of sound or a complete distortion rather than a change of it. Analogue interference sounds more natural, or, one could argue, *organic*. Sonically, digital interference seems to be rather dehumanising in the sense that it impacts on presence and liveness. In the example used above, a listener might tune several analogue radios into the same station so that she can move around the house seamlessly following the continuous, linear signal. On the contrary, the delay effect in digital receivers, often variable depending on the maker of the set, renders them out of sync, which means one cannot follow a broadcast throughout the house in the same way. Whereas the analogue signal is ever-present, continuous and live, the digital signal seems to be spasmodic, disrupted and subject to delays. Surprisingly, then, we may see digital radio as prone to disruption and analogue radio as naturally fluid, uninterrupted. Underneath the analogue crackles there is always a voice, a sound; where analogue interference consists of layered sound, digital interference seems to be more of a *loss* of sound.

Conclusion

With technological innovation there always seems to be a degree of loss as well as gain and often there is an aesthetic price to pay. The differences between analogue and digital radio offer an analogy with those differences between traditional, paper books and e-books, such as Kindles. As with analogue radio, books offer a more tactile, embodied experience than Kindles do. The reader can *interfere* with a book. She can bend it, write on it, tear pages out of it, smell it - and in the same way, the signal of analogue radio can be manipulated by changing the position of the receiver, or its antenna, or even by a listener moving around the receiver. The handling of the book results in an artefact which is not pristine but offers sensory pleasure. Similarly, the fragile relationship of the analogue signal to the matter around it results in non-pristine sound. Listeners, as well as readers, naturally value the benefits of new technologies - in the case of Kindles, a small and light device that can carry a large number of books; in the case of digital radio, a clearer sound and access to additional stations. But audiences, as well as readers, seem to show a certain fondness for a bit of imperfection, as is apparent in the debate about the merits of vinyl records versus CDs and mp3s. Enthusiasts of vinyl value it because of the 'warmth' that analogue recorded sound carries, because of the tactile and visual pleasure that the album covers afford and, crucially, because of the tactile and audible way in which vinyl carries the 'grain' of time and matter. The scratches on a vinyl record may be seen as damage, but they are often treasured by owners because they represent a similar grain to the one that interference represents for radio. They are signs of a journey through actual space and time. Today, even digital devices try to replicate the hands-on experience of analogue technology. Mobile phones and tablets discarded buttons in favour of swipes and taps of the finger on their screens, allowing users, literally, to leave their fingerprint on them.

While celebrating radio's resilience and remarkable ability to adapt to the changes in the media landscape, it may be argued that a healthy dose of interference is not so much a challenge to radio's evocative power and traditional strengths as an affirmation of them. Do not throw away your DAB radios and start looking for stations on short wave! But an understanding of the aesthetics of interference can help the radio scholar as well as the radio practitioner to be more creative in their approach to both theory and practice.

References

Barnard, S (2000) *Studying Radio*, London: Arnold.

Connor, S (2006) 'Atmospherics: The Weather of Sound', paper at *Sounding Out 3*, University of Sunderland, United Kingdom, 8 September.

Crisell, A (1994) *Understanding Radio*, London: Routledge.

Hendy, D (2000) *Radio in the Global Age*, Cambridge: Polity.

O'Neill, B, Ala-Fossi, M, Jauert, P, Lax, S, Nyre, L & Shaw, H (eds) (2010) *Digital Radio in Europe: Technologies, Industries and Cultures,* Bristol: Intellect.

Shingler, M & Wieringa, C (1998) *Methods and Meanings of Radio*, London: Arnold.

Starkey, G (2014) *Radio in Context, Second edition*, Basingstoke: Palgrave Macmillan.

Weiss, S (1995) *Phantasmic Radio*, North Carolina: Duke University Press.

Whitehead, G (1990) 'Principia Schizophonica: On noise, gas and the broadcast disembody', *Art & Text*, issue 37, September.

Part Two
Geographies

Chapter 9

The participative medium: Radio in democratisation processes

Esther Dorn-Fellermann

Abstract

Radio is a resilient medium. It is still an important part of the media repertoire for the younger and more internet-oriented generations. One common assumption is that these generations are interested in interaction with media content and participation in media production. Radio is, however, open for participation on different levels. Some radio stations offer opportunities to participate in media production processes and to participate in society through the media by interacting with media content. As part of my PhD thesis I examined five community radio stations in South Africa, where radio is considered to be the most important mass medium, especially at local level. This chapter will focus on the differences between interaction, participation in and participation through the medium, as well as voluntary participation and opportunities for audiences to get involved in radio programmes. I argue that there is a greater interest in interaction with, than in participation through, the medium, especially in countries where different distribution channels are available. This is one reason why it proves very difficult for alternative radio stations to recruit staff with radio and journalistic skills and the long term commitment needed to ensure the sustainability of the stations.

Keywords: resilience, interaction, participation, community radio, Germany, South Africa

Introduction

Many voices predicted a sharp decline listening to radio. This might be true for listening over the airwaves. However, especially in better developed countries there are different distribution channels in use. Let us begin by focusing on radio as a resilient medium, not only in countries like South Africa where I did my research, but in more developed ones as well. Some 25 years ago each of the mass media depended on a single platform. Today they don't. We find an increase in mobile or smartphones not only in the developed Western countries but elsewhere, such as in South Africa, as well. So media content, not only radio programmes, is highly mobile. I suggest this is an opportunity for radio rather than competition and that is why broadcasters try to attract internet-oriented people with apps and podcasts, audio-on demand, live streams and so on. This vast spectrum of platforms, at least where people have access to the internet, is a challenge for every journalist and producer, and not only those working in radio. Apart from those special characteristics of radio, such as mobility, immediacy, cheapness and ubiquity which contribute to the success of the medium, there are some additional characteristics which are especially important in less developed countries. There is no need to be able to write or to read, so it is quite easy for people who are illiterate to easily access information through radio. It is relatively easy to produce radio programmes, so people can more easily participate in content production.

As regards the role of radio in democratisation processes, in some rural areas of South Africa and in some other African countries, radio is the only source of information. There is no connectivity to the internet and often no newspaper or television. This chapter will also consider the differences between interaction and participation. Radio is open for participation on different levels such as content selection, interaction, participation *in* the medium and participation *through* the medium. One common assumption is that the more internet-oriented generation wants to get involved in shaping media content or that they at least look for information they are really interested in. My question is: are they really interested in participation? Finally, I will also examine the opportunities radio presents in democratisation processes in South Africa.

A resilient medium: no cause for concern

Radio is still an important part of the media repertoire, even though it is used more often for entertainment than for information purposes. Using Germany as an example of a developing country, Arbeitsgemeinschaft Medien-Anlyse (Agma) data show a decrease in the amount of time that the German population spends listening to radio over the airwaves. In 2002 young people from 14-19 years old listened to the radio for more than two hours per day. In 2012 the figures showed a reduction of the time spent listening, down to one hour 30 minutes. What does this mean? Maybe changes have to be made to radio programming make it more attractive to young audiences.

However, in another survey of the duration of media usage in Germany from 2010 published by Engel/Best, we see a difference between total audio consumption and *radio* listening. The youngest group in this survey, 14-29 year-olds, spent 225.5 minutes, or almost 4 hours per day listening to radio programmes, mp3 files, CDs, podcasts and so on. On average 136.4 minutes, or more than 2 hours per day, were spent listening to radio programmes, which represents 60.5 per cent of their listening and clearly more than the amount of time they spent using mp3 files or CDs, which account for less than 80 minutes per day (35.4 per cent), or using audio files (18.1 min per day on average or 8 per cent of their daily listening time). Interestingly, this group listens to radio programmes via the internet for only seven minutes per day, and 5.7 minutes of that time via live streaming (see table 9.1).

| | Total | Gender | | Age | | | |
		Male	Female	14-29	30-49	50-64	65+
All audio	226	228.7	223.4	**225.5**	244.3	225.4	198.6
Radio listening	187.3	185.9	188.7	**136.4**	196.2	204.9	187.5
(above in per cent)	82.9%	81.3%	84.4%	**60.5%**	85.2%	90.9%	94.4%
MD/CD/ MC/MP3	35.3	38.0	32.6	**79.8**	32.6	19.7	11.1
(above in per cent)	15.6%	16.6%	14.5%	**35.4%**	13.3%	8.7%	5.6%
Audio files	6.6	9.5	3.8	**18.1**	6.5	1.4	0.6
Radio via internet	2.8	4.3	1.5	**7.0**	3.2	0.4	0.6
Radio live on internet	2.4	3.6	1.2	**5.7**	2,7	0.4	0.6
Radio podcast	0.5	0.8	0.2	**1.4**	0.4	0.1	0.0
Music	3.6	5.1	2.2	**10.3**	3.3	1.0	0.0
Other audio files	0.4	0.7	0.2	**1.1**	0.5	0.2	0.0

Figure 9.1: Duration of media use in minutes per day in Germany, 2012. (Source: Engel/Best).

Podcasting and audio-on-demand enable listeners to create their own radio schedules, freeing them from the rigid programming of the radio stations, but surveys from Germany do not show much interest in them. Similarly, there seems to be little interest in podcasting or audio-on-demand. In addition to time spent listening to radio programmes, the youngest age group in particular listens to more than an hour per day of music using mp3 files and CDs, choosing to listen to the same music over and over again, rather than select their own choice of radio programme. The advantage of scheduled radio programmes is that people usually listen to the radio while doing their daily routines without switching over to another station. By accident listeners may get information they haven't previously heard and become interested. They may hear more about a subject in depth and so form opinions based on more balanced information. Therefore it is important that radio producers know how to get the attention of their target audiences, especially using the new communication tools which offer increased opportunities for greater interaction with the listeners.

Getting listeners involved in radio programmes is an old idea, one almost as old as the medium itself. Since 1948 community radio stations have offered opportunities to participate in radio stations, or, in Carpentier's words: 'To participate in media production processes and to participate in society through the media by interacting with media content' (2011b: 70). Increasing interaction in well-established media systems mainly means using the different communication tools for getting in contact with the listeners. This means adapting the opportunities offered by multimedia devices. I consider this to be more interaction with the audience than audiences participating in or through the medium. According to Carpentier, interaction is not the same as participation. He noted that: 'Access and interaction do matter for participatory processes in the media – they are actually its conditions of possibility – but they are also very distinct from participation because of their less explicit emphasis on power dynamics and decision-making' (2011a: 28). Interacting with media content and trying to make a contribution to democratic processes in a specific community through the medium is something completely different because there is another idea behind the commitment of the radio station.

Interaction or participation?

The purpose behind participation in community radio stations is to strengthen an internal democratic process by putting decision-making in the hands of the people in the community (Dagron 2001: 25). Access and interaction are pre-conditions for participation in or through the media. Carpentier's analysis further noted:

- Access in the context of participatory processes in the media means the opportunity for people to have their voices heard;

- Interaction is using technical equipment for producing and receiving content, sometimes in groups or communities, and discussing content in an organisational context. It is trying to use the medium as a platform, and co-producing not co-deciding. This is the main difference between interaction and participation;

- Participation means co-deciding on all levels: technology, content, people and organisational policies (2011a: 30).

These definitions are very helpful in describing the different levels of participation in community radio. Participation is one of the special characteristics of community radio stations and varies from differing degrees of audience involvement in programming and management to total ownership of the station (Dagron 2001: 13). The stations provide an opportunity to practise such democratic principles as tolerance towards different-minded people, expressing a view and finding compromises. These are difficult tasks everywhere in the world, not only in South Africa and not only in community radio stations, but, for example, in internet communities as well. Furthermore, the stations provide access to media policy-making, to the selection of media information, to media production and also to feedback possibilities (Berrigan 1977: 17).

Dagron's understanding of participatory communication (2001: 26) is dialogical rather than linear communication. He describes the people involved as dynamic actors, actively participating in the process of social change. They are in control of communication tools and content and they are taking their own future in hand through a process of dialogue and democratic participation in planning communication activities. Urban and rural communities act collectively in the interests of the majority, preventing the risk of handing power to a select few. The communication process is adapted to each community or social group in terms of content, language, culture and media. The emphasis is on participatory and collective processes in research, problem identification, decision making, implementation, and evaluation of change. There seems to be a common belief that media are capable of 'activating' the audience, of stimulating people not only to take part in media processes, but also to become more active in society. It contends that 'the media have a role in informing attitudes, in developing critical awareness, in informing people about the realities of their situation and in stimulating them to improve or change it' (Berrigan 1977: 18). However, access to media production, often seen as 'a passport to freedom' (*ibid*: 15), seems to be only a first step in the democratisation process.

In accordance with the concept of community radio, these stations are supposed to be integral to development processes and democratisation, owned by the communities they serve, operated in a participatory way, often relying on community volunteers to produce and present programmes, develop their own news casts, organise discussions on matters affecting their community and share information in a language they understand (Girard 2007:1). Participation in media means participation in production in terms of content-related-participation and participation in organisational decision-making, or structural participation. Depending on the structural organisation within the station different opportunities for participation may arise in community radio stations. The 'participation in the media' component raises questions about power relations in the broadcasting studio, the newsroom or the management boardroom, for instance. The distinction between maximalist forms, where control and participation become balanced, and minimalist approaches, where participation is reduced to access and interaction primarily to serve the interests of the media organisation, allows us to differentiate between participation in the media and participation through the media (Carpentier 2011b: 69 -70). This distinction is also important for my research. I consider that participation *in* the medium means being involved in content production or technical management, and this not necessarily political or social participation, whereas participation *through* the medium describes the use of the medium for involvement or for having an impact on political and/or wider social decision-making processes.

Considering the audience, Carpentier (*ibid*) combined these two forms of participation with other possibilities for audience activity. He differentiated between participation in media production, participation in society *through* the media and interaction *with* media content. The one is supported by three elements: access to, interaction with and participation in media organisations, such as community media. An alternative model defines media organisations as small, independent of state and market, oriented towards special and possibly disadvantaged communities, accepting their diversity. Carpentier described four ideal typical models:

1) The participation process involves people who organise their own participation that is the way in which the community radio stations should be organised;

2) The media production still takes place in the organisation and the participants do not have to be members of the organisation, the level of participation within the organisation (structural participation) is therefore reduced, examples of which can be found in the digital storytelling sector;

3) The media production becomes detached from the organisation; these are more providers of access. In this model participation is possible on some levels of the organisation, such as wi-fi-communities for instance;

4) As the third model, but only minimal participation within the organisation is possible, for example social networks (2011b: 225).

Content-related participation is possible in all of these models, but with decreasing structural participation from the first to the fourth. The first model, (the maximalist form,) allows participation on both levels, so there is an on-going need for democratisation of organisational structures and protection of the internal power balances within community radio stations organised in this way. Combined with their activities in media production, a permanent discourse about participation in these stations may bring the needed 'knowledge on the practical organisation of participatory processes and how to overcome the many problems these processes encompass' (Carpentier 2011b: 288). For this to work well in community radio stations, in the sense of encouraging community participation in broadcasting and providing horizontal communication in the communities, the stations need participants to be interested in debates about the social, political or even educational demands of the community. Thus they may find a way to satisfy all these expectations while being aware of the needs and interests of the other community members at the same time. For participatory communication there has to be an interested audience as well, coming up with questions or issues they want to discuss. Last but not least the (local) government(s) or municipalities have to accept these stations as independent media organisations. These conditions are not fulfilled everywhere.

Radio in democratisation processes: a case study from South Africa

Rozumilowicz described four stages of media transition and noted that for free and independent media all the institutional, economic and socio-cultural arenas have to support the diffusion of control and access. Referring to the socio-cultural implications, she explained the need for an 'enabling environment' for competing views and tolerance of ideas rather than proliferation of information. For such a culture an educational system instilling values of tolerance within the community is necessary (2002: 17-24). In South Africa many communities have been marginalised, neglected and repressed for decades. According to Ramphele (2008) the burden of the struggle for freedom left deep fissures in relationships between individuals, families and communities, as well as in the wider social system. That is why the South African transformation process rests on a weak social capital base. Ramphele described some dilemmas of the transformation process in South Africa:

- The elite pact that led to the transition of the whole South African system with inevitable compromises and persistent inequalities;
- The scale of the transformation across political, economic and social systems;
- The 'stubborn ghosts of racism, sexism, ethnic chauvinism and authoritarianism';
- The weak base, because of the deliberate underdevelopment of the majority of the population, of this immense transformation agenda (2008: 24-5).

According to *Service Delivery and Conditions of Living in the Eastern Cape*, published by the Eastern Cape Socio Economic Consultative Council (ECSECC), the province is characterised by extreme poverty and its rural nature, having the highest net migration outflow in South Africa, especially among skilled or energetic young people, entrepreneurs and investors. During the period of my research in 2011, the Eastern Cape Province had the country`s second-highest illiteracy level. The majority of the population were not covered by medical aid in spite of the high level of HIV/AIDS. More than half of all households were in receipt of social benefits. Eastern Cape was the province with the lowest percentage of households connected to the mains electricity supply and the highest percentage of households with no access to running water, performing below the average for the country against most transport and telecommunication indicators, especially concerning access to the internet (ECSECC 2011). According to the *Community Survey* (Statistics South Africa 2007: 21) only 3.8 per cent of households in the Eastern Cape had access to the internet at home, but 67.9 per cent of households did have a radio. Radio, therefore, remains the most important mass medium in the area.

Recent approaches to participatory communication focus on structural inequality and social transformation. Participatory communication, as articulated above, is characterised by 'its capacity to involve the human subjects of social change in the process of communicating' (Dagron 2001: 25). Communication for social change is seen as 'a process of public and private dialogue through which people themselves define who they are, what they need, and how they will work together to get what they want and need in order to improve their lives and their communities' (CFSC 2013). In this sense people engaged in the community radio stations find plenty of work to do.

Conducting an empirical comparative analysis of five such stations in Eastern Cape, I examined the different ways in which they operate. There were 19 licensed stations in the Eastern Cape Province during the research period in 2011. The stations I visited during November and December were selected because of their differences of type, (being interest or geographical,) their editorial area, (being rural or urban,) levels of poverty and differences in the Living Standard Measure (LSM) of the target audience. As well as the field research, I interviewed the station manager and at least one volunteer member of the staff in each station. Then I had group discussions with station managers from four other stations and another with students working for a campus radio station. I also collected documents, such as guidelines or constitutions. and I examined websites, programme schedules and Facebook pages. The main focus of my thesis was to what extent may the community radio stations make a contribution to democratic processes in their communities through participatory communication, which opportunities for them existed and where lay their limits.

Community radio stations in South Africa do have an impact on democratic processes, especially through the volunteers working there. There might be an impact through the programme content as well, but I would argue the benefits are to be seen more within the stations themselves than in their wider communities. One reason for this is that there is still no well-defined answer to the question of what exactly constitutes a community, although numerous articles, studies and textbooks dealing with community media have been published and, as Hipfl &Hug found, 'aspects like "community building" have been promoted as one of the most compelling features of the new developments in information and communication technologies' (2006: 10). Considering community radio stations in Kwazulu-Natal, South Africa, Teer-Tomaselli noted that: 'The relationships with the 'community' from which they supposedly spring, and which they represent on air, are oft-times tenuous and contradictory' (2006: 193). In order to examine the participants' willingness to share information, knowledge, trust and commitment in development processes and democratisation, my interviewees in each community radio station were asked to answer such questions as:

- Which topics arise because of this perception of your community?
- How would you describe the community you serve?
- Who decides which topics get airtime?

The answers indicated that the volunteers had considerable freedom in content production but usually had only a vague idea of the community's interests. So they tended to cover topics that they were personally interested in, without any wider reference to the needs of the community. Some of the volunteers who were interviewed said radio is more for having fun than for development purposes or for getting politically involved. I concluded that the volunteers participate more *in* the medium than *through* the medium because the topics which get airtime are mostly about music, relationships and celebrities. These topics are often neither specific to the community nor do they pick up on political or social issues, being more for entertainment than for informational purposes and close to the interests of the younger generation in industrialised countries.

The volunteers interviewed were between 18 and 25 years old and weren't involved in organisational decisions about programming guidelines or financial issues and they showed little interest in this part of the day-to-day running of the station - meeting Carpentier's definition of minimalist dimensions, where participation is reduced to access and interaction. Producing one`s own programmes or newscasts, for instance, may develop an ability to critique the productions and methods of the established media organisations, as well as the opportunity to develop informed opinions and to make informed decisions. Although some of the volunteers did not stay for a long time, hopefully they would keep this in mind and pass these skills to other people in society. The motivation for volunteers to become involved in management as well, is only there as long as gaining skills is seen to be more valuable than earning money, which was the main goal and motivation for the managers that I interviewed. However to expect that the stations should provide these opportunities for everyone belonging to the community, seems to be problematic. As long as there is no clear answer to the question of what exactly constitutes a community, it remains difficult to say who may participate in these stations that serve populations of fifty to two hundred thousand people. One of the main challenges the participative media in South Africa are facing is sustainability, especially in terms of employee turnover and financial management. Having access to media policy making, to selection of media information, to media production or to feedback possibilities is an interesting position to be in, but before the stations may think about community participation and services, they need funding. Community radio stations, and not only in South Africa, are facing a lot of challenges. While the volunteers develop in confidence and skills, and have fun producing their broadcasts, managers complain that the community radio sector is not taken seriously and there isn't enough recognition for the efforts of those participating in the station.

Conclusion and outlook

Radio is still one of the most important media in South Africa, partly because it is cheap to produce and available everywhere. It is mobile and contemporary, it is easy to produce radio content and it is easy to understand even for people with poor levels of literacy. Here it is indeed a resilient medium not only in this area even if distribution platforms may change or evolve. Today it is easier to interact with media content because of the internet, but interaction is not the same as participation. It is co-producing while participation means co-deciding. As long as there is no possibility to get involved in organisational or content-related decision making processes, Carpentier is right to argue that this amounts only to interaction. In this context new communication tools are useful. We can only start to talk about participation when volunteers are actively involved in decision-making processes. It is possible to differentiate between participation *in* and participation *through* the medium, as well as between minimalist und maximalist forms of participation.

Community radio stations in South Africa do have an impact on democratic processes, providing opportunities to practice such democratic principles as tolerance towards different-minded people, expressing an opinion and finding compromises. Broadcasting may develop critical abilities, including to develop informed opinions and to make informed decisions. Although almost everyone agrees that community radio stations are important for South African society, they do not get the financial, ideological and political support they need to survive. Beginning again and again because of the high volunteer turnover demands a very high tolerance of frustration. They see the lack of financial support, of journalistic skills and management ability as well. Acquiring skills seems to be more valuable for the volunteers of the stations than earning money and much more important than getting politically involved. So we see participation *in* the medium rather than *through* the medium. In trying to fill the gap between the high expectations of the concept of community radio and participatory communication on one side and the practical challenges of the day-to-day running of stations on the other, many stations do a very good job, but the benefits are to be seen more within the stations than in their wider communities. The stations are supposed to be independent, but it is very difficult to remain independent while looking for someone to fund the day-to-day running of the station, especially in rural areas. To leave the stations alone to cope with this is not very fair, so if South African society would like to strengthen the community radio sector, because of the potentially valuable contribution of these stations, the fundamental questions are, what kind of community radio is wanted and who is supposed to pay for the services of these stations?

Perhaps each station has its own specific ideas, but some things should be clarified for the whole sector: The definition of what is a community and who are its members has consequences for access to a station and the issue of how to ensure transparent structures within it, not only in financial matters but organisationally too. Many different models are possible, for example:

- Local stations, working like commercial radio stations, where the people living in that area may make daily or weekly programmes to debate issues they are facing, being responsible for their content and their organisation;

- A government-financed system, at least for the cost of studios and transmission, so the stations are able to concentrate on the programme content and meeting the many high expectations of them around participation and democratisation;

- A two-tier system within stations, one responsible for the programme content and the other for the finances, with the community and their interests being represented in both tiers but by different people.

These are only three starting points showing different degrees of participation. Finding the right model for the South African context might be difficult and discussions are necessary not only within the stations but with all the individuals who are interested, involved, engaged in and responsible for the development and sustainability of the community radio sector at all levels. The stations make an important contribution to the democratic process, but they need support and recognition to be able to survive.

References

Berrigan, F (1977) *ACCESS: Some Western Models of Community Media*. Paris: UNESCO.

Carpentier, N (2011a) 'The concept of participation. If they have access and interact, do they really participate? ' *Communication Management Quarterly*, issue 21. http://www.cost-transforming-audiences.eu/system/files/pub/CM21-SE-Web.pdf

Carpentier, N (2011b) *Media and Participation: A Site of Ideological-Democratic Struggle*, Bristol: Intellect.

CFSC (2013) *Communication for Social Change*. http://www.communicationforsocial change.org/mission

Dagron, A (2001) *Making Waves. Stories of Participatory Communication for Social Change. A Report to the Rockefeller Foundation*, New York: Rockefeller Foundation.

ECSECC (2011) *Service Delivery and Conditions of Living in the Eastern Cape*. http://www.ecsecc.org/files/library/documents/ECSECCLivingStandards June2011.pdf

Engel, B & Best, S (2012) *Stream, Audio und Page – die Rezeptionsformen in der konvergenten Medienwelt*. http://www.media-perspektiven.de/uploads/tx_mppublications/02-2012_Engel_Best_NEU.pdf

Girard, B (2007) *Empowering Radio. Good practices in development & operation of community radio: Issues important to its effectiveness*, Program on Civic Engagement, Empowerment & Respect for Diversity, World Bank Institute (WBIST). http://comunica.org/pubs/cr5cs.pdf

Hipfl, B & Hug, T (2006) 'Introduction: Media Communites – Current Discourses and Conceptional Analyses', in Hipfl, B & Hug, T (eds), *Media Communities, Münster et al*, Waxmann Verlag GmbH.

Media Analyse (2013): *Hörfunknutzung nach Soziodemografie. Hördauer in Minuten (Montag – Sonntag)*. http://www.ard.de/intern/medienbasisdaten/hoerfunknutzung/hoerfunknutzung-nach-soziodemografie/-/id=55150/rg70kk/index.html

Ramphele, M (2008) *Laying Ghosts to Rest. Dilemmas of the Transformation in South Africa*, Cape Town: Tafelberg.

Rozumilowicz, B (2002) 'Democratic change: a theoretical perspective', in Price, E, Rozumilowicz, B & Verhulst, S (eds), *Media Reform. Democratizing the Media, Democratizing the State*, London: Routledge.

Statistics South Africa (2007): *Community Survey 2007. Basic results Eastern Cape*. http://www.statssa.gov.za/Publications/Report-03-01-32/Report-03-01-322007.pdf

Teer-Tomaselli, R (2006) 'Community Radio's Impact on Community Building: Case Studies from KwaZulu-Natal, South Africa', in Hipfl, B & Hug, T (eds), *Media Communities, Münster et al*, Waxmann Verlag GmbH.

Chapter 10

Radio as an old and a new medium: Sustaining cultural identities of listeners

Miroslawa Wielopolska-Szymura

Abstract

Traditional radio plays a significant role in expanding knowledge of national culture and society, and it supports cultural creativity and civic participation in the public sphere. Where it does provide some cultural output it demonstrates its most important and specific characteristics and thereby helps sustain the cultural identities of communities both large and small. To what extent can new forms of radio hope to sustain their audiences in the same manner? Internet radio, for example, is very fragmented and its audiences tend to be very diverse. This chapter will compare the formats of some traditional and some web-only radio broadcasters and attempt to resolve some important issues around them. It will ask whether web-only radio might be able to play a role in sustaining the cultural identities of audiences and in creating communities of listeners. It will also consider whether traditional radio will remain as resilient in future, if this is the age of a new form of radio.

Keywords: traditional radio, internet radio, web-only radio, format, identity, Poland

Introduction: traditional radio

When traditional analogue radio began broadcasting in Europe and the United States in the 1920s, it was with similar programmes with similar content for all of its listeners, music and what became known in many countries as 'varieties', largely inspired by the tradition of music hall. In the US this averaged about three quarters of the daily programming (Sterling & Kittross 2002: 86) and non-music content like political and other special news events, religious programming, sports broadcasts, educational programs on a wide scope of topics from cooking to farming, and news commentary made up the rest. Early radio also developed some artistic genres of its own, such as radio drama, literature readings and adaptations, novels and radio series - for example soap opera. In the early 1930s phone-in shows were created by the presenter John J. Anthony and in 1945 radio talks were started by Barry Gray on the American station WMCA. At the same time radio in Poland, Polski Radio, which had started to broadcast in 1926, was creating and developing its own programming, including news bulletins and announcements, reports from cultural events, dramas and literary readings for adults and children, relays of music concerts and shows from opera and theatre, lectures and readings about society, agricultural affairs or sport, as well as satire and sketch programmes. Initially, unlike in the US, the share of music in Polish Radio was around 42 per cent during the daytime, but in the 1930s the amount of music increased and the proportion of words to music became 40:60 (Grzelewska 2001: 237).

Radio connected nations and peoples in many countries, especially in times of crisis. King George VI spoke to the British people to inform them about Britain's involvement in World War II on 3 September 1939, just as the president of Warsaw, Stefan Starzynski, called Polish civilians to battle against the Nazi aggressor on12 September 1939, and Hitler's and Stalin's radio speeches provoked applause from their supporters and aroused fear among the opponents of their regimes. Similarly, during the Great Depression Theodore Roosevelt 'turned to radio to galvanise people behind his administration's plans to reverse the harrowing descent' (Keith, 2007) but paradoxically Orson Welles's radio drama *War of the Worlds* caused panic among its listeners. Such examples amply demonstrate the influence of radio on wide audiences in what some call the 'golden age' of radio. While during World War II radio was often used as a means of propaganda or as governmental messenger providing war information, after the Second World War radio became mostly an entertainment provider with more lightweight content. Peacetime produced the right conditions to re-define a concept of radio in view of both economic circumstances and the simultaneous expansion of television, which started to dominate the world of entertainment and the ways people spent their spare time.

The first radio format, Top 40 was launched by Todd Storz on KOWH radio in Omaha in the early 1950s. 'It was aimed at teenagers, who were the fastest growing segment of the population, had growing disposable income, and had plenty of time to listen' (Sterling & Kittross 2002: 367-8). Many teenagers were less interested in watching TV than their parents, so a new form of radio seemed attractive to them. Radio facilitated access to new music: the era of rock'n'roll began and galvanised youth culture. Soon afterwards, during the late 1950s and early 1960s, radio regained ground as the dominant electronic medium, except during television's 'prime-time' period from

19.30-23.00 when radio was less popular. During the daytime radio had a much larger share of the available audience, mainly in the mornings and early afternoons but also at night, when people switched on the radio after they had watched television, as Douglas noted: 'Listeners included housewives, people driving to and from work, truck drivers and cabbies trapped in their vehicles all day...' (2004: 220).

In parts of Western Europe, until the 1970s the majority of radio stations were state-owned or state-controlled and there the process of radio formatting started in the 1970s and later. Political democratisation of former dictatorships in such countries as Greece, Portugal, and Spain caused deregulation of their media and the development of private radio stations. Deregulation processes in most democratic states spread, for example in the UK where the first commercial licences were granted in 1973, but only for local broadcasters, in France in 1982 and in Sweden not until 1993. In the UK, because of the number of offshore pirate radio stations, in 1967 the British Broadcasting Corporation launched BBC Radio 1 with a Top 40 format directed at young listeners. In Central and Eastern Europe, until 1989 all media were state-owned and subject to censorship, too.

Radio in Poland

Polski Radio launched in 1926. After the communist regime collapsed, five of its channels were transformed into public service media, with an obligation to fulfill the 'mission of public media' enshrined in the Polish media law of 1993, requiring them to ensure high standards of cultural, educational, and informational content.

- **Polski Radio 1** is focused on information and music for a wide audience. Its format is full service or middle-of-the-road (Jędrzejewski 2003; Stachyra 2008). Its programming includes many radio genres, such as drama, documentary, features, satire, literature readings and outside broadcasts including sports. Its format is similar in many ways to that of BBC Radio 2 in the UK.
- **Polski Radio 2** is directed at listeners with high cultural competencies, offering them reports from cultural, musical, and literary events, as well as transmissions of classical, folk, and jazz music. Lectures about composers or classical works, discussions of poetry, musical or literary works are broadcast. It is very similar to BBC Radio 3 and there are no advertisements.
- **Polski Radio 3** offers information on social, cultural, political and economic subjects, and also entertainment content including mostly alternative pop and rock music, with jazz, folk and electronica. There are reports from festivals, cabarets, music and artistic events. It offers drama, features and book readings, organises sport and social events of interest to its listeners and broadcasts programmes for children. It could be compared to a hybrid of BBC Radio 1 and BBC Radio 6 Music (Wielopolska-Szymura 2011: 137).
- **Polski Radio 4** has changed many times in the past, from a strongly educational character for listeners aged nine and above, to the more entertaining model directed at young people aged between 16-39 of today. It was the first Polish radio channel transmitted live with vision on-line, on satellite and on cable (until June 2012), on smart phones, and for smart TV. Its schedule includes music, features, talks, reports, religious content, phone-ins and cultural subjects.

- **The external service** has operated since before the Second World War. It is directed at Polish citizens living abroad and foreigners who are interested in Polish affairs. It broadcasts programmes in several languages, such as German, Czech, English, Hungarian, Italian and Portuguese.

In December 2010 Polski Radio established a web-only radio channel Polski Radio24 (PR24), a twenty-four-hour station based on a news/talk format of news and reports on politics, economics and sport, as well as social and cultural topics. Experimental digital terrestrial transmission was launched for two cities, Warsaw and Katowice in 2013. Five existing terrestrial Polski Radio channels are provided on this radio multiplex together with Polish Radio 24 and Radio Rytm, a Polish radio station broadcast in New York City for the Polish community there. In the near future Polski Radio intends to create some new digital radio channels, a science channel (Radio Eureka), Radio Retro (for older listeners) and a channel for children and parents, Radio Krasnal or Radio Dwarf.

In the early 1990s three national private operators launched, RMF FM, Radio ZET and Radio Maryja.

- **Radio RMF FM** is the most listened-to radio station in Poland, especially by young people aged 25-39. RMF FM has an Adult Contemporary (AC) format consisting of music hits from the last 30 years and news. Programmes include short presenter links, news bulletins each hour, weather and traffic information. There are also talks on lightweight topics, phone-ins and competitions, as well as short talks with studio guests, mainly politicians.

RMF FM Group has some local radio networks. RMF MAXXX is for 18-34 year olds with a Contemporary Hit Radio (CHR) format. RMF Classic has a classical music format for 30-54 year-olds, playing classical and film music as well as a little classic rock. There is news as well as some culture and art. RMF FM Group has also created a large number (102) of web-only radio stations on-line, which are grouped as RMFon. Music formats predominate, for example RMF 50s, RMF 60s, RMF 70s, RMF Beatlemania, RMF Blues, RMF Celtic, RMF Chillout, RMF Baby, RMF Chopin, RMF Classic Rock, RMF Club, RMF Cuba, RMF Dance, RMF Depeche Mode, RMF Flamenco, RMF Francais, RMF Groove, RMF Grunge, RMF Nippon, RMF Love and many more dedicated to one artist or music style, some with Polish language equivalents. The only speech web-radio is RMF Koziołek Matołek, named after Matołek the Billy-Goat, transmitting an audio adaptation of a fable by the popular children's writer Kornel Makuszynski. The adaptation was recorded by RMF FM with Polish actors to celebrate Children's Day, which in Poland falls on 1 June each year.

- **Radio ZET** is a national radio operator with an Adult Contemporary format for mature people aged 28-49. It ranks second in radio listening share in Poland, broadcasting mostly music with news each hour and interviews with politicians on current affairs. It includes some regular longer programmes relating to health, travel, movies, electronic gadgets, and varieties. Programming includes talk shows with celebrities and phone-ins as well. Presenter links are very short in the daytime, being just two minutes long, sandwiched between 15-17 minute-long music sweeps.

Radio ZET Group has two radio networks, ZET Chilli and ZET Gold, in the biggest Polish cities. ZET Chilli oriented toward chillout, soul, and jazz music. It promotes non-commercial artists and devotes a lot of time to culture (concerts, movie, literature, theatre, exhibitions) and lifestyle (food, cooking, design, places, fashion, travel, time out, new technologies). Radio ZET Chilli targets better-educated adults. Radio Zet Gold is for mature people, playing old hits from the past few decades. ZET Gold is a network of several former local radio stations so the news bulletins include some local news, including local politics, cultural and sporting events and current affairs. Some advertisements are local as well. The content includes press reviews, reports from cultural, sport, and other events, radio talks about politics, economics, science, and social matters, phone-ins and competitions. The Radio ZET Group created a number of web radio stations with specific music formats, among them ZET do Biegania (for jogging), ZET PL playing Polish music, ZET Rock, ZET Film, ZET Hits!, ZET Soul, ZET Kids, ZET Beatles, ZET Chopin, ZET Smooth Jazz and ZET Fitness.

- **Radio Maryja** is a nationwide religious (Catholic) station with community radio status. Most of its broadcasts include religious content, which including online prayers, liturgical transmissions both from Polish churches and from the Vatican, the catechism, radio homilies and religious discussions. Radio Maryja transmits practical radio guides to medical, parental, ecological and nutritional problems. There are programs for farmers, parents, children and teenagers.

Traditional radio is listened to by 75.60 per cent of the Polish population. The share of listening to national stations declined between 2012 and 2013 (see table 10.1).

	2012	2013
Radio RMF FM	25.3%	24.6%
Radio ZET	14.8%	14.3%
Polski Radio Program 1	12.9%	11.2%
Polski Radio Program 3	8.5%	6.9%
Radio Maryja	2.2%	1.9%
Polski Radio Program 4	0.5%	0.4%
Polski Radio Program 2	0.5%	0.4%

Table 10.1: Quarterly summary of radio listening by adults aged 15 and over to national radio stations in Poland. Survey periods July-September 2012 and 2013. Source: Radio Track, Millward Brown SMG/KRC.

Internet radio

The history of web radio, also known as internet radio, net radio, streaming radio, and e-radio, began in 1993 in the United States when Carl Malamud 'set up the first community net-only radio station, Internet Talk Radio, in California, North America to stream independent (indie) alternative music that rarely got air play on traditional radio' (Baker, 2009). Web radio appears in two forms, conventional radio streaming online and web-only radio. The first consists of terrestrial radio broadcasters streaming their broadcast programming in parallel over the internet. This type of web radio is typical of Polski Radio's domestic and external services, as well as Radio RMF FM, Radio ZET, and all of the country's analogue local, regional and networked broadcasters. The internet is treated as another way of distributing broadcast services as well as a way of disseminating additional content. The second model, web-only radio, is available only over the internet. In Poland the first is thought to have been launched in 1998, Radio Net (Doliwa, 2010: 112). Currently, in Poland there are several internet platforms offering access to internet radio of both types or the opportunity to create a new one. According to the research organisation Megapanel, in February 2013, 23 per cent of Polish internet users visited radio station websites.The most popular in this group are web sites created by existing terrestrial broadcasters such as Radio Eska and Radio Eska Rock, Polski Radio, Radio Tok FM, Radio RMF FM, Radio ZET, RMF MAXX, and Radio Maryja. Hit rates indicate listening through this platform is significantly below listening to broadcast radio, but they do still attest to some popularity of these services. Radio is still deemed an attractive medium, so its web sites are among those most visited by internet users. The most popular radio websites in Poland are ranked in table 10.2. Web-only radio stations are ranked in 5th, 7th, 10th and 11th positions in the table. The platform Open.fm currently offers a total of 95 stations and another, not included in this ranking, PolskaStacja.pl, offers 77 stations.

1	Eska.pl
2	Polskieradio.pl
3	Tokfm.pl
4	Rmf.fm
5	Rmfon.pl
6	Rmf24.pl
7	Eskago.pl
8	Radiozet.pl
9	Rmfmaxx.pl
10	Tuba.pl
11	Open.fm
12	Eskarock.pl
13	Radiomaryja.pl

Table 10.2: Ranking of the most popular radio websites in Poland. Source: Megapanel PBI/Genuis, February 2013.

Case study: Tuba.pl

Tuba.pl is one of the most-visited internet radio platforms in Poland, and the most-visited by web users in the ranking shown in table 10.2. Owned by Agora Group, one of the biggest media corporations in Poland, Tuba.pl streams three different types of radio station: a bouquet of 30 channels consisting of some traditional radio stations for which it provides parallel streaming and a number of channels of its own; a collection of 235 music streams grouped and sorted thematically by genre and a collection of user-generated web-only radio stations, numbering 47,714 at the time of writing, of which 6,263 were grouped in a section of the most listened, labelled 'Popular'. Among the stations created by Tuba.pl are: Radio Kotek.pl (or 'kitty radio') for teenage girls, which had 457 subscribers identified as fans; Tuba.fm playing Hot Hits and numbering 706 subscribers as fans; and Radio Baobab.pl the only such station with a speech format, which was created by some very well known Polish music journalists, with 85 fans. The second group of streams grouped and sorted by genre includes typical, existing popular radio formats, such as current hits, rock, pop, dance, hip hop and r'n'b. The third type, of user-generated channels, increased in number from August to September 2013 from 46,650 stations to 47,714, and in October increased again to 49,135 channels. The 'Popular' group of such stations includes for example (number of fans in brackets): Romantics of Rock Music (98), La Roux and similar artists (1); Gothic (2); Kaliber 44 (a popular Polish hip-hop group) (2); Rap Poland (2); By zwlec się z łóżka (290); Bestia gra starocie (a beast plays oldies) (231); Grey's Anatomy (the television series soundtrack) (171); Sung Poetry (Polish) (42); Radio Robotnicze (Workers' Radio) (39).

As we can see, there is great diversity in internet radio, which is related to the individualism of the radio listeners, who are at the same time, often the creators of radio content on the internet. A survey conducted in 2011 by the Komitet Badań Radiowych (Radio Research Committee), in cooperation with Millward Brown SMG/KRC, indicated a clear trend. A similar study in 2010 found similar results, with 956 respondents declaring they listened to radio online and among them 46 per cent of online radio listeners were women, and 54 per cent men. The largest audiences consisted of people 20-24 years-old (21 per cent of listeners) and 25-34 (32 per cent), while in the 35-44 bracket the figure was 18 per cent. A total of 61 per cent of respondents declared they listened to the radio on the internet at least once a week, with 22 per cent listening two or three times a week, and 19 per cent listening daily. Respondents most frequently listen to internet radio on weekdays (78 per cent), while 54 per cent listened at the weekend. Respondents most often listened to the radio at home (83 per cent), but 28 per cent listened to the radio at work. Internet radio mostly drew listeners in the daytime, during daily activities (49 per cent), while 40 per cent of respondents also listened to the radio in the evenings. Only 5 per cent of them listened to the radio at night. An overwhelming 76 per cent of respondents had the company of others while listening to the radio, while 24 per cent of them declared they listened to the radio alone.

Internet radio, as well as traditional radio, was often an accompaniment, as 95 per cent of online radio listeners performed other tasks at the same time as listening, including browsing the web (74 per cent), working on a computer (69 per cent), checking e-mail (64 per cent), performing other activities unrelated to using a computer (46 per cent), visiting online social networked sites, forums, and blogs (39 per cent), communicating with friends (37 per cent) and playing computer games or online games (18 per cent). Radio was the medium with the highest degree of parallelism of the media, which is to say the possibility of using more than one medium at a time, such as reading a newspaper, and this parallelism was increasing, with 68 per cent of respondents using other media while listening to the radio online, 94 per cent of them using the internet, 29 per cent reading newspapers, 20 per cent watching television and 5 per cent of respondents listening to traditional radio. The respondents were guided by different criteria for selecting internet radio – 75 per cent were led by music content, among them 21 per cent preferring stations broadcasting only music. Some 36 per cent of radio listeners chose stations broadcasting spoken programmes. The largest number of online radio listeners, 67 percent, selected a radio station which is also available on-air, and 33 percent of online listeners chose web-only radio. Listening to internet radio is not associated with great mobility, since 99 per cent of respondents used a desktop computer or a laptop to listen to the radio online, and only 10 per cent used the mobile phone, which can be explained by the relatively high cost of mobile internet services offered by mobile network operators.

Conclusions

Traditional public or commercial radio stations, providing information, entertainment, and music in a single programme schedule, are more or less able to attract audiences around a mix of programming. Listeners have multiple opportunities to engage with the radio station and with other listeners online, becoming more sociable as sub-communities. They talk about their favorite programmes, music or important events they have in common, they comment on the spoken content, they exchange opinions and feelings, and they connect online to interact with each other. Both public and commercial radio stations can characterised by some common attributes, such as: regular programming which results in the formation of listening habits; the use of a native language, which helps to sustain communication within that society; the use of a public-sphere radio discourse referring to actual social, political, economic and cultural problems, reinforcing social bonds and common cultural identities; including entertainment and interactivity, such as jokes, competitions, satire, music, talking with listeners and messaging, all of which promotes social integration.

Web-only radio stations, however, such as those on the Tuba.pl platform, which are based on music formats alone, do not, however, create communities of listeners exchanging social experiences. They are rather disparate and divided into small groups of fans or lone individuals. If anything, these are temporary social groups without any resilient common interest. Listening to the radio online is more of an individual experience than listening to traditional broadcast radio, even if web radio listeners say they listen with a few other people, because web-only music radio is very fragmented and perhaps should not be treated as a medium of mass communication. Music formatted web-only radio fulfils individual needs and accommodates personal preferences. This kind of communication might be characterised by non-linearity, an absence of simultaneity of listening and a lack of voice interaction as well, lacking, for example, phone-ins and other talk shows with listener participation. We should note that a large number of web-only radio stations in Poland which are based on content other than music radio formats. These are community radio broadcasters transmitting regular programmes of speech and music content, but they are not available on the most visited radio platform Tuba.pl, so they have been omitted from this analysis.

All except one web-only channel on Tuba.pl, have music formats. In this context, stations broadcasting only music do not work like traditional radio stations and do not perform the same social functions. These stations are more like musical jukeboxes. Perhaps only music-formatted internet radio in Polish or other national languages are able to create a cultural identity because of common contexts referenced in songs - music and words which refer to some past or current situations, people, places or events which evoke some shared associations and reflections, emotional or intellectual, and provide a stimulus for social interaction and liaison between listeners in real life. The use of shared languages may reinforce identities, especially if they are in minority groups or displaced geographically. Of course today's national cultures are largely characterised by integration, permeation, and hybridisation, as well as western cultural imperialism. Members of one society may assimilate different cultural patterns from a mulitplicity of non-indigenous societies. Yet, educational and informational radio content based on different influences, including world music, human interest stories, cultural and social events, is able to contribute to sustaining cohesive societies and to creating and sustaining common cultural identities. Web-only radio has great potential, which can be used in the future to contribute to inclusive societies, playing a key societal role, but in order for this to succeed, radio listeners must be willing to listen to radio which does more than just stream non-stop music. Fortunately, it seems that old habits associated with traditional radio listening are transferring to the internet, as demonstrated by the popularity of listening to live streams of broadcast output, which might raise expectations of listeners towards unambitious web-only radio stations.

References

Baker, A (2009) 'Comparing the regulatory models of net-radio with traditional radio', *International Journal of Emerging Technologies and Society*, volume 7, issue 1.

Doliwa, U (2010) 'Radio internetowe – realna alternatywa dla rozgłośni koncesjonowanych?', *Media, kultura, komunikacja społeczna*, issue 6, Olsztyn: Uniwersytet Warmińsko-Mazurski.

Douglas, S (2004) *Listening In: Radio and the American Imagination*. Minneapolis: University of Minnesota.

Grzelewska, D (2001) 'Historia polskiej radiofonii w latach 1926-1989', in Grzelewska, Habielski, Kozieł, Osica, Piwońska-Pykało (eds), *Prasa, radio i telewizja w Polsce. Zarys dziejów*, Second edition, Warszawa: ELIPSA.

Jędrzejewski, S (2003) *Radio w komunikacji społecznej. Rola i tendencje rozwojowe*, Warszawa: Profi-Press.

Keith, M (2007) 'The Long Road to Radio Studies', *Journal of Broadcasting & Electronic Media*, volume 51, issue 3.

Stachyra, G. (2008) *Gatunki audycji w radiu sformatowanym*, Lublin: UMCS.

Sterling, C, Kittross J (2002) *Stay Tuned: A History of American Broadcasting*, Mahwah: Lawrence Erlbaum Associates.

Wielopolska-Szymura, M (2011) 'Program III Polskiego Radia – poszukiwanie nowej formuły programowej', in Pawlak-Hejno, E & Stachyra, G (eds), *Radio i społeczeństwo*, Lublin.

Chapter 11

The obligations of listeners in 'expression-seeking' radio dialogues

Grażyna Stachyra

Abstract

Historically, the presence of on-air dialogue with listeners can be viewed as the one of the first signs of interactivity on the radio. It remains the most significant form of audience participation in radio programmes. Phone-ins, game-shows, musical programmes, commentaries and many other genres treat the presence of listeners as an important element of programming.

This chapter analyses game-show, (sometimes called 'quiz-show',) dialogue in Polish commercial radio, where listeners are rewarded for their participation. The main aim is to discuss the context of 'dummy' game shows, where listeners know from the beginning that they are winners, but are nonetheless obliged to express their joy. This type of dialogue is here termed 'expression-seeking' dialogue. The system of turn-taking is subordinated to the underlying goal of conversation: encouraging the audience to take part in the said game show. Such 'dummy' dialogues could be viewed as a kind of 'resilience' strategy of looking for a conversation opportunity, as formatted commercial radio stations have fewer and fewer occasions to converse with listeners on air and radio itself has to struggle for the listeners' attention in the age of mediated society (Lacey 2013).

Keywords: discourse analysis, communicative obligations, game show, interaction, Poland

Dialogue in radio programmes

On-air dialogue can be pivotal to a number of different radio genres, including any kind of background entertainment on radio, such as general talk or music-based shows with elements of phone-ins, phone-outs and commercials. Radio has long followed the natural tendencies of interpersonal communication, which is based on natural speech. Early attempts at live on-air conversation with listeners were hindered by the lack of suitable technology. There were, however, efforts to overcome this problem: in the 1930s, when German boxer Max Schmeling left for the United States, leaving his elderly mother in Berlin, the Schenectady radio station enabled him to have a conversation of sorts on short wave. Schmeling knew that his mother listened to the radio at a certain time of the day and that there was a telephone nearby. The Schenectady station was able to connect with Stuttgart, which cabled Schmeling's message to Königs Wusterhausen, which then broadcast it on short wave. The son in the US would ask the mother in Europe how she was and tell her about his experiences, his journey and the bouts he was set to fight. She then used the home telephone to answer his questions and send her motherly blessing. The moment when a voice 'from the other side' first appeared on air can therefore be called a watershed in the functioning of radio. The first time a listener could be heard on air was in 1945, when Barry Gray, a presenter working for New York's WMCA station, held a telephone receiver close to his microphone, resulting in the voice of the listener on the line being broadcast. This spontaneous act was the beginning of talk radio, as well as the increasing popularity of on-air dialogue in other radio formats.

A phone-in voice brings radio to life; it endows radio with distinctive characteristics recognisable to the listeners. Dialogue injects variety into radio; it can be a carrier of ideas or, adopting a tabloid mode, it can introduce elements of playfulness, shock or taboo-breaking. Conversation as a social act, (although initially not in its mediated incarnation,) has long intrigued researchers, which has resulted in a number of theories and methods of its investigation. A noteworthy framework is conversation analysis (CA), initiated in the 1960s by sociologist Harvey Sacks and honed by Emanuel A. Schegloff and Gail Jefferson in the late 1960s and 1970s. CA studies the organisation of conversation as social interaction rather than the linguistic dimension of conversation. There are several trends and subdivisions within CA, some researching primarily the organisation of conversation, some exploring the application of CA methodologies to other dimensions of social life, and others dividing interactions into ordinary conversation and institutional interactions (Sidnell 2010).

The focus of this study is the mediated conversation. It was initially dismissed as a legitimate means of analysing media. However, with the use of detailed transcripts of conversations on the radio and television and with recourse to linguistics, philosophy and sociology, researchers have shown that conversation as such is a valid object of media studies. Some of the earliest analyses were published in the *Journal of Media, Culture and Society* (Scannell 1986) and *Broadcast Talk* (Scannell 1991). These studies assumed that, if the mediated conversation is just as much a form of communication as any other, some parallels can be applied to describe its distinctive features. The acknowledgment that 'it is increasingly unrealistic to analyse the structure and content of [mass media] messages independent of the interactional medium within which they are generated' (Heritage, Clayman & Zimmerman 1988: 79–80) pushed forward the study of the mediated conversation. Notable examples include studies of radio phone-ins (Hutchby 1996) or historical research into the formula of the direct address to the listener, indicating its transformation towards sociability and communicative ease. Another field of research has been the institutional dimension of mediated talk, which is frequently disguised (Goffman 1981: 3). The structure of the mediated interaction as a public form of discourse remains a central issue in the study of broadcast talk, as does the analysis of its organisation as a specific phenomenon of the medium reaching its audience.

We might wonder, therefore, what distinguishes mediated conversations constructed in different mass media from any other. A mediated conversation is an instance of public address; at the same time, the audience receive it as a direct and intimate message, intended specifically for them. Essentially, a radio or television broadcast, as opposed to any public speech, is a form of talk oriented at a rapprochement between the interlocutors and at re-creating the conditions of interpersonal communication occurring in everyday face-to-face contact, a tendency Scannell (1989) termed the 'communicative ethos of broadcasting'. The talk of radio and television broadcasters, he argued, can be characterised by a distinctive communicative ethos which seeks to instill a sense of familiarity and, hence, inclusiveness and sociability in the audience. This communicative ethos is something that broadcasters can be understood as working to produce. The talk of radio and television broadcasters is thus not natural speech but rather a performance, into which elements of everyday conversation have been implanted and which has been modified in accordance with the institutional context of broadcasting. The formula of this performance evolved along with the technology of programming and production (Scannell & Cardiff 1991). In their early work on the psychological relations between the auditorium and the broadcaster, Donald Horton and Richard Wohl (1956) posited the concepts of 'parasocial interaction' and 'intimacy at a distance'. Analysing phenomena accompanying early television broadcasts, they explored the reasons why some viewers became fans of certain television personalities. They found that the presenters' strategies of addressing the camera promoted a form of 'non-reciprocal' intimacy: the viewer could feel the talk was addressed directly at him or her, although it was specifically impersonal. Studies of early radio broadcasts (Scannell & Cardiff 1991) showed that the broadcasters constructed lofty, official statements, somewhat akin to sermons, in which they commented on public issues. But these statements were received in the context of the home, during breaks between routine domestic activities. A communicative ethos of broadcasting thus concerned not merely the structuring of the address, but also the context in which it was perceived (Scannell 1989: 156).

Various aspects of conversation analysis confirm the complexity of conversation as a linguistic phenomenon as well as its significance in interpersonal relations, including mediated ones. In its technological and cultural transformations, influenced also by marketing trends, radio underwent the process of formatting, in which the offer for individual target groups was specified. Although the radio is not immune to negative processes typical of infotainment, some of its characteristics allow the radio to retain a 'noble' and audience-friendly status as a medium, to a much greater extent than television or the internet. The apparent weakness of the radio, that is, the lack of visual stimulation, may be an antidote to the trivialisation of the tabloid image culture. Radio has great potential for performing integrative, informative and indexation functions. The extent to which that potential is utilised, however, depends on the properties of the format. Where the programming clock is run by computer software, and the programming is based on music, short news and commercials, little if any space remains to fulfil the abovementioned functions, which are then marginalised and subordinated to marketing. It is in this context that dialogue most often follows the formula of a game show to provoke listeners to speak on air.

The game show as entertaining dialogue

The quiz show, or the game show as it is sometimes known, became popular on US radio in 1939 as an audience-participation programme. *Dr IQ* was the first sponsored radio quiz show, broadcast from large concert halls with audiences coming from surrounding areas. Questions answered correctly were rewarded with money. The game show as a radio genre gained popularity for the simple reasons that the rules were uncomplicated and the audience had a good time as well as an opportunity to win something. Today, the self-advertising of phone-in competitions encourages the listeners to at least listen to others compete, if not personally participate in the competition.

Recent research shows that it is commercial radio that enjoys the most popularity in Poland (Radio Track 2013). The range of genres it offers, however, is restricted, with music taking up most of the programming, and the game show its most important verbal element. In the context of the resilience of radio one might wonder whether the dominance of on-air games in commercial stations is indeed a sign of resilience or flexibility, or perhaps a sign of a crisis of radio, which can be seen as a billboard of sorts, luring listeners in with the promise of winning a fortune, a trip, a computer, a dinner for two, a sandwich - indeed, anything. Would commercial radio stations attract listeners at all if it were not for their 'tempting' competitions? Games, associated with fun and entertainment, have become the key element of programming in Polish commercial radio stations, which have made playfulness, or the ludic quality of their broadcasts, their defining characteristic.

Game shows, or the prizes given away in game shows, need not correspond with current events. For instance, a game show broadcast at the beginning of the holiday season does not need to acknowledge this timing by awarding winners with sleeping bags, tents or T-shirts. The prizes are whatever has been obtained from sponsors. However, for the programme to fulfil the intended ludic dimension, the listener should, in an on-air dialogue, acknowledge his or her status as a winner and obligatorily demonstrate his or her resulting joy. The phatic function is pivotal here. It galvanises the conversation and constitutes the driving factor of a phone-out game show. The message travels in both directions of the broadcaster-listener relationship. The public announcement of the win is aimed at enticing as many listeners as possible to participate and thus fund the prize, (such as by sending premium-rate text messages which generate a profit in which the organiser shares). Communication on the radio is restricted in that it precludes *tête-á-tête* contact but it does enable dialogue. Because this dialogue takes place only in the aural channel, its psychological context is specific. 'Sight isolates, sound incorporates. Whereas sight situates the observer outside what he views, at a distance, sound pours into the hearer' (Ong 2002: 70). Therefore, a natural reflex of the imagination is to 'embody' the voices heard on air. The participant of a game show must be presented to other listeners; at the same time, the participant constructs a 'voice portrait' of the presenter. During the act of communication, the presenter-performer always intrudes into our consciousness with his or her 'corporeality' (Mayen 1958: 127), even without evoking a precise image of self or the character they perform in our imagination. The appearance of a listener on air triggers the 'dispersion' of communication, which is then no longer unidirectional. The entertainment-based conventions of game show dialogue focus the attention of listeners, as 'much of radio's early success was built on the popularity of its light entertainment output' (Starkey 2014: 165). Play, game and entertainment are often expressed on air as competition dialogue: on the one hand it emulates conversation as a natural form of interpersonal communication, while, on the other, it is an opportunity for the radio station to act in its own economic interest.

The organisation of 'expression-seeking' dialogue and its context

In conversation analysis, 'talk is a principal means for accomplishing social actions, is produced in specific interactional contexts, and how people talk is highly sensitive to that context; talk and interaction are orderly: that is, we can find systematic patterns and structures in the ways that people use talk to interact. Talk is organised sequentially; that is, by focusing on how people take turns at talking we can understand how they interpret the immediate interactional context, since turns are related together' (Hutchby 2006: 24). The mediated conversation, (here, conversation on the radio,) has features of ordinary talk, but is a form of institutional discourse, constructed for the sake of the listening auditorium. Interaction in institutional conversation has specific objectives: it 'involves goals that are tied to institution relevant identities; causes special constraints on what is an allowable contribution to the business at hand, and involves special inferences that are particular to specific contexts' (Heritage 2004: 106). Radio dialogue is therefore endowed with specific features of interaction which enable a participant, (a phone-in interlocutor,) to realise in what context, (on-air or off-air,) the conversation is taking place. Phrases like 'We have X on the line', and 'This is Radio Y', signal the start of a conversation where listeners other than the participant are present; in turn, the listener phoning in assumes the role of a person performing in public with all the attendant consequences. It is not always easy for the participant to be psychologically fit enough to cope with the situation and enter the dialogue with ease.

There are dialogues which sound like they are from game shows, although they violate the basic game show principle: the unpredictability of the ending. The player knows right from the beginning he or she has won. The opening of the exchange contains the resolution of this particular game. There is no rivalry or suspense, there are no cliffhangers. 'Expression-seeking dialogue' assumes the form of competition dialogue to harness the ritual power of its formula, for it is the adherence to the rules of the genre that enables the game to be played on air. For example:

1 Presenter: We have Justyna on the line, good morning!
2 L: Good morning.
3 Presenter: Dear Justyna, we have a week's stay in Egypt for two for you!!
4 L: Right...
5 Presenter: We have a live connection with a beach in Egypt for you, can you hear the sea splashing? (waves crashing in background).

6 L: I think I do …(pause).
7 Presenter: It's splashing for you! You'll be on that beach soon!!
8 L: (pause) …Well … I'm sure.
9 Presenter: Of course you will! A five-star hotel! A beach right by the exit! A swimming pool, an aquapark and… that suntan, all your friends will envy you … congratulations!!!!
10 L: Well … (pause) … thank you very much, it's such a surprise.

The broadcaster addresses the listener, constructing an atmosphere of joy, making the message appear extraordinary. The specific nature of the communicative situation means that the broadcaster is trying to strike a balance between shaping the message as primarily commercial and giving the player an opportunity for free expression. The player should act dynamically and creatively to achieve a symmetry between the status of the broadcaster and the participant. But when the participant's linguistic (or communicative) competence is insufficient to take up the conversational convention set up by the presenter (lines 4, 6 and 8), it is the presenter who has to step in and carry the conversation, here emphasising the atmosphere of joy at winning using metaphors, hyperboles, emotive language and exclamations (lines 5 and 9). The listener is slow to interpret the context of the dialogue, which comprises linguistic and social categories, namely metaphor and hyperbole, and public speaking on the radio, respectively. It is worth trying to identify this context. 'Contexts are not "objective" or "deterministic" constraints of society or culture at all, but subjective participant interpretations, constructions or definitions of such aspects of the social environment. …Contexts defined as participant definitions, that is, as mental constructs, are able to function as the interface between situational and societal structures and discourse structures, because they subjectively "represent" relevant aspects of situations and society and directly interfere in the mental processes of discourse production and comprehension' (Van Dijk 2006: 163).

What is common to the various uses of the term 'context' is that they all refer to factors relevant to the understanding of communicative behaviour. The specific context of the dialogue in an apparent competition influences the way it is shaped. The context comprises knowledge, shared by the presenter and the player, about the rules of the game, which stipulate that the telephone call to the player made by the radio station means that he or she has already won something. That knowledge is also shared by other listeners tuning in to the conversation. That context directly affects the underlying goal of the conversation (Bunt 1994), which is not to join the game to win a prize, but to provoke a listener into expressing his or her pleasure and making it public. This public expression of positive emotions is to entice all listeners to participate in competitions. The trivial underlying goal is masked by a turn-taking strategy which directs the listeners to talk about themselves until conforming to the right formula of expressing joy on air. If this fails to happen, the listener will be 'forced' to do so by the presenter.

In 'expression-seeking' dialogues only the expression-seeking participant, (the presenter,) has a communicative goal, while the listener is a kind of tool that is necessary to achieve an underlying goal. The listener-participant serves to provide information for the audience about the permanent possibility of winning a prize from the radio station. How each participant behaves in dialogue depends on the nature of the underlying task, on what they know about each other, on social relations between them, and on what has been said before on the circumstances under which the dialogue takes place. Obviously the linguistic, semantic, physical, social and cognitive contexts (Bunt 1994: 22) will influence the behaviour of participants in 'expression-seeking' dialogue. But in my opinion the most important factors are the linguistic aspects, especially prosody, the physical circumstances in which communication takes place, and the social context, which means roles of participants characterised as rights and obligations to perform a communicative act have a specific form.

All these contexts interact with each other. In telephone communication, the tone of the voice plays a more significant role, allowing the emotions of dialogue participants to be ascertained. The compulsorily joyful, friendly, cheerful tone of the presenter's voice is intended to provoke a similar kind of expression in the listener's response. For example:

> Presenter: With us on the line is the lucky Agnieszka from Gdynia, who is just preparing lunch for her baby. Good morning!

The opening stage of the dialogue also communicates the spatial context of the listener, and this enables subsequent turns on the basis of information passed on to other listeners. This idea has its roots in the turn-taking concept explained by Sacks, Schegloff and Jefferson (1974). They proposed that different forms of talk could be viewed as a continuum ranging from the relatively unconstrained turn-taking of mundane conversation to something much more formal. The listeners are, (including through the stereotyping of the context of kitchen activities,) able to kickstart their imagination, which aids the perception of the entire conversation. Conversation analysis considers that what I shall term 'phone-in-interaction' develops in a sequential way owing to the interpretation of communicative acts occurring in a sequence. The paradigm stresses the immediate sequential context in which a turn is produced. The 'kitchen context' communicated to listeners enhances familiarity: a kitchen is commonly conceptualised as a place where we like to be and where we talk to family and friends. This context also provokes the presenter's subsequent question about the name of the baby, and after this is answered, it enables another question:

> 1 Presenter: So what are you cooking for the little one?
> 2 L: Chicken soup!

Since the context of the dialogue is announced on air, the listener is able to talk about her surroundings while feeling at ease and having a sense of security. 'Understanding turn-taking for conversation and other forms of phone-in-interaction is key to understanding human conduct, because most actions carried out through talking are shaped by the organisation of that talk into speaking turns: it shapes how speakers compose their contributions, it shapes where they position those contributions in the ongoing interaction, and it shapes when they get to participate' (Lerner 2004: 4). If the burden of the conversation does not rest on any single interlocutor, the conversation becomes more interesting and more dynamic, which is in the interest of the broadcaster. As the conversation takes place over the telephone and is further mediated via the radio, the listeners are aware that this is not a private conversation, although its tone is informal. But no conversation is devoid of goals; on the contrary, it has a well-defined objective, one which governs on-air exchanges. A social context is created, ascribing specified roles to the participants of the dialogue. The participants need to act in accordance with their roles, which means producing utterances the broadcaster will find appropriate. This leads to the unequal status of the interlocutors: it is the presenter who stage-directs the conversation, controlling the listener's replies. In fact, the apparent competition dialogue is typologically akin to an interview, where the listener is 'interrogated' by the presenter.

Communicative obligations

'Expression-seeking' dialogue is an entry pass to the listener's private sphere. Verbalising everyday activities or telling stories about family and friends becomes the 'obligation' incumbent upon the listener, who accepts this convention of conversation in order to be rewarded for it. For this is what is being rewarded here: the listener appearing on air and replying in the manner the broadcaster so sorely needs. Commercial radio suffers from a dearth of conversation, which has been marginalised by rigorous formatting and trivialised to the extent that the game show is one of the last excuses to provoke it. Paradoxically, it is not the prize which is central to the apparent game show, but the *dialogic* mode of winning it. The structuring of the individual stages of communication is to be the basis for evoking *emotions*, which draw in listeners. A dialogue consists of turns which follow each other in a sequence and which are created by its participants. Every turn is executed with consideration to the previous one, so that the dialogue is coherent. This generates communicative obligations for the participants. 'These are obligations contracted by the receiver by participating in a dialogue. They regulate the receiver's reaction to the evocative intentions of the sender's preceding contribution' (Allwood 1994: 5). The receiver should consider the sender, (identify the sender and assess how well he or she will be able to continue the conversation,) and then respond in accordance with that assessment of the situation. A communicative obligation is an 'obligation to say something at a given moment and to perform a communicative act with a specific form and function... Taking turns is akin to creating and resolving reactive pressure. When a speaker indicates that he considers his turn to be finished, he puts pressure on his partner to take over' (Bunt 1994: 22-25).

In an 'expression-seeking' game show, the sender is a messenger always bringing good tidings, confirming the player in the belief he or she is lucky right from the beginning of the conversation. The opening stage happens off-air; the listeners are introduced to a specific person who is in a specific place and is busy performing a specific activity. The game show is an element of a compensation strategy, disguising a general lack of interaction between the sender, the (adressor-performer,) and the receiver, (the listener) (Vagle 1997). A competition game reduces the spatial separation between the broadcaster and the audience, giving voice to 'one of many'. A phone-in conversation with one of the listeners is a sign that listeners can relatively easily make it on air; it gives them a pleasant sense of being important to the broadcaster. This is why the news of winning a prize received by the individual player is really intended for all listeners: 'Any one of you can win'. Because audience figures decide on how much value a programme is deemed to have, one way of making a broadcast more attractive is a certain profiling of the presenter, also in terms of language use. This may include the decreased distance between sender and receiver, lack of honorifics, informality and often kitsch. Notably, the influence of mass or popular culture leads to an apotheosis of a mentality which tolerates directness, including on the radio. For example:

1 Presenter: With us on the line is Ewa. Can you hear us OK? Good morning.
2 L: Good morning.
3 Presenter: You wrote: I love my husband, but I can't stand his snoring. Does he snore like wood being sawed or like somebody starting a racing car?

The key communicative obligation in game shows is to express joy at winning. The dialogue is constructed by the broadcaster in such a way as to aid the listener in expressing his or her positive emotions generated by the win. We find it difficult to verbalise emotions. As early as in the 1940s, American linguist Leonard Bloomfield stressed that 'we can define the names of minerals, for example, in terms of chemistry and mineralogy… but we have no precise way of defining words like love or hate, which concern situations that have not been accurately classified — and these latter are in the great majority' (Bloomfield 1970: 39). Research on the linguistic aspect of emotions and metaphors used to express them has since intensified, mainly as a result of developments in cognitive sciences. A participant in a radio dialogue is an ordinary person, whose task is to publicly elaborate on his or her emotions. The need to verbalise emotions on the radio stems from the lack of the visual dimension. Although the telephone call from the radio station means that listeners have won the prize and they are aware of this, they are publicly 'interrogated' by the presenter as to what they feel and whether they are happy. The listener has to confirm the fact of winning.

Arguably, in a competition dialogue devoid of suspense generated by the essence of the game, which is the unpredictability of its ending, the participants of the dialogue need to assume the roles of the player (listener) and the host (presenter). Because the winning of the prize has to be announced on-air in an atmosphere of euphoria, both of them have to negotiate the strategy of the dialogue so that other listeners are reassured it is worth participating in the next round. The participants in on-air dialogue must *play* and *re-enact* the dialogue so that it can be spontaneous. 'Dialogue… allows indeterminacy of meaning and different understandings of the interlocutors and is based on negotiations of meaning and understanding in a game best characterised as a "mixed game"' (Weigand 2009: 238). The participants in the dialogue resort to a number of rhetorical devices to achieve that elusive objective. Sometimes these devices include humour as a means of controlling conversation (Neal & Norrick: 396). For example:

1 Presenter: We have Sebastian from Wrocław on the line. Good morning, Sebastian.
2 L: Good morning.
3 Presenter: Yes! This is real. You are the winner, you have been drawn. I usually ask what the money listeners win will turn into: utility fees, a shopping spree?
4 L: Er, renovation…
5 Presenter: How about a long May Day weekend? A family trip? Entertainment? You'll win money for a renovation project sometime.

Edda Weigand stated that 'speaking is always accompanied by thinking which goes far beyond what is expressed in the verbal utterance' (2009: 273-4). The off-air sphere is a bit like the backstage in the theatre. It is off limits to the audience. What happens there is like a rough draft of a production, a rehearsal before the final version of a performance is ready. The participants in on-air dialogue may negotiate off-air the strategy they will deploy in a moment. This symptom of the resilience of radio should be classified as working to decrease the potential for spontaneity with an on-air exchange. It becomes partly planned, with elements of a screenplay, because the effect has the foremost significance. Thinking about what we are going to say is inextricably connected with what we are not going to say, although we may well be thinking about it. 'Expression-seeking' dialogue is about enacting spontaneity, and though it may evoke ambivalent feelings, these may not be articulated on air. For example:

1 Presenter: On the line now we have our listener Iwona. Good morning.
2 L: Hello, good morning.
3 Presenter: You told me off air that you completely couldn't believe you'd won anything
4 L: No, really.
5 Presenter: So I hereby confirm you have! Yes!! You have won 1000 zl!
6 L: Gee, I'm so happy!!! Really!?
7 Presenter: Really!!!
8 L: I'm shocked!

There is no better means of negotiating the expression of emotion than dialogue. The presenter reveals the off-line confession of the listener (line 3) deliberately, to provoke her disbelief in her good fortune (lines 6, 8). She intuitively takes up the exclamatory tone of speech suggested by the presenter (line 5). 'We will always use dialogue, as our most intuitive semiotic system, to articulate and express what we think, share our thoughts and ideas with others, and collaboratively create meaning and understanding to make joint inquiries or solve common problems. We may be doing these things in more immediate, participative or multimodal ways, but the deep psycho-social imperatives are more impervious to change' (Ravenscroft & Boyle 2010). Dialogue on the radio is 'a game within a game': the awareness that the conversation will be made public and the wish to obtain the prize impose on the listener certain tasks they must fulfil. The on-air performance seals the win. Imagine that a listener refuses to talk on air, or that he or she admits to being disappointed with the prize. These dialogues must take place, but they occur off air, in the backstage. When the listener hears the following down the phone line: 'Good morning, Ewa, you already know you're a lucky woman', she mobilises to confirm that this is indeed the case.

Occasionally, emotional difficulties are compounded by ethical problems. When contestants enter a game at work and there are witnesses to this fact, they are often embarrassed and struggle to overcome any reluctance to publicising the temporary suspension of their work duties. This presenter appears to ignore this resistance and insists on obtaining an on-air 'testimony':

1 Presenter: You are a teacher, who is in the middle of teaching a class now.
2 S: Yes.
3 Presenter: But you left the classroom?

4 S: No … my students are busy drawing just now …
5 Presenter: Well then, you have to tell them: Dear students, you are now live on
            air! (She repeats the message, students audibly applaud).
6 Presenter: Here's your prize! An i-Pod Shuffle!!
7 (No reaction, silence).
8 Presenter: Ok, we're not interrupting anymore, bye for now.

A forceful insistence on an on-air reaction stems from game show rules on the radio. The formal structure of dialogue gives the presenter the right to ask questions which may be awkward, but it is difficult not to answer them. Arguably, the influence of social roles we acquire in the process of socialisation is at work here. In an aural message, the prosody of a statement, which must cohere with the sense of the words being uttered, has an increased importance. Living up to the demands of public speaking can be a source of satisfaction for an individual, and overcoming psychological obstacles to a successful utterance can facilitate functioning in contemporary society. The convention of the game does, however, assume an element of fiction, which signals to other listeners that they need not believe in the genuineness of the feelings revealed on air. To alleviate the discomfort caused by this awareness, the 'flexible' radio gives away prizes to maintain an atmosphere of good fun.

Conclusions

An encouragement of the public display of emotion brings to mind strategies typical of the tabloid press. Nevertheless, we may wonder whether it is valid to equate it with the lowering of standards by radio. Does it sometimes become an excuse for certain cultural tendencies functioning beyond the media realm? Does the radio actually shape this culture or merely reflect it and, if so, to what extent? It is difficult to give a conclusive answer to these questions. It seems that, depending on the issues which researchers want to emphasise, the problem may have different dimensions, ranging from the anthropological to the purely technological ones. What one actually deals with here is a large array of dynamic changes, in the axiological sphere of today's culture or in the economic or technological sphere. Commercial radio utilises 'expression-seeking' dialogue to 'bring to life' the automated, computer-controlled programming on the one hand, and on the other to obtain a marketing objective. Undoubtedly, an obligation to express emotions on air is an indication of exhibitionism in contemporary culture, which is often complemented by the faking of real emotions for the sake of the media. The ritual of the programme genre enables the assumption that neither the listener nor the presenter show their true feelings in apparent competition dialogues. The rules of the game, however, force them to enact these feelings to a set plan so that others, the listeners, may be entertained.

References

Allwood, J (1976) 'Linguistic Communication as Action and Cooperation', *Gothenburg Monographs in Linguistics*, issue 2, Göteborg: University of Göteborg.

Allwood, J (1994) 'Obligations and Options in Dialogue', *Think*, volume 3.

Allwood, J (1980) 'On the Analysis of Communicative Action', in Brenner (ed) *The Structure of Action*, Oxford: Blackwell.

Allwood, J (1984) 'On relevance in spoken interaction', in Kjellmer, G & Bäckman, S (eds) *Papers on Language and Literature. Gothenhurg Studies in English*, issue 60, University of Göteborg, Department of English.

Allwood, J & Haglund, B (1991) Communicative Activity

Allwood, J, Nivre, J & Ahlsén, E (1990) 'Speech management - on the nonwritten life of speech', *Nordic Journal of Linguistics*, issue 13.

Allwood, J, Nivre, J & Ahlsén, E (1992) 'On the Semantics and Pragmatics of Linguistic Feedback', *Journal of Semantics*, issue 9.

Bloomfield, L (1970) *Language*, London: Allen & Unwin.

Brückner, A (1985) *Etymologiczny słownik języka polskiego*, Warszawa: Wydawnictwo Wiedza Powszechna.

Bunt, H (1994) 'Context and dialogue control', *Think*, volume 18, issue 1.

Bunt, H (1995) 'Dialogue control functions and interaction designs', in Beun, Baker & Reiner (eds) *Dialogue and Instruction Modelling Interaction in Intelligent Tutoring*, *Series F: Computer and Systems Sciences*, volume 142, Berlin: Springer.

Clark, H (1996) *Using Language*, Cambridge: Cambridge University Press.

Couldry, N (2000) *The Place of Media Power: Pilgrims and Witnesses of the Media Age*, London: Routledge.

Craig, R, Karen, T (eds) (1983) *Conversational Coherence: Form, Structure and Strategy, Sage Series in Interpersonal Communication*, Beverly Hills: Sage.

Dayan, K (1992) *Media Events. The Live Broadcasting of History*, Harvard University Press.

Esslin, M (1981) 'The mind as stage' in Shingler, M & Wieringa, C, *On Air. Methods and Meanings of Radio*, London: Arnold.

Gibbs, R (1999) *Intentions in the Experience of Meaning*, Cambridge: Cambridge University Press.

Gloger, Z (1972) *Encyklopedia staropolska, przedruk z wydania 1900-1903*, Warszawa: Wydawnictwo Wiedza Powszechna.

Goffman, E (1981) *Forms of Talk*, Philadelphia: University of Pennsylvania Press.

Grice, H (1975) 'Logic and conversation', in Cole, P & Morgan, J (eds), *Syntax and Semantics III: Speech Acts*, New York: Academic Press.

Hall, Hobson, Lowe & Willis (eds) (1980) *Culture, Media, Language*, London: Hutchison.

Heritage, J (2004) 'Conversation analysis and institutional talk', in Fitch & Sanders (eds) *Handbook of Language and Social Interaction*, New York: Lawrence Erlbaum.

Heritage, J (1985) 'Analyzing news interviews: Aspects of the production of talk for an "overhearing" audience', in van Dijk (ed) *Handbook of Discourse Analysis, Volume 3, Discourse and Dialogue*, London: Academic Press.

Herzog, H (1944) *What Do We Really Know About Daytime Serial Listeners, Radio Research 1942-43*, New York: Duell, Sloan, and Pearce.

Hobbs, J (1979) 'Coherence and Coreference', *Cognitive Science*, volume 3.

Horton, Wohl (1956) 'Mass communication and para-social interaction: Observations on intimacy at a distance', *Psychiatry*, volume 19.

Hutchby, I (1991) 'The Organization of talk on talk radio', in Scannell, P (ed), *Broadcast Talk*, London: Sage.

Hutchby, I (1996) 'Confrontation talk. Arguments, asymmetries, and power on talk radio'.

Hutchby, I (2006) *Media Talk: Conversation Analysis and the Study of Broadcasting*. Glasgow: Open University Press.

Hutchby, I & Wooffitt, R (1998) *Conversation Analysis: Principles, Practices and Applications*. Malden: Polity.

Hutchby, Wooffitt (2008) *Conversation Analysis*, Cambridge: Polity Press.

Kehler, A. (2002) *Coherence, Reference and the Theory of Grammar*, Stanford: CSLI Publications.

Lacey, K (2013) *Listening Publics: The Politics and Experience of Listening in the Media Age*, London: Polity.

Lerner, G (2004) *Conversation Analysis. Studies from the first generation*. Amsterdam: John Benjamins Publishing Company.

Levinson, S (1983) *Pragmatics*, Cambridge University Press.

Lewis, P (1981) 'Radio Drama', in Shingler, M & Wieringa, C, *On Air. Methods and Meanings of Radio*, London: Arnold.

Mann, W (1988) 'Dialogue games: Conventions of human interaction', *Argumentation*, issue 2.

Mayen, J (1958) 'Monolog i dialog radiowy', *Dialog*, issue 12.

McKenzie, J (2001) *Perform or Else: From Discipline to Performance*, London: Routledge.

Hutchby, I (1986) 'Media talk: Conversation analysis and the study of broadcasting' *Media, Culture and Society,* volume 8, issue 4, London: Sage.

Neal R, Norrick, A (2009) 'Theory of humor in interaction', *Journal of Literary Theory*, volume 3, issue 2.

Ong, W (2002) *Orality and Literacy. The Technologizing of the World*, London: Routledge.

Radio Track (2013) MillwardBrown SMG/KRC, Warsaw.

Ravenscroft, A, Boyle, T (2010) 'A dialogue and social software perspective on deep learning design', *Journal of Interactive Media in Education*. http://www-jime.open.ac.uk/article/2010-12/html

Sacks, H, Schegloff, E & Jefferson, G (1974) 'A simplest systematics for the organization of turn-taking for conversation', *Language*, volume 50, issue 4.

Scannell, P (1989) 'Public service broadcasting and modern public life', *Media, Culture & Society*, volume 11.

Scannell, P (1991) *Broadcast Talk*, London: Sage.

Scannell, P (1996) *Radio, Television & Modern Life*, Massachusetts: Blackwell Publishing.

Scannell, P & Cardiff, D (1991) *A Social History of British Broadcasting, Vol. 1*, Oxford: Blackwell.

Schegloff, E (2002) 'Beginnings in the telephone', in Katz, J and Aakhus, M (eds), *Perpetual Contact: Mobile Communication, Private Talk, Public Performance*. Cambridge: Cambridge University Press.

Severinson Eklundh, K (1983) *The Notion of Language Game: A Natural Unit of Dialogue and Discourse*, Linkoping: University of Linkoping Press.

Sidnell, J (2010) *Conversation Analysis: An Introduction*, Chichester: Wiley-Blackwell.

Sławski, F (1952-1956) Słownik etymologiczny języka polskiego, Vol. I, Kraków: Towarzystwo Miłośników Języka Polskiego

Starkey, G (2014) *Radio in Context, Second edition*, Basingstoke: Palgrave Macmillan.

Traum, D & Allen, J (1994) 'Discourse obligations in dialogue processing', paper at the 32nd Annual Meeting of the Association for Computational Linguistics.

Vagle, W (1997) '"Ways of Speaking" on Norwegian Radio 1935-1980. A study of text norm evolution'. www.nordicom.gu.se/common/publ

Van Dijk, T (1997) *Discourse as Social Interaction*, London: Sage.

Van Dijk, T (2006) *Discourse, Context and Cognition*, Discourse Studies.

Weigand, E (2009) *Language as Dialogue. From Rules to Principles of Probability*, Amsterdam: John Benjamins.

Wittgenstein, L (1953) *Philosophical Investigations*. New York: Macmillan.

Chapter 12

Narcissism in Western Australia's community radio sector

Simon Order

Abstract

Community radio in Australia is well established and an important part of the radio sector. Yet, in today's economically driven world, it sits at the bottom of the media money pile. In order to argue for community radio's continuing existence and funding in a competitive media landscape, a way of capturing its value is essential. This paper summarises the development of a theoretical framework of value for community radio from the existing literature and the testing of that framework at three community radio stations in Perth, Western Australia. Volunteer participation by the wider community in the operation of community radio has been a normative value for the sector. In particular, this chapter discusses the importance of one key finding around that value of participation in the research. Study participants at all stations frankly asserted that often, their motivation to participate in community radio sprang from a purely selfish motivation. If participants in this study perceived the value of community radio from a purely selfish motivational standpoint, the wider community benefits could potentially be considered as pure side effects. Subsequently, any attempt to argue for the wider community benefits of community radio, and thus support and funding, could become much harder to substantiate.

Keywords: community radio, participation, volunteering, Australia

Introduction

This paper reflects on one aspect of a larger seven year-long research project that developed and tested a theoretical framework of value for community radio to aid in the understanding of value for the sector (Order 2013). This introduction offers some context to the reader about that larger work and sets the scene for the chapter's main contribution, which focuses on one key result from the testing of that framework at the site of community radio. The development of the draft theoretical framework of value for community radio was achieved through a detailed literature review of notions of value, and an exploration of the history and policy development of the Australian sector. A research methodology was then developed, in order to apply the draft framework of value at the station level, at three different community radio stations in Perth, Western Australia, 6RPH Information Radio, RTRFM and Radio Fremantle. Data collection methods included semi-structured interviews, listener feedback in the form of focus groups, and observation/participation at each station to gauge volunteer, staff and audience views about the station's performance.

This data was then analysed, firstly to identify the extent to which the values from the draft framework of value were evident in the sample stations. Did they match or were they different? Were there new ideas or aspects that extended the concept of value? Were there factors unique to each station that impact on the study participant's perceptions of value? Did the results of the field testing suggest adjustment of the framework? Secondly, because the data collection methods provided a snapshot of current operational practice, the framework may offer community radio stations one approach to potentially examine and quantify their own worth. These snapshots, in the form of rich and descriptive narrative case studies, could include evidential recommendations from the study participants about future station policy-making.

A theoretical framework for community radio: A meta-analysis

The framework was developed through five theoretical lenses, which corralled the sometimes contested and divergent theoretical terrain (Order 2011) into more useful subject areas. The five lenses are: the Lens of the Public Sphere, the Lens of Media Ownership, the Lens of Contested Value, the Lens of Australian Community Radio Policy and the Lens of Financial Challenges Facing Australian Community Radio (Order 2013). The Lens of the Public Sphere focuses on the concept of the *bourgeois public sphere* of Jurgen Habermas (1989) as a valuable contribution to participatory democratic social theory (Calhoun 1992 vii; Fraser 1992). Because Habermas' work resonates strongly with the core values of community radio, Australian community radio theorists, such as Van Vuuren (2006: 381) and Forde, Meadows, and Foxwell (2002a: 56-57), have acknowledged the contribution of his work in informing community media theory. The values that emerge from this lens focus on community radio as an agent of democracy (Fraser 1992: 123) or representation and as a medium for alternative voices to be heard in the public sphere (Zhao & Hackett 2005: 11; Hood 1980: 25; Forde, Foxwell, & Meadows 2003: 317; 2002b: 56-7; Downing 1984: 17; Downey & Fenton 2003: 187-9; Fraser 1992: 124; Habermas 1989: 171).

The second lens, The Lens of Media Ownership, rests on an assumption that the animation of democracy occurs within the mass media (Dahlgren 1995: 2). This lens views the value of community radio in the context of today's concentrated mainstream media. The concentration of media ownership is described as responsible for reducing the number of viewpoints available in the media (Bagdikian 2000; Taras 2001: 24) for the homogenisation of content (McChesney 2004: 7) and for the reduction in content diversity (Jolly 2007; Foyle 2006: 19; Wasko 2004: 315; Barr 2000: 6-7; Given 2006; *Convergence* 2012) and community representation (Downing 1984: 5). The principal value of community radio shown by this lens is the notion of media content diversity. The third lens is The Lens of Contested Value and this is where notions of value from community media theorists are most divergent (Atton 2007: 17; Van Vuuren 2009: 175). This lens has four foci: the focus of *definitions* of community/alternative media, the focus of *oppositional power*, the focus of *social power* and the focus of *participation*.

The first focus, the *definitions* of community or alternative media, reveals a lack of consensus around terminology. For example, John Downing believed that: 'to speak of *alternative* [media] is almost oxymoronic. Everything, at some point, is alternative to something else... (Downing *et al* 2001: ix). Rodriguez's preference is for the term *citizen's media*. She believes that citizenship is not a passive legal right but something to be enacted on a daily basis via participation in media production (2001: 19-22). In the Australian context, Forde *et al* prefer the terms *independent* or *community media*, suggesting such terms offer a clear 'alternative to the mainstream' (Forde, Foxwell & Meadows 2003: 316). Where theorists cannot agree on definitions, it is clear that the value of community radio is not clearly understood. The second focus, *oppositional power*, examines community media as challenger to the mainstream media. The approach paints the mainstream media as 'monolithic and unchanging' where 'the power of the mass media marginalises ordinary citizens: not only are they denied access to its production, they are marginalised by its reports' (Atton 2008: 215). Another approach is the propaganda model of Herman and Chomsky where market concentration has reduced citizens to mere consumers incapable of contributing to genuine public discourse (Herman & Chomsky 1988: 2-19).

The third focus of *social power*, explores ideas around personal or political empowerment that may emerge from involvement with community media. Researching alternative media at the grassroots reveals more about social power than oppositional power discussed above. Rodríguez discussed how 'multiple streams of power relationships are disrupted in the everyday lives of alternative media participants' (Rodriguez 2001: 16-17). The power of personal and community identities is constantly in flux as they move between participation in groups and their individual everyday lives. The fourth focus, *participation*, challenges the notion that participation in community media in itself is to be celebrated and that other factors should be considered before assigning significant value to the activity of participation. In particular, broadcaster ideology and participant production skills are important considerations if the act of participation is to be valued (Atton 2008: 218-9). Atton's arguments about the benefits of participation are shared by other researchers in the field. Sandoval *et al* stated that alternative media should be *critical* media to have maximum effect (2010: 142). Secondly, they are critical of participatory, not-for-profit, collectively-governed media operating on a shoestring and tending to dispense with professional organisational practice and production values (*ibid*: 142-3). Taken together, the four foci of the Lens of Contested Value reveal how heterogeneity, a widely valued characteristic, may be hampering a clear understanding of value for community radio.

The fourth lens is The Lens of Australian Community Radio Policy and examines the community radio sector as the product of a muddled Federal Government communications policy that saw the establishment of the third sector of public radio, the term initially used to describe community radio during its inception in the 1970's. David M. Barlow's *The Promise, Performance and Future of Community Broadcasting* explored the objectives and the political machinations leading to the initial legislation of the sector in 1978. He painted a picture of the 'journey from concept to legislation [that] was somewhat haphazard' (1998: 43), riding out changes in government and suffering from the most frustrating ad hoc policy making process. These sentiments are supported by Phoebe Thornley (1999), whose more historical work traces the political and governmental influences in the establishment of public broadcasting until 1992. This muddled and confused birth has left a lasting legacy on notions of value for the Australian sector today. The Lens of Financial Challenges Facing Australian Community Radio suggests the relationship between funding and the value of community radio is by no means a simple one. As AMARC stated, there is a need to demonstrate community radio's 'value for money' in meeting their community goals (2007: 50). Their argument suggests that funding for stations should follow if there is a clearer model of value and stations can demonstrate that value. However, as Griffiths, an early advocate of Australian public radio (1975), argued at the inception of the sector, it may be that funding is required to bring the station to a professional standard or perceived level of value. This kind of 'chicken and egg' dilemma is difficult to resolve. It adds weight to the argument that a clearer model of value is long overdue.

Methodology

From these lenses of analysis, a new draft theoretical framework of value for community radio was derived via a qualitative meta-analysis, aggregating existing studies, extracting the pertinent elements and distilling the results into a new conceptualisation (Paterson *et al* 2009: 23; Schreiber, Crooks, & Stern 1997: 314; Walsh & Downe 2005: 204). The literature on qualitative meta-analysis offered no universal guidelines for analysing the studies under scrutiny. However, as a general guiding principle, whatever process of analysis was conducted, the literature agreed that the preservation of meaning from the source studies was essential, as far as possible (Sandelowski 2004: 893; Timulak 2009: 595; Walsh & Downe 2005: 208). This study chose to follow Timulak (2009: 595) who offers a more prescriptive process, at least in its description.

The *generic descriptive interpretative* approach uses a four-phase system. In the first phase, the collected data were assigned into domains, (the domains represent a conceptual framework that the researcher brings to or observes in the data). This phase was accomplished by corralling theoretical ideas by overarching *higher level constructs* of value within the lenses of analysis. These were the values of *access, diversity, alternative, independence, representation* and *participation* (see table 12.1). In the second phase, meaning units were delineated, being the smallest units of the data that can stand on their own while conveying a clear meaning. This phase was achieved by distilling *specific values*, (more operational or implementation notions,) that had emerged from the lenses of analysis. Initially there were 82 specific values. In the third phase, categories are generated through the comparison of meaning units among themselves and through the distilling of the essence of similar meaning units, the categories abstracted and meaning units clustered on the basis of inherent similarities. There was a fair amount of duplication and overlap among the 82 specific values that had to be addressed. Thirdly, there was a simplification and improvement of the quality of some of the descriptions that give more specificity to the specific values. Fourthly, some of the descriptions were expanded to include the sense of any eliminated specific values. Six iterations of these processes were used to ensure that they occurred incrementally with the highest level of validity. This resulted in a refined set of 27 *specific values* (see codes 1a - 6c in table 12.1). In the fourth phase, the main findings are abstracted, often in the form of figures or narratives (Timulak 2009: 595). This is the draft theoretical framework of value for community radio in table 12.1.

High level construct	Code	Specific value name	Description
Access	1a	Connection between the media and local communities	Offering community-centred/local programming. Content is drawn from, and aimed at, the community. Caters to the broadcasting needs of states, cities and/or suburbs, rather than nation-wide content. Thus, local issues, arts and culture are emphasised.
	1b	Represent communities of interest not adequately represented by mainstream media	Providing services to people from a particular niche, ethnic or cultural background, for example music enthusiasts, ethnic language, indigenous, gay, religious, trade union, educational groups.
	1c	Community information and community promotion	Broadcasting information especially relevant at the local level and also promotion of community events, etc.
	1d	Community development and social outcomes	Facilitating the promotion of positive social change via social inclusion, cultural diversity and civic participation. Creating social capital through building connections among individuals to produce social networks based on the norms of reciprocity

			and trustworthiness that arise from them.
	1e	Participatory democracy in society	Promoting more active participation in public sphere discourse beyond the range and reach of increasingly concentrated mainstream media.
	1f	A resource for community cultural production	Offering a forum for cultural identity formation through diverse modes of cultural production.
Diversity	2a	Promote harmony and diversity and contribute to an inclusive, cohesive and culturally-diverse Australian community	Promoting a positive view of cultural difference in Australia via community radio presenting diverse perspectives.
	2b	Content diversity	Presenting diversity in programme formats, voices & content.
	2c	Diversity of viewpoints/ ideological diversity	Presenting a plurality of ideas rather than a narrow mainstream perspective to serve the needs of diverse audiences.
	2d	Foreign language content	Including foreign language programs to appeal directly to ethnic sectors of the audience.
Alternative	3a	Alternative dialogues, voices & content	Featuring alternative voices and content to mainstream media, especially relevant to those groups and issues inadequately represented by the mainstream media. This involves both the selection of stories and the treatment of stories, as well as alternatives to mainstream programme formats and norms of broadcasting.
	3b	Credible source of alternative/local content	Aspiring to professional broadcasting standards to enhance appeal and credibility of the service as an authoritative alternative to mainstream media.
	3c	Political media alternative	Presenting political views alternative to the mainstream.

Independence	3d	Internal democratisation pre-figurative politics, transparent governance	Running stations with internal governance structures in line with community radio principles of democratisation, pre-figurative politics and transparent participative governance and decision-making.
	3e	Alternative media literacy	The shared and interactive nature of community media production produces enhanced media literacy within listeners.
	3f	Oppositional power	Contributing to a counter public sphere that can potentially undermine the dominant representations of society presented by mainstream media and provides a training ground for oppositional activities towards the mainstream media.
	4a	Independence in programming	Providing programming free from commercial or government influence. Stations should be legally constituted as owned and controlled by the community to ensure that they are accountable to and serve the community.
	4b	Not-for-profit status	Depending on a not-for-profit revenue generation model via commercial sponsorship, listener subscription, and/or sale of airtime, with clear guidelines to ensure equity of access and independence from commercial interests.
	4c	Professional /amateur media production values, programming and broadcast quality	Professional programming and broadcast quality may contribute to financial independence through increased listenership and thus sponsorship. The absence of slick, dynamic professional production values can be perceived as a negative attribute to the sector but also a positive for listeners preferring a 'relaxed' style of community broadcasting.
	4d	Audience participation	Proactively fostering audience participation and avenues of listener feedback.
Represent ation	5a	Representation of the community	Facilitating access to the airwaves to all segments of society to ensure that a wide range of views are represented. This includes representation of otherwise marginalised groups, (for example based on

			ethnicity, gender and class,) to provide a democratic balance.
	5b	Specialist representation	Relating to stations devoted specifically to the representation of a niche or specialist community group.
	5c	Generalist representation	Relating to stations devoted to the representation of a wide range of community groups under one station umbrella.
	5d	Audience reach	Reaching as high a percentage as is practical of the intended station audience.
Participation	6a	Citizen participation	Involving community members as contributors to the selection, production and delivery of broadcast content, usually as volunteers, rather than paid employees.
	6b	Communications managed by the community	Fostering community participation in station management at all levels.
	6c	Personal development and possible political empowerment at a personal/group level	Enhancing participants' sense of identity, personal satisfaction and education through involvement in broadcasting. May also be manifested as increased sense of political empowerment or emancipation. This also may include the development of broadcast skills through training.

Table 12.1: A draft theoretical framework of value for community radio

The case study approach

The research questions in this study examined community radio stations in the present moment, as alive and breathing social worlds of the now. It is the perception of value by the stakeholders of community radio, (staff, volunteers, and listeners,) that interested this study. The advantages of the case study in exploring this world is that it includes a wider range of evidence, including interviews, observations, documents and participation. In addition, the case study has distinct advantages as a research strategy in a world where the investigator has no control over events, and where a 'how' or 'why' research question is posed about contemporary matters (Yin 2009: 9). Case studies were a suitable approach for the world of the community radio station and offered the best chance to test the draft theoretical framework of value for community radio in the field and record a rich snapshot of station operations. Within the case study strategy three field methods were selected, namely observation/participation by the researcher, open-ended interviews and audience focus groups.

While the purpose of the data collection was to see how the values from the draft framework were operationalised, the use of the *specific value* terminology in framing the questions for participants raised three issues. Firstly, this would assume that study participants understood the nature of their participation and the nature of community radio in these theoretical terms. Secondly, mention of the framework of specific values within a question might, using legal parlance, 'lead the witness'. For example, in the context of validating the draft framework, it would lead study participants to use that same terminology. Thirdly, the specific values have been shown to often be overlapping and difficult to define. Their meaning, in the context of community media, is often conflicted and contested (Order 2011). Allowing the respondents to use their own terminology would permit the greatest flexibility in later assigning their responses to specific values in the draft framework. In addition, this approach would enable new values and themes to emerge. These three issues were addressed in the following ways. Firstly, the questions were formulated to address operational, rather than theoretical, issues and specific value terminology was avoided where possible. There are occasional questions where the specific values do arise and this is because it is difficult to ask the question another way. Secondly, the questions were deliberately open in nature. They were devised to encourage the participants to express their undirected thoughts and opinions. In this way, the perceptions of participants are approached as valuable and meaningful within themselves, rather than purely in terms of how they might relate to pre-existing theoretical constructs. Thirdly, the open nature of the questions provided flexibility to associate interview responses with more than one specific value when multiple references were embedded within them, during the analysis phase.

The results

There were approximately twelve interviews at each station with staff and volunteers and each station audience focus group contained approximately twelve participants. The methodological differences between interviews and focus groups means the data favours the contributions of station volunteers and staff. Station volunteers and staff were more articulate around operational station issues, while focus group members from the station audience were more invested in content and programme quality. This meant focus group members generally brought less to the data than station participants. The study used a qualitative content analysis to indentify themes from the data, (that is, values from the theoretical framework of value for community radio,) and a tabulation strategy to determine the frequency of occurrence of the themes (Namey *et al* 2008: 137). Drawing conclusions from the data occurred in a three ways. Firstly, the total mentions of values across all case studies were considered. Secondly, emergent (new) values were considered across all case studies and thirdly, occurrence of values at individual stations was considered. In summary, this content analysis assisted in validating the draft framework of value for the stations, and showed where value was perceived by the study participants. This chapter is primarily concerned with the highest mentioned specific values. The five most frequently-mentioned specific values across the whole study were, with the number of mentions for each shown in italics:

- (6c) Personal development and empowerment at a personal/group level *67*

- (1a) Connection between the media and local communities *46*

- (1d) Community development and social outcomes *44*

- (4c) Professional/amateur media production values *38*

- (3d) Internal democratisation and transparent governance *36*.

That these five specific values were mentioned the most across all three stations justifies their inclusion in any community radio framework of value. These specific values also give a strong indication of the priorities of stakeholders at the three community radio stations in Perth, Western Australia. The highest mentioned specific value, (6c) personal development and empowerment at a personal/group level, suggests that community radio is not an altruistic activity. Study participants at all stations were quite frank in their assertions that often it was a purely selfish motivation that led to their involvement or listening. Neither station participants nor audience members significantly mentioned the more political or 'oppositional' values from the theoretical framework of value, (see figure 12.1 for full value occurrences). This indicates that community radio is as much about the benefits for the volunteers as the benefits for the listening community. Motivations of participation were examined by Van Vuuren (2001), and these results corroborate her contention that the benefits of social capital are a major motivation for community radio participants and listeners. The following remark from a 6RPH volunteer from this study was not uncommon:

> 'They are fairly selfish reasons. When I'm asked what I'm doing in my retirement, I can promote the radio station and listen to me. It has given me some purposeful identity outside being a retired person. I identify my retirement activity as reading on the radio. I'm aware of the community need to help visually impaired people and this is what the station provides but I am not consciously driven by the need to help them. It is purely egotistical.'

The second highest mentioned specific value, (1a) connection between the media and local communities, indicates a belief in the benefits of community radio for the listening community. Community radio is filling a communication gap between the mainstream media and the wider community. There are echoes here of the much-discussed public sphere of Jurgen Habermas (1989), where it was proposed that the wider public could contribute to societal discourse on matters of the day. Volunteers often described disenchantment with the mainstream media, especially the commercial sector, as their interests and concerns were largely ignored. This was especially the case for minority groups. Community radio offers a connection for those communities to and from the media, as one participant from Radio Fremantle commented:

> 'The Afghan community here [in Fremantle], they need a radio show. I like my people, to help them, to give them a bit of something and as a journalist I have been living here seventeen years and I am happy to present this show. During the Taliban years, our community divided into two. We had a very hard time as a community. We tried to tell the truth as a show and we had some part of community against us but when things calm down, it has become easy. Our community is at peace now.'

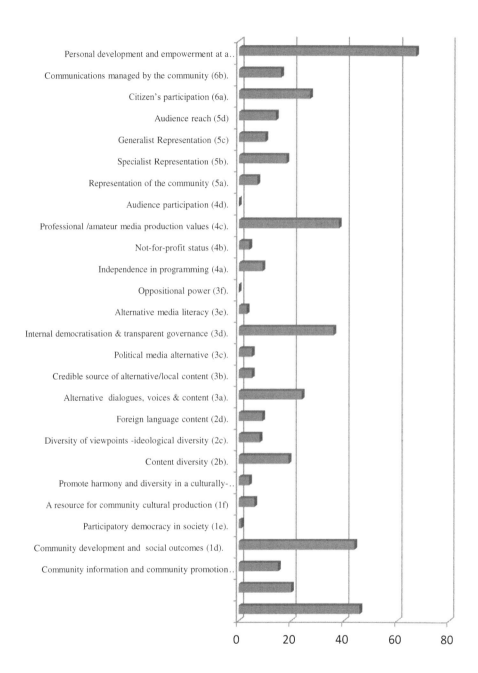

Figure 12.1: Positive mentions of specific values (sum of all three stations)

There is a strong sense here that this specific value originates from personal empowerment motivations. So, 'connection between the media and local communities' created by community radio is a way to enact 'personal development and empowerment' (6c) for the participants. Their belief in the power of a 'connection between the media and local communities'(1a) is likely to be impacted on by their own motivations for volunteering. Even though at first glance this specific value appears to be of benefit for the audience community, there is a high likelihood that it also benefits the participants in community radio. The third highest-mentioned specific value, 'community development and social outcomes' (1d), indicates a strong belief by study participants in the benefits of community radio for the listening community. In the case of 6RPH, (6c) 'personal development and empowerment at a personal/group level' was rated highest, and (1d) 'community development and social outcomes' was also rated highly. Although motivations for participation were strongly personal, there was also a belief that their contributions were beneficial to their listening community. However, at a station where the primary activity of volunteers is to read newspapers and magazines on-air for the print-handicapped community, there was a fair amount of personal satisfaction gained by volunteers from doing a fairly mundane task as well as they could. Interestingly, volunteers and the audience knew the work was valuable to the print-handicapped community, hence the high number of mentions, but no volunteers cited this as a primary motivation for volunteering. For participants, the value to the print-handicapped community was a fortunate side-effect of their volunteering.

The fourth highest mentioned specific value, (4c) 'professional/amateur media production values', further highlights the personal motivation theme. This was a largely discursive value in the theoretical framework, where opinion in community radio over the importance of professional production values was contested in the lenses of analysis (Order 2013: 137). The contested and sometimes divisive nature of this specific value is reinforced by the high frequency of mentions. Participants at 6RPH generally bemoaned the amateur production values that were the norm, while participants at RTRFM generally had a more professional approach to broadcasting, and at Radio Fremantle the broadcasting standards are generally low. However, what is more interesting is that the majority of participants thought of broadcasting professionalism as a matter of their personal pride. Participants at RTRFM and 6RPH were especially keen to explain that they wanted to do good a job for their own sense of achievement. The reasoning behind the high frequency of mentions of this specific value again point to the personal motivations of participants, as was suggested by a participant from RTRFM:

'There is a sense of fulfilment when everything goes right and that is in quite a selfish way. Primarily that's what drives me through the course of the day, there's the pressure of producing a show, lining up stories minutes before a show goes to air, finding the right person to talk about it, the interview goes well, the show goes well; there is a sense of satisfaction in the wheels running smoothly on the machine, that's the primary satisfaction and reward that you get. When people phone up and say they enjoyed listening to you that's always nice. It is quite selfish isn't it?'

The fifth highest-mentioned specific value, (3d) 'internal democratisation and transparent governance', suggests that community radio participants felt that this was a desirable aspect to their involvement. At 6RPH volunteers suggested that the flatter personnel structure contributed to a relaxed and enjoyable working environment. At RTRFM volunteers and staff alike talked about a palpable sense of family at the station, which was a by-product of their more collective form of station governance. One said:

> 'It's a good environment, like everybody's hearing it. It's a positive reinforcement of what they are all doing and things are getting done. Also everybody's very approachable and there is a lot of camaraderie… Everybody really understands what the station is trying to do, so nobody is out there trying to do their own thing, they are there working for the station, they want the station to be held in high regard.'

This specific value was not mentioned much by volunteers at Radio Fremantle, but there was a sense that volunteers were left to run their own shows without any interference. This suggests some satisfaction with their personal autonomy, which was also apparent at RTRFM and 6RPH. This specific value is also strongly linked to the personal motivations of community radio participants, with some participants suggesting the 'alternative' work environment was a deciding factor in their participation. In tune with the disenchantment of many participants with the content and style of mainstream media, there was also dissatisfaction with mainstream corporate and hierarchical workplace structures.

Conclusion

In summary, strong evidence was demonstrated by the five highest-mentioned specific values that the value of community radio at the grassroots level significantly resides in the personal benefits for community radio participants, in addition to community values. The conclusion drawn from these highest mentioned specific values is probably unsurprising considering the limited scope of the study. The data is drawn from stakeholders at three community radio stations in the relatively affluent and politically stable city of Perth, Western Australia. At this time, there are not so many community or political issues there, compared to other times and/or places. The political or 'oppositional' values from the framework were virtually non-existent, which has been suggested in previous research. Forde, Meadows and Foxwell stated that the Australian community radio sector is 'relatively conservative in its outlook, possibly caused by a significant shift to the "right" in the past 10 years' (2002b: 1). Participation and access to the airwaves have remained valuable aspects of community broadcasting, but there has been a noticeable decrease in the notion of 'progressive political action, such as epitomised by "left-wing" and student-run stations' (*ibid*: 7). It can also be argued that this reflects the increasing narcissism most evident in recent decades in Western societies (Twenge & Campbell 2010). This is a small study based on three stations, but the conclusion from the data that the 'personal' outweighs the 'political' suggests an interesting realignment of community radio values. One focus group participant at Radio Fremantle commented:

> 'There is an assumption that the primary goal community radio has is to serve an audience. I don't think that is necessarily true. I think that community radio can serve the participants as well and Radio Fremantle is the only station in Perth that is like that. Radio Fremantle is the only station you can walk into and have a chance of getting a show and feel supported in that by the station. That is just as significant a reason for funding a community station [rather than representing the community]'.

References

AMARC (2007) 'Community Radio Social Impact Assessment: Removing Barriers, Increasing Effectiveness', in *Challenges, Findings, Reflections, Experiences, Lines of Action for Community Radio Stakeholders: AMARC Global Evaluation*, Montreal: Wold Association of Community Radio Broadcasters.

Atton, C (2007) 'Current Issues in Alternative Media Research', *Sociology Compass* volume 1, issue 1.

Atton, C (2008) 'Alternative Media Theory and Journalism Practice', in Boler, M (ed) *Digital Media and Democracy: Tactics in Hard Times*, Cambridge: MIT Press.

Bagdikian, B (2000) *The Media Monopoly*, sixth edition, Boston: Beacon.

Barlow, D (1998) *The Promise, Performance and Future of Community Broadcasting*, La Trobe: Bundoora, Department of Media Studies, School of Arts and Media.

Barr, T (2000) *Newmedia.com.au: The Changing Face of Australia's Media and Communications*, Winchester: Allen and Unwin.

Calhoun, C (1992) 'Introduction: Habermas and the Public Sphere', in Calhoun, C (ed) *Habermas and the Public Sphere*, London: MIT Press.

Convergence Review (2012) *Convergence Review: Final Report*, Canberra: Department of Broadband.

Dahlgren, P (1995) *Television and the Public Sphere*, London: Sage.

Downey, J & Fenton N (2003) 'New Media, Counter Publicity and the Public Sphere', *New Media and Society*, volume 5, issue 2.

Downing, J (1984) *Radical Media: the Political Experience of Alternative Communication*, South End Press.

Downing, J, Ford, T, Gil, G & Stein, L (2001) *Radical Media : Rebellious Communication and Social Movements*, London: Sage.

Forde, S, Meadows, M & Foxwell, K (2002a) 'Creating a community public sphere: community radio as a cultural resource' *Media International Australia* incorporating *Culture and Policy*.

Forde, S, Meadows, M & Foxwell, K (2002b) 'Community radio, radicalism and the grassroots: Discussing the politics of contemporary Australian community', *Transformations* issue 4, September.

Forde, S, Foxwell, K & Meadows, M (2003) 'Through the Lens of the Local: Public Arena Journalism in the Australian Broadcasting Sector' *Journalism* volume 4, issue 3.

Foyle, L (2006) 'In the hands of a few', in Warren, C (ed) *The Media Muzzled: Australia's 2006 Press Freedom Report*, Redfern: MEAA.

Fraser, N (1992) 'Rethinking the Public Sphere: A Contribution to the Critique of Actuallly Existing Democracy', in Calhoun, C, *Habermas and the Public Sphere*, London: MIT Press.

Given, J (2006) 'Should we rely on the regulators? ' in *Research and Resources in the Public Interest*: AustraliaPolicyOnline.

Griffiths, D (1975) 'Democratising radio: the long revolution', *Media Monograph 3*, Sydney: Department of Government and Public Admin, University of Sydney and ARA).

Habermas, J (1989) *The Structural Transformation of the Public Sphere*. Cambridge: MIT Press.

Herman, E & Chomsky, N (1988) *Manufacturing Consent: The Political Economy of the Mass Media*, Pantheon Books.

Hood, S (1980) 'Bertolt Brecht, Radio as a Means of Communication', *Screen* number 20 (3/4).

Jolly, R (2007) *Media ownership deregulation in the United States and Australia: in the public interest?* Canberra: Parliamentary Library.

McChesney, R (2004) *The Problem of the Media: US Communication Politics in the Twenty-First Century*, New York: Monthly Review Press.

Namey, E, Guest, G, Thairu, L & Johnson, L (2008) 'Data Reduction Techniques for Large Qualitative Data Sets', in MacQueen, K, *Handbook for Team-Based Qualitative Research*, AltaMira Press.

Order, S (2013) *Community Radio in Western Australia: Notions of value*. PhD thesis, School of Arts, Murdoch University, Murdoch University.

Order, S (2011) 'Community radio and the notion of value: a divergent and contested theoretical terrain', paper at the Cultural ReOrientations and Comparative Colonialities: CSAA Annual Conference, Adelaide.

Paterson, L, Dubouloz, C, Chevrier, J, Ashe, B, King, J & Moldoveanu, M (2009) 'Conducting Qualitative Metasynthesis Research: Insights from a Metasynthesis Project' *International Journal of Qualitative Methods* volume 8, issue 3.

Rochester, C, Paine, E and Howlett, S (2010) *Volunteering and Society in the 21st Century*, London: Palgrave Macmillan.

Rodriguez, C (2001) *Fissures in the Mediascape: An International Study of Citizens' Media, Hampton Press Communication Series*, New Jersey: Hampton Press.

Sandelowski, M (2004) 'Qualitative Meta-Analysis. In Lewis-Beck, M, Bryman, A & Futing Liao, T (ed) *The SAGE Encyclopedia of Social Science Research Methods*, New York: Sage.

Sandoval, M & Fuchs, C (2010) 'Towards a critical theory of alternative media', *Telematics and Informatics* volume 27, issue 1.

Schreiber, R, Crooks, D & Stern, P (1997) 'Qualitative meta-analysis', in Morse, J (ed), *Completing a qualitative project: Details and dialogue*, Thousand Oaks: Sage.

Taras, D (2001) *Power and Betrayal in the Canadian Media*, second edition, Peterborough: Broadview Press.

Thornley, P (1999) *Broadcasting Policy in Australia: Political Influences and the Federal Government's Role in the Establishment and Development of Public/Community Broadcasting in Australia - A History 1939 to 1992*, Adelaide: University of NSW.

Timulak, L (2009) 'Meta-analysis of qualitataive studies: A tool for reviewing qualitative research findings in psychotherapy', *Psychotherapy Research*, volume 19, issue 4-5.

Twenge, J & Campbell, K (2010) *The Narcissism Epidemic: Living in the Age of Entitlement*, New York: Free Press.

Van Vuuren, K (2006) 'Community Broadcasting and the enclosure of the public sphere', *Media, Culture and Society*, volume 28, issue 3.

Van Vuuren, K (2001) 'Beyond the studio: A Case Study of Community Radio and Social Capital', *Australian Community Broadcasting Series*, volume 1, number 4.

Van Vuuren, K (2009) 'The Value and Purpose of Community Broadcasting: The Australian Experience', in Gordon, J, *Notions of Community: A Collection of Community Media Debates and Dilemmas*, Oxford: Peter Lang.

Walsh, D & Downe, S (2005) 'Meta-synthesis method for qualitative research: a literature review', *Journal of Advanced Nursing* volume 50, number 2.

Wasko, J (2004) 'The Political Economy of Communications', in Downing, J, *The Sage Handbook of Media Studies*, London: Sage.

Yin, R (2009) *Case Study Research. Design and Methods*. London: Sage.

Zhao, Y & Hackett, R (2005) 'Media Globalization, Media Democratization: Challenges, Issues, and Paradoxes', in Zhao, Y & Hackett, R, *Democratizing Global Media*, New York: Rowan and Littlefield.

Chapter 13

The strengths of radio journalists working in lesser-used European languages: Between convergence processes, specialisation and social responsibility

Irati Agirreazkuenaga, Ainara Larrondo and Koldo Meso

Abstract

The development of new technologies has multiplied the possibilities for radio journalists to enhance the importance and influence of their medium. This paper focuses on radio journalists working in public broadcasting corporations using minority languages, such Euskadi Irratia, which is part of the Basque Public Broadcasting Corporation (EITB), and Radio nan Gàidheal, operated by the British Broadcasting Corporation (BBC). The research aims to take an in-depth look at how the routines and professionalism of radio journalists are affected by convergence processes, by content specialisation and by the concern of the journalists themselves about their responsibility towards the society they serve. In line with other studies with similar characteristics, it employs a mixed methodology incorporating mainly qualitative methods, ethnography and semi-structured interviews, and quantitative ones, surveys. The results indicate, among other things, that the more specialised radio journalists are, the more satisfied they feel in their everyday job and tasks. In the same way, comparing situations where radio news journalists work only for radio with those working for radio and television, we conclude that the bi-media journalists consider their radio product is enriched by the incorporation of television, especially with respect to the variety of sources.

Keywords: public radio, journalists, profiles, routines, Radio nan Gàidheal, Euskadi Irratia, Spain, Basque Country, Scotland

Introduction: European lesser-used languages and public radio stations

In Western Europe there are 30 minority languages which each have speakers numbering between 50 and one million. These include minority languages within their own nations as well as those within larger nation-states. Some have official status and some do not, and naturally there are languages that have varying numbers of speakers. Nearly 82 per cent of the world's languages have fewer than 100,000 speakers, and 56 per cent 10,000 or fewer speakers (Manterola & Berasategi 2011: 17). The most widely spoken languages in the world are Chinese, Spanish and English. This research involves speakers of minority languages and their communities who each have to co-habit with dominant, major languages. The Basque language mostly co-exists with Castilian Spanish, the majority language of the Spanish state, but also with French in the French state. Scottish Gaelic mainly co-exists with English in the nation of Scotland, a semi-autonomous region of the United Kingdom.

The sociolinguistic surveys conducted in 2011 by the Siadeco company on behalf of the Government of the Basque Autonomous Community provide information on the situation of the Basque language today, and cover four areas of research: the language competence of Basque citizens, transmission of the language, Basque use in a range of spheres, (in the home, among friends, at work and in formal spheres,) and attitudes towards Basque. So it can be asserted that there are 714,136 bilingual Basque speakers – who speak Basque and Castilian Spanish or Basque and French – throughout the Basque Country (Eusko Jaurlaritza 2012: 8). That is, if we combine the Basque Autonomous Community (the provinces of Bizkaia, Gipuzkoa and Araba-Alava), with Navarre and Iparralde (Northern Basque Country administered by France). In addition, in this geographical area there are 388,255 passive bilinguals, or people who cannot speak Basque but who understand it and who may consume Basque-language media among others (*ibid*). In the case of *Gàidhlig*, or Scottish Gaelic, there are fewer speakers. The Scottish nation has a surface area of 78,782 square kilometres and 5,222,000 inhabitants according to General Register Office for Scotland 2001 data. The Scots were asked four questions: whether they can write in Gaelic, whether they can read it, whether they can speak it and whether they can understand spoken Gaelic. In 2001, 92,400 people over three years could speak some Gaelic (General Register Office for Scotland 2005: 5).

Therefore, one of the important elements in our case studies is that they are based on minority languages, but an equally important feature is that they are situated within public media. It has already been affirmed that local media play an important role in the development of lesser-used languages (Jones & Piette 2003), but in this chapter rather than focusing on the contribution that can be made to the language, we have focused on media that are currently in a referential position for the society they are geared towards in order to establish the objects of study. They are Euskadi Irratia and Radio nan Gàidheal, and are part of two public broadcasting companies which are EITB, supported by the Government of the Basque Autonomous Community, and the BBC, a British public service broadcasting corporation operating under a Royal Charter. The concept of public service broadcasting (PSB) was initially developed in the 1920s in the UK. Although a universal definition did not emerge from it, there are some models available (Tunstall 2010: 145-157). According to some authors (Debrett 2009: 807-827; Chan 2012: 898-912), there are three main normative functions which can be assigned to PSB in Western European democratic countries. Firstly, in terms of political needs, it serves democracies through the independent and impartial coverage of news. Secondly, from a social viewpoint, it promotes inclusion, satisfying diverse groups in society. Thirdly, in terms of culture, it preserves high programming standards and plays an important role in enforcing national cultural resources. The functions of the PSB are geared towards working for 'common' interests above the interests of particular individuals (McQuail 1992), and thus accomplishing social objectives, such as attaining solidarity through the embracing of diverse cultural identities and the promotion of tolerance and inclusion (Schlesinger 2004). In the same way, public journalism is understood as a normative set of journalistic ideals and practices that underlines the value of citizen involvement in journalistic process and in public discussion (Avha 2012: 1-17).

For over a decade the media have been seen as sellers of the knowledge model we call information (Basterretxea 1999: 39-50). This information is taken as a product that can be sold and bought, and that works according to the louder public demands. Some authors also speak of the 'commodification of information' (Toral 1998: 104). Embedded in these processes, to some extent, the media have become part of the political and economic elite (Ramirez de la Piscina 2004). Even when it comes to local radio in Europe, which, as mentioned above, has been crucial for the support and expansion of minority communities, while they might be better equipped to resist homogenisation (Starkey 2012: 167-178), since the mid-1990s they have often fallen victim as well to the globalising tendencies of the wider political economy. Faced with those practices then, we advocate that public media have another degree of responsibility for the society that sustains them. Public media organisations are regulated by internal editorial guidelines that every journalist is required to follow. These guidelines deal with classic values of public journalism such as accuracy, impartiality, fairness, offence, privacy and funding, as is the case with the BBC *Editorial Guidelines*, and the arguments for PSB are still based on the key principles of educating, informing and entertaining (Schlesinger 2004). Public bodies appear to be committed to meeting the information and entertainment needs of their audiences with high-quality, creative and challenging output. Hence, in this context social media and civic journalism will be deliberately employed to challenge those values by the very taxpayers who fund public media. The reason is that, as some authors have stated (Garnham 1993: 251-265), in Europe the public service broadcasting model, strongly linked to the protection and propagation of national cultures, has confronted an institutional crisis in the face of growing commercialisation and the loss of regulatory power. It was considered interesting to observe to what extent the journalists in this research are aware of, or are linked to, these processes.

Another intrinsic characteristic of the journalists in this research is the fact that they work in radio, and more specifically, on general content or generalist radio stations. The second of these deals with diverse programme types, news, features, radio magazines, fiction, music programmes and science programmes, among others. However, in a study of the programming provision of the general content stations in Spain (Gutierrez & Huertas 2003: 117-135), the authors concluded that homogenisation is the concept that best defines these radio models. From Monday to Friday, generalist radio schedules coincide for more than fifty per cent of their daily broadcasts. In Spain, therefore, conventional radio is supported by an outdated structure underpinned by years of conservative attitudes. According to Rodero and Serrano, the Spanish radio scene is not encouraging either for specialised radio, and, as they noted: 'while it is true that at one time it brought an air of renewal, today we see how it has drifted towards the conventional trend' (2007: 170-81). *A priori* this is not an isolated problem affecting a specific state, as experts in the neighbouring country of France have also warned of the risk of the collapse of pluralism (Cheval 2006) in French commercial as well as public radio stations, due to the concentration of radio formats and structures. What is true is that specialised radio in Spain is growing at a much slower rate than expected, compared with other countries. As clearly stated by Keith (2000), in order to be successful, a radio station has to cultivate a strong and distinct personality.

Along the same lines, one might wonder why radio has been chosen from among the audiovisual media, in view of the fact that it is regarded as the poor relative of television. Radio has been chosen for the study not only because it is more democratic than television (Thomas 1970), but also because it can handle 'ideas and abstraction better than television' (Starkey & Crisell 2009: 126), and because, overall, it has undoubtedly had a very significant influence on the development of the world's minority-language speakers. Radio was the first electronic medium when only the press existed, and it initially made all kinds of entertainment and information more available to a broader public, both in respect of its audience - because the sense of hearing is *a priori* all that is needed for consuming radio - and from the perspective of its producers, because it does not need the big budgets of television. In addition, both historically and now, the languages that did not or cannot find a place on television are on radio, which is considered to be a medium that promotes pluralism and supports multiculturalism (Checa 2002: 1-5) . Indeed, thanks to radio, the concept of minority is not limited to an ethnic or religious group that occupies a small area, since it includes international minorities that are united with each other by the radio broadcasts that survive on the internet and offer free listening.

Hence, the authors of this chapter considered it to be time to explore which strategies are followed by journalists working in European public radio with respect to their working habits and attitudes, to enable them to survive and maintain their essence in a transforming environment. Now here comes the term 'professionalism'. That is, regardless of the language or the external or internal crises, radio journalists have to create their content and serve their audience on the basis of professional standards. In the digital revolution the discussion surrounding journalists' professionalism is again being challenged with the emergence of citizen journalism or user-generated-content where 'everybody can be a journalist' (Harrison 2010: 243-56). Yet, a recent study (Blaagaard 2013: 1076-90) analysed the thoughts of 25-year-old international journalism students at London City University, who considered that citizen journalism will only be useful for the public sphere when it is done by professional journalists. So they were reinforcing that idea of professionalism in journalism culture.

Aims and case studies

This chapter aims to take an in-depth look at some of the most important factors that shape the routines and attitudes of two groups of radio journalists, and ultimately, discuss how these factors can be modified to get a better level of resilience for these radio stations working in minority languages. In order to establish their habits and attitudes, after examining the studies of previous scholars of journalists of different kinds, we will be focusing on the four pillars that influence radio journalists' habits and behaviours. They are: convergence strategies established in the newsrooms, along with their role at work regarding the content they create; professional standards achieved; social responsibility and job satisfaction. We will also be looking at the interrelationships between these elements. As explained in the introduction, the case studies are of journalists who are working on the public radio station at EITB, Euskadi Irratia, and at BBC Alba, Radio nan Gàidheal.

Regarding the convergence process, very briefly it can be stated that the related strategies can take place simultaneously within the same media organisation, and they can display a different level of development. In this respect, while technology represents an elementary requirement of any convergence process, a kind of a driving force, the level of innovation reached in the newsroom usually offers a more precise idea of the convergent progress achieved by the media organisation, as well as of the type of managerial mindset on convergence. In fact, several authors have addressed the technological and managerial dimensions of convergence, from the standpoint of its implications for newsroom production, in terms of 'increasing cooperation and collaboration between formerly distinct media newsrooms and other parts of the modern media company' (Deuze 2004: 140). In this sense, digitisation *per se* is not a determining factor for cross-media journalistic routines (Erdal 2007); convergence depends on the ability of the media organisation to transgress traditional routines and it does require a factual synergistic dialogue between different media divisions, not only the cross-promotion, cloning or sharing of resources (Dailey, Demo & Spillman 2005). In this study we will see how much of the convergence strategies have been applied in the working groups of the radio journalists in question, if they have been applied in any way, and under what conditions.

Methodology

A methodological triangulation was applied in this research. Tools derived from ethnographic methods were used to create descriptive data, to collect 'peoples' own spoken words' (Taylor & Bogdan 1984: 20). Certainly, qualitative methodologies prevail in this research - the direct observations in the newsrooms and radio studios, and the in-depth interviews being of great importance. Researchers performed active non-participant observations, which means that they did not take part in the phenomena being observed (Juaristi 2003: 201) so we were able to record the journalists' routines, attitudes and viewpoints without distractions (Domingo 2008). In Scotland, the observation technique was implemented at the main headquarters of BBC Alba in Inverness during May 2011, although less ambitious observation days were also carried out in BBC Scotland's main headquarters at Pacific Quay in Glasgow, as the Gaelic TV newscast *An Là* is produced there and so are some radio features for Radio nan Gàidheal. At Euskadi Irratia observations were mainly accomplished at the radio station's main headquarters in Donostia-San Sebastian during February 2011 and 2012. Yet, as in the case of Radio nan Gàidheal, some days were spent in Bilbao where the head offices of the Basque Radio and Television Corporation (EITB) are located. This stage was planned to cover the main elements and relationships taking place in the broadcasters' daily routines and decisions. Researchers shadowed journalists in the preproduction meeting rooms, editorial meetings, live broadcasts and post-transmission meetings. The field diary was of significant value in this phase as it involved both the bringing together of previously prepared criteria to the observation points and keeping a record of what the researcher was collecting from the experience. In-depth interviews with journalists were also performed inside the aforementioned spaces, and a digital voice recorder was used as the main tool; in total 44 in-depth interviews were completed, 22 in each radio station.

Nevertheless, the quantitative data was enriched and contrasted with statistical analyses that were undertaken by means of surveys. When designing a survey, it is essential to bear in mind the method chosen for the data gathering and to come up with questions in line with it, because the questionnaire format will largely limit its effectiveness (Wimmer & Dominick 1996: 115). Thus, the survey coped with a range of variables that measure the perception some journalists have of a range of factors influencing their professionalism and job satisfaction. For this purpose, a revision of the methods used in the past and present by pioneers (Stepinska & Ossowski 2012: 857-67; Nygren & Degtereva 2012: 732-43; Demers 1994: 914-25; Pollard 1993: 193-208) was used to try and measure journalists' views in various contexts. In our version for this research, the journalists were shown eight statements which they were asked to respond on a scale of 1 to 5, where 1meant 'totally disagree', 2 meant 'disagree', 3 meant 'so-so', 4 meant 'agree', and 5 meant 'totally agree'. Dealing with subjects in a set of questions makes the questionnaire lighter. Nevertheless, in such statements, it is a good idea to combine positive phrases with negative ones, to discourage respondents from answering the questions in an automatic way without thinking (Díaz de Rada 2005: 119).

The eight sentences dealt with the following issues: 1) The level of appreciation they feel that journalists of other mass media have towards their current work;   2) Considerations towards the money they earn [we first tried to test this subject with a question that could provide an approximation of the salary of journalists, but we found that it was not effective owing to the filters that the survey had to pass before reaching the journalists, and, on the other hand, previous studies suggested that the question of pay be removed from the questionnaires, given the high percentage of non-responses (Amurrio & Martín Sabarís 2005: 434)];   3) Perceptions about how much their profession gives them the capacity to influence society; 4) Perceptions about not having enough time to reflect on the content they work on; 5) Perceptions of the need for more technical resources to carry out their work better; 6) Freedom to work on their daily content creation processes; 7) Thoughts on receiving comments from their superiors directly; 8) The perceived job satisfaction on content creation, which we measured by asking how significant the difference was between the work they do and what they would like to do. In the case of Euskadi Irratia, 50 journalists out of 74 responded to our survey (68 per cent) and at Radio nan Gàidheal 32 out of 63 (50.8 per cent). All were working on different kind of contracts in different roles within the stations. Applying a specific sociological surveys technique (Fuentelsaz Gallego 2004: 5) showed that the samples selected for the surveys enjoyed a level of reliability of 99.9 per cent. To make the most of the semi-quantitative data, a statistical analysis was performed between variables to determine the degree of correlation, using the Spearman correlation index (Hollander & Wolfe 1973), in which the latter correlation coefficient assessed how well the relationship between two variables can be described. Merging different research tools allowed us to achieve greater scientific verification of the results.

Results: journalists' convergent and divergent perspectives

Firstly, the profiles of the journalists in both public radio stations. Most of the broadcasters worked in news. At Radio nan Gàidheal this was 60 per cent of all the editorial staff on the station, and at the Basque-language station 45 per cent. However, there were very few specialised-content journalists, (around 8.4 per cent at Euskadi Irratia and 4 per cent at Radio nan Gàidheal). These journalists worked specifically on political issues, cultural matters, international affairs, and so on. Furthermore, there was a remarkable difference when it came to the multimedia aspect of each group of journalists, as Euskadi Irratia journalists worked only for the radio and conversely, in Radio nan Gàidheal, broadcasters, (be they presenters, reporters or producers,) worked for both radio and television, producing daily content for *An Là*, the evening newscast on the television channel BBC Alba.

The fact that Gaelic broadcasters at the BBC are bi-media journalists is related to the launch of the TV channel in 2008; the staff who were then working in Radio nan Gàidheal were trained in bi-media skills in order to be able to produce TV content for the first Gaelic television channel. Naturally, this new milieu required a dramatic change in the working routines of the Gaelic journalists. This means that while nowadays in the Basque-language public radio station no systematic convergence strategy has been established. That is, there are content exchanges between journalists working on the radio and in the Basque-language TV or in the Spanish-language radio for instance, but always in an unsystematic way. The Gaelic journalists working in news are producing and presenting news content on BBC Alba at the same time, so they work with a convergent approach to both. The Gaelic Department developed its own working process, which is based on a rota system where the back, day and night shifts are changed weekly but so are the tasks carried out by each broadcaster, and they may vary between beginning on a producer shift, a reporter shift or a presenter shift. It is thanks to this fully convergent process in which the radio and TV can go forward jointly that the BBC was able to create the Gaelic TV station. This means that the two radio newscasts, *Aithris Na Maidne* and *Aithris an Fheasgair*, and the TV newscast, *An Là*, are brought together in the same editorial meetings.

This situation has had an effect on the use of sources by broadcasters, particularly among first-hand and second-hand sources since the use of first-hand sources has increased at Radio nan Gàidheal ever since they started working for TV as well. Once radio broadcasters were required to create media content for the TV newscast *An Là*, the way stories were put together had to change; for instance, they could no longer conduct an interview over the phone, as the TV involves images. Face-to-face interviews are always of a better quality, not only technically but in content terms, too, because they involve the freshness of being with the actual interviewee, and that, of course, has an influence on the quality of the interview offered on radio. By contrast, in the Basque-language public radio there is a predominance of second-hand sources; yet in favour of these broadcasts, we should underline that they use varied sources, not just pertaining to the political and administrative unit of the Basque Country, but also to all the seven provinces forming the Basque-language cultural unit. Certainly, it is important to outline that the agenda of both groups of journalists goes beyond the confines of their linguistic and geographical limits.

In this context, we argue that the professionals prioritise professional journalistic behaviour over linguistic militancy. Hence, the speech community is not the only influential factor when it comes to deciding on the radio content. 'A newscast is a newscast, that's it, whether it's in one language or another, the aim is to inform' the editor-presenter of the daily Euskadi Irratia midday newscast told us. In Radio nan Gàidheal, although great importance is attached to the sources coming from the Gaelic world, they consider they are very focused on their 'broadcaster profile', and not just the 'Gaelic-speaker one' (newsroom observation, 2011). Nonetheless, prioritising journalistic skills is not the only factor we have to explore when talking about professionalism. Furthermore, in the literature about the factors that determine the professionalism of a journalist, autonomy at work has been considered to be essential to it, 'particularly in the sense of freedom from faction' (Singer 2006: 14). That is, from particular ideologies. In this study, autonomy at work has been observed and studied, and we can state that there are internal and external dynamics playing a role in the level of independence that journalists feel in their daily content decision and creation processes. To research the internal process, we used direct observations and interviews but also surveys, through which journalists were asked how much freedom they have to determine the content. We found 39 per cent of Basque journalists and 48 per cent of Gaelic journalists asserted that they did have freedom. Hence, from an internal dynamics approach, Gaelic journalists feel more independence when deciding the content they are going to work on due to their less hierarchically-fixed way of working and because they have developed 'distinct professional norms' related to autonomy (Hallin & Mancini 2004: 37). However, in the specific case of the Basque journalists, the few specialised journalists, 16.8 per cent of them, covering politics, international news, culture, sport or specialised programmes on ecology, science, social problems, music or humour, have a sense of greater autonomy when deciding their content compared with those who work in just any subject, (regardless of whether it is news or features). Even if in Radio nan Gàidheal there are no significant differences, a Basque general-content magazine journalist will give a score of 2.7 points out of 5 with respect to the autonomy statement, and the specialised ones a score of 3.8 points out of 5.

Yet, this context also needs to be enriched by the knowledge on the external dynamics that occur in the media in general in a specific society. The public media broadcasting companies in Spain, including in the Basque Country, are very ideologically dependent on the Government in power at any time, so strong political bonds tend to be detrimental to journalists working for those public media, too. In this sense, the research confirms the tendencies previously described by other authors, that public journalism tends to be more partisan in southern Europe (Schudson 2003). In that respect, the different ways of seeing professionalism will be due, to a significant extent, to the differences in the national media and political systems, which affect the social and cultural practices of journalism (Zabaleta *et al* 2010: 191). Apart from professionalism, valuing issues of social responsibility is vital for journalists working in public radio stations. In this study, the perception of the social responsibility of public radio broadcasters was measured through the combination of the following variables: '*Journalists of other media value my work*' and '*This work gives me the capacity to influence society'*. The journalists working in Euskadi Irratia felt they have a greater capacity to influence Basque society, and that is due to the wider target audience they seek, as we gathered from the observations and in-depth interviews with them. In other words, their ultimate goal is to reach all the Basque speakers that are located in the seven provinces of the Basque cultural territory. That desire prompts in them the thought that they will gradually achieve the goal of being a 'national radio station', and that means they will have a greater perceived influence on society than if they were only aiming to satisfy a specific geographical region. In Radio nan Gàidheal, however, even if journalists think that they can exert considerable influence on the people within the Gaelic community, (with 73 per cent of the Gaelic community as listeners,) nevertheless, the levels of acceptance and professional self-esteem appear to be lower according to the data from the observations. At a basic level, for instance, this could be deduced from their perception of their counterparts in English radio.

Notwithstanding the above, in the measure of the overall satisfaction with the content they currently produce, the Radio nan Gàidheal journalists appeared to be more satisfied compared with the Euskadi Irratia ones, even if there is a difference of just five points between the two, as they gave 3.8 and 3.4 points out of 5 points, respectively. Furthermore, at Radio nan Gàidheal there were hardly any differences between the three groups, that is, specialised content (2.3/5), news (2.7/5) and general magazines (2.3/5) among the broadcasters regarding job satisfaction. Then again, at Euskadi Irratia, journalists who are devoted to specialised content appeared to be more satisfied than the rest of the journalists (2.5/5), an impression that coincided with their perceived level of autonomy. The journalists on general content newscasts and feature programmes expressed the same degree of satisfaction (3.1/5). In that regard, it should be pointed out that by 2006 previous research showed that among 201 journalists who were working in broadcast media located in the Basque Autonomous Community, 21.4 per cent, (which was the highest percentage,) said their main professional wish was to produce specialised news content (Martin Sabarís & Amurrio 2006: 29-52). Therefore, this study confirms that idea because the autonomy and job satisfaction variables appeared to be related to the type of content production on Basque public radio.

Finally, by applying Spearman's correlation index (Hollander & Wolfe 1973), the most relevant correlations when taking into account both groups of journalists were found among the perceived value from other journalists and their satisfaction at work (Radio nan Gàidheal, $R=0.64***$ $p<0.001$); and the felt value from other journalists will be determined by how much they can exert an influence in society (Euskadi Irratia, $R=0.64***$ $p<0.001$). This means that the variables that most influence the trends of variation of these journalists are the ones that measure the social responsibility journalists have towards the society they serve.

Conclusions

This study, based on two specific case studies in which empirical research methods were applied, can confirm that journalistic convergence processes, if applied bearing in mind the particular context of a medium and its main actors, can be very beneficial for the journalists' level of professionalism. One of the main pillars that public corporations have to follow to achieve a high level of resilience is not to remain isolated, and for this purpose, the connections with other media are essential. The journalists studied work within large media organisations such as the BBC and the EITB, and if working for two media enriches their information sources or the exchange of information with other journalists in the same organisation and feeds into their daily media content, the strategy of convergence is for them a very positive experience. Fostering convergence processes among different groups of journalists within the same corporation helps to build networks, and if at any time a journalist or working group fails, there will be other support to cope gracefully with the upheaval. Convergence, as pointed out already, when applied in an efficient and specific way, ought to be able to develop the connections among the group of journalists. Certainly, the fact that journalists advocate maintaining their own media agendas but without being completely detached from those of the other mass media in society, (hence using sources that come from their communities but integrating them with national and international stories,) shows awareness of not remaining marginalised, and therefore, renders them less vulnerable to external pressures. However, there are some pressures which are harder to control, the external ones, and in particular, those related to wider, usually deeply established, structures of society. In this regard, the heads of public corporations located in Southern European countries should reflect deeply about how much the disproportionate ideological connection of their enterprises with the ideas of the political party in power might harm the quality of their journalists' work.

Finally, the social responsibility of the journalists studied working in public media can be raised or improved by fostering higher autonomy levels in their daily content decision practices. At the same time, the level of autonomy is related to the category of journalists, which considers the type of journalists, specialised or general, they are meant to be. The data obtained showed that the more specialised journalists are, the more time they will have to reflect on daily content production, and so create a more relaxed relationship towards editors or other superiors during the creative process. We must also draw attention to something we saw directly, *in situ*, in direct observations in newsrooms and editorial meetings: how the specialised journalist in politics, culture or international affairs senses greater independence from the editors' power leadership. When they specialise in a subject, the editors will respect that status.

References

Ahva, L (2012) 'Public journalism and professional reflexivity', *Journalism*, volume 13, issue 6.

Amurrio, M & Martín Sabarís, R (2005) 'Ikus-entzunezko kazetarien lanbide soslaia', in Arrieta, M, Basterretxea, J, Gonzalez, M, Gutierrez, A, Ramirez de la Piscina, T, Torregarai, I, Urkiza, A & Zuberogoitia, A (eds), *Kazetaritza euskaraz: oraina eta geroa*, Bilbao: Euskal Herriko Unibertsitateko Argitalpen Zerbitzua.

Basterretxea, J (1999) 'Masa-komunikazioaren funtzio eta pragmatika sozialak identitateen eraikuntzan', *Uztaro*, volume 29.

Blaagaard, B (2013) 'Shifting boundaries: Objectivity, citizen journalism and tomorrow's journalists', *Journalism Theory, Practice and Criticism*, volume 14, issue 8.

Chan Chin, Y (2012) 'Public service broadcasting, public interest and individual rights in China', *Media, Culture & Society*, volume 34, issue 7.

Checa Godoy, A (2002) 'La radio y las minorías al inicio del siglo XXI', *Razón y palabra*, volume 27.

Cheval, J-J (2006) 'The French radio broadcasting between permanency and transformation, diversity and concentration', paper at the Mutations des industries de la culture, de l'information et de la communication international conference, Paris.

Dailey, L, Demo, L & Spillman M (2005) 'The convergence continuum: A model for studying collaboration between media newsrooms', *Atlantic Journal of Communication*, volume 13, issue 3.

Debrett, M (2009) 'Riding the wave: Public service television in the multi-platform era', *Media, Culture & Society*, volume 31, issue 5.

Demers, DP (1994) 'Effects of organizational size on job satisfaction of top editors at U.S. dailies', *Journalism and Mass Communication Quarterly*, volume 71, issue 4.

Deuze, M (2004) 'Journalism studies beyond media: On ideology and identity', *Ecquid Novi*, volume 25, issue 2.

Díaz de Rada, V (2005) *Manual del trabajo de campo en la encuesta*, Madrid: Centro de Investigaciones Sociológicas.

Domingo, D (2008) 'Inventing online journalism. Development of the internet as a news medium in four Catalan online newsrooms', thesis, Barcelona: Universitat Autònoma de Barcelona.

Erdal, J (2007) 'Researching media convergence and crossmedia news production. Mapping the field', *Nordicom Review*, volume 28, issue 2.

Eusko Jaurlaritz, (2012) *V. Inkesta Soziolinguistikoa*, Vitoria: Government of the Basque Country.
http://www.erabili.com/zer_berri/berriak/dokumentuak/2012/V_inkesta_soziolinguistikoa.pdf

Fuentelsaz Gallego, C (2004) 'Cálculo del tamaño de la muestra', *Matronas Profesión*, volume 5, issue 18.

Garnham, N (1993) 'The mass media, cultural identity, and the public sphere in the modern world', *Public Culture Winter*, volume 5, issue 2.

Gutierrez, M and Huertas, A (2003) 'La programación de las radios generalistas en España', *Zer*, volume 15.

Hallin, D and Mancini, P (2004) *Comparing media systems: Three models of media and politics*, Cambridge: Cambridge University Press.

Harrison, J (2010) 'User-generated content and gatekeeping at the BBC Hub', *Journalism Studies*, volume 11, issue 2.

Hollander, M & Wolfe, D (1973) *Nonparametric Statistical Methods*, New York: Wiley.

Jones, E & Piette, G (2003) 'Panorámica de medios de comunicación local en lenguas minorizadas de la Unión Europea', paper at the Tokiko Hedabideak Etorkizunera Begira conference, Zamudio.

Juaristi, P (2003) *Gizarte ikerketarako teknikak: teoria eta adibideak*. Leioa: Euskal Herriko Unibertsitateko Argitalpen Zerbitzua.

Keith, M (2000) 'El futuro de la radio en el mercado global', paper at the Jornadas Internacional de Comunicación conference, Pamplona.

Manterola, I & Berasategi, N (2011) *Hizkuntza gutxituen erronkak* (The Challenges of Minority Languages), Bilbao: Udako Euskal Unibertsitatea.

Martin Sabarís, R & Amurrio, M (2006) 'Euskal irrati eta telebistetako kazetarien soslai soziologikoa', *Uztaro*, volume 58.

McQuail, D (1992) *Media Performance. Mass Communication and the Public Interest*. London: Sage.

Nygren, G & Degtereva, E (2012) 'Russian and Swedish journalists. Professional roles, ideals and daily reality', *Journalism Practice*, volume 6, issue 5-6.

Pollard, G (1993) 'Social attributes and job satisfaction among newsworkers', *International Communication Gazette*, volume 52.

Ramirez de la Piscina, T (2004) *Ikus gaitzazuen bestelako komunikazioa: alternatiba kritikoak*, Irun: Alberdania.

Rodero Antón, E & Sánchez Serrano, C (2007) 'Radiografía de la radio en España', *Revista Latina de Comunicación Social*, volume 62.

Schlesinger, P (2004) 'Do institutions matter for public service broadcasting?', London: Office of Communication.
http://stakeholders.ofcom.org.uk/binaries/consultations/psb2/annexes/wp2schles.pdf

Schudson, M (2003) *The Sociology of News*, New York: Norton.

Scotland's Census Gaelic Report 2001 (2005), Edinburgh: General Register Office for Scotland. http://www.gro-scotland.gov.uk/press/news2005/scotlands-census-2001-gaelic-report.html

Singer, JB (2006) 'The socially responsible existentialist', *Journalism Studies*, volume 7, issue 1.

Starkey, G (2012) 'Live and local no more? Listening communities and globalising trends in the ownership and production of local radio', in Oliveira, M, Portela, P & Santos, L (eds), *Radio Evolution: Conference Proceedings,* Braga: University of Minho.

Starkey, G & Crisell, A (2009) *Radio Journalism*, London: Sage.

Stepinska, A & Ossowski, S (2012) 'Three generations of Polish journalists. Professional roles and identitites', *Journalism Studies*, volume 13, issue 5-6.

Taylor, S & Bogdan, R (1984) *Introducción a los métodos cualitativos*, Barcelona: Ediciones Paidós.

Thomas, N (1970) 'The air over Europe', *Planet*, December 11-14.

Toral, G (1998) 'Radio, sociedad e información', in *Actas del XIV. Congreso de Estudios Vascos*, Donostia: Eusko Ikaskuntza.

Tunstall J (2010) 'The BBC and UK public service broadcasting', in Iosifidis P (ed) *Reinventing Public Service Communication: European Broadcasters and Beyond*, New York: Palgrave Macmillan.

Wimmer, RD and Dominick, J (1996) *La investigación científica en los medios de comunicación. Una introducción a sus métodos*, Barcelona: Bosch.

Zabaleta, I, Xamardo, N, Gutiérrez, A, Urrutia, S, Fernandez, I & Ferré, C (2010) 'Between language support and activism', *Journalism Studies*, volume 11, issue 2.

Chapter 14

Narrative elements in *The Archers*: An analysis of a long-running radio soap opera

Emma Rodero, Lluís Mas, Olatz Larrea and María Blanco

Abstract

First broadcast on BBC Radio in 1951, *The Archers* is the oldest radio soap opera in the world that is still running. It celebrated its 60th anniversary in 2011. This chapter presents an analysis of the main narrative elements of the series. It will show how different sound elements recreate three-dimensional spaces and actions, and how atmosphere depicted in the story is created. It will study characterisation in *The Archers*, paying special attention to the definition of the drama's personalities online. These characters have been born, have grown and in many cases have died as if they were real people, becoming very well-defined individuals in the minds of the listeners.

The study will also define the use of time in the series. Listeners rarely forget the events portrayed, and a timeline is available online, amongst other web content.

Finally, the podcast of the radio drama will be analysed as a relatively recent innovation. With it, it is possible to listen to *The Archers* any time and anywhere, including through a mobile device.

Keywords: radio fiction, soap opera, narrative elements, broadcast, BBC, United Kingdom

Introduction

First broadcast on BBC Radio in 1951, *The Archers* is the oldest and longest-running radio soap opera in the world, with over 17.000 episodes broadcast. It celebrated its 60th anniversary in 2011. In terms of content and genre, *The Archers* can be classified as continuing radio drama, an important genre which began to appear in the programme schedules of the major radio stations around the world in the early 1930s and 1940s. Such programmes rely on the potential of sound to generate mental images in the minds of radio listeners, using a variety of the different elements of radio language available to radio producers (Lewis, 1981). The creative potential of this genre is considerable, and in the series creativity is used to depict life in the fictitious village of Ambridge.

The Archers can be framed within the classic British fiction genre coming from the theatre tradition, with topics focused on real life from a courtesan or a genuinely picturesque regional custom perspective (Thomas 2009). It is a contemporary soap opera, in which a British middle-class rural ambience is reproduced: from the very beginning (Toye 1998), it has been based on family life and the wider social community of an English village, strongly connected to the idea of a nation-state (Reeve & Aggleton 1998). Its locations, constantly dichotomised between the traditional home, the field or the farm, relate to a society that is strongly attached to the countryside, but connected to the working class through the industrial revolution in Great Britain, a country where modernity always embraces customs and roots.

Place in *The Archers*

The village of Ambridge, in the county of **Borsetshire**, is the location of the different settings in which the various plots and sub-plots of *The Archers* are located. This imaginary county is placed between the real counties of Worcestershire and Warwickshire, to the south-west of Birmingham and the West Midlands. Ambridge takes its name from the River Am. The main economic activity is farming. Home Farm is the biggest. Brookfield Farm is owned by the main characters of the story: it has been passed from generation to generation, from Dan to Phil Archer and now it belongs to David Archer and his brother and sister, Kenton and Elisabeth. The other farms are Bridge Farm, acquired by Tony and Pat Archer in 2008, Grange Farm, owned by Oliver and Caroline, and the Grange Spinney farmstead. One can also find the cider bar, Grundy's Field, and two former farms, Hollow Tree and Marney's which, currently, serve Brookfield Farm. Finally, Nightingales Farm is no longer functioning as such.

The council houses in Ambridge that are featured in the series are Number 6 The Green, and Number 1 The Green. St Stephen's Church, with an old cemetery next to it, dates from 1281. The Vicarage was built in 1970 to replace its Georgian predecessor. Ambridge also has a facility for community events, the Village Hall, where the annual flower show takes place. The Village Shop is managed by volunteers. Ambridge also has a hotel called Grey Gables and an area of dwellings for elderly people called Manorfield Close. Ambridge Hall, home to Linda and Robert Snell, is a charming guest house, and Arkwright Hall is an old Victorian house dating back to the sixteenth century. Matt Crawford and Lillian Bellamy live at The Dower House, Susan Carter and Neil live at Willow Cottage, which was built by Neil and is situated next to Willow Farm. The Archers also have a summer house called Glebe Cottage. Peggy lives at The

Lodge, and Shula Hebden Lloyd lives and works at The Stables. The Glebelands are smaller houses located on the Village Green, where we can also find the bungalow of Bert Fry, a worker at Brookfield Farm, and his wife Freda, who works in the Bull, a bar and restaurant serving homemade food. Finally, there are several cottages, such as April Cottage, built in 1960 by the land-owner Charles Greenville, Blossom Hill Cottage, where Peggy Woolley lived, Honeysuckle Cottage owned by Adam Macy and Ian Craig, Rickyard Cottage which used to be for vacation rentals, and finally Woodbine Cottage.

Spaces depicted in *The Archers* can be classified as indoors or outdoors, such is the variable space created by the writers for the characters to evolve and interact in (Rodero 2010: 85). The outdoor locations are pictured in a very general manner, that is to say the 'farm-outdoors' are described as totally connected to the work in progress, with animal effects, mainly cows, pigeons, gates and machinery effects, or the sounds of specific actions of the characters, their footsteps, tying ropes, holding and moving great objects. This space gets bigger with the plotting of various characters moving and doing things. The space depicted as being next to machinery, (by placing in the foreground spot effects of a specific mechanical noise,) is not usually dwelt upon. On the other hand, other outdoors space is described by street sounds, such as cars passing by every once in a while, and birds singing in the background, plus some action from the characters. For instance, there could be a car approaching and stopping, someone who gets out of a car, with brakes and a stopping sound, then a car door effect and footsteps of the character approaching, giving the listener a 'hearing perspective' described as the *point ici* by Fuzellier (1965). That *point ici* might be alongside a lone character or, more often, with a character who is already chatting with someone else. In general, the background sound of birds singing, although in different intensities, depending on the outdoor location, is the most commonly-used descriptive ambient sound feature of the series.

Paradoxically, indoor spaces are quite varied. One could classify them as public and private. Amongst the former, there are many scenes set in the pub – conversations and background music, chair effects, drinking effects, voice reverberation. In the laundry we hear characters' moving and washing actions. There are locations for livestock competitions – we hear reverberating voices over the tannoy and crowd noises. A great variety of rooms are located in the different private houses of Ambridge. In general, the place of interaction par excellence is the kitchen. This is an intimate location where, quite commonly, close chats between characters occur - whispered talks with no acoustic description, or phone conversations with one voice processed electronically to create an earpiece effect. Another very common space in *The Archers* is the office, with the background sound of computer hardware, paper sounds, telephone rings and so forth, especially in what may be called the 'in front of the computer' subspace, with a lone character or two characters exchanging whispers above a keyboard typing effect. Some action is placed in the farm-indoors by placing the sound of machinery in a suitably distant background. In addition, the house-indoors is also depicted by placing characters in different rooms for dialogue that quite often involves children. Lastly, the 'inside-car' location is used very often in the plot by simply placing the engine sound in the foreground and sounds of passing cars as background, using the stereophonic effect of the left and right channels creatively.

Action and interaction

The Archers defines not only some physical spaces where different plots evolve, but also some specific spaces where characters perform tasks, move and talk. Interaction can be the sole occupation of two characters in a scene. When an interaction involves two or more characters, they might be in any one of two different positions:

1   Standing: this is more common outdoors as time out before or after some farm-specific work, such as grooming a horse or feeding hens. The action sounds for two or three seconds before an approaching character intervenes, approaching the foreground. Subsequently, the parallel action fades out progressively. Indoors, the positioning of voices is often complex as it depends on the movements that the parallel action in question implies; it is often the case that a character enters the space by raising his or her voice from afar and projecting it forward before reaching the 'close-chat space'.

2   Seated: in this case, the intensity and rhythm are lower, and the hearing perspective tends to be central and close to all characters heard. It is often used for coffee or tea time, so the sound of sipping is important, as well as the sound of a chair or a settee when someone sits or lies down beforehand, or the sound of a table when someone rests on it to create the intimate space for conversation. Furthermore, voices tend to be in a close foreground and very narrowly directed to the other character. Sometimes a third character comes in, raising voices and making the space heard more clearly (reverberation).

In both cases, when there are more than two speakers placed in a scene, a central hearing perspective is used. When seated, conversation can be combined with other tasks both in the farm-outdoors and in the house-indoors. The latter is more common and enriches the spaces as action, giving more information on the space's size and shape, and the objects there. In fact, the former is treated as just a conversation while standing outdoors: the main parallel action is set aside, as the noisier sound would be too high in the mix for the conversation to be heard properly by the listener. Characters may adopt different positions in these interactions, and they often make a contribution to the definition of the characters' psychological state, the context of the situation and the relationship between them (Crook 2001). Such positions include:

•   Seated focused: a character is perhaps working on handicraft, cooking or watching television. The character either keeps on doing the same activity and speaks downwards, or temporarily pauses the task and directs the voice up towards the incoming character joining the scene.

•   Standing still: brief and occasional conversations between two characters who stand, so one can hear some foot sound effects: a few isolated steps and movements.

•   Standing and moving: this is very common in *The Archers*. In this case, the hearing perspective is placed in the space created between both characters, so the changing distance in between is noticed. This happens a lot when someone is preparing tea, looking for something, gathering things or preparing to leave.

- Already in the middle of a conversation: two characters speak calmly about a topic when a third one comes in through the door, greeting them from afar, gets closer and can be heard sitting down, starting a three-way conversation.

Characterisation

The construction and adaptation of the characters, besides reflecting the spatiotemporal changes that occur in the scenes of dramatic programmes, are particular issues in radio narrative (Rodero & Soengas 2010). Therefore, in a radio fiction such as *The Archers*, a strict characterisation is essential to achieve identification and empathy with the audience. A character with a defined personality will always be outlined as more appealing and attractive to listeners. Most of the characters we remember are those provided with strong characterisation, otherwise, they would have gone unnoticed or they would simply have been forgotten (Rodero 2012). Moreover, good characterisation is always a useful way to avoid behavioural contradictions. Adequate knowledge of a character's personality, as a consequence of strict design, prevents incoherent ways of acting or improper comments by that character.

By analysing the episodes and also the website, we can observe that *The Archers* develops well-defined characters. On the site listeners can access two sections, for 'major characters' and 'all characters'. There, users can find a detailed description of all the characters who appear in the series and also the names of the actors (Rodero 2011). The site shows the large number of characters who appear in the series, 118 in total, 63 of whom can be considered major characters. The 63 are divided according to families and branches of families currently being depicted in the narrative:

- The Aldridge family, with eight key characters.
- The Archer family, Bridge Farm branch, consisting of five characters.
- The Archer family, Brookfield Farm branch, consisting of five characters.
- The Carter family, with five key characters.
- The Frank family, with three key characters.
- The Grundy family, with seven key characters.
- The Lloyd family, with four key characters.
- The Pargetter family, with four key characters.
- The Perks family, with two key characters.
- The Snell family, with two key characters.
- The Sterling family, with two key characters.
- The Tucker family, with two key characters.
- Other characters: 10 individuals.

A well-defined portrayal of characters in radio drama includes personal, physical, psychological, social and cultural data. In the specific case of *The Archers*, we found detailed information in the online bibliographies (Rodero 2005), as follows:

1 *Personal data* are fundamental to making the characters act and speak coherently, and include birthplace or home, birth date, age and marital status. Every biography shows the name of the actor who plays the character. There is a genealogy of close relatives and finally, the place where the character lives.

2   *Physical data* define the physical image of the character, which includes race, height, weight, constitution and the colour of the eyes and hair, in addition to any personal feature that might be particularly significant. However, for *The Archers*, this physical description is not needed, as the website includes a picture of each actor in character, even though they normally have only to sound like them.

3   *Psychological data* define personality, tastes, desires and hobbies. Every character's biography on the website includes a brief start-up description of their personality, as well as their likes and dislikes, and also the best and worst moments of their lives.

4   *Social and cultural data* further deepen the characterisation with social class, career path, education, work, hobbies and cultural background and, in general, how characters connect with their environment.

It is interesting to highlight the importance given to the actors playing the characters. Not only are their names and pictures shown but brief biographies with favourite actors, books and films. Finally, each biography includes an audio clip of a scene featuring the character. We concluded that *The Archers* characters are very well defined and promote authenticity because of the following features:

1   They seem very real due to the extensive biography on the website.

2   They are believable and authentic as their reactions and feelings are natural and coherent with the features described on the website.

3   They have well-defined temperaments and personalities, tastes and hobbies. In addition, these features appear in the characters' performances in the audio clips.

4   They are generally appealing, which helps hold audience attention and increase identification by frequently appealing to listeners' emotions.

The timeline

The Archers website includes a section which acts as a table of contents or index. Actually, it has become a very useful tool for the programme's fans. Since its inception, listeners have become witnesses to the growing up of the characters and the economic and cultural life of Ambridge. Many of those characters were born on air, have grown old and in some cases died just as if this were real life, leaving behind them new generations of characters. So, both the listeners themselves and the characters in the series have grown up in parallel, sharing a common interest in the series, and a dependency on the village. Over the period, so many things have happened that, sometimes, listeners need a reminder of the details of a storyline, so a timeline is available online. It reinforces the notion that *The Archers* is not just an everyday story of country folk. Most of the characters have had relationships with each other and, while some of the storylines are frenetic, others are just plain odd. New listeners wanting to know the past of *The Archers* or the beginning of a particular narrative can access a visual outline of the highlights of the series in chronological order. It has been built from the script archives of the series and it allows the user to scroll back and forth in search of the desired information. Its design is based on a traditional timeline, and its content orders the major events from 1951 to the present and embellishes them with numerous archival photographs, as well as audio clips of selected highlights.

An additional function of the website is community building. Often, old and new listeners debate in the website forums the origin of a particular memorable event and, usually, they can find the answer to their questions in the timeline. Its design is quite simple. It is divided by labels for every single year since the series began, and within them, all 12 months of the year pop up. In addition, each event features a short abstract.

We found that events reflected in the timeline can be classified as listed below.

1 *Obituaries* Both actors and characters dying have consequences in different ways for the series and, therefore, appear in the timeline. A number of major deaths have been included in the index as among the most dramatic moments of the series, including:

- (1955) Phil Archer's first wife, Grace, died in a barn fire, trying to save a horse;
- (1982) Polly Perks was killed in a crash between Pat's car and a milk tanker;
- (2005) An especially sad year, as script writers had to deal with the deaths of actress Mary Wimbush (Julia Pargetter) and Pamela Craig (Betty Tucker);
- (2009) Norman Painting, the voice of Phil Archer, died. He features in the *Guinness Book of Records* as the longest-serving actor in a soap opera.

2 *Weddings and births* These are also generational markers. Sometimes the union of two characters can mean the merger of two farms or rural properties, so that the event transcends the union of the newlyweds. Sometimes these couples give birth to new generations of residents and heirs of Ambridge, for example:

- (1951) Peggy gave birth to her third child, Tony;
- (April 1955) Phil Archer married Grace Fairbrother;
- (September 1968) Jennifer Archer married Roger Travers;
- (September 1985) Shula Archer married Mark Hebden.

3 *Rural life issues* Some of the most dramatic events of the series concern the professional life of the farms. The purchase of land, changes of ownership and infrastructures, plagues or diseases that affect livestock, parties and market days, all affect life in Ambridge and therefore are considered to be important events with consequences for the future. For example:

- (1972) The Perks took over The Bull, selling the shop to Jack Woolley;
- (1981) A difficult year for Tony, getting tetanus and swine vesicular disease;
- (2012) The e coli virus arrived in Ambridge.

4 *Social life issues (gossip)* The essence of Ambridge's social life revolves around what is accepted or rejected in contemporary society. The soap opera has not stopped treating, at any time during its existence, some of the hottest topics in society. Abortion and racism also exist in Ambridge. Sometimes, contentious issues are reflected in the conversations of the characters, which also reveal their impact and the reactions of the characters, many of whom gossip. Finally, the departure or return of characters from or to Ambridge also disrupts life, generating new events.

- (1967) Jennifer's pregnancy shocked the Archer family. Jennifer named her baby boy Adam, and escaped village gossip by moving to Bristol. She refused

to name the father, but Adam's shock of red hair suggested it might be
Brookfield cowman Paddy Redmond.

- (1976) After an affair with a colleague, Paul Johnson quit his job in London and
returned to Ambridge, The Stables and Christine.
- (1989) Vicar Jerry Buckle scandalised half the village by taking in Clive
Horrobin and his pregnant girlfriend, Sharon Richards. Clive disappeared soon
after the birth of baby Kylie.

5   *Cameo*s The appearance of a celebrity in the cast constitutes a form of promotion of
the series, as well as a remarkable event in the timeline. Examples include:

- (2011) Camilla, Duchess of Cornwall took part in two episodes of *The Archers*.
Her first appearance commemorated the National Osteoporosis Society's 25th
anniversary, and the second commemorated the show's 60th anniversary;
- (1991) BBC radio presenter and disc jockey John Peel appeared as himself;
- (1984) Princess Margaret and the Duke of Westminster appeared during a
fashion show to celebrate the centenary of the National Society for the
Prevention of Cruelty to Children.

However, lack of budget and new technologies mean that the timeline is not always
updated on the website. In order to overcome this disadvantage, editors use such other
updateable sources as Facebook or Twitter, where users can discuss any issues. These
sources were supplemented by the official blog of the series, called Diamond Decades,
in order to celebrate the 60th anniversary, which includes highlights and provides
graphic documents and sound archives. Finally, fans add historical data to their own
web pages. Archers Addicts has been the official fan club since 1995.

The Archers podcast

Finally, in 2007, the *The Archers* began distribution as a podcast (Gibson 2007). The
main advantage of having this format is that listeners can hear the episodes wherever
and whenever they want. Due to syndication and portability they do not have to log in
each time an episode is posted online, once they have downloaded a player. So the
podcast offers independence, mobility and the freedom of personal scheduling. *The
Archers* is a clear example of how conventional radio has adapted to modern times,
offering the series as a podcast and creating a new community of listeners (Herschmann
& Kischinhevsky 2008; Kelly 2006). It uses the mp3 format and is available on the
BBC website and iTunes, with each episode lasting 13 minutes, like the broadcast.
Each episode is structured as follows. The first 20 seconds consist of the signature tune,
Barwick Green, during which time the podcast includes an extra announcement, saying:
'You're listening to Friday's episode of *The Archers*, from BBC Radio Four'. Then, the
various scenes follow in a sequence determined by the day's narrative and then a reprise
of the signature tune signals the end of the episode.

Conclusions

Radio is the resilient medium and should be considered as such. From the analysis of
the narrative elements in *The Archers* in this paper, we can infer that *The Archers* is still
a contemporary drama, connected to British society to the extent that many consider it
to be in fashion. Key characteristics are the ways in which spaces, both literal and

metaphorical, are constructed, characters evolve based on action, action occurs along a temporal continuum, and the drama adapts to new platforms - with online content, podcasting and clips to be consumed in different ways and on different platforms. Although Ambridge is an imaginary village set in an imaginary county, we know it is supposed to be in the rural Midlands, so neither the village nor the region are difficult to imagine. In that specific location, *The Archers* has succeeded in creating a particular atmosphere in which everything Britain represents, both inside and outside the United Kingdom, is implicit. They do this by putting characters in action in different locations, mainly indoors, (in public or in private,) and outdoors, (on the farms or in the countryside,) and building psychological spaces of interaction as a unique task or a shared one, depending on the location of the action and the characters' situations and movements. All this evokes places and environments to be imagined by the listeners.

In *The Archers* characters are closely defined, in both sound and on the website. The website provides biographies, in which each character's physical, personal, social and psychological data are visible. In general, faithful characterisation of the characters in *The Archers* contributes to a sense of reality, credibility and attractiveness to listeners. The website has developed several ways to keep the audience updated, the timeline, links to social networks and fan blogs. Designed as a visual representation of the narrative, the timeline and social networks each have additional goals of indexing the content and community building. Many online users access the blog and the web page every day in order to express and share their opinions about past episodes. In those comments participants interact with each other and the media, creating online discussions and developing a feeling of a virtual community. Since podcasts of *The Archers* were launched, followers have been able to access any episode at any time.

This is a challenging context for radio producers as very frequently they face new big decisions regarding technology, programming and distribution. However, the magical formula for a piece of sound to be successful is still the same: content. Content is about storytelling, and the blindness of the medium is exploited in the sense that every imagined space, situation, character or timeline can be portrayed in sound. The code of radio drama, based on voice, music, effects and silence being sequenced or simultaneous and taking certain combined perspectives, should be the lexicon of every script. However, we all know this code of communication is enriched daily as long as quality radio and quality productions such as *The Archers* are made. This code is all but exclusively iconic, so it can be imagined. Indeed, radio can be literal, concrete, specific and visual, as much as abstract, complex and literary. Finally, we strongly believe that, through storytelling, content based on emotions can be the basis for other radio genres to progress: news, sport, magazines, debates or advertising should take advantage of this communicative visibility for the benefit of information, entertainment and persuasion.

References

Arnot, C (2010) 'The Archers at 60', *The Guardian*, 6 October.

Brindle, D (2011) 'Young people log on for shared headspace', *The Guardian*, 9 February.

Barea, P (2000) *Teatro de los sonidos, sonidos del teatro: Teatro-radio-teatro, ida y vuelta,* Bilbao: Universidad del País Vasco.

BBC blog (2013) 'Six diamond decades'.
http://www.bbc.co.uk/blogs/thearchers/posts/six_diamond_decades_-_the_1990

Crook, T (1999) *Radio Drama: Theory and Practice,* London: Routledge.

Fuzellier, E (1965) *Le Langage radiophonique,* Paris: Institut des Hautes Etudes Cinématographiques.

Gibson, O (2007) '*The Archers* becomes an everyday story for iPod folk', *Guardian.co.uk.* http://www.guardian.co.uk/media/2007/oct/13/radio.apple

Herschmann, M & Kischinhevsky, M (2008) 'A "geração podcasting" e os novos usos do rádio na sociedade do espetáculo e do entretenimento', *Revista Famecos,* volume 37.

Kelly, W (2006) 'Podcasting drama: The golden days of radio serials are returning'.
http://blogcritics.org/scitech/article/podcasting-drama-the-golden-days-of

Lewis, P (1981) *Radio Drama,* New York: Longman.

Reeve, D & Aggleton, J (1998) 'On the specificity of expert knowledge about a soap opera: an everyday story of farming folk', *Applied Cognitive Psychology,* volume 12.

Reynolds, G (2009) 'Norman Painting's death marks the end of an era in Ambridge', *The Telegraph,* 30 October.

Rodero, E (2011) 'Welcome to pod-drama-cast and to a new listening experience: The virtual community of The Archers', *Comunicaçao e Sociedade,* volume 20.

Rodero, E (2012) 'Stimulating the imagination in a radio story: The role of presentation structure and the degree of involvement of the listener', *Journal of Radio and Audio Media,* volume 19, issue 1.

Rodero, E & Soengas, X (2010) *Radio drama, how to tell a story on radio,* Madrid: IORTV.

Rodero, E (2005) *Radio Production,* Madrid: Cátedra.

Thomas, L (2009) 'The Archers: an everyday story of old and new media', *The Radio Journal. International Studies in Broadcast and Audio Media,* volume 7, issue1.

Toye, J (1998) *The Archers 1951-1967: Family Ties,* London: BBC.

Chapter 15

Free and community radio in Spain: Waves in a global village

Carmen Peñafiel

Abstract

This chapter discusses from an historical perspective the origin, evolution and current status of free and community radio in Spain. It is a history that has led to the development of a range of different collaborative initiatives across the country. They include federations of free broadcasters, such as in Aragón, free broadcaster coordinators, such as in Cataluña, free broadcast networks as in Galicia and Valencia province, and federated and non-federated broadcasters as in Madrid, as well as a number of different approaches in Andalucía, Euskadi and elsewhere. The history of free radio in Spain has nonetheless been one of a heterogeneous movement with common goals and defined objectives. The chapter will focus on the role of these third sector broadcasters within the media landscape in Spain, where 75 per cent of broadcasters are owned by big companies, of which 75-95 per cent have national audiences.

Keywords: free radio, community radio, radio history, internet, Spain

Introduction

Free radio has been understood as an independent and non-profit form of broadcasting, whose management and programming decisions are made collectively. Such stations are not promoted by public, private or other types of commercial institutions, but by groups of people or non-profit associations. The concept comes from the experiences of the free radio stations in Italy and France that began broadcasting in the 1970s. The history of Italian free radio stations dates back to 1968 when the Danilo Dolci Group began clandestine broadcasting to denounce the deplorable living conditions of the residents of Belia, Sicily. In the 1970s the movement spread as a result of enormous social pressure, under which broadcasters emerged among different groups, such as ecologists, separatists, Christian Democrats and radicals. In 1979 there were already about 2,500 broadcasters in Italy. British pirate radio had no political links and stations concentrated their efforts on economic benefits. Free broadcasters in France appeared in response to a stream of aspirations, beliefs and social and moral changes of the sixties, which advocated a more direct voice and libertarian conditions (Cheval 2009). The phenomenon of free radio emerged later in Spain than in several other European countries. It was one that erupted spontaneously in the late 1970s in neighbourhoods of cities and towns as a means of giving a voice to minority groups, peaking in the first half of the 1980s. In 1987, with the passing of the new telecommunications law, many free radio stations were shut down. Currently, the number of free radio stations in Spain is fewer than one hundred. Significantly, the broadcasters of the third sector in Europe, both free and community, try to play an important social ideological role, demanding higher levels of participation and social justice in a global context (Chaparro 2008).

In France free stations emerged after the crisis of May 1968 and as an alternative media. In Italy, they spread as a means of expression for those groups who had never had a voice. However, in Great Britain they lacked political connections and focused their efforts on financial profit. In Spain they showed up on the radio dial as an alternative for minority groups and social movements who felt the need to express their views with freedom of expression which could not be found in conventional, legalised public or private broadcasting. According to Jean-Jacques Cheval, the free radio movement in France 'is also the emergence of an aspiration to speak out, with more direct speech that is free from constraints and more in line with the fears, aspirations, and social and moral changes of the 1960s. A reference point in an evolution that took place over several years, in an ambiguous situation, the place and the role of radio in the events of May of 1968 highlight the contradiction of a French media system that is reaching its end at the same time it announces, but does not realise, the changes of the 1970s and particularly the Free Radio stations of the future' (2009).

This study begins by providing an historical perspective, which is then complemented by an analysis of qualitative interviews with experts from community and free radio stations, interpreted in such a way that produces new knowledge about such third sector broadcasters. Six in-depth interviews of managers and employees of free radio stations were conducted between July and September 2013. Some of those interviewed preferred to remain anonymous or use a pseudonym. The chapter ends with an overview of the most recent legislation in Spain and a number of collaborative efforts to protect and preserve this third sector of broadcasting.

The Spanish radio landscape and the right to communicate

'The Spanish constitution recognises and protects the right to freely express and disseminate thoughts, ideas and opinions through words, writing, or any other means of reproduction, to freely communicate or receive truthful information by any media.' *Article 20.*

Free radio stations are contemporaries of the Spanish Constitution, being born just over 30 years ago. The ending of the news monopoly of the state broadcaster RNE in the late 1970s was taken advantage of by numerous citizen initiatives that were the driving force behind the creation of 'free' radio stations in 1979, following the European trends set by Italy and France. Most of these groups brought their concerns to local city councils when faced with forced closures and the seizure of equipment ordered by the Spanish government in the late 1980s. The first station in Spain to call for the freedom to broadcast and the right to communicate dates back to 1970 in Barcelona with the creation of Onda Lliure. However, it was short-lived. It was closed four times and became a pioneer in the democratic struggle it would have with Onda Verde in Madrid, Radio Paraíso in Pamplona, and Radio Klara in Valencia, the main champion of a citizen movement that spoke out and expressed itself over the airwaves. The spirit of all free radio stations was inspired, no doubt, by the thoughts of Beltolt Brecht who said that: 'Radio would be the finest possible communication apparatus in public life, a vast network of pipes. That is to say, it would be if it knew how to receive as well as to transmit, how to let the listener speak as well as hear, how to bring him into a relationship instead of isolating him. It would be necessary for radio not only to be a means of dissemination but also a major means of communication for listeners' (1932). Brecht's suggestion of an active, citizen use of radio, dovetails with Enzensberger's, which is based on the proliferation and multiplication of the number of stations in order to increase the production of culture and information (1974), and both relate to social democratisation in the development of community radio broadcasting internationally.

The early history of community radio stations takes us further back to the workers' radio clubs in 1930s Germany, the popular Latin American stations, the liberation and independence stations in the Third World, and Paolo Freire's theories on popular education. These experiences fueled the development of community radio broadcasting around the world, giving rise to a participatory, democratic communication experience for the citizens in which UNESCO declared itself to have 'a special social interest due to its participatory practice, culture and promoting of human rights and pro-human development and sustainable democratic solidarity' (2013). In Spain, in the 1980s there was a boom in community radio linked to neighbourhoods, communities or eco-pacifism that, along with other cultural and social stations, initially emerged as a reaction to the trends of concentration and a response to some uniform news and cultural content that did not reflect the expressive diversity of society. In Spain the number of free radio stations currently remains small, although it has significantly increased as a result of greater tolerance. There are now approximately a hundred active free and community radio stations, which share the radio waves with other public, private, and municipal stations, as follows:

Private Three major private broadcasting groups, Prisa/Unión Radio, COPE and Onda Cero, plus numerous small, private and independent groups.

Public RNE (RTVE Group) covering the whole country; autonomous regional community radio stations licensed by the 17 autonomous communities of Spain, (such as Andalusia, Cataluña, Galicia and the Basque Country,) in an autonomous radio and television federation called FORTA; municipal stations licensed by various local and city government authorities.

Private, non-profitmaking A third sector of free and community radio stations.

The coordinator of free radio stations in Cataluña stated that: 'Free radio stations should not be simply all rolled into the so-called community media or non-profit sector. They are not stations broadcasting religious content, they do not have a political or financial group behind them that is seeking to obtain another station on the dial through an alleged "social project". Free radio stations give a voice to those who would otherwise not be heard combating sexism, xenophobia, and social exclusion and which, at its foundation, champions the right to communicate... However, it is worth mentioning the opinion of Guatemalan Frank La Rue, United Nations Rapporteur on the Promotion and Protection of the Freedom of Expression, who deemed it imperative that governments set aside at least one third of the radio spectrum for community and citizen media, (which would include a place for the free stations)' (Nodo50 2011).

The history of radio has been marked by the deregulation of the radio spectrum, leaving all the transfer processes at the discretion of the market and executive power. Ideological re-balancing and the intention to promote a more pluralistic map that favors radio diversity and supports local agendas have been failing in all calls for tenders. Hundreds of broadcasters have been unable to survive in a landscape monopolised by the centralisation of the advertising market and the combination of their interests with the stations. It is estimated that 41 per cent of commercial licenses are held by independent entrepreneurs, but they have clearly opted to rent their broadcasting slots to other stations. The most favoured of all in this transfer market has been Cadena SER, which has the biggest audiences among Spanish listeners in its different formats.

Free radio stations in Spain: alternative communication

'Radio Chicharra 102.4 FM is a free radio station. It does not depend on any company, political party, or other body. It is characterised by freedom and autonomy, both economically and ideologically. Its management and programming are created collectively.'

https://www.facebook.com/pages/Radio-Chicharra/122114251140701

The concept of free radio stations is understood to mean those that are promoted mostly by social groups, institutions or small-scale economic groups and make use of the airwaves without a broadcasting licence. In Spain the majority appeared between 1983 and 1986. Interviewed in July 2013, Ernesto Che Majara of Contrabanda FM in Barcelona, said: 'They were born at a time when it was vital to, on the one hand, broadcast and lend strength to grievances and more or less militant struggles, and on the other, provide a space for artistic expressions that were absent from other media. Hence their rapid spread in a multitude of neighborhoods and towns, at least in Cataluña'. José Luis Terrón suggested that free radio stations soon evolved into 'laboratories for testing new uses of radio language' and in Barcelona a range of different formats appeared, with some existing stations adopting ideas previously broadcast by the free radio stations. He said: '...free radios offered few formal innovations, and they were more as the result of spontaneity rather than of a calculated strategy. The differences are seen, more than ever, in the content, in the word' (1993). Therefore, free stations have been recognised as one of the clearest examples of the fundamental right to freedom of expression and recognised by such international institutions as UNESCO and the European Union. They have been legalised for decades in such countries as France, Italy and Holland.

As alternative media, the free and community radio stations in Spain have needed to defend and give a voice to a number of different values over the airwaves. These include widening participation and access through plurality of speech, giving citizens the ability to express themselves in the public sphere, promoting horizontal communication and environmental decentralisation and highlighting the concept of proximity to citizens. They were created by the people, for the people, often broadcasting content in different languages and using programme formats that in many cases would never be broadcast on conventional public service and commercial radio stations. By definition, a community station is one that has been created with the intention of favouring one community or population centre, whose main interest is its own social and cultural development. Some assumed great importance in autonomous communities, such as Andalusia and Cataluña, until legal proceedings were initiated by the department of transportation and telecommunications, which resulted in their closure in 1989. At present, some free stations stream on the internet where no licence is needed, so they can reach many more people than before and have a broader reach, although their goal is to continue broadcasting localised content and report on issues concerning citizens. Manuel Chaparro, a professor at the University of Malaga and director of the municipal broadcasters association of Andalusia, commented that: 'Radio stations in the non-profit sector in Europe try to play an important role in social re-ideologisation, demanding greater levels of participation and social justice in a global framework' (2008).

The Spanish audiovisual law allows for regulating and recognising the existence of free and community media, intellectual property rights and management companies, technological advances, social networks and the involvement of social movements and participation in non-profit sector media. Free radio stations are characterised as being self-managed, non-profit projects that offer local programming with a strong focus on citizens that promotes citizen involvement. Generally, they are projects that have a certain complicity with social and/or cultural organisations in a local environment. They are popular media fulfilling a strong public service obligation to the community in disseminating information. In their programming they include music programmes that build bridges between the alternative music groups from different countries and regions. In their self-management system, they also govern themselves horizontally with a collective decision-making system. They are primarily funded by membership fees, with no advertising or dependency on external financing, and under the guidelines of their own members, who accept certain bylaws, pay a fee, and contribute some of their time to joint activities. Their activities are based on the work of volunteers and professionals dedicated to these communication projects. They are usually low power stations with a small geographical coverage, however, thanks to the internet, they form collective networks and larger movements. One can say that the free stations add 'color' to the radio dial, making it more pluralistic.

Interviewed during the summer of 2013, Javier Serrano of *Radio Topo-Zaragoza* stated that: 'Most of the free stations still have this theoretical and organisational point of view, with the original principles regarding self-management, non-professionalisation, independence from institutions or parties, commitment to society and no advertising. We continue to be funded by membership fees and joint ventures. Using this system, we have managed to cover our expenses and rent, and continue to improve our equipment. We haven't hired any staff nor requested subsidies to cover their wages, and we have opted to take much less advertising or commercial sponsorship than we could take'. Their primary objective is to try to give the public the ability to transmit and receive ideas, tastes, and concerns directly from other citizens as well as participate in the formation of public opinion that is free, supportive, and aware, far from the major power groups. Javier Serrano stated that: 'If we were to talk about a common goal for everyone, it would be to maintain a channel of communication between citizens'.

Meanwhile, Victor Lopez of Radio La Granja, in Zaragoza, considered that: '...freedom of expression is the most important thing. Offering an opinion over the airwaves, as long as it is non-violent, respects human rights, and is not xenophobic, is essential for participating in a radio station like ours'. Social and cultural projects are common. Programmes are made by groups in society to spread their own initiatives and alternative activities. Examples include the internationalist committee for solidarity, Colectivo Pedalea, the trade union CGT, the Gusantina occupational workshop (for children), the prisoners' support association of Aragon (ASAPA), AISA (Association of Sahrawi Immigrants), *Bloque Independentista de Cuchas*, Stop, and DRY. There are also programmes that involve different groups in society, including people with mental health problems and migrants. Nonetheless, most of the programming is music and entertainment. These stations are also often involved in other external activities if they own large premises such as cinemas, theatres, lecture theatres, or concert venues. In some cases they also have digital magazines that are sent via email with reviews, comics, articles by individuals, poetry, and information about the station itself.

In the interviews we conducted, some managers of free radio stations criticised a number of ongoing challenges as adding problems to their work, including, according to Ernesto Che Majara, of Contrabanda FM, Barcelona, '...an ongoing battle with pirate commercial radio stations since they see us as the smallest fish in the pond and want to take our spot on the dial, the harassment of copyright management organisations, and the helplessness (at best) of public administration'. He continued: 'It is the greatest daily threat for Catalán right now, which is not to say that sometimes we don't have to deal with other problems'. Many of these free, community, and association stations have to leave the airwaves after many years of continuous broadcasting, due to financial problems and the difficulties that arise when attempting to achieve stability. This was the case with the veteran station Tas-Tas Irrati Librea, which was founded in 1992 with the intention of being the free radio station of the greater Bilbao area, but stopped broadcasting in 2013 after 21 years on the air. Tas-Tas was one of the stations which entered the competition sponsored by the Basque Government in 2006 for the allocation of 34 licences to broadcast on FM, but was unsuccessful. The station was the result of other horizontal communication projects, such as the alternative news agency *Tas-Tas* and free radio stations like *Iluna, Ortzadar, and Txomin Barullo*. Its programmes and activities were the work of both volunteers and professionals.

Adapting to new technologies

As with other sectors of the radio industry and other media, the free stations have undergone a dizzying technical evolution. They started building their own transmitters and now have adapted well to the new technologies. In general, technical standards have been reached that would have seemed incredible 20 years ago: they have seized the opportunities offered by audio management software, they use global communication networks for obtaining information, broadcasting, and exchanging programmes via streaming or podcasting and of course, they use free software, in many cases creating it. Víctor López at Radio La Granja said that: 'Now people listen to the radio a lot via the ivoox portal. Any time you want, you can download the programmes in excellent quality. We can see that active listeners are online'. Meanwhile, Ernesto Che Majara said: 'Although streaming has facilitated reaching more places or being able to broadcast from any space, it is still imperative to be present on the FM dial to reach people of all ages and social classes who are still not familiar with the internet. The free radio stations are still necessary because they maintain the immediacy that other media do not have, and at the same time, they have endless creative possibilities'. The development of audio broadcasting via the web has had a big impact on content. 'Sound already transforms voices, words, music into objects rich with representations. The disembodied voices of broadcasters already excite our imagination, curiosity and desire for more. They are related to the borders of sound that cannot become visible. Web radio loses the sound-centric nature of traditional radio broadcasting and this kind of convergence raises issues about the quality and the type of content' (Gazi, Starkey & Jedrzejewski 2011).

New legislation for community radio

'It is precisely through the active and peaceful involvement of the whole society in the country's democratic institutions in which the exercise of freedom of expression is fully manifest and enables the condition of marginalised sectors to improve.'

Advisory Opinion 5-85, Inter-American Court of Human Rights.

Social media have become vitally important in modern societies characterised by huge volumes of information, leading to the 'information society' and the 'knowledge society'. In the Spanish legal system, various forms of television and radio broadcasting services were regulated in terms of their geographic scope, the technology used, and other distinguishing characteristics. However, non-profit free radio stations had no place in the legal system and were in a 'legal limbo', so for thirty years they have been under threat of government shutdowns and vulnerabile to commercial stations. Until now, they lacked a legal framework that regulated their services. General audiovisual law is now a reality. Article 4.1 of the Spanish law on audiovisual communications now covers community audiovisual communications services, stating that: 'Everyone has the right for audiovisual communications to be provided through a plurality of media, whether it be public, commercial, or community, which reflect the ideological, political, and cultural pluralism of society'. Article 32 established a legal regime of not-for-profit, community audiovisual communications services. It not only recognises and protects the non-profit citizen stations, but also urges the state government to guarantee a publicly owned space on the dial for them and promote the exercise of citizens' rights to the freedom of expression through them.

This legal regime defines non-profit community audiovisual communications as: '...*those that are provided by private entities which are legally considered non-profit entities and which aim to address the social, cultural, and specific communication needs of social groups and communities and promote citizen involvement and the structuring of the associational fabric*'. To provide this type of service, a licence must be obtained beforehand, which is granted by public tender that is organised and determined by the competent body of the Autonomous Community. These licenses are granted for a period of fifteen years and the content to be broadcast shall always be open. The service area of non-profit community radio frequencies may not exceed the borders of the municipality concerned. For cities with more than 100,000 inhabitants, coverage may not exceed 20 per cent of the population. Each Autonomous Community has to fulfill its duties and develop specific regulations to ensure the existence of free radio stations and other citizen media, both now and in the future.

The Aragonese federation of free radio stations asked its regional government:

'To develop a census of non-profit communications initiatives that clearly set them apart from the commercial pirate stations or other types of stations with financial interests.

To develop regulations that guarantee the current and future existence of non-profit social communications projects in Aragon.

To consult with these communications projects, as stakeholders, regarding their needs, proposals, concerns, and technical constraints when it comes to developing regulations on non-profit citizen media in our autonomous community.

To have the Autonomous Community support the necessary technical upgrading of the existing free radio stations to meet the constraints arising from the aforementioned regulations with the technical and human resources they have.'

http://www.diagonalperiodico.net/aragon/Las-radios-libres-tenemosla.html

Many of the stakeholders closely related to the free radio stations felt that the enactment of this law is not enough. They acknowledge that the law has served to dignify the activity of these stations and recognise the altruistic nature of the people who with their hard work have made these alternative channels possible. This is a first step towards achieving some of the long-standing abitions of the free stations. There are many groups of cultural, community, and non-profit broadcasters in Spain that are raising their voices in protest due to the risks they face and their possible closure. These broadcasters have spent years demanding a fair and dignified legalisation of their status. They demand spaces and workshops to reflect on a new model of social, independent, and non-profit radio because they believe they are a necessary complement to the presence of public and private media. This is the case with fifteen radio stations in the union of cultural radio stations of Madrid. In the Canary Islands around 25 stations with an uncertain future formed the Canary Islands community radio stations federation (FERCCA). They all have in common intensive collaborative work based on voluntary participation, the promotion of access for all persons to the media spectrum and the goal of plurality of information and freedom of expression. The situation in the Canary Islands, which began with the passing of a royal decree in the summer of 2010, was preceded by similar conflicts in other regions. The most famous is the case of Madrid, where the supreme court rejected the awarding of licences due to a complaint by the community radio stations union. In a previous setback, the Supreme Court also repealed the local television decree of 2005. Currently, the free radio stations perceive a need to join together in associations or under coordinators to find common ground in the world of alternative communication. Hence, there have been joint projects between stations, programme exchanges, joint broadcasts and training projects, to name a few examples.

Other examples of collaborative work include: the association of public radio and television broadcasters of Andalusia (EMARTV), which has operated as an umbrella organisation for 20 years; the Aragonese federation of free radio stations; the coordinator of free radio stations in Catalonia, and the Galician network of free and community radio stations. The union of free and community radio stations of Madrid (URCM) promotes understanding among broadcasters to prevent unnecessary battles for the airwaves, thus facilitating broadcasting agreements for sharing frequencies that allow for complementarity for all stations. Its purpose is to get social radio stations to participate in a networking project that aims to create an alternative information space linked to social projects along with other organisations and social institutions. Thanks to the internet, much larger networks have also been formed in the Basque Country due to a more homogeneous culture there. These media share aspects of diversity and culture and share their own minority language. According to Gutierrez: 'Initiatives like Arrosa and NIES are understood within the context of these claims. In the first, several radio stations in the Basque Country have created a collective work network. Using a server, these stations exchange some programmes and produce others together. The first goal was for the project to go beyond that in order to make programmes as a producer, but this required a solid structure and a large investment and, although the idea hasn't been rejected, it has not yet been possible to carry it out. They have a website which, in addition to information about the network, offers the audience the opportunity to access the programming of all of the radio stations broadcasting on the internet, (and not on the air,) as well as each station's website' (2008).

Conclusions

Free radio stations play a substantial role in society, at least for certain parts of society that want to express their concerns and make their voice heard through the media without any intermediaries or economic, political, social, or spatial limitations. True free radio not only makes contributions to society, but also thrives on it. Free radio stations are a thermometer of social movements. When they are on the rise, it is because society is active and transforming. Social movements seek speakers and convergence points for their own independent ideas, such as free radio stations. They develop in programming and impact, driven by that rise in grassroots social activity. Radio is the only common broadcasting platform for the groups involved in it, both inside and outside the station. The social groups that make up the station and the struggles and mobilisations that, at each moment, have carried it forward set the content. Some still exist, others have disappeared and others are new.

There is also an important aspect to programmes that give a voice to social concerns or movements. Examples include the feminist movement, immigrants' struggles, the environmental movement, anti-repression, Occupy, anti-militarism and labour struggles. There is also a very important aspect that is focused on disseminating artistic and cultural expressions which in practice find no place on conventional radio stations. They are primarily funded by fees from members, those who work on the programmes and support organisations and, occasionally, organise events and sell merchandise. Free radio stations open up a space where people can comment and participate with fewer restrictions. They are self-managed and people who want to communicate can participate without being a journalist. They are characterised by collectivism, self-management of the content, and independence from any financial or political pressure group. Currently there are a greater number of faultlines and battlefronts in society, which obviously free radio stations echo. These are mainly stations that are located on the internet. In recent years, they have joined different types of associations in order to strengthen their position.

In short, they are stations that, despite all the adversities they face, continue to have the same principles as three decades ago, promoting citizen involvement. They are stations that are far removed from the mainstream media and economic power. They give a voice to numerous citizen movements. They have been introduced to the digital domain via the internet. They provide a reference point in their coverage that has adapted to the current circumstances by promoting cultural and social activities. These are broadcasters that promote citizen involvement and they are financed in a variety of ways, with the contributions of partners and activities supported by an extreme form of extended citizenship. Free radio stations have joined with community radio stations in different kinds of associations.

'I disagree with what you say, but I will defend to the death your right to say it.'

Javier Serrano, Radio Topo-Zaragoza

References

Brecht, B (1932) 'Teoría de la radio', reproduced in *Revista de Economía Política de las Tecnologías de la Información y Comunicación*, volume 5, issue 2.

Carpentier, N (2007) 'The on-line community media database: Radio stationswap as a trans local tool to broaden the communicative rhizone', *Observatorio,* issue 1.

Chaparro Escudero, M (2013) 'Construcción de un imaginario perverso: la comunicación del desarrollo', *Telos*, issue 94.

Chaparro, M. (2009) 'Comunicación para el empoderamiento y comunicación ecosocial. La necesaria creación de nuevos imaginarios', *Perspectivas de la Comunicación*, volume 2, issue 1.

Chaparro, Manuel (2008) 'Los déficit democráticos de los medios audiovisuales', in Del Valle, C (ed) *Contrapuntos y entrelíneas sobre cultura, comunicación y discurso,* Chile: Universidad de la Frontera.

Chaparro, M (2007) 'Los déficit democráticos de los medios audiovisuales' in Peñafiel, C (ed), *Transformaciones de la radio y la televisión en Europa*, Bilbao: UPV/EHU.

Cheval, J-J (2009) 'Mai 68, un entre deux Dans l'histoire de la radio en France', *Comunicación,* issue 26.

Cheval, J-J (2008) 'La radio, parôles données, paroles à prendre', *Mediamorphoses,* issue 23, Paris: INA.

Day, R (ed) (2007) *Bicycle highway: celebrating community radio in Ireland*, Dublin: The Liffey Press.

Day, R (2009) *Community radio in Ireland: Participation and multi-flows of Communications.* Cresskill: Hampton Press.

Dexter, L (1970) *Elite and specialized interviewing,* Evaston: Northwestern University.

Enzensberger, H (1974) *Elementos para una teoría de los medios de comunicación,* Barcelona: Anagrama.

Gazi, A, Starkey, G & Jedrzejewski, S (2011) *Radio Content In The Digital Age. The Evolution of a Sound Medium*, Bristol: Intellect.

Gutiérrez, M (2008) 'En el mapa radiofónico de Euskal Herria predominan las cadenas estatales y el castellano', Euskonews.com, May 30.

Nodo50 (2011) 'Catalunya: La Coordinadora de Radios Libres frente a los gigantes', 1 January. http://info.nodo50.org/Catalunya-La-Coordinadora-de.html

Palomé, P (2009) *Les médias sur internet*, Toulouse: Milan.

Peñafiel, C & Palazio, G (2009) 'El periodismo digital móvil en la época de la multiplicidad de emisores', in Pérez Herrero, P, Rivas Nieto, P & Gelado Marcos, R, *Periodismo ciudadano, posibilidades y riesgos para el discurso informativo*, *Estudios de Periodística XIV*, Salamanca.

Peñafiel, C (2007) 'Los retos de la radio en el entorno multimedia', in *Transformaciones de la radio y la televisión en Europa*, Bilbao: UPV/EHU.

Rede Galega de Radios Libres (2013). http://radioengalicia.blogspot.com.es/2013/10/rede-galega-de-radios-libres-e.html

Santos, M & Pérez da Silva, J (2011) 'Ondas libres en el Gran Bilbao : el salto de la radio tradicional a la red', paper at the third Congreso Internacional de Ciberperiodismo y Web 2.0: La transformación del espacio mediático, Bilbao.

Taylor, S & Bogdan, R (1987) *Introducción a los métodos cualitativos de investigación: La búsqueda de significado,* Barcelona: Paidós Básica.

Terrón, J (1993) 'Ràdios Lliures : 15 anys recorrent el buit', *Annals del periodisme catalan,* issue 23.

Vallés, M (1999) *Técnicas cualitativas de investigación social. Reflexión metodológica y práctica profesional,* Madrid: Síntesis.

UNESCO (2013) 'World Radio Day' http://www.unesco.org/new/es/world-radio-day (13/02/2013)

Chapter 16

Public broadcasting in Brazil: Images and perspectives of the audience - challenges to overcome the passive symbolic and achieve social credibility

Carlos Eduardo Esch and Nélia R. Del Bianco

Abstract

One of the biggest challenges for Brazilian public broadcasting lies in changing public perceptions of such stations. This chapter will explain how an initial analysis of data obtained in an ongoing research project shows that respondents tend to have negative images of public media. At times they are in favour of the principles that should define the performance of public radio stations and television channels, such as diversity, independence and differentiation from commercial media, but which are not always followed. At other times they criticise the quality of programming and the way these stations are not simply run by the state, but are seen to be *of* the state, in that they are widely perceived as closely associated with the government. Within such a critical context, the chapter presents a discussion of the challenges facing the public broadcasting sector in Brazil, considering the complex circumstances around history, culture and economic policy that have contributed to the continuation of this 'symbolic liability' between media and the audience as citizens. The chapter also reflects on some possible strategies to address the problem.

Keywords: public broadcasting, Observatory of Public Broadcasting, audience, symbolic liability, Brazil

Introduction

Change and change quickly. That is probably the biggest challenge currently faced by the Brazilian public media, as identified by listeners and viewers who participated in research entitled Citizens and Public Media, conducted by the Observatory of Public Broadcasting in Latin America. The investigation began in July 2012 and it will continue until the end of 2015. The objective is to evaluate the level of satisfaction of Brazilian citizens regarding radio and television belonging to the public domain. For this, we created a virtual research platform, available 24 hours a day, containing a list of open and closed questions on four main themes: the amount and nature of media usage by respondents; the share of that usage achieved by public media; the levels of participant satisfaction in relation to the programming and the programmes offered, and the image of public radio and television in the minds of the audience. At the time of writing, 548 people had participated in the research. The goal is to achieve a sample of two thousand people through wide dissemination including through social networking sites and non-governmental bodies related to the protection of the democratic nature of communication in general and public radio and television broadcasting in particular. As respondents are self-selecting, without the establishment of quotas by age, education or place of residence, the largest group of respondents so far, 46.8 per cent, are 20 to 35 years old. In total 34.6 per cent live in the south east, the most developed region of the country, and 42.9 per cent in the midwest. In terms of social class, 37 per cent of them have a monthly household income between one to three thousand dollars. Most have a relatively high level of schooling compared to the Brazilian national average, that is, higher education.

The first stage of information gathering and analysis allows us to discuss the image of the Brazilian public radio and television stations among a segment of a relatively young audience with a high level of schooling and income, allowing us to draw some significant conclusions. It can be argued, based on preliminary data, that there is a huge symbolic liability in the relationship between public media and the audience in Brazil. The image of public radio and television has always been tied to government. While some of them have made efforts in the last 10 years to be bound by the principles of independence and diversity and offer differentiated content through renewed programming, brand repositioning and the establishment of mechanisms for social participation in management, the audience still perceives them as being of inferior quality and lacking in credibility. From the data collected, it is evident that the audience still resists changing the perspectives they have about these media, which are consolidated in the collective mind, a denial that prevents them from realising the extent of the changes underway. This image of government has historical origins and to change this situation, which we call 'symbolic liability', requires change to be effected by managers, strategists and the production professionals of public broadcasting stations.

A brief context of public broadcasting in Latin America

For more than 80 years, in Latin America public broadcasting has been perceived, particularly in Brazil, as a synonym for government media. In most countries in the continent, the concept of public broadcasting applied to the stations has been built by the operators of the communication channels under the control of government agencies belonging to the world of public administration. Public broadcasting systems were structured in the subcontinent based on two traditions, either a public system associated with the educational and cultural sectors or one that is connected to the government and state agenda. In an analysis of the situation of public media in the sub-continent, the Chilean researcher Valerius Fuenzalida (1998) identified three structural reasons for the crisis that hit the sector with greater intensity in the 1990s. Firstly, mismanagement due to an executive board subject to political interference, which generated discontinuity of goals, several cases of corruption and irresponsibility with impunity. Secondly, a lack of economic sustainability, exacerbated by a strategy of subsisting, ignoring the interests of the audience and not establishing mechanisms to diversify the financing. Thirdly, unattractive programming, of appeal only to marginal audiences, which does not attract many listeners. According to Fuenzalida, in the context of the 1990s, in which the administrative capacity of the state was not trusted, there was no political support for investment proposals using public money on inefficiently operated channels with audiences too small to justify such spending. The structures of public broadcasting were traditionally on the margin of investment policies and government budgets. This occurred over time and continues to happen for lack of financial capacity, lack of strategic vision, projects and government planning or, in more severe cases, the adoption of policies that offer favours and privileges to private media based on large entrepreneurial conglomerates.

Another aspect to be considered is that the state-funded broadcasting station emerges as a 'private place' in contexts where the mediatic structure works harder for the benefit of the political group that controls a transitional government and to the detriment of the real interests of the population. This occurs in broadcasting stations due to four reasons: the absence of a culture of public practices and policies supported by procedures and actions that are effectively democratic and encourage the consolidation of public values; the absence of a set of professional rules that would protect the public communication structures from influences and political excesses of the time; the lack of interest in promoting legislation that would ensure economic independence and reliable financial arrangements included in government budgets, and finally inadequate professionalisation of the technical, managerial and operational staff in the public stations. We should also remember that in the early twentieth century, with the rise to power or reaffirmation of power of governments from left wing parties, such as in Brazil, Bolivia, Paraguay and Ecuador, the process of reorganising educational, cultural or state channels began bringing them closer to precepts that characterise them as public services. Despite the conflicts and resistances observed in each national context, it is clear that there are consistent attempts to implement changes, some modest but others bold, in the regulatory frameworks in several countries and in the reorganisation of the management of broadcasting stations. This process of transformation is an indicator of the degree of preparedness of each country in establishing a social consensus around the proposition of a public service of independent and democratic communication.

The Brazilian public broadcasting system seems at present paradoxical. On the one hand, it has intensified the discussions about the role that public radio and television stations, funded by government resources, should have in Brazilian society and about the limits of the influence that governments should exert on these media. On the other hand, the social context is one marked by the unawareness, rejection and prejudice of most citizens, of and towards the real role that has been played by government and the public sector throughout history, and even about the imagined possibilities for the future. With the coming into office of Luiz Inácio Lula da Silva (2003-2010), the government tried to promote, together with civil society organisations, actions with the aim of redirecting the discussion on the role and functioning of the means of communication in Brazil. Although in 2009 the government had supported the creation of the first national conference of communication in the country, the proposal for a regulatory framework approved at that meeting, which had an attendance of more than 1,200 people has not yet been enacted in law. In the sphere of public broadcasting, the creation of the Brazilian communication company (EBC) in 2007 can be considered a milestone in this process. With the approval of the law creating the company, the government could set goals and principles that would govern the behaviour of broadcasting services operated by the federal executive branch. Among its objectives are: to provide mechanisms for public debate on issues of national and international relevance; developing critical awareness of citizens through educational, artistic, cultural, informational and scientific programming; to support processes of social inclusion and socialisation of the production of knowledge, ensuring spaces display regional and independent production; to seek excellence in content and language and develop creative and innovative formats, becoming a centre of innovation and talent training, directing their production and programming for educational, artistic, cultural, informational and scientific aims, and promoting citizenship, without detracting from their competitive nature in seeking the greatest number of listeners or viewers.

The institutional model of EBC includes mechanisms typical of public broadcasting. The company's management is focused primarily on the existence of three councils, administrative, financial and curatorial, and an executive boardroom. The idea is that the councils regulate each other and regulate the operation of the company - financially, administratively, and especially in relation to the fulfillment of its social commitment in the production and transmission of content or the availability of its television capacity. The Board of Trustees is the deliberative body within the management structure of the company. Among its duties are the approval of the annual work plan of the company, the ratification and monitoring of the implementation of the editorial line and monitoring the programming, as well as making recommendations. Their members, especially the Board of Trustees, are representatives of civil society with direct involvement in the operation of the station. Despite fighting for editorial autonomy from the government, the close relationship with the executive is evident because the CEO and general manager of the company is directly appointed by the president. The government also holds a majority of seats on two of the three councils. At the same time their sustainability through public funds faces resistance. The law creating the EBC predicted that its funding be made up in part by a subsidy from the Telecommunications Supervision Fund. Besides its representing a new tax for operators, telephone companies in Brazil filed a direct action of unconstitutionality to question the use of financial resources allocated for telecommunications for public broadcasting. The action remains pending in court awaiting the final decision. Meanwhile, the EBC remains dependent on the resources of the Treasury, prevented from advertising goods and services from private companies, despite carrying advertising for public agencies and receiving support for some cultural productions.

Admittedly, the EBC is an important example of what occurs in public broadcasting in Brazil, but it signifies just a small portion of the system. In the country about 200 radio stations and 90 television channels are operating, linked to such institutions of political power as the state and local governments, as well as public universities. Channels are defined by Brazilian law as exclusively for educational purposes, neither being commercial in character, nor being for profit. According to the analysis of the Observatory of Public Broadcasting of the operating and management model covering 30 television stations and 70 radio stations in the country, most of them work much more like government institutions than independent entities that have closer ties with the population, who participate in them, and in which some of the citizens perceive their interests to be reflected in the content of the programmes offered (Bianco, Esch & Moreira 2012). Apart from the EBC, only four other public companies and foundations were identified in the country, which established councils with representatives of civil society in a position to oversee the management of the stations. The operation of these councils is not always transparent, with, for example, clear criteria for choosing representatives from civil society or disseminating the minutes of meetings. It was also noted that although the legislation creating EBC had established such principles of action guided by public interest as autonomy, independence, diversity of content and social participation, stations subordinate to federal institutions, like public universities, for example, had not substantially changed their organisation or management. In the analysis of the functioning and the routines of the institutions it is clear that there is a 'deficit' between the regulatory framework of some broadcasting stations and the way they function on a practical day-to-day basis. Many still retain a strong relationship with the government that is directly responsible for their funding, thus perpetuating their dependence on a system built on political and editorial subordination.

Understanding what the audience thinks

To understand the meaning of the image lag between public media and the audience, we start from a perspective analysis that considers the conditions of origin and operation of public radios and televisions, their actions, schedules, productions and their own historical trajectory in a social context constructed from interaction amongst its members and institutions. This interaction occurs at different levels and in different ways, but it is fundamentally the characteristic that marks life in society and living in groups. The relationship between public media and the audience is immersed in the field of interactions that occur in everyday life. It is part of a larger phenomenon that characterises contemporary societies based on the presence of the strong and progressive electronic communication that occurs in contemporary society.

The fundamental idea from which our analysis started is that of interaction. Etymologically, the word interaction expresses primarily the notion of developing a mutual action, that is, it assumes reciprocity among all those who participate in it. In a relationship it is not enough to perceive the other to establish interaction. A change in the perception of the subjects who appreciate means of communication should be effected, taking into account what the subjects who observe offer, faced with the action of using the media. Likewise, the fact that the subjects studied feel they have been observed, may make them wish to change their appearance, change their attitude, the way they talk, their conduct or any other element that serves as a reference for judgments made by the subjects who perceive, changing their perception. In short, this continuous process of observation and response underlies the relationship that unites the media, whichever it might be, and their audiences as possible consumer segments. Therefore, it can be seen that interaction is essentially a dialectical relationship because the nature of the feedback of the action between the parties involved allows interaction to be the moment in which social relations are reproduced and updated continuously. It can also be a space for intervention and innovation and where, at each moment, it is grounded in and reshapes social ties (Mead 1982). These ties shape society based on the activities of social groups formed by a variety of individual consciences, which act and react on one another from the established communication.

It is the existence of these actions and their consequent reactions, namely the set of interactions established, in which we recognise a particular society (Mauss 1969: 141). Therefore, interaction can be seen as a 'total social phenomenon' in the sense that Mauss understood a phenomenon implicated in the whole of society and its various institutions that interact concurrently in psychological, cultural and social dimensions. This perspective developed by symbolic interactionism is based on three assumptions. The first considers that human beings acquire a position faced by the things that they come across in the world, according to what these things mean to them. The second is that the meanings acquired by such things are the result of the social interaction that each of us has with the others who share the same social space. And finally, the third assumption states that meanings emerging from these interactions are manipulated and changed through a process of interpretation performed by the people, as they confront the universe composed of things deriving from their living as human beings (Blumer 1982: 12; Perrotta 1988: 30-31 and Baert 2001: 91-92). The interactionist view holds that meaning does not emanate from the object and neither does it 'sprout' from the perception of human beings, but it is the result of a process of interaction amongst individuals. In this process, the meaning that one thing carries for a person is the result of the different ways in which other people act in his or her presence in relation to that thing. The acts of others produce the effect of defining the thing for this person (Ritzer 2002). In other words, for symbolic interactionism the meaning is mainly socially constituted by means of a set of defining actions that are performed by individuals as they interact (Mead 1982: 81). Given this perspective, so as to clarify the circumstances around the establishment of images by Brazilian citizens about public means of communication, it is necessary to bear in mind, firstly, the procedural nature of the communicative everyday action of radio and television broadcasting stations. On speaking of images, we are referring to the senses that emerge from a daily, continuous and historical performance, in which the means of communication are brought face to face over time with a series of situations and facts that occur in the world and invade - or not - programmes and programming in the form of news, opinions and even content derived from the audience itself.

Thus, the media elaborate on a number of meanings about all these events, which feed the daily mediatic discourse transmitted to listeners and viewers. Throughout this process images and symbolism are also composed, tied to the media and constituted from what the audiences of these media think, believe, criticise and praise. The development of these images and the burden of meanings that they contain can be understood from two resulting moments. The first has to do with how the media operate and hence with the potential roles they perform for the public. The significance that each medium develops for the public is the direct result of a dynamic process of evaluation that the audience performs about what is done by the medium – what it offers, defends or omits in its programming and how it does it. The second belongs exclusively to the audience and emerges from this process of appreciation in which each of its members, based on their needs and valuations, assigns the meanings that the media and its programmes take on in the context of individual experiences. This phenomenon of the constitution of symbolic representations corroborates the idea that the fundamental characteristic of humanity and the processes that shape social life is the use of a variety of symbols with different degrees of complexity (Saperas 1998: 136). The communication performed by the media is not abandoned. Rather, it presents itself as an action of the senses and is characterised as a further instance in the social process, in which a series of reciprocal relationships amongst individuals and institutions are continuously established, including those that are mediatic. In this context, media and audience interact with facts, people, ideas and situations that end up somehow regularising attitudes, positions and behaviours that both may adopt. From this, it follows that because of differences in the contexts and individual and collective processes of social interaction, a greater or lesser acceptance of the media themselves and what they present their audiences can be produced.

Therefore it is true that the tone of the actions, programming and products that they produce ultimately influences, favorably or not, the emergence of feelings of respect, admiration, evaluation and approval by the public in relation to certain radio or television stations. Ultimately, let us remember that the programmes are produced and broadcast in different social environments with significant variations of needs and desires on the part of an audience that is segmented by multiple differences. Thus, it is in the midst of these complex interactive dynamics established among various actors of the social scene - here represented by listeners/viewers and the public media - that 'meet' in the discursive spaces prepared by their programming, where mediatic actions are set and acquire meaning and establish their real and/or symbolic repercussions. And it was to reveal some of the meanings that shape the image of the public media that we set out to hear the Brazilian public, their ideas and concepts about this particular mediatic universe.

Levels of satisfaction of the audience with the public media

The relationship between public media and audience encompasses 'fundamental' interaction that is established in the context of media usage. Among the participants of the survey, it can be observed that the internet and mobile telephones have become the newest platforms for listening to music, acquiring information and entertainment previously only offered by traditional media. While 97 per cent used the internet daily and 93 per cent used cellphones, the levels of watching broadcast television (57 per cent), cable television (50 per cent) and radio (46 per cent) fell by almost half. This is an audience that uses the internet anywhere: at home, at work, at school and in public places. On radio, their interest is listening to music and news. While on broadcast television the preference is for news, on cable television the largest use is of movies, documentaries and international series. The level of importance attributed to the media by the respondents was between 3 and 5 on a *Likert* scale where 1 is unimportant and 5 very important. The internet was the most rated as very important level in everyday life (87 per cent), followed by mobile phones (66 per cent). Regarding their use of public media there were significant differences from the answers provided about commercial media. When asked what the first idea that comes to mind was, of public radio and television, two-thirds made negative comments because they believed these media to be historically linked to governments. Examples included:

'A place of government politicking.'

'A place of shameless advertising by governments.'

'Directed programming for the government of the moment.'

'They are extremely controlling in nature, being anything but public.'

'They are focused on transmitting news on what interests the government.'

'All façade. They should be reliable and more independent than the private media, but this is not reality.'

'Despite being public, they are broadcasting stations controlled by the government.'

'They are broadcasting stations connected to the government and their policies of opportunism, but not the least public.'

'The majority of the programmes are bad, focused on a not very critical audience with the aim of promoting the government.'

These perceptions are formed from a low level of use of public media itself. While the large numbers regularly watched television (54 per cent) and listened to commercial radio (29 per cent), 41 per cent declared they watch public television only sometimes and 27 per cent said they rarely listened to public radio stations. The low frequency of public media usage is significant: 52 per cent watch television and 41 per cent listen to public radio upto three times per week. However, it should be stressed that nearly 30 per cent said they never listen to public radio and 18 per cent never watch public television. Although this sample is not the entire audience, it made negative comments about public media. It is likely that this opinion has been formed over a length of time, and assumptions about public media as government-controlled may be hard to dispel. Most of the participants of the survey believed that public media do not represent them, yet many had strong opinions as to how these media should act. For example, some respondents said:

'They should be creative communication tools that act according to the public interest; something difficult in our country.'

'They should be spaces where the voice of the community has a seat. Or rather, where the media focus on the production of content that would enhance society.'

'From my point of view, they should be broadcasting stations that disseminate programming that is alternative to that already available. The very few that exist in Brazil should be more democratic, which is something that does not exist in our country.'

'I think they should be a means of communication that disseminates actions and products aimed at public interest, such as educational, cultural and citizenship action and products... they are still lacking in Brazil.'

'They should be creative places for freedom of speech.'

Based on the research it was also possible to interpret a third way of criticism of public media, now associated with the language adopted by programmes that are part of their schedules. Generally speaking, 41.4 per cent of those who listen to the radio and almost half, 48.8 per cent, of those who watch public television say they are partially satisfied.

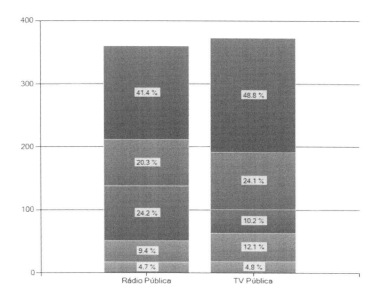

Figure 16.1: Levels of satisfaction with the quality of educational and cultural content on Brazillian public radio and television. (Shading shows, in descending order, partially satisfied, satisfied, no opinion, partially unsatisfied and unsatisfied.)

Those who watched public television frequently said they were partially satisfied with news (48 per cent), interview programmes (41 per cent), films (36 per cent) and documentaries (35 per cent). As for radio, they said they were satisfied (42 per cent) only with the musical programming. In relation to the journalistic programmes, the majority were partially satisfied with news (38.4 per cent) and interview programmes (38.1 per cent). The partial satisfaction could be explained by the perception that the programming is not appealing to them. Some of the respondents commented:

'Boring and dull.'

'Poor quality programming.'

'Programme schedules with little diversity or investment.'

'Boring and tedious programmes.'

'Broadcasting stations with poor programming, as well as being boring.'

'Public radio stations do not appeal to listeners in the way they are produced and transmitted, becoming tiresome. Public TV only serves niche interests and therefore ends up being accessed only, and merely when you share that minority interest.'

'The standard of both TV and radio is very like that of other stations. They need to be more daring, to invest in languages, to produce content in partnerships, such as real movies and animation, to be open to people with new proposals, to innovate, to renovate, to have the courage to actually reflect the communities they serve, warts and all. They need to invest in and stimulate Brazilian audiovisual production.'

Journalism in public broadcasting stations was criticised by the audience for not offering substantial and significant news that could be an alternative to that found in commercial media companies. When asked if their journalism was of good quality, 47 per cent said they agreed partially. They agreed with such statements as 'discusses topics of interest to the population' (44 per cent), 'discusses topics of interest to the government' (34 per cent), 'offers different perspectives in news' (36 per cent) and 'it is impartial' (26 per cent). The lack of editorial independence is seen as a problem for half of the participants who said they watch public television. Some typical responses were:

'Journalism and talk shows on television *Cultura* have the tradition of being of excellent quality, but in recent years have proven to be biased in favor of the state government of São Paulo, having deteriorated more since mid-2012.'

'TV *Brasil* still presents a large amount of coverage for the Dilma government.'

'I see the same standard of journalism as on private commercial stations. There is a lack of boldness and being open to experimentation. They should encourage more national coverage with emphasis on the news of all the regions of Brazil.'

Although criticism was made based on the idea that the broadcasting stations should follow the principles of diversity, independence and plurality of views, the audience recognised the merits of the programming. For example, the majority observed that neither public television nor public radio showed tabloid-type programmes (58 per cent), that the content of the programming was varied (37 per cent) and that with news they could still manage a deeper approach than the commercial stations (30 per cent).

Defending public media in democratic societies

Broadcasting in Brazil was structured around the commercial stations because of a contiguous relationship established between media companies and political agents. This proximity allowed, over time, the development of a system of public concessions operated for the interests and convenience of the political parties, whether in obtaining tax incentives and subsidies, privileged participation in the distribution of government advertising budgets, obtaining benefits from the targeted development of telecommunication infrastructure and the establishment of regulatory acts that ensured the free flow of capital. The symbiotic model between communication and politics favored a strong concentration of economic, political and symbolic power in the hands of private entities. In contrast to the hegemony of private media, public stations remained in the background, a condition exacerbated by, in particular, the coupling of government broadcasting stations, lack of investment in infrastructure and for the production of content, as well as structural and bureaucratic difficulties in renewing professional staff. While this environment of exclusion has contributed to the establishment of negative public perceptions, respondents understood (68 per cent) that public radio and television stations are important for democracy and therefore their existence should be supported and guaranteed. Almost half (45 per cent) recognised a significant difference in quality between the schedules of public television and radio stations and their commercial counterparts. They believed that there is potential in this sector to offer diversity of content about Brazilian culture (41 per cent), presenting programmes that increase knowledge about Brazil and viewers' own cities (43 per cent) and, finally, they believed that the public broadcasting stations are also capable of being both entertaining and educational (32 per cent).

However, recognising this potential does not lead the audience to agree with the possibility of implementing traditional models of financial sustainability of public media, by imposing specific taxes on citizens. For 43 per cent of the respondents, it was unacceptable to levy specific taxes for the running of these stations. They also refused to accept the idea of maintaining them exclusively by advertising (55 per cent). The solution would be to establish a mixed form of financing. The largest group (37 per cent) agreed entirely with the idea that the public broadcasting stations should be maintained by public funding and advertising. There are historical reasons for this attitude, which can be seen in some comments of the participants of the survey:

> 'There are no problems advertising, provided the advertisements are not of products harmful to health or that cause avoidable damage to the environment, and especially provided that they do not interfere with the impartiality of programmes shown. To pay a tax now seems impractical in Brazil. However, at a future time, it could be viable, as long as production makes the most of potential collaboration and there is participation of the audience in the definition and analysis of the content produced.'

> 'Although history shows the difficulty of maintaining public broadcasting stations with only public money, on the other hand, I find it uninteresting having to fight for audiences and finding a lowest common denominator to get sponsorship. Surely, with so many taxes that we pay, if everything functioned well, if all employees were taken on by merit, (so there is no employing of friends, who swap over at every change of government,) there would be no lack of money. We already pay so many taxes, we should have a quality public broadcasting system without any politicking.'

> 'I think taxes are an interesting option, provided that public television gains independence from government. But anyway, this is double-funding, since we pay already taxes to fund the actions of the government and the state.'

Conclusions: symbolic liability

These first data to be analysed allow us to elaborate on some initial reflections about the meanings that are contained in the objective and subjective opinions collected from Brazilian citizens by the Observatory of Public Broadcasting in Latin America. They indicate that the major challenge for Brazilian public broadcasting is to try and overcome what we call 'symbolic liability' with regards to the national audience. This detachment is demonstrated by the doubts that people have about independence from the government that finances and administratively subordinates the broadcasters, as well as the real nature of their programming in terms of quality of content and the attractiveness of the programmes. This clash of perspectives generates a paradox from the differences between the public image that the media have of themselves and that which the audience has of them. The predominance of disconnection ends up causing a significant portion of the population to consider these means of communication in a kind of 'symbolic ghetto' that qualifies and sets the value, importance and representativeness that they occupy in the Brazilian media and cultural scenario and that isolates and differentiates them qualitatively from the commercial media. From the perspective of symbolic interactionism, the subject is conceived as a human being who acts in the present, being influenced not only by what happened in the past, but also by what happens at the time of interaction. This view has been encouraged by various forms of social exclusion experienced by everyday citizens, (lack of housing, health, education and many others,) and an inability of the government to provide basic services satisfactorily. Another phenomenon that undermines the notion of the state as a promoter of good public welfare is the practice of patrimonialism, which occurs when the ruling elite treat political management as a personal privilege, while exploiting ownership of political power as if it were their private property.

We conclude that the connection of public media to a negative perception of government influence on them has produced a social significance that created a distancing between audience and media. Even when the stations are already making some changes in the programming and guiding themselves more clearly by the principles of diversity and plurality, there has not been enough time for new images to be constituted and internalised by citizens. One of the barriers for citizens to symbolically perceive and understand the changes that are underway in the industry is what we define as 'symbolic liability', a kind of 'historical stability of negative assessments' that connects the collective imagination of public media to the lack of quality and autonomy with respect to instances of governmental power. The existence of this perspective of dissatisfaction results from a sum of non-affirmative actions undertaken by public broadcasting stations. Throughout history, they have managed to develop processes that have shaped negative perceptions among the population. The fact that a significant portion of the research participants were dissatisfied with these stations cannot be justified as something momentary and of little importance. It is reinforced, in part, by the interaction with the programming in a sporadic manner, and also by the image formed in minds from negative opinions spread by word of mouth. The problem seems much deeper because, although part of the respondents presented themselves as potential consumers of public media, they have a contrary view in relation to them and worse, without the will to change this critical view.

This distance between citizens and public media can be perceived in the data of audiences of the sector. In the case of EBC, the best audience ratings in their own television network did not even reach an average of 1 per cent in Rio de Janeiro and São Paulo, the two largest cities in Brazil. The situation presented in these two urban centers is representative of the poor penetration of public media. The context tends to get worse if we also consider that in many other Brazilian cities a significant amount of public radio stations and television channels do not even get rated in audience surveys. This is a situation that demonstrates the serious crisis of representativity experienced by public media which anticipates the challenges that these means of communication will have to face, to become a viable option in the media landscape for the different sectors of the population, especially the younger age groups. Hence, the sector seems to be at a stalemate, as representative portions of the population do not use them and others even express their previous rejection in watching them, despite not knowing what the most recent programming is. For example, some respondents said:

'...if it is public, I don't care as I'm not going to watch it anyway'

'...I don't really know them very well, but if public, they will certainly be boring'

In this context, the data collected and analysed so far indicate we should highly recommend that leaders and managers of public media firstly become aware of the complexity of the current picture that defines the relationship between media and audience, and create multiple strategies of reconciliation with the audiences, aiming at earning more credibility, and increasing their levels of acceptance. It is necessary to face the situation, which we have named symbolic liability, and not just with declarations of intention linking them to the universal principles of public broadcasting. It means establishing analyses and evaluations in the scope of the media, about what and how they do their work, setting new attitudes in their programming and presenting a profile of production that would be appropriate to the daily routines of the audience, and thus create a better identity and closeness to the citizens. In this way, the fostering of a more positive image could facilitate a process of re-signification of public media, returning them to the collective mind in more positive ways. The social connection, between the listener or viewer and the media, involves the media inserting themselves into the way of life in society, sharing common heritage like language, music, work, sport and events. Ultimately, the imaginary that represents the way we live. It means transforming the media in a space where people recognise each other as belonging and as participants of a certain social context. It would be a place of cultural identity, of social integration with a plural view of the world. It would entail adopting an affirmative attitude, something that cannot be done only based on discourse constructed around oneself. Audience, seen not as a monolithic block with a single way of thinking, but as, essentially, complex, multifaceted, unequal and plural. Based on the logic of identification, it is possible that the public media will find their place in daily life, contributing to the mutual recognition and identification of people who live in the same place, who share a common way of life, interests, likes, and ultimately a culture.

References

Baert, P (2001) *La teoría social en el siglo XX*, Madrid: Alianza Editorial.

Bendix, R (1986) *Max Weber: um perfil intelectual*, translation by Hanna, E & Viegas Filho, J, Brasília: UnB.

Bianco, N, Esch, C & Moreira, S (2012) Radiodifusão pública: um desafio conceitual na América Latina, *Estudos em Comunicação*, volume 12.

Buarque de Holanda, S (1995) *Raízes do Brasil*, São Paulo: Companhia das Letras.

Blumer, Herbert (1981) *El Interaccionismo Simbólico: Perspectiva y Método* Barcelona: Editorial Hora.

Fuenzalida, V (1998) 'Situación de la televisión pública en América Latina', *Diálogos de la comunicación*, issue 53, December.

Mauss, M (1969) *Oeuvres, 3*, Paris: Editions de Minuit.

Mead, G (1982) *Espíritu, Persona y Sociedad*, Barcelona: Paidós.

Perrota, R (1988) *Interazionismo Simbolico. Concetti sensibilizzanti e ricerca empirica*, Catania: CUECM.

Ritzer, G (2001) *Teoría sociológica moderna*, Madrid: McGraw Hill.

Saperas, E (1998) *Manual Básico de la Teoría de la Comunicación*, Barcelona: CIMS.

Chapter 17

Religious radio stations in Poland: A community-oriented Catholic ghetto? A case study of Radio Niepokalanów

Urszula Doliwa

Abstract

Religious radio stations take up a large proportion of the Polish airwaves. Most of them are Catholic stations and one national station is particularly well-known, Radio Maryja. In total, archdioceses, dioceses, parishes and convents have about 50 licences to broadcast. A large number of them belong to the Plus network, under the auspices of a large media concern, Eurozet. This chapter will characterise the non-commercial, local religious broadcaster existing independently of the commercial Plus network, Radio Niepokalanów and examine to what extent this station follows the model of community broadcasting within the meaning of the Declaration of the Committee of Ministers on the role of the community media in promoting social cohesion and intercultural dialogue passed on 11 February 2009 by the Council of Europe. The main research methods are observations made during a visit to the station and interviews with the managers, as well as with one volunteer working for the station. In addition, a content analysis of the weekly programme sample was undertaken.

Keywords: religious radio, community radio, Catholic media, Poland

Why community broadcasting is important

Communication rights, such as access to information and freedom of expression which is independent not only from government but also from commercial factors, constitute a cornerstone of democracy. In classical liberal theory, the media are seen as a very important and very positive element of democracy – as a fourth estate performing control functions, serving as a source of information and a sphere in which public debate takes place (Curran & Seaton 2000: 121, 127, 129; Goban-Klas 1989; Jędrzejewski 2003). However, in the twentieth century this attitude towards media, which has its roots in the eighteenth century, proved to be too idealistic. Profit has become the main factor stimulating the development of media. As noted by Richard Butsch, today companies may have a similarly devastating effect on media systems as states which control the public sphere in their own interest (2007: 8). Furthermore, John Downing drew our attention to the fact that in the case of the mainstream media, autocensorship and unreflective acceptance of commercial media schemes play an important role (2001: 16). Yet, democratic public life cannot develop, if the important issues are not discussed by citizens. The public sphere concept of Jürgen Habermas, creates an ideal theoretical framework for studying the relationship between democracy and communication (Habermas 1989: 24).

This concept is also useful when talking about community media and their role in democratic systems. As stressed by Kevin Howley, community media create part of the public sphere, in which members of society may gather to debate about public issues, promote local heritage and participate in communities (2005: 35). The significant role of the community radio as a medium providing a sphere for public debate is also supported by Susan Forde and Michael Meadows, according to whom this medium effectively attracts local societies because of concentrating on local issues. It serves as a catalyst in the process of civil participation in the democratic system (2012: 193). It is worth stressing that community radio usually has a more democratic organisational structure, in which there is a place for different points of view represented by several social groups often marginalised in the mainstream media. As Habermas himself underlines, in order to consider a public sphere as healthy, there should be small community media which are not profit-driven. An opportunity for media participation is another interesting aspect often discussed in the community media context. As underlined by Peter Lewis and Susan Jones, social participation of ordinary people - amateurs who, thanks to such activities, become more self confident - is one of the key features of community radio (2006: 3). Julia Fröhlich, Daniel Däschle, Andrés Geerts and Sofie Jannusch recognise four different aspects of participation: in programming, management, ownership and funding (2012: 1). To make such participation possible a form of education is also needed. That is why, apart from broadcasting, community radio stations are very much involved in media training (Günnel 2006: 49).

The other aspect which is worth studying in the community media context is social inclusion – giving a voice to the voiceless, who are marginalised in the mainstream media and public discourse as a whole. Peter Lewis stressed, 'Community media can provide the opportunities for social groups excluded or misrepresented in the mainstream to come in from the margins and give voice to their cultures and concerns' (2008). Building the community is another of the social functions often discussed in the community radio context (Day 2008: 63). A 'community' in the radio context may function on several levels. On the one hand, we can talk about a community of listeners, while on the other hand a community of employees and volunteers also plays a significant role. In stations which are based on volunteering it is very important to develop such a model of cooperation, which is satisfactory for both sides – the audience and the volunteers (Doliwa 2013). These two communities cooperate and create a new dimension of a radio community. As observed by Donald Brown, a special attitude in community radio towards listeners is seen primarily in interviews and talk shows. The pace of such broadcasts is significantly slower than in commercial media. There is time for additional questions and an attitude of respect towards listeners prevails, no matter what kind of views they present (Brown 2012: 158). Community radio representatives try to maintain close contact with their listeners and know them as well as possible. The small scale of such initiatives even allows a degree of genuine face-to-face contact with significant numbers of listeners. Internet-based communication via Facebook and Twitter also plays an increasingly important role.

This chapter will try to assess to what extent the above-mentioned theories and observations are true in the case of Polish religious radio stations. The oldest religious radio station in Poland - Radio Niepokalanów - will serve here as a case study.

Religious radio stations as community broadcasters

The history of religious broadcasting in the world is as long as the history of radio as a medium itself (Stout 2011: 89). Radio benefits from many advantages which make this medium especially suitable for religious broadcasting. One of the most important is its blindness – listeners use their imagination to create an image of the message which encourages reflection and mediation (*ibid*: 89). However, there remains a question of whether religious radio stations are or are not community broadcasters. In the Declaration of the Committee of Ministers of the European Union on the role of community media in promoting social cohesion and intercultural dialogue agreed on 11 February 2009 by the Council of Europe, stations run by religious institutions were explicitly excluded from the community media definition, as being too dependent on the Church. In the declaration the features of community media are characterised as follows:

> 'Independence from government, commercial and religious institutions and political parties; a not-for-profit nature; voluntary participation of members of civil society in the devising and management of programmes; activities aiming at social gain and community benefit; ownership by and accountability to the communities of place and/or of interest which they serve; commitment to inclusive and intercultural practices'. (Council of Europe 2009)

In practice, in many countries the religious radio stations officially belong to this sector. As noted elsewhere by a number of scholars of radio, this is the case in, for example, the UK (Gordon 2009: 65), South Africa (Teer-Tomaselli 2006: 193) and Australia (CMA 2012). The legally-recognised third tier of broadcasting in Poland called 'social broadcasting' is actively and exclusively used by religious radio.

One of the key features of community radio is the fact that it serves a particular community. However, to define such a community is not an easy task. In community media regulations the community is often divided into two main types: the geographic community and the community of interest. For example, one can find such a differentiation in the Community Radio Order in the UK (British Parliament 2004) or the Independent Broadcasting Authority Act in South Africa (IBA 1993). In this act serving a community of interest means that the station is addressed at a community with a specific common interest, and its common interest is the distinctive feature of this kind of broadcasting service. In the act possible kinds of community of interest have also been specified: those that serve 'institutional communities', 'cultural communities' and 'religious communities' (Teer-Tomaselli 2006: 193).

It is certain that 'exclusive' community radio stations run by communities of interest – religious groups, cultural groups, creative groups and so on – have a natural operational advantage. It is easier to motivate and organise a group who share similar attitudes to a project and have similar social or cultural values (Fogg, Korbel & Brooks 2005). However, the real challenge is how to 'answer to the needs of groups at present marginalised or ignored by mainstream radio while at the same time avoiding the ghettoisation that separate channels might create' (Lewis 1984: 148). On the one hand, a community radio station that refuses to engage with religious groups risks alienating itself from a significant section of the population and their needs. On the other hand, religious broadcasting can alienate, (and often infuriate,) people of different or no faith (Fogg, Korbel, & Brooks 2005). Sometimes the social gain from such 'exclusive' stations 'stretches well beyond their specified communities'. Another important question for this chapter is, is that true in the case of Radio Niepokalanów?

Catholic media and religious broadcasting in Poland

When talking about religious radio stations in Poland we are mainly talking about Roman Catholic stations. This is partly because of the importance of the Catholic church in Polish society, which is one of the most religious in Europe - significantly more so than Western Europe, but also other post-communist countries - as 95 per cent of Poles declare themselves to be Catholics (Mtw/PAP 2011). The Polish Catholic church is very active in the field of media. The most important Catholic media sector seems to be the press. It is worth noting that the most popular weekly newspaper in Poland in 2010 and 2011 was the Catholic *Gość Niedzielny*. Another important Catholic weekly, addressed to the upper class of society is *Tygodnik Powszechny*. The most important Catholic monthly is *Rycerz Niepokalanej*. The only Catholic daily newspaper is *Nasz Dziennik*. The most important initiative in the Catholic media market was in 1993 – when the Catholic Press Agency (KAI) was established, and it is now the third largest religious news agency in Europe. There is also one nationwide television station, Telewizja Trwam. The Catholic church is also active on the internet. There are plenty of portals and websites devoted to the Roman Catholic Church, among which opoka.org.pl is the most popular.

There are also plenty of Catholic radio stations. The first attempts to start radio broadcasting in Poland took place in the interwar period. However, after World War II the Catholic church, as well as other religious institutions, were completely cut off from access to the airwaves. The state monopoly of broadcasting was broken when the Polish Parliament passed an Act about the relationship of the State to the Catholic Church in the Polish Republic of Poland on 17 May 1989 (Polish Parliament 1989). The Church was given a right to broadcast, as well as a right to obtain frequencies to take advantage of this right. Thanks to this regulation, the first legal non-public radio stations in Poland were established. Most of the religious stations in existence today started broadcasting in the early 1990s – it was a period when religious radio broadcasting was shaped in Poland. Today, the number of licences for the Catholic church is similar to the number of such licences in 1999 when there were 46 active Catholic radio broadcasters (Habryń 1999: 129). They were established in almost every diocese in Poland. Such a dynamic development of the radio sector was to some extent dictated by the willingness to compensate for the Catholic church persecutions before 1989 and in recognition of the involvement of the Catholic church, which actively supported Polish society in its democratic struggle. These days some experts are of the opinion that there are too many religious broadcasters on the Polish airwaves, (almost a quarter of the total number of licences in Poland belong to the Church). The fear among politicians that any kind of change to this special status of the Catholic church in the broadcasting market may cause dissatisfaction among the Catholic voters results in the system being left alone.

Catholic radio stations take up a large part of the Polish airwaves. There is one nationally well-known station, Radio Maryja. Radio Maryja is a Polish religious, conservative Roman Catholic radio station and media group, describing itself as 'patriotic'. It was founded in Toruń, Poland, on 9 December 1991 and it has been run since its inception by the Redemptorist rector Dr Tadeusz Rydzyk, who is often called Father Director. The station has been criticised by other media, and by academics, notably for the misuse of Catholic doctrine as a political tool. The functioning of this station is also widely discussed in literature (Krzemiński 2009), (Frelichowska 1999). However, in Poland one can find many other religious broadcasters on the airwaves. In total, archdioceses, dioceses, parishes and convents have 44 local licences to broadcast. Half of them constitute a part of the Plus network, under the auspices of a large commercial concern. There are also some active broadcasters from other religions. These are the evangelical Radio CCM in Śląsk and Radio Orthodoxia from Bialystok for Orthodox Christians, part of the Bialystok-Gdańsk Orthodox Diocese.

In Poland, the third tear of broadcasting is not fully recognised by the law. However, in the Media Law there is a special regulation included for so called 'social broadcasters' which are non-commercial and may be treated as a stub of community broadcasting in Poland. This status was established in the Polish Broadcasting Act of 2001. However, such a status is associated with exclusion from the advertising market and any other recognised financial support, which makes the existence of non-religious stations within this legal framework really difficult (Doliwa 2010). As a result, in Poland there are only eight social broadcasters and all of them are connected to the Church. The most similar to the community radio model are independent local religious broadcasters – those with and without 'social broadcaster status' - which are not members of the commercial Plus network. They have rather a large combined coverage area. However, the listenership of such stations is rather small and usually is not bigger than two to three per cent of the population in the area they cover.

Radio Niepokalanów - a case study

Radio Niepokalanów has a long and interesting history, which is closely related to the beginnings of non-public broadcasting in Poland. The first religious broadcasting initiative in Poland dates back to the interwar period. In 1938 the Conventual Franciscan friar Saint Maksymilian Kolbe had attempted to start a non-public radio station in the monastery in Niepokalanów. He was so sure that one day the station would obtain permission for broadcasting that he had built a special building for the radio station. There were also three experimental programmes broadcast (Sotowski 2012). Then World War II interrupted work on this project. During the war Kolbe volunteered to die in place of another man in the Nazi death camp at Auschwitz. He was canonised in 1982. The building is still the headquarters of Radio Niepokalanów today.

The main idea behind Radio Niepokalanów, as well as being the biggest difference between this station and more mainstream media, was well summarised by its director Damian Karczmar in one of the interviews broadcast during the week analysed. He said:

'Meeting people who listen to Radio Niepokalanów, I hear that this station is different from others, that we actually are fed up by the big politics, which we cannot influence, that we are fed up with tracking scams, tricks and scandals. We would like to see that in this world it is a place for good. This is exactly what you can see in our radio station, that a human being is good and can do good things. Even in our programmes dealing with local government issues... There was a new refinery built, there was a new fragment of the road created, a school was saved, a shelter for dogs was opened... These are small things, which are not present in the mainstream media, because contemporary media chase after something which is abnormal, this means bad things like suicides, robberies, rapes, financial scams – this is all very current. But we would like to show that these are not things by which man lives. The human being is fed up with it; he or she would like to see good things around, that somebody helps somebody else cross the street'.

The author visited the station on 24 February 2012. During the visit, Agnieszka Goleniak – the programme director of Radio Niepokalanów - was interviewed. There was also an interview with Malwina Szymańska, a vice-programme director. Additionally, on 27 February 2012 there was a telephone interview with a chaplain in a Lodz hospice for children, Andrzej Partyka. He is a volunteering author and presenter of one of the most moving broadcasts in the weekly schedule of this station, *Hospice – A Hospitality Of The Heart*, about children who are terminally ill. The interview was conducted on 27 February 2012. There was also a one-week programme sample of Radio Niepokalanów analysed, which was broadcast from Monday 13 February to Sunday 19 February). The programme sample was downloaded during the visit.

The study of Radio Niepokalanów in Poland was a part of a bigger research project about non-public stations which try to fulfil non-commercial goals. In the framework of this project there were also other religious radio stations researched. One of the main goals of this project was to check to what extent these stations fulfil the model of the community radio station. The interviews took place at six religious radio stations: four with 'social broadcaster' status and two with commercial licences. Among them was one non-Catholic radio station run by the Orthodox Church, Radio Orthodox. One of the elements of the research was a request to the managers of these stations to evaluate on a scale of 1 to 5 to what extent the elements of the community media definition included in the declaration of the Committee of Ministers on the role of community media in promoting social cohesion and intercultural dialogue were true in their case. The results are shown in Table 17.1, in which 5 meant 'very true' and 1 'not true at all'.

Council of Europe Declaration	Radio Niepokalanów	Radio Fara	Katolickie Radio Płock	Radio Rodzina Wrocław	Radio Anioł Beskidów	Radio Orthodoxia
Independence from government, commercial and religious institutions and political parties	1	1	1	1	1	4
A not-for-profit nature	5	5	5	5	5	5
Voluntary participation of members of civil society in the devising and management of programmes	3	3	3	3	3	4
Activities aiming at social gain and community benefit	5	5	5	5	4	5
Ownership by and accountability to the communities of place and/or of interest which they serve	3	1	2	5	4	3
Commitment to inclusive and intercultural practices	5	5	5	5	5	4

Table 17.1: Religious radio stations measured against the Council of Europe definition of community media, 2012

As we can see from the table, the representatives of all the researched stations gave very similar answers. Such stations seem to fully follow some elements of this definition, such as their non-for-profit nature, broadcasting aiming at social gain, and inclusive and intercultural practices. However, there are some other points of this definition which are for representatives of religious radio stations not so certain. For example, religious radio stations do not feel 'independent from religious institutions' – yet, they are usually financed by, accountable for and owned by these institutions. So, Radio Niepokalanów may be treated to some extent as representative of the whole sector.

Radio Niepokalanów – building the community

The main target group of Radio Niepokalanów is definitely a community of interest which may be defined as a group of active Catholics. However, there are also some elements of the functioning of the station, as well as the programmes which are targeted at the local community. Yet, it is possible to formulate a thesis that the members of the local audience who are not so religious may feel excluded from the audience. The main reason is a very religion-oriented programme schedule. This feeling of 'otherness' may be escalated by the fact that the community is often built by the use of the oppositional 'we' and 'they'. It was Rudyard Kipling who wrote that people judge those outside their community as 'other' (1926). In this particular case, the group described as 'we' may be defined as very committed Catholics, (although Agnieszka Goleniak declared that this group is broader and consists of believers from other Christian faiths,) and 'they' may be characterised not only as people who are not Catholics but also as people not so deeply involved in the life of the Catholic church.

There are several masses, prayers and religious broadcasts in the weekly schedule, which may make representatives of other religions or people who are not so devout feel excluded from the audience. Every day at 11:00 there is a mass from the basilica in Niepokalanów. An exception is Sunday, when the transmission of the mass takes place earlier - at 08:30. During every mass retransmitted by the station, the radio listeners are blessed from the altar. In the week there are plenty of different prayers broadcast. Some of them are presented regularly, every day. This is the case with a Franciscan prayer from the nineteenth century which is broadcast at 06:13. This prayer is followed by another one called Hours of the Immaculate Conception, which has a celebratory nature. At midday there is The Angelus. At 15:00 the Chaplet of Divine Mercy is transmitted from the Church in Cracow Łagiewniki or from the sanctuary in Ożarów Mazowiecki and at 19:30 the Rosary from the basilica in Niepokalanów. Interestingly, the meeting in the church is correlated with the radio programme. In the last part of the prayer people assembled in the church prey for radio supporters. Some of the prayers, such as the Chaplet of Divine Mercy or the Rosary are preceded by intercessions. The listeners may send the intercessions they would like to pray for by email, by post or by phone. Some of them are rather general, such as requests for salvation, health, faith, the dead, strength or help in difficult moments. Others are more descriptive, such as requests for luck during exams, healing from cancer or ear disease, freedom from pornography for somebody's husband, having a good job and so on. The intercessions before the Rosary are divided into three different categories: 'general intercessions' (for example for access to water for everyone), mission intercessions (for example for support for health workers who take care of people in the very poor regions), intercessions of the Militia of the Immaculata (for the gifts of the Holy Spirit, for the Pope, bishops and priests) and the intercessions of prayer (for example for listeners to Radio Niepokalanów).

In the daily schedule there are also plenty of other religious elements. Twice a day there are Bible readings. On Sunday the reading is followed by a comment. Furthermore, some elements of John Paul II's teaching are reiterated in the form of recordings of the former Pope's homilies. Every day a priest, Jacek Pędziwiatr, prepares a short story about a saint. Such a story is also broadcast twice a day. There is also a series about people in the Bible. One of the key religious elements in the schedule is religious radio programmes. On Tuesday evening an evangelistic team made up of young people prepares a broadcast dealing with issues for the younger generation. On Wednesday evening there is a phone-in, *Important Questions*. In the broadcast analysed, presented by a Franciscan and a married journalist, a long discussion took place about happiness. On Thursday evening another religious radio show is broadcast, entitled *The Time For Nicodemus*, with friar Michał Misiak. In the broadcasts analysed there was a discussion about the role of acolytes in the Church. On Fridays the programme *Hand In Hand With St. Maksymilian* is broadcast. One of the most interesting religious radio shows is *Handheld Catechism* with friar Piotr Pawlukiewicz. It is an example of radio not avoiding difficult questions. The questions are sent in by listeners and the priest tries to answer them from the point of view of the Catholic church. In the broadcast analysed, from Sunday 19 February 2012, among the questions asked were: Where are the limits of necking before the wedding? Is the touching of the breast allowed? Is videoing childbirth moral? Is expressing grief to God for your existence a sin? What will the Judgement look like? Do we have a right to honor national heroes whose behavior was immoral? These are only few examples of religious elements of the programme. The whole list of such elements is so long that makes it impossible to characterise all of them. However, it is worth mentioning that there are also programmes on religious news, press reviews, books and religious music shows. One can also find religious elements in other programmes which do not have a strictly religious character, such as in the local government programmes.

However, what constitutes the religious character the most are greetings. The most popular form of greetings among presenters, as well as listeners is the Franciscan greeting 'peace and well-being'. Another frequently-used form of greeting is 'God bless you'. More universal forms of greeting, like for example 'Hello' and 'Good morning' are a rarity. In the author's opinion this is one of the key elements of the programme which make the inclusive character of the programme questionable. Such forms of greetings sound like a declaration: I am one of the members of the group of committed Catholics. A non-catholic listener entering the discussion is not officially forbidden, but in practice people from the outside of the Catholic community may have a feeling that they are not welcome on air. Furthermore, it might be also a problem for Catholics who are not so deeply involved in the Catholic community and are not familiar with these forms of greetings or do not feel comfortable using them. This problem is escalated by the fact that the person who leads the discussion on air and has a dominant position in the conversation is a presenter (Kaszewski 2006: 51) and when this person starts the communication with one of the religious forms of greetings it is very difficult not to follow the style of the conversation imposed by the journalist. Such forms of greeting are used not only in explicitly religious broadcasts but also in other parts of the schedule devoted to, for example, music or local issues.

Radio Niepokalanów - media participation

As already discussed, when talking about community media we can recognise four different aspects of participation: participation in programming, management, ownership and funding. In the case of Radio Niepokalanów two of these aspects may be reported as present. These are participation in programming and participation in funding. There are two organised groups which have supported Radio Niepokalanów constantly. One of them is a prayer group, thanks to whom the daily transmissions of the Rosary from the basilica in Niepokalanów are made possible. Another is the group of young people from Łódź called Firm in the Spirit who prepare one broadcast every week, *Talking About God*. In total about ten people work for the station as volunteers. People who would like to volunteer for the station are instructed how to do it on the station's website. The working team is also recruited from the church. One of the volunteers is the author of the broadcast *Hospice – A Hospitality Of The Heart*, about children who are terminally ill. He is a hospice chaplain, Andrzej Partyka. In the interview Partyka stressed that for him it is very important that he can introduce his children's wards and their stories on the airwaves.There are also plenty of phone-in radio shows on air. What distinguishes this genre from those in commercial, as well as in public radio stations, is the time the listeners may spend on the air. The programme *Important Questions* broadcast on 15 February can serve as an example. In this radio show the discussions with each listener could last three to four minutes. The listeners also communicate via text, email and letters, and during this broadcast there were as many as 20 texts sent to the presenters. There is still some face to face contact, which plays an important role. In the programme *The Time Of Nicodemus* broadcast on 16 February, the presenter, who is a priest, mentioned people who discuss his programme with him after the Sunday Mass. Sometimes people not only send letters to the station but also other items, mostly things they have themselves - an example may be a picture sent by one of the listeners. Listeners are also very active in financing the station. Money for its functioning only partly comees from the Franciscan monastery. It is also collected in churches and through the Foundation of Good Media Message, started by the director of the station. Only a little money comes from advertising, which is allowed but limited to only two per cent of the output. Unfortunately, the author did not receive an answer to a question about the proportions of the different sources of finance.

Radio Niepokalnaów - social inclusion

It is easy to find broadcasts which are rare on commercial radio stations in the programme schedule of Radio Niepokalanów - talking about people who are underserved by other media. The main group which may feel supported by the station are the elderly people who are not attractive for advertisers and as a consequence, the whole commercial sector. This group is recognised by the managers as one of the most important groups for whom the schedule is organised. Programme director Agnieszka Goleniak explained in the interview that these are not only old but often also ill people who cannot get out of their homes. Not surprisingly, it is mostly elderly people who take part in the phone-in programmes, send letters to the station and send in handmade pieces of art as a way of saying thank you to the Radio Niepokalanów journalists.

On the station there are also other groups and problems represented who are a rarity on other radio stations. These are, for example, weak and poor people at whom the programme *Betel* is aimed. This programme is produced by another religious radio station from Częstochowa, however it is rebroadcast by Radio Niepokalanów. Another group who may feel underserved by the mainstream media and yet are included by Radio Niepokalanów in their target group are definitely children - as are the sick and the alienated from society. The programme *Hospice – A Hospitality Of The Heart* is a good example. In this programme children who are terminally ill have a voice, as do children who are connected to a respirator and have problems with everyday communication. On Sundays there is also a chart show especially for children. Another group often omitted in mainstream discourse are the Polish friars who have their own broadcast *Behind The Enclosure*. The station also broadcasts a one-hour-long daily programme for the Polish minority in Chicago, which is rebroadcast live by one of the Chicago radio stations, WPNA 1490 AM.

Conclusions

In conclusion it is worth noting that independent religious radio stations, which occupy a good deal of space on the airwaves, may be to some extent treated as community broadcasters – they follow in some ways the community media model. Radio Niepokalanów, which served here as a case study, broadcasts a very diversified programme with plenty of spoken word present on air. It is also a place where public debate about socially-important issues takes place. What seems to be important is the fact that such debates are run at a very slow pace. Spoken word elements in such programmes sometimes last 20 minutes without a break for music, or even longer, which might be impossible on a commercial radio station. However, the programme is fully subordinated to the religious radio format which makes the possibility of gaining listeners from outside the religious community almost impossible. The station has significant achievements in the field of social inclusion, serving groups which may feel underserved by other media: elderly people, children, ill and poor people, clergy and the Polish minority in Chicago. However, taking into account the whole society, the programme formula seems to be more exclusive than inclusive. People who do not believe in God or whose faith is not so solid may feel excluded from the audience.

Compared with community media in other counties, which have a long tradition of community broadcasting, the participatory nature of this medium may be characterised as limited. The station is supported by the volunteers but only to a limited extent. Such a possibility is not open for everyone – volunteers, as well as employees are recruited from declared Catholics. The community plays a role in funding, but definitely not in the management of the station, which officially belongs to the Franciscan Convent and the director of the station is a friar of the convent. The listeners have little influence on the programming and rules of operation of the station. The station seems to be community-oriented but definitely not community-run. The existence of Radio Niepokalanów seems to be especially important for elderly religious people – the largest group of listeners are aged over 60. Without this station the life of these people might be significantly poorer.

References

British Parliament (2004) Community Radio Order 2004, London: Parliament.
http://www.publications.parliament.uk/pa/ld200304/ldhansrd/vo040716/text/40716-05.htm#40716-05_head0

Brown, D (2012) 'What is 'Community' in Community Radio?', in Gordon, J (ed), *Community Radio in the Twenty First Century*, Oxford: Peter Lang Publications.

Butsch, R (2007) 'Introduction: How are media public spheres', in Butsch, R (ed), *Media and Public Spheres*, Basingstoke: Palgrave Macmillan.

Carpentier, N (2011) *Media and Participation: A Site of Ideological-democratic Struggle*, Bristol: Intellect.

CAM (2012) *History*, Christian Media Australia. http://christianmedia.org.au/index.php?option=com_content&task=view&id=31&Item id=60.

Committee of Ministers of the Council of Europe (2009) Declaration of the Committee of Ministers on the role of community media in promoting social cohesion and intercultural dialogue, Brussels: Council of Europe. http://www.connexx-av.de/upload/m49a288b318ab0_verweis1.pdf

Curran, J & Seaton, J (2000) 'Rethinking media and democracy', in Curran, J & Gurevitch, M (eds), *Mass Media and Society*, London: Arnold.

Day, R (2008) *Community Radio in Ireland: Participation and Multiflows*, New Jersey: Hampton Press.

Doliwa, U (2010) 'Elektroniczne media społeczne w Polsce. Stan obecny i perspektywy rozwoju', *Studia Medioznawcze*, volume 43, issue 4.

Doliwa, U (2013) 'Radio społeczne a idea partycypacji społecznej na przykładzie Radia Spark w Wielkiej Brytanii', *Studia Medioznawcze*, volume 54, issue 3.

Downing, J (2001) *Radical media: Rebellious communication and social movements*, Thousand Oaks: Sage.

European Parliament (2008) Resolution of 25 September 2008 of the European Parliament on Community Media in Europe, Brussels: European Parliament. http://www.europarl.europa.eu/sides/getDoc.do?pubRef=-//EP//TEXT+TA+P6-TA-2008-0456+0+DOC+XML+V0//EN.

Fogg, A, Korbel, P, & Brooks, C (2005), *Community Radio Toolkit*, Radio Regen.

Forde, S & Meadows, M (2012) 'Facilitating public conversations: The role of the "citizen" in community radio and alternative journalism', in Gordon, J (ed), *Community Radio in the Twenty First Century*, Oxford: Peter Lang Publications.

Frelichowska, D (1999) *Ojcowie Redemptoryści i ich Radio Maryja*, Toruń: Adam Marszałek.

Fröhlich, J, Däschle, D, Geerts, A & Jannusch, S (2012), *Community Participation at Local and Community Radio Stations. An explorative study in Africa, Asia, Latin America and the Pacific.* http://www.cameco.org/english/publications/CAMECO-Practice-Series/.

Goban-Klas, T (1989) *Prasa lokalna i środowiskowa w Stanach Zjednoczonych w cieniu gigantów*, Kraków: Polska Akademia Nauk.

Gordon, J (2009) *Notions of Community: A Collection of Community Media Debates and Dilemmas*, Oxford, New York: Peter Lang.

Günnel, T (2006) 'Action-oriented media pedagogy' in Lewis, P & Jones, S (eds), *From the Margins to the Cutting Edge: Community Media and Empowerment*, Catskill: Hampton Press.

Habermas, J (1989), *The Structural Transformation of the Public Sphere: An Inquiry into a Cathegory of Borgeois Society*, Cambridge: MIT Press.

Habryń, M (1999) 'Polskie media katolickie 1989-1999', *Zeszyty Prasoznawcze*, volume 159/160, issue 3-4.

Howley, K (2005) *Community Media. People, Places, and Communication Technologies*, Cambridge: Cambridge University Press.

IBA (1993), The Independent Broadcasting Authority Act (South Africa). http://www.wipo.int/wipolex/en/text.jsp?file_id=218750

Jędrzejewski, S (2003) *Radio w komunikacji społecznej,* Warszawa: Vespa-Druk.

Kaszewski, K (2006) *Język dyskusji radiowej. Analiza wypowiedzi słuchaczy w Programie III Polskiego Radia*, Warszawa: Semper.

Kipling, R (1926) *We and They: Debits and Credits*, London: Doubleday Page & Co.

Krzemiński, I (2009) *Czego nas uczy Radio Maryja? Socjologia treści i recepcji rozgłośni*. Warszawa: Wydawn Akademicke i Profesjonalne.

Mtw/PAP (2011) 'CBOS: 95 procent Polaków to katolicy'. http://wiadomosci.radiozet.pl/Polska/Wiadomosci/CBOS-95-procent-Polakow-to-katolicy

Lewis, P (1984), 'Community Radio: the Montreal conference and after', *Media, Culture, and Society*, 6.

Lewis, P, & Jones, S (2006) *From the Margins to the Cutting Edge: Community Media and Empowerment*, Catskill: Hampton Press.

Lewis, P (2008) 'Finding and funding voices: the London experience', *Information, Society and Justice*, volume 2, issue1.

Polish Parliament (1989) *Ustawa o stosunku Państwa do Kościoła Katolickiego w Rzeczypospolitej Polskiej*. http://mateusz.pl/dokumenty/ustawapk.htm

Sotowsk, P (2012) *Próba uruchomienia Radia Niepokalanów*, *http://www.radioniepokalanow.pl/o-nas/historia.html.*

Stout, D (2011) *Media and Religion: Foundations of an Emerging Field*, New York: Routledge.

Teer-Tomaselli, R (2006) 'Community Radio's impact on community building: case studies from KwaZulu-Natal, South Africa' in Hipfl, B & Hug, T (eds.), *Media Communities*, Munster: Waxmann.

Part Three

Histories

Chapter 18

Comedy shows: Humour, crisis and the resilience of radio

Madalena Oliveira

Abstract

Being a part of many radio stations' programming, comedy shows are also available on radio websites as audio on demand. Often topical, many of these shows are based on everyday news. With a strong aesthetic sense, comedy shows are often brash as well as funny, but they can also play an important role as a barometer of social, political, economic and cultural life.

The history of comedy shows on radio in Portugal began in the 1940s. Since that time, humour has been inspired mainly by news and current affairs, not only in terms of content but also in terms of format. Many comedy shows parodied news genres. Like news bulletins, these shows normally feature an anchor who presents the comedic news. The scripts for these programmes are written in a satirical way and present a caricature of society.

This chapter will identify some characteristics of comedy shows on the radio, consider the relationship between comedy shows and real news output and reflect on the role humourous narratives may play in contributing to the resilience of radio.

Keywords: radio comedy, humour, news parody, spectacle, Portugal

Introduction: the frequency of laughter

One of the most successful radio genres is probably comedy. Comic sketches on the radio are almost as old as radio itself. The first such programmes had begun in the United States by the end of the 1920s. Since then, radio comedy has been part of many stations' programming. Considered by Henri Bergson (1983) as inseparable from the human being, laughter is today one of the most important ways of reflecting on daily life. According to Verena Alberti, 'laughter and comedy are literally indispensable to know the world and to apprehend reality' (2002: 13). Every society of every epoch had its own forms of humour and its own forms of satire, comedy demonstration and public exhibition. Many different comedy genres, from comic theatre to stand-up comedy, have appeared during the history of radio. Most use the same approach, making fun of situations, people, historic episodes and political strategies, while simultaneously provoking thought and stirring opinions. Taken as a version of the ordinary, worldly understanding of our social life (Meredith 2014), comedy performances are much more than entertainment formats. Although sometimes using the unrealistic, their main goal is to portray real life. If in the past, comedy shows were, as with all other forms of art, intended for certain groups in society, such as more educated and wealthier people, today, humour formats are widely targeted at all social groups. To a large extent, due to the appropriation of this kind of discourse by the mass media, comedy plays and humourous sketches are nowadays among the most-consumed media productions. Generally defined as 'laughter-provoking', these narratives have a particular characteristic on radio. That is, their power is exclusively found in the audio, in both words and sound effects. Despite such an apparent disadvantage, they are very popular.

In Portugal, for example, humour is almost an obligatory genre on national radio stations. In some commercial radio programmes, even the language used by the entertainers is deeply influenced by humour styles, as a way of making audiences feel good while listening. Detailed studies of specific audiences of humour programmes on Portuguese radio are unknown, Marktest, the company that produces audience data for industry, does not publish information detailed enough to show genres. Instead, radio stations seem to intuitively feel that listeners like this kind of programme. In general terms, all the national stations have slots in their programming dedicated to humour, usually short sketches. These programmes are, in almost all cases, also available on the stations' own websites, or on other audio-on-demand platforms, where they can be downloaded to be listened to outside of the broadcast schedule. The popularity of these formats is evident, though, in their being widely shared on social networks, where links to this kind of audio content are exchanged between potential new listeners. Sometimes people linked in these networks comment on excerpts too, contributing to a wider distribution by triggering a viral effect across the country.

Compared to comedy programming on television, where programming also includes comedy narrative genres, humour on the radio is normally in shorter bursts and very often broadcast on a daily basis. More fleeting than the television programmes, the humour sketches on Portuguese radio have, however, a particular dynamic and seem to have the capacity to win over audiences. Aesthetically pleasing, with a vivid structure and direct references to current political, social, economic and cultural news, these sketches can be considered to be an interesting barometer of communities that correspond to the audiences of the stations. Quite intentionally a form of social and political criticism, humour is in various ways one of the most produced genres on radio. The genre exploits to the full the creative power of the word and the significance of sound. This chapter will consider the frequency of laughter of two Portuguese national radio broadcasters and, taking two specific programmes, identify the main characteristics of humour shows. This approach has three main objectives. Firstly, to determine whether there is a narrative pattern to comedy sketches, secondly to understand what the framing of these programmes is within the stations' programming and finally to ask what is the Portuguese sense of humour. Putting comedy narratives into perspective, both in general and in the specific context of radio, has a special relevance in the current creative industries. Today, much more concerned with spectacle and entertainment, creative industries represent, both in economic and cultural terms, the level of innovation societies are experiencing. The analysis is focused on the connection between comedy narratives and programming strategies. At the same time, the examination of two particular programmes aims to provide some insight into the interpretation of humour as an expression of a joyful culture, delivered to give pleasure and to cause laughter. As signs of the times, and emblems of what Guy Debord identified as the 'spectacle society' (1995), comedy sketches are content-oriented, for provoking thought and nurturing affective connections, but also representative of the parodic and satirical character of post-modern societies.

A history of Portuguese comedy on radio

The history of comedy on radio in Portugal begins in the late 1940s. In 1912 a weekly satirical newspaper of significant national impact, *A Bomba* (The Bomb), was published for about three months. With explosive and audacious headlines, this publication was provocative and brave, not only in its textual content but also in the illustrations, (very often caricatures,) published on its pages. Many years after the last edition, this newspaper inspired the creation of the group Parodiantes de Lisboa, or Parodists of Lisbon, a group for comedians that produced some iconic programmes for Portuguese radio. *Parada da Paródia* (Parody Parade) and *Graça com Todos* (Joke with All) were probably the most significant productions broadcast by the group. According to their website, *Parodiantes de Lisboa* first aired in March 1947. At first, the group was on air once a week, starting with *Parada da Paródia*, which was broadcast by Rádio Peninsular on Tuesdays at 20:00. Later, with the programme *Graça com Todos*, the Parodiantes de Lisboa extended their activity to new audiences in Porto, Madeira, Angola and Mozambique, as well as various foreign radio stations dedicated to expatriates. The group was populated by some of the most popular comedians, who later became very well-known television stars. The Parodiantes de Lisboa distinguished themselves because they produced different kinds of comedy programmes, including soap operas, especially for radio, although they also produced shows for television. In August 2005, the Portuguese daily newspaper *Diário de Notícias* published a special feature on the parodists, saying they had captured the imagination of Portuguese people over 30. In the publicity for the programme, the newspaper revealed that the group had always used the same approach to writing comedy: they would open the newspapers and news magazines to get ideas from each day's news and current affairs.

At around the same time, there was also a programme called *A voz dos ridículos* (The Voice of Ridiculous), which was broadcast for the first time in April 1945. This show came out of a proposal aimed at 'transposing' to radio a humorous column someone from Porto used to publish in the newspaper *Os ridículos* (The Ridiculous) entitled Piadas à moda do Porto ('Jokes Oporto's Way'). Some historical notes gathered from the press of that era state that, in the first episodes, the programme was composed of funny songs and words, which were biting, sometimes caustic, and had above all a function of social criticism. Today, *A voz dos ridículos* is still on the air and is broadcast by a regional radio station in northern Portugal. The programme retains almost the same structure of the first broadcasts, with jokes, satire and jocular comments on daily life. Running for about seventy years, the programme is not only a reference point for comedy programmes in Portugal but probably the oldest regular programme of Portuguese radio that is still on the air.

This chapter will not pretend to present a detailed genealogy of radio comedy in Portugal. The history of such productions is extraordinarily rich, made of abundant examples of sketches that, commenting on daily life, used the language of laughter to create characters that became symbols of certain generations. Some of these characters were born in the newspapers, in the caricature press where the burlesque caricatures of some public personalities were drawn. They were later transformed into aural language, and in some cases, they were also taken further to the small screen in television shows. Classics of the Portuguese media scene, many of these programmes contributed to the consolidation of a Portuguese style of comedy programming. With a strong affective connection with the audiences, mainly in the period preceding the spread of television in Portuguese homes, this kind of production was then resurgent in the last few years, sometimes appearing in advertisements. Icons of the creative industries, they were used for marketing campaigns, having a further impact that is not picked up by audience statistics. According to Jorge Guimarães Silva, who publishes the blog *A Rádio em Portugal* (Radio in Portugal), 'comedy programmes are the last blast of the golden age of radio in Portugal'. The Parodiantes de Lisboa were on the air for many decades. The public imagination of the second half of the twentieth century is strongly associated with this memory because they became national icons through the national radio stations Rádio Clube Português and Rádio Renascença. During their history, this group of comedians produced some radio drama, in addition to the brief comedy sketches. Because of their wide experience, the group can today be taken as the inspiration for much modern comedy, such as that of Produções Fictícias, a Portuguese company appearing on radio and television as well as theatre, cinema and the press.

Satirical news or reflections of real life?

Although today there are more programmes, and therefore more diversity, than in the past, one great difference between the early forms of radio comedy and those of today is that, unlike then, today, comedy is more often produced as monologues. Parodiantes de Lisboa was a group effort, with dialogues between the parodists, who used to play different characters. Today, however, daily comedy sketches on radio are more focused on one single comedian or on a dialogue between two of them, and very often they are celebrities who are already well known from television and advertisements. Ángel Nieto agreed, adding that: 'Comedy programmes on the radio used to exist in very distinct formats, although almost all in tune with the drama genre. Comedians usually played one or more characters. Monologue was not used like it is used today' (2008: 106). Although relatively small, Portugal has almost three hundred radio stations, many of them with their own comedy shows, while others broadcast shows produced by production houses or individual comedians, some distributed through networks. For this research the programming of two national radio stations was examined: the public service broadcaster Antena 1 and the commercial news station TSF. According to December 2013 data from the Bareme Rádio of Marktest, r/com has the highest audiences in Portugal, with a weekly reach of 48.8 per cent and a 36.4 per cent share of listening. Over the same period, audiences were lower for the two stations analysed for this research. TSF registered a weekly reach of 9.4 per cent and a 4.4 per cent share of listening, while Antena 1 had a weekly reach of 11.4 per cent and a 7.1 per cent share. Nevertheless, stations of the r/com group focus more on music with presenter links and entertainment. Their comedy output seldom consists of individual, built programmes. By contrast, choosing to analyse Antena 1 and TSF for this study reflects a decision to analyse stations which are based on news content rather than entertainment.

Antena 1 is one of the three main national broadcasters. It is part of the public service broadcast group and is the station most expected to follow principles established in the public service contract, which states that the group should include a plurithematic broadcaster, with diversified options and a strong informative component, as well as some entertainment, targeted to serve the majority of the population. It should be aware of the regional realities and engaged with the broadcasting of Portuguese music, Portuguese singers and composers, as well as popular culture and sport. With very diversified programming, which encompasses news programmes, cultural shows, the showcasing of Portuguese music, literature and such specialised musical genres as jazz, in 2013 this broadcaster had only one comedy programme. *Portugalex* is presented as 'a comedy magazine, which combines the main news stories with other diverse items'. Amusingly, the text introducing the programme announces that: 'what they [the presenters] say is all invented, with rigour and journalistic exemption'. Produced by Produções Fictícias, this programme sets out to satirise the news itself and genres of mediatised news. The script includes traffic information, in a bulletin entitled *Já bateu* (It Crashed), and a public opinion slot called *Gosto muito do seu programa* (I Love Your Programme). There is also futurology, within a segment called *Previsão do estado da atualidade* (The Current Forecast). *Portugalex* is a three-minute programme - the producers say it can also be four minutes 'if many things happen' - broadcast every weekday in the morning and at lunchtime, which is of course prime time for radio in Portugal because it is also drive time, at least in the main towns and cities.

Being at the forefront of Antena 1's programming, *Portugalex* features two comedians whose purpose is 'to sum up Portugal in three minutes'. Adopting the register of a news bulletin and presented by two different voices, this programme is a funny take on the day's news. It picks up some real events in a satirical way, and sometimes even an unrealistic way. The format is pseudo-informative since the programme presents a kind of sound caricature of some public figures as well as of other media programmes. In this sense, *Portugalex* produces a discourse that might be labelled as meta-discourse. Specially inclined to treat everyday news in a mocking way, the programme is consistent with the profile of the station. If news constitutes a strong component of the programming, in *Portugalex* the comedians scoff at current affairs but also, in a more indirect way, at the journalism itself through reinterpretations of some of the news values which determine the production of real news bulletins. The style is not original in terms of the international media landscape, and it rephrases some formulas already tried and tested in television. However, it seems to be extremely successful, as it is followed by more than 12 thousand people on Facebook.

TSF, on the other hand, is the sole broadcaster of Controlinveste and the only broadcaster with a profile close to a national news radio station. Its programming includes mainly news content, with breaking news every thirty minutes. It produces different kinds of news bulletins, mainly on sports and economics, and also has programmes aimed at listener participation. In terms of humour, TSF has invested significantly in these formats in the last two decades, with, in the second half of 2013, at least two specific comedy shows, one broadcast daily and another weekly. Although different in many respects, these two programmes had in common the purpose of satirising social behaviour and presenting topical news in a humourous way. Both programmes were inspired by real news formats and commented satirically on stories. *Tubo de Ensaio* (Test Tube) is a sketch show presented by Bruno Nogueira, one of the top comedians of the current generation of humourists. The programme, with its online archive on the TSF website, was created by Produções Fictícias and it is presented as a space for 'stand-up news, fictional interviews, "hot" topics, things that may irritate, projects for the future, public figures who present some abilities on the radio, solutions for the main problems of humanity and many other experiences'. It is a three-minute programme, broadcast every day at three different times, 09:20, 18:25 and 20:25. *Tubo de Ensaio* is a monologue, during which the presenter makes personal comments on recent events and news stories, caricaturing some public figures, making some funny remarks about incidents of the day or the week and joking about media reporting.

Governo Sombra (Shadow Cabinet) is also broadcast by TSF, but it is a very different programme, being fictional content produced in a comedic style. This project brings together three men, all closely involved in the media either as columnists or a comedian. The programme flows as if a talk show or a debate, led by a real journalist. Each week, each comedian assumes the character of a minister of the real cabinet and participates in a dialogue with the group, commenting on the political agenda in a satirical way. As with the previous programmes, *Governo Sombra* is also inspired by the news, although mainly politics. Once again, this programme fits the genre of programmes that attempt to make humour using a typically journalistic style. The programme is much longer than the others, lasting 45 minutes, and broadcast on Fridays at 19:15, when a significant part of the working audience is driving home or going out. *Governo Sombra* was originally created for radio. The programme is available on the TSF website, and more recently, a version is made for a TV channel. Both *Tubo de Ensaio* and *Governo Sombra* are available as podcasts and the latter also has a blog, although little used since 2011.

A detailed comparison of the three comedy shows described in this chapter would, of course, be constrained by the very different structures of the programmes. There are, in fact, big differences, mainly between the daily and the weekly formats. However, some similarities can be noted and the extent to which they might depict any pattern in comedic radio content considered. Notwithstanding the specific characteristics of each programme, at least seven features might define some trends in this genre: 1) the source material being news and current affairs, 2) the emulation of journalistic media genres, 3) the reinterpretation and caricature of political and social agents, 4) the leg-pulling over current events, 5) the bitingly critical nature of the humour, 6) the objective of provoking a critical stance concerning social and political news stories and 7) the creative capacity to make people laugh at their own lives. Today, adapted to new lifestyles and to a more complex society, contemporary radio comedy programmes in Portugal follow some traditions that have shaped several comedic narratives since the 'Parodiantes de Lisboa'. The focus on episodes of everyday life and on the public social and political agenda is probably a tendency of all forms of humour. Today, as in the past, these programmes show how risible some news is and how reality is often experienced as a spectacle.

Conclusion

According to Alison Ross, comedy is always something related to '...an ambiguity, or double meaning, which deliberately misleads the audience' (2005: 7). In Simon Critchley's opinion, '...comedy is produced by a disjunction between the way things are and the way they are represented in the joke, between expectation and actuality' (2002: 1). This is what radio comedy shows still have in common with stage comedy. Besides, now just as in the past, there is in comedy something that comes mainly out of the way words are articulated. This may be why comedy is so suited to aural media and why '...radio became a widely popular vehicle for humour' (Havig, 1990: 5). Comedy is related to crisis by nature. Crises of moral values, political crises or economic crises are very inspiring for comedians. Every era has its own crisis. Thus, comedy is intrinsic to history. It represents the capacity a certain society has to laugh at itself, and it consists of a kind of criticism that is above the capacity of producing a joke. Bergson considered that comedy signifies a 'diversion of things'. He explained that: 'Comicality can be defined as a diversion of things, like the individual comicality is also due to a certain diversion of the person' (1983: 50). Which does not mean comedy is outside reality. Diversion is otherwise a way of interpreting it. Sometimes more destructive than constructive, comedy is meant to work as a way of dismantling and disconcerting, being in all these forms an expression of excess.

Contemporary societies have been described as excited but depressive. Comedy is one of the most significant expressions of such a contradiction. By mixing carefully chosen words, sound effects and the use of the human voice, comedy on radio completes, in some ways, the companion function this medium performs for many people. It reinforces the power and the resilience of radio. Besides engaging listeners in mainstream broadcast radio, comedy programmes have been very successful in attracting audiences on the internet who comment on and share extracts. If comedy can provoke laughter, stimulate thought and build audiences, then radio comedy might well deserve to be recognised as a language that entertains but remains essentially radio.

References

Alberti, V (2002) *O riso e o risível na história do pensamento*, Rio de Janeiro: Jorge Zahar Editor.

Ángel Nieto, M (2008) 'Dramáticos', in Borreguero, M (ed), *Nuevas perspectivas sobre los géneros radiofónicos,* Barcelona: Editorial Frágua.

Bergson, H (1983), *O riso. Ensaio sobre a significação do cómico*, Rio de Janeiro: Zahar Editores.

Critchley, S (2002) *On Humour. Thinking in Action*, London: Routledge.

Debord, G (1995) *La société du spectacle,* Paris: Gallimard.

Havig, A (1990) *Fred Allen's Radio Comedy*, Pennsylvania: Temple University Press.

Meredith, G (2014) *An Essay on Comedy and the Uses of the Comic Spirit*, Adelaide: The University of Adelaide. http://ebooks.adelaide.edu.au/m/meredith/george/on-comedy/

Ross, A (2005) *The Language of Humour*, London: Routledge.

Chapter 19

Noise, soundplay, extended radio: *Bugs & Beats & Beasts* as an example of resilience in the German *Hörspiel*

Ania Mauruschat

Abstract

This chapter highlights *Bugs & Beats & Beasts* (1999) by Andreas Ammer and Console to explore the development of the special German radio art *Hörspiel* through soundplay and even beyond towards the concept of 'extended radio'. It argues that the unique openness of the *Hörspiel* as a special kind of radio art makes it possible to respond almost instantaneously to cultural and technological transformations and contributes to the evolution of the medium of radio in doing so. Consequently this soundplay was able to dramatically articulate the rise of the network society, its swarm logic, and the evolution of the medium at a time long before these significant changes were understood by a wider public. It did so by using 'noises' in different meanings and pushed the resilience of the medium of radio forward on three levels, aesthetic, technological and spatial.

Keywords: noise, *Hörspiel*, extended radio, network society, Germany

Introduction

Bssssssshshshhhssssss. The noise of an insect in a room. Perhaps a fly trapped in a glass? In parallel with it another track starts with a strange 'boing' sound – the sound of a jew's harp might come to mind. Next, on a third track, we hear a cello, which slowly, slowly becomes louder and louder, and its tone develops into a more complex melody. Meanwhile the buzzing of the fly fades out into the distance. Suddenly a very, very quiet and deep humming sound underneath the cello can be heard, like an acoustic pad. Then, a track with a male voice starts to describe in German the scenery of a landscape without human beings. The last two words, *leise Geräusche* (quiet noises) are difficult to understand because they are almost totally faded into the sound of the cello. By then, underneath the cello, there is a track with deep, fat bass beats, which sound like 'wupp wupp'. Suddenly, the noise of the fly in the glass occurs once again – at first only briefly, then longer and with more intensity, almost desperate. After a while a track starts with a second male voice reciting a text in Latin. On another track, the noise of an insect can be heard that sounds strange, as if it is somehow defamiliarised electronically, somehow echoing and a bit looped. Every now and then the fly in the glass buzzes again. At the end of the Latin recitation, a female voice says 'natural techno', followed by a short buzzing of the fly. Then the cello cross-fades into the loud chirping of cicadas.

This is how one could translate the aural experience of the first track *Natural Techno* of *Bugs & Beats & Beasts* into words. It is the beginning of that *Hörspiel* – or perhaps more precisely, 'soundplay', as will be explained later – which was the first genuine cooperation between Andreas Ammer, the most successful contemporary *Hörspiel* writer in Germany, and the well-known electronic musician Martin Gretschmann, who is also known as Console. *Bugs & Beats & Beasts* was commissioned and finally broadcast on 15 October 1999 by the radio drama department Hörspiel & Medienkunst of the public Bavarian broadcasting station Bayerischer Rundfunk in Munich. It was produced on the laptops of Ammer and Console and mixed at the independent uphon-Studio in Weilheim, Upper-Bavaria, where most of the voices were also recorded.

The main idea for this radio drama, for which Andreas Ammer was able to acquire Martin Gretschmann as his co-writer, was to create a *Hörspiel* out of 'bugs' – a *Hörspiel* that would consist almost entirely of electronically-remastered original recordings of insect noises. Approximately 95 per cent of the beats in this radio drama are real insect noises, sampled and defamiliarised, which were taken from such CDs as *Insect Noise in Stored Foodstuffs*, a CD that was produced for 'sonic warfare' (Goodman 2010). Its purpose was to help farmers to detect, identify and eliminate parasite infestations in grain silos, such as rice weevil larvae that are invisible but not inaudible due to sensitive microphones with narrow frequency responses. Only five per cent of the beats were generated electronically. The German texts were taken from entomological encyclopaedias, as well as a Latin text that even dates back to Pliny the Elder and his famous book *Naturalis Historia* from the first century AD (Mauruschat 2012a). One could regard *Bugs & Beats & Beasts* as being merely a modest little production that is easily missed as it apparently only deals with something as annoying and mundane as insects and their noises. Nevertheless, one ought not to underestimate this *Hörspiel* – or insects either. What makes the award-winning *Bugs & Beats & Beasts* so interesting from a media aesthetic perspective, is that it sums up not only Ammer's achievements and developments in his own *Hörspiel oeuvre* of around 25 radio plays, which he created in the last 25 years. The piece also sums up the almost 90-year-long debate on the German *Hörspiel* and fulfils an almost 90-year-old vision of a true soundplay in the very best sense of the term, for which German radio art is well known for all over the world (Cory 1992; Sá Rego Costa *et al* 2013). *Bugs & Beats & Beasts* even points beyond that, towards media art or maybe more precisely 'expanded radio art' and the theoretical concept of something called 'extended radio'. This concept, as formulated by the media theorist and media historian Bernhard Siegert (2002), argues that there never was and never will be a stable definition of what exactly radio is, because radio is impossible to define due to the permanent evolution of the medium. As Marshall McLuhan and Edmund Carpenter characterised the audio space of the electronic age as being 'dynamic, always in flux' (1960: 41) one could say that its primary medium, radio, is dynamic, always in flux, developing and evolving since its beginning, since the invention of gramophone, telephone, telegraphy and short-wave.

By reflecting all of these aspects in an artistic way, *Bugs & Beats & Beasts* touches on crucial contemporary aesthetical questions and opens up new spaces of perception, production and distribution. This is why *Bugs & Beats & Beasts* could be considered on three levels as an appropriate example to use to demonstrate the resilience of radio on three levels, aesthetic, technological, and spatial. On each level of resilience, the epistemological and aesthetic category of 'noise' (Schüttpelz 2003: 15-229; Sigert 2002; Sigert 2004) plays a key role because it is noise which pushes the resilience of a medium. As Michel Serres, the philosopher of *The Parasite* put it: 'The noise, through its presence and absence, the intermittence of the signal, produces the new system, that is to say oscillation' (2007: 52).

Aesthetic resilience

Due to the rise of electronic media from the end of the nineteenth century, Marshall McLuhan predicted a return of the acoustic space, as he called it, adding: 'We are back in acoustic space. We begin again to structure the primordial feelings and emotions from which 3000 years of literacy divorced us' (1954: 18). He argued that mass media as 'extensions of the mechanisms of human perception' are responsible for how people perceive their environment, how they experience it and how they relate to it. McLuhan regarded the telephone, gramophone, and especially radio as the 'mechanisation of postliterate acoustic space'. Aural media such as radio and audiovisual media such as television, 'the omnipresent ear and the moving eye... have abolished writing, the specialised acoustic-visual metaphor which established the dynamics of the Western civilisation' (1954: 17). In this sense, electronic media have to be regarded as a disturbance of the order that was installed by the linearity of the literary culture. Or as Erhard Schüttpelz put it: 'The dissemination of a new medium... disturbs the modes of perceptions that were installed by an older network of media, it disturbs the whole modality of a medium and its modes of storage, usage and reflexion' (2003: 20). The point of this observation is that it is not only the new medium that disturbs the order of the old medium, but it is also the order of the older medium that often stands in the way of the breakthrough of the new.

The history of German *Hörspiel* is an important example first and foremost of an aesthetic struggle in the sense of perception of two different kinds of order that go hand-in-glove with different kinds of media. This example can be especially well traced and investigated by looking at the history and traditions of Ammer's most important broadcasting station department, the radio drama department of the public Bavarian broadcaster Bayerischer Rundfunk in Munich, one of the six public broadcasters established in the Federal Republic after World War II by the Allies with the aim of re-educating the German population. One of the Nazis' 'most dangerous weapons', radio, which they centralised and used for their propaganda, had to be turned back into a 'normal' mass medium. In fact, the editors in charge at Bayerischer Rundfunk responded quite openly to these efforts (Zeyn 1999: 31–39), perhaps also because the history of Bavarian broadcasting was tainted by Nazi ideology. One name to note is Richard Kolb, a deeply committed Nazi from the very beginning. He was *Hauptschriftleiter* (editor-in-chief) from 1930 to 1932 of the *Bayerische Radiozeitung* (Bavarian Radio Newspaper) (Hasselbring 1999: 26) and one of the most important conversational partners for Joseph Goebbels, later the Nazi Minister for Propaganda, when Goebbels was trying to understand the new medium of radio and its challenges and possibilities. Goebbels even once said of Richard Kolb: 'I am indebted to him for numerous ideas, I am indebted to him for a wealth of thoughts, which were later integrated into works when we were given control of broadcasting' (Döhl 1992: 39).

In 1932, just before the Nazi takeover, Richard Kolb published a collection of his essays on the artistic potential of the new medium of radio under the title *Das Horoskop des Hörspiels*. In it he declared that his aim was to free the radio drama from 'noise' and the dominance of technology (Kolb 1932: 69). His vision was a veritable 'cult of the word', which praised silence as proof of a literary masterpiece. Bernhard Siegert once called this notion of radio art 'negative radio aesthetics', which can be understood as a special version of McLuhan's famous dictum 'The medium is the message'. In the case of 'negative radio aesthetics', as propagated by Kolb and his influential post-War successors (Schwitzke 1963; Siegert 2002), it was not the medium that was the message; rather, it was the neglecting of the medium that was the message. In this sense, Kolb's radio concept could be regarded as the struggle to keep up the aesthetic ideas and values of the Age of the Press (or the Gutenberg Age). It was this suppression of the medium which implicitly promoted the reason that radio developed into a literary genre (Siegert 2004: 863–65). This notion of radio art as a literary genre was very prominent in Germany up to and including the 1960s, and to a certain extent it still is today, following the rise of audio books in recent years. However, under the circumstances of the end of the Weimar Republic, Kolb's literary radio aesthetics had specific political implications. He propagated the absolute primacy of the word and the human voice as a so-called '*körperlose Wesenheit*' ('bodyless essence' or 'entity'), as a neutral transmitter of the ideas of the poets (1932: 48–69). Of course, one also could substitute 'poet' with 'spiritual leader', or maybe even most precisely by '*Führer*', whose words and ideas should be rearticulated and internalised as purely as possible on the part of the listeners. In this respect Kolb's radio aesthetics could be regarded as the theoretical foundation of the idea of merging the radio listener with the radio device with the aim of synchronising the audience with the broadcaster and the listening population with the will of the broadcasting management. In this sense Richard Kolb's rejection of 'noise' and his promotion of the literary tradition of the Gutenberg Galaxy within the new medium of radio can also be regarded as a declaration of war on the radio avant-gardists in Berlin and Frankfurt; namely the radiophonic experiments of Hans Flesch, Bertolt Brecht, Kurt Weill and others (Hagen 2005: 67–120).

Since the very first radio show in Germany on 29 October 1923, broadcasting of any political content was strictly prohibited by the authorities in charge. Due to the social and political confusion following World War I, they feared a revolutionary uprising and therefore allowed the new medium to broadcast only cultural entertainment and education (Hagen 2005: 67–75). Of course, on the one hand this political restriction was viewed by some of the German radio pioneers as a pure provocation, while on the other this restriction was taken up as a challenge to explore the artistic potential of the new medium to its fullest extent. So, for example, the composer Kurt Weill developed his influential ideas of the 'possibilities of an absolute radio art' (1925: 264–70). These restrictions also led to highly-advanced, self-reflexive aural experiments, notably *Zauberei auf dem Sender: Versuch einer Rundfunkgroteske* ('Wizardry on the Air: An Attempt at a Radio Grotesque') in 1924 by Hans Flesch, writer of the first German radio drama and later director of the broadcasting station Funk-Stunde AG in Berlin. As perhaps the most advanced radio pioneer of the Weimar Republic, Hans Flesch was especially interested in the technical aspects of the new medium of radio. Inspired by the silent movies of his time, by the first theories of cinema and by Kurt Weill's considerations of 'the possibilities of absolute radio art' Flesch tried to derive for radio from its special technological characteristics and possibilities a genuine new art form. Hans Flesch's vision was to achieve by the means of radio an artistic impact that neither literature nor theatre, neither cinema nor concert could achieve. This led him to the insight that true radio art has to be derived from the apparatus. Its genuine artistic effects could only come from the mechanics of this electronic, mechanical instrument. In search of this new radiophonic art form, he supported as director of the Berliner Funkstunde the so-called Rundfunkversuchsstelle, that he founded in 1928, a laboratory for the creation of new instruments like the trautonium, new 'noises' and eventually new sound, that became part of the Berlin conservatory. This Rundfunkversuchsstelle can be regarded as one of the first studios for electro-acoustic music, an early precursor of Pierre Schaeffer's *studio d'essai* in Paris, Herbert Eimert's and Karlheinz Stockhausen's Studio für elektronische Musik in Cologne or Desmond Briscoe and Daphne Oram's BBC Radiophonic Workshop in London. Soon after the establishment of the Rundfunkversuchsstelle, for Hans Flesch all experiments came to an end. He was dismissed in August 1932, was accused in two Nazi broadcasting trials and received orders to go to war as a military doctor. Flesch was reported missing in April 1945 (Hagen 2003) and Kurt Weill and many others had to flee Germany. The Nazis won the struggle over the country and the medium, at least in the first round, and so, also over Richard Kolb's 'negative radio aesthetics'.

It was not until 1961 that the Austrian-born German media researcher Friedrich Knilli published his book *Das Hörspiel: Mittel und Möglichkeiten eines totalen Schallspiels* (*The Hörspiel: Means and Possibilities of a Total Soundplay*) as an intervention into the acoustic self-limitations propogated by Richard Kolb's influential tradition of German literary radio drama. Knillis' prescription was: 'The *Hörspiel* writer today can only free himself from the narrowness of the verbal *Hörspiel* (*Worthörspiel*) by expanding the sonic dimension of the traditional *Hörspiel* and by experimenting with the means and possibilities of both electronic music (Meyer-Eppler, Eimert) and *musique concrète* (Pierre Schaeffer)' (Cory 1992: 352). It was Knilli's achievement to take up the pre-War ideas of Hans Flesch and Kurt Weill, for example, and thereby to challenge the entire establishment of the radio drama scene in the young Federal Republic. Knilli's vision was '*Ein echtes Schallspiel*', meaning a true soundplay instead of a literary radio drama, just as Hans Flesch speculated around 1930 regarding the possible aesthetic effects of electromagnetic and acoustic waves. Knilli's ideas were taken up at first by the German author Paul Pörtner, who in 1965 created his first *Schallspielstudie*, literally a 'soundplay study'. Pörtner's experiments were supported by the radio drama department of the Bavarian broadcasting station in Munich, notably by its open-minded editor Hansjörg Schmitthenner. As Mark E. Cory put it: '...the *Hörspiel* became accessible and interesting again to the avant-garde through the constellation of Knilli, Pörtner, and Schmitthenner' (1992: 355).

By then it was possible once more for artists to regard and use text, sound and noise as equally important elements in their experimental and avantgardistic radio art. In addition to that, the electronic studio and its equipment became their instruments, while stereophonics made it possible for them to choreograph acoustic space. Thus, some of the radio drama departments in Germany became important collaborators in the avant-garde experiments of writers, musicians and artists like Peter Handke, Ernst Jandl, Friederike Mayröcker, John Cage, Mauricio Kagel and Ferdinand Kriwet, to name but a few of the most famous ones (Schöning 1982). Of course, this re-invention or rejuvenation of the German *Hörspiel* brought forth much criticism, too. For example, these soundplays, that became well known as what Klaus Schöning termed '*Neues Hörspiel*', were called 'empty experimentations' at best, and 'anti-humanistic verbal acrobatics' at worst. Anxiety developed around a '...suicidal flight away from plot, theme, and character... poised for surrender to peripheral areas such as electronic music and sound poetry'(Cory 1992: 332). Such objections could not stop avant-garde artists experimenting with new media, looking and longing for new artistic means, possibilities of expression and perception and a contemporary re-invention and understanding of their own identity as artists. In this respect Paul Pörtner stated: 'I trade the desk of a writer for the studio of the sound engineer, my new syntax is the cut, my product is recorded over microphones, mixers, and filters on magnetic tape, the principal of montage creates a playful composition out of a hundred particles' (Cory 1992: 331).

It is in this tradition of German *Hörspiel*, (or better, soundplay avantgardists from Hans Flesch and Kurt Weill to Paul Pörtner,) that Andreas Ammer and his musical collaborateurs, such as FM Einheit and Console, are situated. It is in soundplays like the *Hörspiel Bugs & Beats & Beasts* that the struggle of old and new media, of the old order that stands in the way of the breakthrough of the new order, to evoke McLuhan and Schüttpelz, is summed up in a 'radiophonic nutshell'. To express his criticism of the centuries-long institutionalised hierarchy of word over sound, all of the radiophonic art of Ammer and his colleague stand under a special licence, which promotes the equality of text and sound, author and musician. This is written in the artists' contract with the broadcasting stations, so that the musician gets the same repeat fees as the writer and therefore can better afford to invest time and energy in the creation of such a subtle, noisy symphony as *Bugs & Beats & Beasts* (Mauruschat 2012a).

Technological Resilience

The aesthetic resilience of the *Hörspiel Bugs & Beats & Beasts* is very much related to electricity and its artistic consequences. Its technological resilience is especially related to the consequences of digitalisation and the rise of home electronics. Since *Radio Inferno,* the first major *Hörspiel* collaboration of Andreas Ammer and FM Einheit in 1993, Ammer and his musical partners use digital tools extensively for their productions. As they always aimed at producing *Hörspiel* by using the latest technologies, they were often confronted with programming bugs that even the software engineers could not resolve. Trying to solve the problems they were confronted with, they had to respond creatively to them. In this sense the term 'bug' always had a double meaning for Ammer and Console. It stands for the insects but also for the technological mistakes, the glitches, that can be regarded either as disturbing noise or as a challenge for creativity. It just depends on the point of view of the observer (Mauruschat 2012a/b).

In the case of *Bugs & Beats & Beasts*, Ammer and Console also relied on the advanced technologies of bio-acoustic engineers, namely on the highly sensitive microphones that allowed recording even noises of insects with such deep or low frequencies that a human ear normally cannot hear them. 95 per cent of the beats in this *Hörspiel* were such insect noises and were recorded for scientific reasons. Only the characteristic starting noise of the fly trapped in a glass at the beginning was recorded by Console himself, and only five per cent of the beats were created purely electronically by him. All of these noises were finally edited with the help of the audio-software Logic and the hardware sampler Kurzweil K2000, a synthesizer with a sampling option that could be controlled via MIDI and that was so cheap that even an independent electronic musician like Console could afford one. Most of the voices and the cello were recorded at the small, independent music studio uphon-Studio in Weilheim, Upper Bavaria. Once the material was set, Ammer and Console arranged it on their laptops into the kind of symphony they had in mind and mailed the files to and fro between their 'bedroom production studios' until they decided they were ready to go to the uphone-Studio again for the final mix and mastering. The whole production was far removed from the traditional high standards of a classic studio at a broadcasting station, and it was also free of its restrictions. In this respect *Bugs & Beats & Beasts* can be regarded as being paradigmatic or a significant example of the vanishing of the radio studio as we know it: the traditional radio studio as a laboratory for the creation of new noises or sounds has been dissolved by digitisation. The old monopoly and authority of broadcasting stations in the realm of electroacoustic aesthetics has not only been disturbed but in some respects, it has even been destroyed and abolished and substituted to some extent by the 'network studio' as a virtual 'non-place' and 'non-space' (Théberge 2004: 773).

The resilient effects of digital technology are obvious, not only on the production side, but also in respect of archiving and distributing content. Due to the mp3 format and the internet, Ammer and Console offer their productions online as a webstream for free and as a cheap download. Thus, instead of only being broadcast once and then perhaps only every now and again, (but most of the time being locked away in the archives of broadcasting stations,) this radiophonic art work remains accessible after its transmission. This transgression of the traditional limitations of the *Hörspiel* to create acoustic art at a certain, ephemeral moment by a radio station, and its immediate reception via a radio receiver, was an idea that Andreas Ammer and FM Einheit took up even before the breakthrough of digital technology and the internet. Inspired by the general trend of multimedia art in the early 1990s and in the spirit of an expanded radio art as promoted, for example, by the Kunstradio department of the ORF in Vienna since 1987 (Grundmann 2006), Ammer came up with idea of a so-called 'radio opera'. Their *Hörspiel Apocalypse Live* in 1994 was a complex multimedia installation with screens and all different kinds of technological gadgets that was performed in front of an audience at the municipal Marstall Theater in Munich and a few weeks later a recording of it was broadcast on radio (Bachmann 2013). This new format of a 'radio opera' in the sense of a classical *Hörspiel* that contains scenic elements and is performed in front of an audience, was taken up by Ammer and his co-authors a few times since then. For example, *Have you ever heard of Wilhelm Reich?* (2009) and *Die Vögel nach OSCAR SALA* (2010), are two further collaborations between Andreas Ammer and Martin Gretschmann. Both plays could easily be called 'radio operas' due to their huge amount of musical and scenic elements, although they do not have very much in common with the idea of a traditional bourgeois opera. As FM Einheit used to be the drummer of German post-industrial noise band Einstürzende Neubauten, and as Martin Gretschmann, alias Console, is responsible for the electronic part of the Bavarian independent band The Notwist, these radio operas sound more like techno performances than like operas, and their sound, of course, might be regarded from the point of view of certain bourgeois concepts of music as – noise.

Spatial Resilience

In many respects, the noises of *Bugs & Beats & Beasts* do open up new spaces, in a concrete as well as an abstract sense, and therefore do also demonstrate the spatial resilience of the medium of radio. Due to its modes of production and distribution, this *Hörspiel* overcomes the classical radiophonic spaces of the broadcasting station and the radio set as a receiver and player. *Bugs & Beats & Beasts* is in some respects a true digital production of the age of 'social networking' (Bonini 2014). Its home is not the infrastructure of a large broadcasting institution but the 'network studio' of contemporary independent producers. Its destiny is not the institutional archive but the permanent accessibility of the internet. Its audience is not only the realm of the more or less contingent number of radio listeners at a certain moment in time when this *Hörspiel* is broadcast, but also a kind of a global community of fans who share a special interest in the works of Ammer and Console. Due to its electronic aesthetics, this 'natural techno symphony' also opens up the realm of pop culture. Thus, Console plays some of the tracks either as a warm-up before concerts of his band *The Notwist* or as a chill-out track at one of his DJ sets. In this respect, it is the club and the concert hall as subcultural spaces that are opened up by this kind of radio art (Mauruschat 2012b). However, that which Andreas Ammer and the radio drama department of the Bavarian radio station declared as their aim in the early 1990s, '*Hörspiel in die Hitparade!*', or '*Hörspiel* in the charts!' (Krug 2008: 126), has not yet come to pass. The club is perhaps an even a better place to reach the community of actual and potential fans.

Finally, *Bugs & Beats & Beasts* opens up a very special space that is not easy to name as it can be understood as opening up a new space of perception (Holl 2012). The fact that bio acoustic engineers developed such highly sensitive microphones that are able even to record and make audible noises that human ears alone cannot hear, such as the sound of rice weevil larvae, was the premise for this very specific artistic experiment, one that arranged different tracks and the mutual interference of different noises in such a way that listeners, who can hear and perceive it all, get thrown out of their anthropocentrism. The noises of the insects interact with the male and female voices, the dialogue of the cello and the electronic beats with the Latin and German texts and the noises of 'sonic warfare' were turned into a 'natural techno symphony'. The artistic, skilful arrangement of insect noises challenges the listener and questions the idea of human superiority, not in an anti-humanistic way but rather in a post-humanist way that might in the best case mean more modesty of mankind. This is probably the highest art of disturbance that noises can achieve, or in other words, after truly hearing *Bugs & Beats & Beats*, anyone will look very differently at all insects.

Conclusion

If *Bugs & Beats & Beasts* by Andreas Ammer and Console is a *Hörspiel* in the broadest sense, we must conclude with the famous definition of a *Hörspiel* that was coined by the writer and radio producer Helmut Heissenbüttel in 1968: '*Hörspiel* ist eine offene Form', or *Hörspiel* is an open form in which everything is possible, everything is allowed (1968: 222-3). This openness makes this acoustic art form able to respond almost instantaneously to crucial changes in technology and society by making them audible and presenting them to a broader public. It is the perfect tool, not least because it is funded through fees for artistic research at the forefront of medial, technological, cultural and political changes, artistic research in the sense of a seismographic articulation of the disturbing noises of the new, of the unknown to come. It was the aim of this chapter to show how resilient the medium of radio has always been, still is and probably always will be, as envisioned in the theoretical concept of 'extended radio'. The historical investigation on the aesthetical level showed how even conventional radio was always able to open up to new technologies to make new sounds heard, despite different, mainly political hindrances. The investigations at the technological level focused on the changes of the last few decades, including the development of highly sensitive microphones that make new aesthetic experiences possible, the network studio with its hybrid equipment that implicates other forms of collaborative artistic work as well as more independence from broadcasting stations, and finally the internet. It is both a platform where, at least theoretically, content is always accessible instead of being broadcast only once and, with luck, afterwards being locked away in an archive, and a platform where a global network of fans can be established in addition to a local community of listeners. These technological examples of the resilience of radio form the premise of its spatial resilience. Digital technology and the internet are the prerequisites for contemporary radio to be unconstrained by time and space. But these technological premises on their own are not enough to open up new spaces of understanding and consciousness, therefore one needs art and reflection, especially about something as subtle and ephemeral as sound.

In this respect, the fact that the main subject of the natural techno symphony, *Bugs & Beats & Beasts*, is the noise of bugs with the inherent *double entendre* there of insects and errors, makes even more sense. Insects have in the last few decades been of significant interest to many researchers and media theorists in parallel with the rise of digital technology, the internet, and the network society (Castells 2010). Through listening one acquires an aesthetic experience of something that cannot yet be fully understood with all its consequences. Or as Eugene Thacker put it: 'What is interesting in the case of sonic swarms is the way in which the incorporeality of the swarm as a phenomenal entity in itself is tied to a materiality that is unseen, unbodied, and only reductively localisable' (Thacker 2007). We can hear the swarm way before we can see it and then finally we also can start to investigate the phenomenon systematically with our eyes in our urge to tame it. However, at the beginning we only have our ears and the opportunity to listen if we want to understand. Listen to the noises of bugs, of insects, as uncanny as they may be, uncanny as any disturbing noise which heralds the new. Bssh.

References

Bachmann, A (2013) 'Andreas Ammers *Apocalypse Live*. Transmediales Erzählen und intermediale Situation', in Renner, K *et al* (eds), *Medien. Erzählen. Gesellschaft. Transmediales Erzählen im Zeitalter der Medienkonvergenz*, Berlin: de Gruyter.

Bonini, T (2014) 'The listener as producer: The rise of the networked listener', in Bonini, T & Monclús, B (eds), *Radio Audiences and Participation in the Age of the Network Society*, London: Routledge.

Castells, M (2010) *The Rise of the Network Society*, Malden: Wiley-Blackwell.

Cory, M (1992) 'Soundplay. The Polyphonous Tradition of German Radio Art', in Kahn, Douglas *et al* (eds), *Wireless Imagination. Sound, Radio, and the Avant-Garde*, Cambridge: The MIT Press.

Döhl, R (1992) *Das Hörspiel zur NS-Zeit. Geschichte und Typologie des Hörspiels*, Darmstadt: Wissenschaftliche Buchgesellschaft.

Gilfillan, D (2009) *Pieces of Sound. German Experimental Radio*, Minneapolis: University of Minnesota Press.

Goodman, S (2010) *Sonic Warfare. Sound, Affect, and the Ecology of Fear*, Cambridge: The MIT Press.

Grundmann, H (2006) 'Expanded Radio. Radiokunst im Spannungsfeld zwischen Sendemedium und Kommunikationstechnologie', in Thurmann-Jajes, A *et al* (eds), *Sound Art. Zwischen Avantgarde und Popkultur*, Bremen: Schriftenreihe für Künstlerpublikationen.

Hagen, W (2003) 'Der neue Mensch und die Störung. Hans Fleschs vergessene Arbeit für den frühen Rundfunk', in Kümmel, A *et al* (eds), *Signale der Störung*, München: Wilhelm Fink Verlag.

Hagen, W (2005) *Das Radio. Zur Geschichte und Theorie des Hörfunks – Deutschland/USA*, München: Wilhelm Fink Verlag.

Hasselbring, B (1999) 'Am Anfang war Dorfrichter Adam', in Kapfer, H (ed), *Vom Sendespiel zur Medienkunst. Die Geschichte des Hörspiels im Bayerischen Rundfunk. Das Gesamtverzeichnis der Hörspielproduktion des Bayerischen Rundfunks 1949 – 1999*, München: Belleville.

Heissenbüttel, H (1968) 'Horoskop des Hörspiels', in Heissenbüttel, H, *Zur Tradition der Moderne. Aufsätze und Anmerkungen 1964 – 1971*, Neuwied: Luchterhand.

Holl, U (2012) 'Medien der Bioakustik. Tiere wiederholt zur Sprache bringen', in Nessel, S *et al* (eds), *Der Film und das Tier. Klassifizierungen, Cinephilien, Philosophien*, Berlin: Bertz + Fischer.

Karathanasopoulou, Evi (2014) 'Ex-static but not ecstatic: Digital radio and the end of interference', in Oliveira, M, Stachyra, G & Starkey, G (eds) *Radio: The Resilient Medium*, Sunderland: Centre for Research in Media and Cultural Studies.

Kapfer, H (ed) (1999) *Vom Sendespiel zur Medienkunst. Die Geschichte des Hörspiels im Bayerischen Rundfunk. Das Gesamtverzeichnis der Hörspielproduktion des Bayerischen Rundfunks 1949 – 1999*, München: Belleville.

Kapfer, H *et al* (ed) (2006) *Intermedialität und offene Form. Hörspiel und Medienkunst im Bayerischen Rundfunk. Gesamtverzeichnis 1996 – 2005*, München: Belleville.

Knilli, F (1961) *Das Hörspiel. Mittel und Möglichkeiten eines totalen Schallspiels*, Stuttgart: W. Kohlhammer Verlag.

Kolb, R (1932) *Das Horoskop des Hörspiels*. Berlin: Max Hesse Verlag.

Krug, H (2008) *Kleine Geschichte des Hörspiels*, Konstanz: UVK Verlagsgesellschaft.

Mauruschat, A (2012a), Transcript of an interview with Andreas Ammer.

Mauruschat, A (2012b) Transcript of an interview with Martin Gretschmann, alias Console.

McLuhan, M (1954) *Counterblast*, Berkely: Gingko Press.

McLuhan, M *et al* (1960) 'Acoustic space', reproduced in McLuhan, M (1997) *Media research: technology, art, communication*, Amsterdam: G+B Arts International.

Parikka, J (2010) *Insect Media. An Archeology of Animals and Technology*. Posthumanities 11. Minneapolis: University of Minnesota Press.

Sá Rego Costa, M *et al* (2013) 'The arts on the radio and radio art in Brazil', paper at the ECREA Radio Research Conference, September, London.

Schöning, K (ed) (1982) *Spuren des Neuen Hörspiels*, Frankfurt/Main: Suhrkmap.

Schüttpelz, E (2003) 'Frage nach der Frage, auf die das Medium eine Antwort ist', in Kümmel, A *et al* (ed), *Signale der Störung*, München: Wilhelm Fink Verlag.

Schwitzke, H (1963) *Das Hörspiel*, Köln: Kiepenheuer & Witsch.

Serres, M (2007) *The Parasite*, translated by Schehr, L, *Posthumanities 1*, Minneapolis: University of Minnesota Press.

Siegert, B (2002), 'Das Hörspiel als Vergangenheitsbewältigung', in Schneider, I *et al* (eds) *Diskursgeschichte der Medien nach 1945: Bd. 1, Medienkultur der 50er Jahre*, Wiesbaden: VS Verlag für Sozialwissenschaften.

Siegert, B (2004) '1953, March 26 – Coming to terms with the past', in Wellbery, D et al (eds), *A New History of German literature*, Cambridge: Harvard University Press.

Thacker, E (2007) 'Pulse Demons' in *Culture Machine 9*.
http://www.culturemachine.net/index.php/cm/article/view/80/56

Théberge, Paul (2004) 'The Network Studio: Historical and Technological Paths to a New Ideal in Music Making', *Social Studies of Science*, volume 34, issue 5.

Weibel, P (2012) 'Einleitung', in Gerlach, J (ed) *Sound Art. Klang als Medium der Kunst*, Karlsruhe: ZKM.

Weill, K (2000) 'Möglichkeiten absoluter Radiokunst', in Weill, K, *Musik und musikalisches Theater*, Mainz: Schott.

Wolfe, C (2007) 'Introduction to the New Edition', in Serres, M, *The Parasite*, Minneapolis: University of Minnesota Press.

Wolfe, C (2009) *What is Posthumanism? Posthumanities 8*, Minneapolis: University of Minnesota Press.

Zeyn, M (1999) 'Alles war möglich. Das Hörspiel im Bayerischen Rundfunk von 1949–1973', in Kapfer, Herbert (ed), *Vom Sendespiel zur Medienkunst. Die Geschichte des Hörspiels im Bayerischen Rundfunk. Das Gesamtverzeichnis der Hörspielproduktion des Bayerischen Rundfunks 1949 – 1999*, München: Belleville.

Chapter 20

Breaking the taboo of avisuality: When pure audio theatre is not enough

Karolina Albińska

Abstract

The tendency to compare and contrast visual and non-visual means of artistic expression is as old as radio itself. This is clearly visible when one analyses the history and the directions of the development of this 'music box' and the genres that were, (and still are,) broadcast through it – particularly a phenomenon called the 'Theatre of the Imagination' or the 'Theatre of the Mind'. Hence even in the times when radio drama was not treated as an independent form of art, practitioners and theoreticians who created and examined radio plays tried to find elements that were common to this kind of radio programme and film – for example their methods of creation and perception. In the twenty-first century this trend has become even stronger because pictures have been physically added to the radio content. As a result the demarcation line between visual and non-visual media is very hazy.

This chapter describes the forms and existence of radio drama in both the pre-convergence and convergence eras. It discusses concepts of full and partial visualisation of the audio theatre and presents the examples of different methods that have recently been used to give Polish and British media users new media products that can not only be heard, but also seen.

Keywords: audio theatre, radio drama, visualised radio, radio with pictures, Poland

Introduction: The shift of radio's ontological status

According to the authors of *Programming for TV, Radio & the Internet,* 'In electronic media nothing is forever' (Perebinossoff, Gross, & Gross 2005: xvii). They have used a concise sentence that serves as the motto of this article to comment on the past and present situation of the media market. However, they are not the only propagators of this view. There are few scholars, if indeed any, who would claim the contrary. In fact, it is very hard to disagree with this statement, especially when one examines the vigorous development of radio – the first technological invention that has been ascribed to the group of means of mass communication mentioned in the above quotation - the ways of its existence through the ages and the change of its identity. Ultimately, it is the 'wireless music box' that has constantly had to keep pace with media trends typical of different eras and, thereby, meet the shifting requirements of both mediasphere and audience (Pleszkun-Olejniczakowa 2012: 240-86).

What is more, radio's adaptability as well as its ability to reinvent itself and, in consequence, to survive in a competitive environment have always depended not only on social, cultural and economic factors but also on how well broadcasters have adjusted to technological change (Fleming 2012: 181-237). This fact was painfully discovered in the late 1940s and early 1950s of the previous century when television entered the scene for good to steal radio listeners and turn many of them into viewers. Since this pivotal time, in different historical periods, radio has resorted to various tricks so as not to disappear from the media landscape. Certainly, its every innovation was a milestone and they include: the invention of stereo transmission that offered a new, richer sound experience; the appearance of transistor receivers that liberated listeners from indoor, static, sedentary and group listening in favour of their mobility to the accompaniment of portable, smaller and cheaper sets; the installation and widespread use of car radios that contributed to greater flexibility and immediacy of listening on the move or the introduction of headphones that personalised broadcasts and made them more intimate (Albińska 2011a: 75-7). This is all the more true in the current century because – as Martin Shingler and Cindy Wieringa noted – 'new technology has a principal role to play in radio's recent and on-going renaissance' (1998: xii). Analysing this issue in a broader context, it can even be said that the digitisation process has opened a new chapter for radio and has become the driving force for its rejuvenation. Because of this, today this medium, instead of a single 'analogue face' characteristic of a bygone era, has many incarnations as its content is disseminated via different platforms. Moreover, it is no longer perceived merely as 'transmission of sounds converted into electromagnetic waves directly through space to a receiving device which converts them back into sounds' (Danesi 2008: 246). Instead, modern digital broadcasts, sometimes known as 'Radio 2.0', go far beyond traditional AM and FM transmissions and may adopt many forms, such as digital terrestrial radio (DAB, DRM, IBCO), digital terrestrial TV (DVB-T), satellite radio, web-based radio and television broadcasting systems (internet radio, streaming, podcasting, video casting), mobile-phone systems, Wide Area Networks and various hybrid systems (see chapter 2). For this reason, distribution techniques no longer represent an adequate criterion for differentiating between what is radio and what is not.

Perhaps one of the most serious complications with media categorisation is that 'finding a stable definition for radio in the multiplatform age – as Carole Fleming suggests - is increasingly difficult (2010: 42). Even though from a technological angle it is not at all clear where one medium ends and another begins, three things are obvious. Firstly, digitisation has become a catalyst in the transformation process from 'old-fashioned' to 'modern' radio. Secondly, the opinions about the technological future of radio are contradictory. Some people strongly support the idea that, with time, this means of mass communication will be fully entwined in the computer world, and change into a metamedium (O'Neill 2007). Others – for example Henry Jenkins - deny the myth of the 'black box' (2007) by pointing at media divergence rather than convergence as the end of the radio's historical development since, according to him, we have witnessed the tremendous multiplication of audio reception devices. Last but not least, the very definition of radio transforms as fast as the media world itself, not only due to the cross-fertilisation of different media on the most general, 'environmental' level, but also because of the mixing of the means of artistic expression for given media.

With time people simply started to realise that there is considerable truth in Marshall McLuhan's thesis that 'the medium is the message' (1975: 45), yet content may be 'king' as well (Ramsey 2008: 72). Referring to Joshua Meyerowitz's approach, it goes without saying that media intermingle also in regard to the secondary sphere that comes down to the metaphor of 'media grammar' (2013). Therefore, in contrast to the thesis presented in the books *On air: Methods and Meanings of Radio* (Shingler & Wieringa 1998: xii) or *Understanding Radio* that such audio codes as speech, sounds, music and silence have remained constant because 'in radio all the signs are auditory' (Crisell 1996: 42), nowadays it is more and more noticeable that the standard classification that takes into consideration the raw material of which media content is made is, in fact, not as unambiguous as it may seem at first glance. Given this, there is no denying that in what concerns radio, it is no longer possible to fully preserve its most distinctive feature – 'blindness' – because now non-visual and visual media freely transgress the boundaries that for ages have acted as an unwritten demarcation line between them, irrespective of whether the 'blindness' of traditional radio has been regarded as the most prominent of its strengths or its worst limitation (De Fossard 2005: 30). Thus, in accordance with the so-called 'anthropological tendency' (Levinson 2006: 114) that aims at a union between 'eye-centered' and 'ear-oriented' media, (a harmonious, biological cooperation between human senses,) radio 'enhances' its content by physically adding visual components to fit better into the 'audiovisual culture' (Hopfinger 2008: 26-7). With this goal in mind, Andrew Crisell explained that: 'In the context of convergent tendencies in the mass media, some of the essays attribute its [radio's] resilience to an ability to preserve its distinctiveness, others to the ease with which it can incorporate features such as interactivity and *visual texts*' [my emphasis] (2006: viii).

In short, to satisfy the needs of contemporary media users, a specific hybrid has been created that combines the distinctive features of both sound-based and vision-oriented means of mass communication. This 'enriched' output is labeled 'radio with pictures', 'radio with sight', 'visualised radio' or 'radiovision' and usually is explained by means of very broad and inclusive definitions. Therefore, 'visualisation' is simply using images to enhance radio, visualising radio is 'enhancing an audio-only broadcast with visual material, to garner a richer understanding of the subject matter' (Radio with pictures 2012) and 'visualised audio is part of what we need to offer with any program to reach the audience that we want to reach... It is the right content on the right platform for the right audience' (Radio Talk 2012). Of course, nowadays consumption of traditional radio broadcasts still prevails but radio with added visual value – although it is not always seen as radio *per se* (Goban-Klas 2011: 119) - is an alternative that cannot be ignored, at least by less conventional listeners with such sophisticated artistic tastes as might listen to radio drama. Those who can appreciate the potential of exploiting the synergy between visual and non-visual media probably find the 'visualised' option quite attractive since 'today... it is common practice for a generic program presented in one primary medium to work in tandem with other media to take advantage of the characteristics of each medium' (Silverblatt 2007: 17). Nevertheless, this statement is just sheer conjecture because to draw more general conclusions additional scientific research on the reception of 'visualised' radio plays is needed.

On the other hand, visualisation may also represent a threat to radio drama, a specific genre that by its very nature is based on audibility and invisibility, especially as this audio form is considered to be the one in which radio's most distinctive qualities are to be found (Mayen 1965: 30). This opinion is reflected in Michał Kaziów's definition of a radio play as 'a radio work of art whose raw material consists entirely of audio elements... its structure is subordinated to literary poetics and its dominant feature is invisibility. Its action is not played on stage, despite the participation of actors; it is constructed as an imaginative reality in the productive listener's imagination. In view of radio's specificity it seems obvious that invisibility and audibility are the most important factors that impinge on 'audio theatre' (1973: 93). If so, the most important question that should be posed in this context is this: is it really possible to bring together two contradictory tendencies and force radio drama to take a visual path?

Visual arts and the artistic dependence of the 'Theatre of the Imagination'

Interestingly enough, long before the recent convergence era that is tantamount to the most untrammeled development of the visualisation of the audiosphere, scholars who searched for the origins of radio plays also made the first attempts to combine this type of work of art with a visual dimension. With a high degree of certainty, the taboo of invisibility was partly broken when theoreticians and practitioners started to compare and contrast radio plays with other forms of visual artistic expression, in the middle of the 1920s. Paradoxically, the more people's attention was drawn to these interrelationships, the more invisible, in the literal sense, radio plays became. This artistic form of radio transmission was gaining its independence quite slowly. At first, radio drama could not escape its predecessors, and as Irzykowski said, 'every art contains within itself the elements of other arts' (Laskowicz 1983: 39). In other words, at first, radio drama was seen as subordinate to 'older' arts since it was strongly believed not to have its own, separate identity. Such broadcasts were for years treated as nothing more than 'literature for peformance', 'theatre crammed onto a machine' or 'cinema for the ear' - to use the nomenclature coined by Aleksander Małachowski, Krzysztof Eydziatowicz and Antonii Bohdziewicz respectively, who focused on the problem of the lack of the independence of radio plays in the years 1925 to 1970 (Pleszkun-Olejniczakowa 2000a; Albińska 2012; Bardijewska 2001; Bachura 2011).

However, the issue of the hazy boundaries that divide this artistic genre from works that are based mainly on vision has also been echoed by more contemporary authors. For obvious reasons, it is impossible to enumerate all of them, therefore, only a few are mentioned here, by name and in alphabetical order: Sława Bardijewska (2001), Tim Crook (1999), Andrew Crisell (1996), Jerzy Limon (2004), Dermot Rattigan (2002), and Jerzy Tuszewski (2002). We should not forget either the members of the Łódź School of Radio Studies, Professor Elżbieta Pleszkun-Olejniczakowa, Joanna Bachura and Aleksandra Pawlik who wrote about the tight links between radio drama and vision-based works in *Dwa Teatry: Studia z zakresu teorii i interpretacji sztuki słuchowiskowej*, among others (Bachura 2001). They said that at present, when audio theatre has finally gained its independence, in the eyes of the general public there is still a deep sense of doubt whether the 'Theatre of the Imagination' is a sub-category of written literature and traditional scenic theatre or, if in contrast to its name, it simply shares common characteristics with productions that are screened in cinemas and broadcast on television (Pleszkun-Olejniczakowa 2011).

On closer examination, many authors of specialist literature tried to find a common denominator for radio drama and other works that incorporated visual components as a key part of their structures. Their views may be briefly summarised in a few essential points. Taking into account the conditions under which radio drama emerged, scholars wanted to establish a common plane of understanding between this aural genre and eye-centered, written literature. In so doing they created different classifications of radio plays by referring to the classical literary genres of prose, poetry and drama that had been well known since the times of Ancient Greece. They also emphasised the importance of a script that served as the outline for a final radio production that, only thanks to a director, actors and sound effects specialists, takes its radiophonic shape. Overall, there was a general consensus, with respect to the written text of a would-be radio drama, that radio as a transmitter of literature resembled, to the greatest extent possible, the most traditional and prestigious means of mass communication - books (Pleszkun-Olejniczakowa 2000b: 363).

Not surprisingly, theatre influenced radio plays not only through adaptations of written stage plays. It is easy to realise that the shared platform for both arts was the presence of actors. But here the similarities ended because in order to adapt to the imperatives of an 'invisible scene', people who worked in radio theatre had to completely change their attitude to acting. In radio there was no scenery and no lighting. There was no point in wearing costumes or make-up. That is why only when prototypes of radio plays were transmitted in real time from theatre buildings via the so-called *théatrophone* and during a short period when they were already transferred to radio studios, did actors hang on tightly to scenic attributes. With time, they got used to the 'naked' voice playing the leading role (Albińska 2012) and the practice of wearing costumes and playing roles in front of a live audience was not recommended anymore (Bachura 2012). The new tasks of performers and the change of their working conditions provoked comparisons between radio drama actors and film actors as well (Pleszkun-Olejniczakowa 2011). The complexities of the issue of radio drama's inferior status were also noticed by Val H. Gielgud who drew a very different, though interesting, line of investigation by comparing classical theatre with the 'Theatre of the Mind'. To show that the differences between these two are so great as to be larger than their similarities he wrote the following: 'We are all accustomed, in everyday phraseology, to going "to see" plays, as opposed to going "to hear" them. In consequence the mere juxtaposition of the words "radio" and "play" must imply for many people a contradiction in terms' (1957 : 85). The same problem was also reflected in the writings of Grażyna Pawlak who claimed that radio dramas once functioned as a counter-proposal to visible theatrical spectacles (2000: 383).

Radio drama, with its dependency on sound alone, was also compared with cinema and television productions, especially as regards the methods of their production. Some scholars, like Antonii Bohdziewicz, were convinced what united them was the relationship of souls and blood that stemmed from their historically-conditioned origin (1935: 11). Others, for example David T. McFarland, focused more on the technological aspects and said that editing techniques that were used by the creators of radio programmes, not excluding radio drama, that is, the 'segue', 'cross fade', 'silence', 'stab/shotgun' and 'drop in' had their exact functional equivalents on the ground of visual arts called 'cut', 'dissolve', 'fade', 'wipe' and 'key' (1997: 113-17). Still others described different types of montage or acoustic plans. Nonetheless, all media experts agreed on one thing: these two kinds of works of art were in many respects alike because 'quite a lot of similarities between the grammar of radio language and the grammar of film language can be noticed in the relationship that occurs on the line of film - radio drama' (Pleszkun-Olejniczakowa 2011: 70-1). The topics of the perception and reception of radio drama also represent fertile territory for comparing and contrasting these artistic works with the visual arts. The first notion goes far beyond the scope of this chapter. What is more, the question concerning the nature of radio images still remains without a satisfactory answer. Initially, radio drama could not free itself from film or theatre because some media commentators postulated that radio plays had to be consumed in a very similar way to that in which visual performances were watched. As a result they insisted on creating 'radio salons' or 'radiocinemas' (Bohdziewicz 1935: 61), where listeners, plunged into darkness, could sit in silence and listen to radio plays. When television appeared on the media scene for the first time, the situation did not change much because its audiences were still treated as listeners who were able to watch programmes, not as viewers who were able to listen to them (Mayen 1965: 26). Today, this method is only used during such festivals as the Two Theatres Radio and TV Drama Festival in Sopot or such artistic exhibitions as the visualisation of the *Become A Member* radio drama by Alexander Doliner and Nikola Tasic, presented during the Alias in Wonderland event organised by the University of Applied Arts, Vienna.

'Visualised' radio plays – case studies

Fundamentally, the success of radio drama has depended, first and foremost, on the 'blindness' of the medium and its ability to stimulate the listener's imagination, as spoken words and sounds have remained central to its generic identity. The fact remains that the most meaningful union of radio and vision-based means of mass communication happened well over 80 years ago, when early image-receiving devices that worked in tandem with radio sets were introduced. Thanks to technological inventions such as Rayfoto, Radiovisor, (from which the word 'radiovision' was derived,) or the Fultograph, (that from 1929 was used by a regional station of Polish

Radio in Poznań,) that images in their physical form could be broadcast to listeners' houses to accompany gramophone records and, later, radio. In this way, as Krzysztof Michalski remarked, Poland became the third country in Europe to have this kind of equipment and during one year carried 364 'visualised' transmissions, disseminating 850 pictures (2004: 14-15). Significantly, with time, the term 'radiovision' applied not only to facsimile paper images but also to a broad spectrum of different products of the visualisation process, namely pictures, drawings and posters printed in the press, photographs, lantern slides and filmstrips for use with a still projector and tape recorded audio soundtrack (Albińska 2013: 156-7). As so often happens, these techniques of visualisation were also very eagerly adapted by radio drama producers, especially when they served as an educational tool for schools. Therefore, at the beginning of the 1960s, 'France, Holland, Norway, Sweden, Niger, all projected still, bright, large colourful pictures as an integral part of a radio broadcast' (Williams 1968: 11), which were no less popular in Australia, the Netherlands, Cameroon, Turkey and the UK (Foxall 1972). For instance, the auditory codes gained visual value in the case of the BBC radio play *Vincent Van Gogh* that, in 1967, won a Japanese Prize for the best radio program and consisted of the sound of the radio drama and a filmstrip depicting 26 reproductions of the famous painter's works. Listeners could also go on the 'visualised' trip to Pompeii and see before their eyes the ancient city, before and after the huge natural disaster, due to the illustrations prepared for broadcast. The painted illustrations provided also a visual accompaniment to *Cook's Second Voyage* (Williams 1968), while a six-page folder of twenty 35mm colourful slides with self-portraits, portraits, landscapes, religious paintings, etchings and drawings was used as visual material to make a dramatised program about Rembrandt more attractive (*The Listener* 1969).

Examining methods that in the past were used to translate radio messages not only for the ear but also for the eye, it is evident that radio entered the next era of the visualisation process when radio/TV simulcasts were initiated. What is surprising is that there is every likelihood that radio drama, in contrast to morning shows (Albińska 2011b: 146-51), skipped this phase and moved directly into the internet age, as the author has not managed to find any examples of such bi-media broadcasts. The prominent saviour of radio plays in the audiovisual era may be the computer. Two or more media interact in harmony, to a greater or lesser extent, bringing additional 'visual' stimuli to radio content. This possibility was quite quickly noticed by media innovators who stressed that radio drama is very much a team production and started to cooperate with web designers. They wanted to take the next step toward better visualisation, to provide not only live-streaming and listen-again facilities but also visual elements that could be effectively mixed with audio. The first wave of non-traditional producers experimenting in this way appeared in the 1990s (Albińska 2011b: 157-63). One pioneer in this field was the Swedish Radio Theatre in Finland that in 1997 broadcast *Särskilt de Primitiva* – an on-demand science fiction radio play about an experiment made by alien anthropologists who conducted research on primitive races. Definitely, the real breakthrough was that this dramatised radio program was supported by visual elements in textual form that could be seen on a computer screen. The concept of creating a revolutionary broadcast of this type using an interactive game was discussed by the same company two years earlier, but at that time the internet was not well-developed or popular enough to guarantee success, so therefore, this brave vision was not turned into reality. The much more advanced version of 'visualised' radio drama, addressed to children, was produced by Estonian Radio in 1997. *StrawBully-TarBubble* gave listener/viewers the chance to enter a site to listen to the radio play in Estonian, synchronise the broadcast with its written text or read the subtitles in Russian and English. They could also experience hypertextuality by clicking on selected words to get additional information but, what is more important in the context of this chapter, they were also encouraged to 'animate' the visual presentation by rolling the text on the screen. Additionally, they could admire the pictures that served as the visualisation of the audio content (Crook 1999: 26-7), which deserves a special mention here. Sometimes visual materials performed the function of additional information. For example, in Poland, the drama serial *Motel w pół drogi* (2006-8) was very popular. At the same time, on the website **motelwpoldrogi.wp.pl** visual components were featured, including the texts of four blogs written by the director (Janusz Kukuła) and actors (Joanna Wielopolska, Marcin Kamiński, Marek Wagner); articles full of personal finance tips as well as culinary art, health and fitness advice; photo galleries showing what was going on behind the scenes of particular episodes and videos of chats with the authors and producers (Pawlik 2012).

Alternatively, visual images depicted the location of a given radio drama's plot. Thus, the visualisation was going hand in hand with the development of the plot of a story. Among radio plays whose producers focused on the visualisation of the storyline were some created in Britain from 1989 to 2003 by Independent Radio Drama Productions (Albińska 2011: 148) and the American radio dramas produced by Seeing Ear Theatre such as *Tripping Astral* by Brian Smith, *Murder Mysteries* by Neil Gainman, and *City of Dreams* by Michael Straczynski (Willis 2010). What, at that time, struck everyone, broadcasters and listeners alike, was the change to the method of visualisation. Instead of traditional, paper pictures, electronic photography in the form of a slide show was used. There is, more than ever, a need to remember that this seemingly perfect method of visualisation that was born at the end of 1990s proved to be far from ideal. The pace of 'visualised' presentation was very slow and, as a result, for most of the duration of transmissions of radio dramas viewers saw nothing other than the 'blackness' of the computer screen. To put it another way, their exposure to 'visualised' elements was sporadic, so a few pictures that were added to audio output were treated as imprecise clues, while the rest of a story had to be imagined on the basis of words and sounds that were heard by audience of a radio play.

This 'primitive' visualisation did not preclude working on more advanced editing techniques resulting in the creation of so-called photo films. That is, digital storytelling, where photography is a dominant way of expression. According to Peter Rudge: 'We don't like the term "audio slideshow" because it's more complicated than this. It's not just slapping in some photos with audio on top; it's about trying to craft a film, an experience, a narrative – all those good things. But still images have a power to affect people that's hard to beat, so we certainly don't do things without photography' (2013). Building on this assumption, 'photo film' can be thought of as a visualisation method that combines techniques traditionally used by photographers and film makers and, in practice, it can be created in multiple modalities. Usually, it is a series of static strips that resemble a comic in which individual images are put into a multi-panel audio-visual sequence or as visual elements that give the impression of movement because separate, 'frozen', shots are set in motion due to editing techniques, not the movement of depicted characters. Examples of this method include *Pushing* and *Dublin One Way* (Pawlik 2011: 273-85). The first, despite its audio-only radio transmission, could be consumed in visualised form via TV and computer. It was one of six 15-minute radio plays that were broadcast in 2008 as a part of *The City Speaks* series. Transmitted by the BBC on 19 March in the *Afternoon Play* slot, it told the story of a cheeky boy who was helping a reclusive Gulf War ex-soldier to push from Lewisham to the City a huge, broken down fridge, in which 'a dead man's heart' was hidden. Tellingly, this short radio play was a joint work of a team of three people: the scriptwriter, Lin Coghlan, the BBC radio producer Jessica Dromgoole, who was responsible for the acoustic sphere and the film producer Alnoor Dewshi, who created visualised content. At first they developed the script, recorded it and then added the 'photographic visiontrack' to exactly match the audio narrative. The same was done for the rest of the plays in the series, although the production teams were different (Albińska 2012b). The second photo film prepared especially for a premiere in the S-1 concert studio of Polish Radio, *Szczecin* by Grzegorz Skalski was about a Polish emigrant who went to Ireland to find a better job. It was directed by Krzysztof Czeczot who also played Kris, the protagonist. The music producer was Marcin Borys but the songs themselves were written and performed by the Pogodno music band. As with *Pushing*, *Dublin One Way* was designed as multi-platform production that was presented in sound-only form via radio and in a 'visualised' form that was screened, among others, during the eighth Two Theatres festival where its producers won two awards. Later, it was available as a videocast online. It was the first Polish radio drama in the Dolby Surround format (Dublin One Way 2012).

Parallel to this, contemporary radio drama producers have adapted 'moving pictures' to serve as a visual complement to audio. This manifestation of a smooth flow of images can in less pretentious language be called a movie, since audio content is in fact only a soundtrack. It is impossible to distinguish what was designed first, sound or image, or which component was an after-effect and which came first. In *Yalda*, the next of the six 'playlets' of the *The City Speaks* series, Mehrdad Seyf, Sam Hoyle and Esther Johnson – as in the case of *Pushing* - took their inspiration from the religious-themed novel by Peter Ackroyd about the apparition of the Virgin Mary in London, to make the visualisation in a feature film style. However, visual content responded indirectly to the story presented by a first-person voiceover because, as described in a review, 'some key lines are actually pumped up onto the screen, part blurb, part slogan, whilst the dramatic climax – the revelation that Yalda's miracle is the surgical restoration of her virginity – is offset against shots of synchronised swimmers' (Malkin Towers 2008). The *Dickens in London* series that was broadcast from 6 to 10 February 2012 on BBC Radio 4's *Woman's Hour* drama strand, via BBC Red Button and online should also be included in this analysis. However, this time five radio plays written by Michael Eaton, but based on Dickens's journalistic essays, showed that visualised radio dramas could be a whole, a biographical portrait of life, that included a blend of animation, footage and puppetry arts that had been melded together by Chris Newby (Albińska 2012b).

For highly practical reasons, this analysis could not be complete without raising the issue of 'full' and 'partial' visualisation. These subcategories often, although not always, signify the length of radio content that undergoes the transformation process to become both sound and vision. *Głosy do wynajęcia* and *Bóg zapłacz* are excellent cases in point here, since Polish Radio Olsztyn decided to enhance only small fragments of them. In brief, internet users could track the kinetic rhythm of still photographs depicting actors and get samples of radio voices. The adaptation of Włodzimierz Kowalewski's book was accompanied by subtitles in English at the bottom of the screen. All these innovations show radio drama in a favourable light and direct listeners back to the full-length dramatised programme that was broadcast in the traditional way, that is, via radio and without visual clues (Albińska 2013a).

Today, increasingly, additional visual content is generated through audience responses because digital technologies have democratised the production and distribution process. *Flickerman*, is an example of radio drama visualisation that was constructed from audio-visual elements in collaboration with contemporary media users. Hence, the originator of this innovative project, Lance Dann, decided in 2009 to put the creative process into the hands of the audience, at least to greater extent than ever before. The corollary of this was a visualised radio play in the form of a still photography interactive presentation that was designed with the use of photographic materials that had been supplied for the internet by the on-line viewers who responded to an initial appeal for help. This was issued by the main character of the radio drama: 'Watch the intro film, download each episode to your MP3 player and listen, check the links for the pictures – realise that this all might be true, read the journal – look through the maps – dig around... and find out what you can..., contact me (or Travis), contribute photos – help tell my story. Cornelius Zane Gray and Travis Deetoo'. The audience was asked to send links to their folders on Flickr, then the main author of the play chose the most interesting listener-producer proposals and on the basis of them built the next episodes. Audience contributions could be assessed by the general public since the private photos that changed into public content were available for further exploitation. The links to them were displayed under the audio content so that after listening to the play online or on radio, (it was broadcast on Resonance 104.4 FM in London from 15 to 17 April 2009,) they could click on them and in this way integrate the verbal and the visual. As a result, radio drama fans could just listen to the sound in the background or stay glued to a computer screen to face the visualised adventures of Cornelius Zane-Grey, his girlfriend and friends (Dann 2012).

'Visualised' audio theatre in the eye of critics and advocates

Broadly speaking, the transmission of visual images alongside audio content was done with varying levels of success, as both proponents and adversaries treated the visualisation process as a contentious issue. Theoreticians and practitioners who wrote about the first 'visualised' radio plays believed that productions of this type compared very favourably with traditional dramatised programmes that were devoid of visual aspects. In its experimental stage when printed illustrations, lantern slides or filmstrips were used as visualisation tools, people noticed their advantages as well as disadvantages, although the former prevailed. Consequently, Anne Foxall reckoned that colourful illustrations were of good quality, therefore, they added interest and clarity to the audio output. What is more, according to her, the appliances that helped to display images were portable, easy to operate and accessible because they could be found in most schools or public institutions. Additionally, the cost of radiovision strips was low (approximately £1.60) so many people could afford them, even though not many of these audio-visual publications were put on sale. The virtue of radio plays with visual components was also that usually they were independent of the radio schedule as they were often pre-recorded and could be listened to whenever media users wanted. On the other hand, she emphasised the need for better teacher training so that visuals could be used in more effective ways as well as animation, although she believed that the high standard of illustrative material for broadcast partly eliminated the effects of the lack of motion (Foxall 1972: 301-8). Lloyd N. Williams also indicated classroom organisation problems but at the same time criticised radio drama composition. For instance, incorrect sound clues that indicated where illustrations had to be changed or the information about it interwoven into a story (1968: 11-14).

The alliance of visual elements and radio transmission was also praised when visualised radio dramas arrived on the internet. This claim is best illustrated by means of the following comment by Anne Karpf who wrote in *The Guardian*: 'Is it a bird? Is it a plane? No, it's the first UK Internet Play of the Month, accessible to anyone with a computer and a modem. It even stars the PM's father-in-law, Tony Booth. Modern or what? For the listener, too, although at first it seems perverse to put an aural genre on to what is still primarily a visual medium, there are evident benefits' (Crook 1999: 29). Richard Rudin also spoke favourably of on-line radio plays with added visual value: 'IRDP has scored a remarkable first in putting their productions on the internet... The play can be downloaded in five files, each of around ten minutes. Well worth listening! Elsewhere on the IRDP site you can download pages of related information, such as how to write radio drama, details of radio drama competitions, the background to the prestigious Prix Italia, awards won by IRDP... All of this is very well written, researched and presented' (Crook 1999: 28).

However, it is hard not to get the impression that with time, the novelty wore off and 'enhanced' technologically advanced versions of radio plays started to attract criticism. The following quotation from *The Spectator* summarised the problem: 'The rest of the plays [apart from *Pushing*] were all rather flat, as if something was missing. As if they lacked a sense of purpose, of deciding whether this was meant to be a visual or an aural experience... None of these plays could have worked on TV without the radio soundtrack. Maybe with hindsight, *The City Speaks* will be seen as the moment when TV suddenly gave in and admitted it can't keep up' (Chisholm 2008). A similar view was expressed by Robert Hanks: 'What baffles me is that when I first heard about *The City Speaks*... I thought it sounded a rather interesting idea. What was I thinking of? The best explanation I can come up with is that I was seduced by the fact that Peter Ackroyd's name was attached to this project... But oh, how wrong I was... The big, bold twist was that these plays were all accompanied by optional pictures, which you could see by pressing the red button, on a digital television, or by logging on to the website. You might object - the idea of doing radio with pictures has been tried already, and has proved a modest success under the name of "television". To be fair to the team behind *The City Speaks*, they were trying to do something slightly different, in which the balance of power lay with the words rather than the images, but what they ended up with was a series of uncomfortable compromises' (2008). Elisabeth Mahoney, who also took a critical look at 'photo films' and 'films for radio', pondered: '... the experiment

252 | R a d i o :   T h e   R e s i l i e n t   M e d i u m

increased my appreciation of the best conventional radio drama for pictures it effortlessly creates. I felt lazy, looking at the small screen as I listened, and oddly cheated. There is an immense pleasure in conjuring up the visuals for yourself' (2008). For Gillian Reynolds, who, in turn, focused on the *Dickens In London* series, it was also indisputable that '…I tried the computer route where I saw a Dickensian puppet, made of papier-maché, trot across floors, silhouetted scissors threatening its strings to symbolise eight-year-old Charlie, visiting London with his uncle, being separated, scared, rescued. My pictures were better' (2012). Admittedly, some reviewers disagreed and considered that 'occasionally, sound and image combined in a way that was more than the sum of their parts' (Trilling 2008), because 'Radio 4 has been working hard to expand the scope and remit of its plays, which have dulled for England for many moons now' (Sawyer 2008). Others were even saying that: 'it's exactly the kind of innovation that the BBC – and for that matter Dickens – is all about' (Drive in Bingo 2008).

Generally, opinions about 'visualised' radio drama were not entirely optimistic and even the radio play in an interactive version raised mixed emotions: 'Last week (Resonance FM) did something 'radical and groundbreaking' (their words) or 'new and amazing' (mine). Maybe this kind of thing happens on experimental art radio all the time, it never happens on Radio 4. *Flickerman* was a classic drama serial. The acting was good and bad, the writing sometimes brilliant, never awful. It had a quality of fashionable compulsiveness… in which the author knows that "plot" and "whodunit" and "pace" are very old-fashioned, but puts them in ironically; because they are so self-aware, there is no pressure on these devices to succeed and, for that reason, I think, they are bizarrely successful…It spins texture into what would otherwise be standard paranoia-conceit…it all makes you feel involved. This is what people hope to create when they say 'interactive' but I've never seen it work. It is a strange and exhilarating project' (Dann 2012). So, were these radio experiments with visualisation worth making? I believe they were, even though the producers didn't always manage to get the mixture of the aural and the visual right. All in all, visualisation of the 'Theatre of Imagination' has shown that contemporary radio is something more than 'the playground for the proven' (Perebinossoff, Gross & Gross 2005: 155). Therefore, it should not be labelled a 'dinosaur medium' since in the digital, multi-platform age it still is such a brave, creative and 'energetic old man' (Goban-Klas 2011: 111).

References

Albińska, K (2011a) 'Kilka uwag o przeobrażeniach środowiska medialnego współczesnego radiosłuchacza. Szkic przeglądowy', *Media i społeczeństwo. Semiologiczne aspekty komunikacji medialnej*, volume 6, issue 1.

Albińska, K (2011b) 'Słuchowisko w erze 'nowego radia'. O współczesnym sposobie istnienia teatru audialnego i jego statusie', *Kultura i edukacja*, volume 80, issue 1.

Albińska, K (2012) 'Teatr do słuchania', literatura do grania', kino dla ucha'? – o rodowodzie gatunkowym słuchowiska radiowego', *Kultura i Historia*, volume 21, Issue 1. http://www.kulturaihistoria.umcs.lublin.pl/archives/3400

Albińska, K (2012a) '(TOP)kultura czy (POP)kultura? Słuchowisko na rozdrożu', paper at the Języki popklutury conference, Łódź, September.

Albińska, K (2013a) 'Visualised Radio? Research findings from Britain and Poland', paper at the FILM and Media 2013: The Pleasures of the Spectacle conference, London, June.

Albińska, K (2013) 'Did pictures kill the radio star? "Radiovision" as a new/old incarnation of radio in the audiovisual era', in Stachyra, G (ed), *Radio. Community, challenges, aesthetics*, Lublin: Maria Curie-Skłodowska University Press.

'Alias In Wonderland' (2009) http://digitalekunst.ac.at/index.php?id=132

Bachura, J (2011a) 'Kategorie filmowe w teatrze radiowym', in Pleszkun-Olejniczakowa, E, Bachura, J & Pawlik, A (eds), *Dwa Teatry. Studia z zakresu teorii i interpretacji sztuki słuchowiskowej*, Toruń: Adam Marszalek.

Bachura, J (2011b) 'www.motel.wp.pl jako przykład konwergencji różnych form komunikacji', in Pleszkun-Olejniczakowa, E, Bachura, J & Pawlik, A (eds), *Dwa Teatry. Studia z zakresu teorii i interpretacji sztuki słuchowiskowej*, Toruń: Adam Marszalek.

Bachura, J. (2012) *Odsłony wyobraźni. Współczesne słuchowiska radiowe*. Toruń: Adam Marszałek.

Bardijewska, S (2001) *Nagie słowo. Rzecz o słuchowisku*, Warszawa: Elipsa.

Bohdziewicz, A (1935) 'Przyszłość słuchowiska radiowego', *Pion*, issue 15.

Chisholm, K (2008) 'Death of television. The City Speaks (BBC Radio 4)'. http://www.spectator.co.uk/arts-and-culture/featured/563941/part_2/death-of-television.html

Crisell, A (1996) *Understanding Radio*, London and New York: Routledge.

Crisell, A (2006) *More than a Music Box*, Oxford: Berghahn Books.

Crook, T (1999) *Radio Drama. Theory and Practice*, London: Routledge.

Danesi, M (ed) (2008) *Dictionary of Media and Communications*, New York: M E Shape

Dann, L (2012) 'One Half the Story: Radio Drama, Online Audio and Transmedia Storytelling', in Oliveira, M, Portela P & Santos, L (eds), *Radio evolution: Conference Proceedings*, Braga: University of Minho.

De Fossard, E (2005) *Writing and Producing Radio Dramas*, London: Sage.

Drive In Bingo (2012) 'The BBC Dickens Season: Post-Mortem'. http://thedriveinbingo.wordpress.com/2012/02/26/the-bbc-dickens-season-post

'Dublin. One Way' (2012). https://www.szczecin.pl/UMSzczecinSwiat/files/.../dublin_info_pdf.pdf

Fleming, C (2010) *The Radio Handbook*, London and New York: Routledge.

Foxall, A (1972) 'Radiovision' – A Survey and Discussion', *Programmed Learning and Educational Technology*, volume 9, issue 6.

Gielgud, V (1957) *British Radio Drama, 1922-1956: a survey*, London: Harrap.

Goban-Klas, T (2011) *Wartki nurt mediów. Ku nowym formom społecznego życia informacji*, Kraków: Universitas.

Hanks, R (2008) 'While the city speaks, the listeners sleep'. http://www.redorbit.com/news/entertainment/1312092/while_thee_city_speaks

Hopfinger, M (2008) 'Kultura: scalanie i wybór', in Kluszczyński, R & Zeidler-Janiszewska, A (eds), *Perspektywy badań nad kulturą*, Łódź: Wydawnictwo UŁ.

Jedliński, R (2001) 'Słuchowiska radiowe w kształceniu polonistycznym', in Budrewicz, Z & Uryga, Z (eds), *Drogi i ścieżki polonistyki gimnazjalnej*, Kraków: Wydawnictwo Naukowe Akademii Pedagogicznej w Krakowie.

Jędrzejewski, S (2006) 'Radio', in Pisarek, W (ed), *Słownik Terminologii Medialnej*, Kraków: Universitas.

Jenkins, H (2007) *Kultura konwergencji. Zderzenie starych i nowych mediów*, Warszawa: Wydawnictwa Akademickie I Profesjonalne.

Kaziów, M (1973) O *dziele radiowym. Z zagadnień estetyki oryginalnego słuchowiska*, Wrocław: Zakład Narodowy im. Ossolińskich.

Kwiatkowski, M (1975) *To już historia. Felietony o dziejach Polskiego Radia*, Warszawa: Wydawnictwa Radia i Telewizji.

Laskowicz, K (1983) *Świat za drzwiami*, Poznań: Wydawnictwo Naukowe UAM.

Levinson, P (2006) *Miękkie ostrze, czyli historia i przyszłość rewolucji informacyjnej*, Warszawa: Muza.

Limon, J (2004) *Trzy teatry*, Gdańsk: Słowo/Obraz Terytoria.

MacFarland, D (1997) *Future Radio Programming Strategies*, London: LEA.

Mahoney, E (2008) 'Radio review. The City Speaks', *The Guardian*, 21 March. http:www.guardian.co.uk/media/2008/mar/21/radio.tvandradioarts

Małachowski, A (1969) 'Słowo wstępne', in Krzysztoń, J (ed), *Teatr Wyobraźni słuchowiska radiowe*, Warszawa: Iskry.

Malkin Towers (2008) 'An experiment in convergence. The City Speaks, BBC Radio 4, digital TV and online'. http://malkintowersmediablog.blogspot.com/2008/03/city-speaks-bbc-radio-4-digital

Mayen, J (1965) *Radio a literature*, Warszawa: Wiedza Powszechna.

McLuhan, M (1975) 'Przekazem jest przekaźnik', in Krzymowska, K (ed), *Marshall McLuhan. Wybór Pism*, Warszawa: Wydawnictwa Artystyczne i Filmowe.

Meyerowitz, J (1998) 'Multiple Media Literacies'. http://www.fritt-ord.no/images/uploads/Multiple_Media_Literacies.pdf

Michalski, K (2004) 'Narodziny radia – technika', in Kunert, Krzysztof & Andrzej (eds), *Z dziejów polskiej radiofonii rocznik 2004/2005,* Warszawa: Polskie Radio.

O'Neil, J (2007) 'Mix/Remix as Epistemology: The Implications of the Metamedium, Digital Media'. http://www.jamieoneil.net/images/oneil_remix_epist.pdf

Palczewski, M (2012) 'Rozmowa dnia - 26 lipca 2012. Z Waldemarem Modestowiczem o reżyserii słuchowisk, Hamlecie i młodym pokoleniu rozmawia Marek Palczewski'. www.sdp.pl/rozmowa-dnia-waldemar-modestowicz

Pawlak G (2000) 'Teatr radiowy', in Fik, M (ed), *Teatr. Widowisko*, Warszawa: Instytut Kultury.

Pawlik, A (2011) 'Słuchowisko w zmieniającej się rzeczywistości medialnej (wybrane zagadnienia)', in Stachyra, G & Pawlak-Hejno, E (eds), *Radio a społeczeństwo*, Lublin: Wydawnictwo Uniwersytetu Marii Curie-Skłodowskiej.

Pawlik, A (2012) 'Seriale radiowe w Internecie', in Oniszczuk, Z & Wielkopolska-Szymura, M (eds), *Konwergencja mediów masowych i jej skutki dla współczesnego dziennikarstwa*, volume 1, Katowice: Uniwersytet Śląski.

Perebinossoff, P, Gross, B & Gross, L (2005) *Programming for TV, Radio & The Internet*, Boston: Focal Press.

Pleszkun-Olejniczakowa, E (2000a) *Słuchowiska Polskiego Radia w okresie piętnastolecia 1925-1939. Fakty, wnioski, przypuszczenia*, Łódź: Biblioteka.

Pleszkun-Olejniczakowa, E (2000b) 'Intencje interpretacyjne wpisane w słuchowiska za pomocą słów i dźwięków', in Michalewski, K (ed), *Regulacyjna funkcja tekstów*, Łódź: Wydawnictwo Uniwersytetu Łódzkiego.

Pleszkun-Olejniczakowa, E (2011) 'Jak jest zrobione słuchowisko? O morfologii i znaczeniu, o kreacji znaku', in Pleszkun-Olejniczakowa, E, Bachura, J & Pawlik, A (eds), *Dwa Teatry. Studia z zakresu teorii i interpretacji sztuki słuchowiskowej*, Toruń: Adam Marszałek.

Pleszkun-Olejniczakowa, E (2012) *Muzy rzadko się do radia przyznają. Szkice o słuchowiskach i reportażach radiowych*, Łódź: Primum Verbum.

'Radio Talk: Visualising Radio'. http://youtube.com/watch?v=Kht_8uV5HOo

'Radio with pictures - it's not just crap telly'. http://www.youtube.com/watch?v=Q0_Nwdi8tK4

Ramsey, M (2008) *Making Waves. Radio on the Verge*, New York: iUniverse.

Rattigan, D (2002) *Theatre of Sound. Radio and the Dramatic Imagination*, Dublin: Carysfort Press.

The Listener (1969), 'Rembrandt', Issue 2077.

Reynolds, G (2012) 'Radio review: Broadcasting House, Radio 4, and the last week's highlights. http://www.telegraph.co.uk/culture/tvandradio/9064543/Radio-reiev

Rosińska, Z (2001) *Blaustein. Koncepcja odbioru mediów*, Warsaw: Prószyński I S-ka.

Rudge (2013) 'Duckrabbit's Peter Rudge on how to make photo films'. http://www.ideastap.com/ideasmag/the-knowledge/duckrabbit-peter-rudge-hoe-to-make

Sawyer, M (2008) 'Radio with pictures? It'll never catch on'. http://www.guardian.co.uk/media/2008/mar/23/radio

Shingler, M & Wieringa, C (1998) *On Air. Methods and Meanings of Radio*, London: Arnold.

Silverblatt, A (2007) *Genre Studies In Mass Media. A Handbook*, Armonk, London: M.E. Shapé.

Sopot (2013) 'XIII Festiwal Teatru Polskiego Radia i Teatru Telewizji Polskiej Dwa Teatry - Sopot 2013'. http://www.trojmiasto.pl/festiwal-dwa-teatry

'The Flickerman. Intro Film' (2009). http://www.theflickerman.com/intro-film/

Trilling, D (2008) 'A day to remember. Peter Ackroyd is behind a series of supernatural events on London's streets'. http://www.newstatesman.com/radio/2008//03/london-streets-ackroyd-city

Tuszewski, J (2002) *Paradoks o słowie i dźwięku. Rozważania o sztuce radiowej*, Toruń: Adam Marszałek.

Williams, L N (1968) 'Radiovision', *Audio-Visual Media*, volume 2, issue 4.

Willis, J (2010) 'Seeing Ear Theatre. Home to the finest online audio drama'. http://www.sffaudio.com/?p=19883

Chapter 21

Radio documentary in times of media convergence

Monika Białek

Abstract:

Convergence in the technology of radio broadcasting has already been recognised as a fact. It is clearly visible on many levels, but it can be seen within particular journalistic genres too, including that known as radio reportage. By definition, a radio reportage perceived as a sound document should present an image of reality as faithfully as possible. Recently, however, in Poland the genre of reportage has been changing. It is slowly adopting a means of expression that used to be typical of radio drama. Using actuality as sound is becoming less important than creativity and production, which was once more a characteristic of radio plays.

In this chapter we consider whether the contemporary radio feature may still be perceived as a sound document. Does this noticeable transformation into an artistic form lead to the death of what we might term 'radio non-fiction literature'? We will also note changes to the role of the journalists – reporters ceasing to act like recorders of events and starting to create stories. They are turning into creative producers, while radio features dangerously teeter on the edge of radio theatre, presenting not just a set of true facts, but 'a story based on true facts'.

Keywords: reportage, radio documentary, feature, radio drama, Poland

Introduction

For 45 years, Polish radio broadcasting functioned in accordance with the rules imposed by the communist regime, (censorship, isolation and a subservient role to the party). In the so-called 'People's republics', the media operated on different principles. No wonder then, that such a reality demanded distinct forms of particular genres of journalism. 'Reportage' is no exception here. The distinction between 'radio documentary' and 'feature' has been present in European broadcasting for many years. The first is understood as a documentary record of reality, while the second puts strong emphasis on artistic elements. Polish literature refers to the first features, recorded for the German and British broadcasting companies, as 'dramatised reportages' or 'documentary audio dramas'. In Polish broadcasting, such a term was used sporadically, rather as a description of a musical/poetic montage. To this very day, there is a dispute among media researchers over the true nature of the feature genre, whether it can be classified as a form of journalism or rather as an artistic work. Journalists themselves have some difficulty stating their own opinion. There are some who firmly negate this term and those who want to create features at all costs. Probably, the reason for such a terminological confusion is that over several decades of broadcasting history in an isolated Eastern block, a distinct radio form was created - known as the reportage. Moreover, academic publications on both media and texts prepared by radio practitioners highlight the existence of the so called Polish school of reportage. The distinction hinges around solely authentic sounds. Until the 1990s, the feature genre was virtually absent in Poland. In the *Polish Radio Journal* of 1957 one may find a division of radio forms into literary reportages, (texts written by a writer and read in front of a microphone,) sound reportages and documentary montages (Jankowska 1996: 103). Literary reportages were created in the literary department and were considered to be artistic works prepared for radio purposes. The aforementioned radio reportages and documentary montages were recorded in the politics and information department , and primarily played an informational role. Over time, along with technological development, (such as the appearance of portable tape recorders,) the genre of literary, written reportage gave way to the radio reportage. Eventually, the latter took over the artistic function of the utterance.

Production practices

Therefore, in Polish broadcasting, the term 'reportage' is used to describe a form of aural report on reality, composed in accordance with its author's - that is, the reporter's - idea, and made up of different sounds. The specificity of the Polish school was based on the use of real, actual recordings - or 'actuality'. The artistic dimension of the form could be achieved only through a thoughtful montage and composition and by using radio's own means of expression, including music, reverb and acoustic effects. Some practitioners insisted even on using the authentic acoustic effects, recorded during the process of collecting materials for the needs of the reportage. Over the course of time, effects taken from radio archives or CDs prepared by, for example, the BBC, became acceptable. A model reportage should constitute an acoustic report of reality, where sound should be used to create a complete narration. In an ideal situation, all the reporter's questions should also be cut out. The main task of the experienced journalists was to convince their interviewees to build their stories in such a way as to enable the elimination of all of the reporter's questions. Just an acoustic recording of space and protagonists was needed to form a legible, coherent story. Among other characteristics of Polish reportage were length, (in most cases about 30 minutes although this rule was never strictly observed,) and subjects. Possibly due to the restrictions imposed by censorship, reporters used to focus on depicting people in the modern world, together with their problems, dreams and passions, instead of investigating socio-political issues. As noted by Kinga Klimczak, a researcher of the genre: 'Polish reportage... appeared as a result of a social need, as a document presenting the current human problems, addressed to an average audience, not necessarily educated. In western countries, where the radio feature was already formed as a kind of an artistic audition for the chosen, artistically exquisite... listeners, the situation was quite different' (2011: 69). Reportages forced their audiences to reflect on the substance of human existence. Such a model was the norm in Polish broadcasting until the mid 1990s.

After 1989, the whole communist block underwent political change. In Poland, this transformation was accompanied by substantial changes to the radio market. Its structure was transformed, and private broadcasters begin to appear. On the other hand, in what appears to be the most important factor in the case of the reportage, producers were given new possibilities of cooperation with journalists and broadcasters from all over Europe. Polish reporters gained the ability to participate in grant programmes and workshops organised in Western Europe. International competitions also became available. Due to these new contacts, Polish radio terminology gained the term 'feature'. However, its status is not strong enough for it to replace the word 'reportage'. The two terms co-exist, but there are no unambiguous criteria to determine the exact meaning of the newer of the two. Until now, practitioners of the genre have problems in explicitly stating what the feature is. It is especially visible at radio reportage competitions. Awards are granted in various categories, among others for artistic and social reportage, while the competition rules talk about artistic radio documentary and reportage, using these terms interchangeably. However, the term 'feature' cannot be found anywhere. Surely, Polish researchers, (possibly together with their colleagues from other former communist countries,) need to specify their terms more clearly, especially because of international meetings and problems with translation of their terminology. Exchanging the word 'reportage' with 'feature' is not entirely justified. Analysing the properties of the genre, one may state that both forms of the utterance possess artistic elements, but the feature includes elements of creation, while the reportage does not. Taking this into consideration, we need to propose an explanation. This chapter uses the terms radio reportage, audio reportage, radio documentary and documentary broadcast. We will use them interchangeably, as the terms for radio forms of documentary based on an authentic event. Radio drama is another form of audio production, located at the opposite end of a spectrum: both use sounds from the world around us, but the main difference between them is that reportage is based on authentic events, while radio drama normally involves a degree of fiction.

Let us now examine the genre of reportage itself. Some practitioners and researchers claim that the genre of reportage is as old as human speech. They believe that a story about mammoths grazing on the clearing could be the first reportage ever, which is the favourite statement of Melchior Wańkowicz (1892-1974), one of the most important Polish reportage producers. Some consider Homer and Herodotus the first, ancient reporters. Others look for the earliest reportage forms in the journey letters, chronicles or diaries. Regardless of the date we accept as the beginning of the genre, we all need to agree on one distinctive property of the reportage – authenticity. Probably, we can also state that the primary function of the reportage is to provide information. One of the popular handbooks for Polish students of journalism included radio reportage in the category of informational genres of journalism (Wolny-Zmorzyński, Kaliszewski & Furman 2006). Therefore, its informational function was acknowledged as primary and all other determinants of the genre, (such as timeliness and attractiveness,) were judged to be subordinate to it. In theory, reportage should also quote documents, eyewitness reports and personal opinions of the protagonists. All that in order to make it seem more reliable, so the listener should not doubt the authenticity of the story presented.

However, a detailed analysis of radio reportages recorded in Poland during the last decade revealed that this form of expression has undergone some substantial changes. By definition, the sound reportage, perceived as a radio documentary, should present an image of reality as faithfully as possible. In the last couple of years however, Polish broadcasting exhibited some signs of significant transformation of this genre. Radio reportage is slowly adopting some forms of expression that used to be typical only of radio theatre. Actuality is becoming less important than creativity and production values that are characteristic of radio drama. Fictional elements are starting to appear more and more frequently in radio reportage. They are becoming a significant part of the genre. They are no longer merely elements that add attractiveness to the story, they are becoming its structural axis. The rules postulated by the Polish school of reportage are being abandoned. The authors add to authentic sounds with created or borrowed audio. Fiction is becoming as important as the real recording. In the course of time, reportage makers started to use various elements of creativity, often using more than the actuality. Radio reportages have now begun to introduce creativity: dramatic reconstruction, fictional situations, fictional characters, fictional documents and extended narration.

This means that professional actors are recruited to record the reportage. Their task is to act a specific role. In most cases they read letters or documents that are important to the narration. Sometimes they act as narrators or commentators. However, frequently they impersonate specific characters, becoming their aural representatives. For example, in a reportage about Korean orphans secretly brought up in a Polish orphanage, child actors were used to read the letters written by little Koreans to their carers, after the children returned to their homeland (Kysowata 2003). Another example is a reportage about the fate of a former Auschwitz inmate, who was imprisoned by the Polish security service after the war (Gruszyńska-Ruman 2009). The story is based on the memories of a woman sentenced to death by the communist authorities. When the reportage was recorded, its protagonist was already dead. That is why an actress was needed to act her role. She reads the very personal entries from the protagonist's diary. Being a professional actress, she personally interprets the text. These fragments are accompanied by reports of the protagonist's fellow inmates and her daughter. By way of digression, the elements which have been acted in front of a microphone last longer than the real recordings used in this reportage.

Theatrical styling is another fictional element beginning to appear in the radio reportage genre. The journalist recruits professional theatrical producers to record the reportage, resulting in a reportage with extended dramatic sequences. They are produced in accordance with theatrical conventions and can be recognised immediately. Their main task is to achieve a particular style, designed to constitute a frame for the real story. For example, the sounds of a street, of a horse-drawn carriage or shouting newsboys that are meant to take the listeners to pre-war Warsaw, or of a jungle with screams of wild animals to introduce a story about exotic animals in a zoo.

Fictional elements in reportage

Situations These are found in most examples of historical reportage. Obviously, it is impossible to report from the point of view of an observer or participant in the events. Historical stories can be told only on the basis of reconstruction. In order to make the story more interesting, authentic and reliable, the authors very often decide to introduce extended theatrical sequences. In the course of production, actors record specially-written lines following stage-specific situations. For example, the author of a reportage about the forgotten Polish composer who lived in the nineteenth century and is extremely popular in Japan nowadays, introduces scenes that are characteristic of radio drama (Michalak & Hałasa 2009). Together with the producers, she creates an audio image of nineteenth-century Warsaw. She creates a scene in which the young, novice composer tries to sell her first works. Of course, we do not know whether such a situation really happened. We do not have access to any documents that could confirm this event. It is a product of the writer's imagination, created only for the purpose of the reportage. Paradoxically, this fictional situation was created to make the whole story more reliable. Fiction was made up for the sake of 'reality'. In another historical reportage, for a story about a Polish aviator who died in Normandy, the authors constructed the scene of a dogfight, during which a plane is shot down (Czyżewska-Jacquemet 2010). The listener is not informed about the fictitious character of this scene. The reportage does not include a word of explanation. On the contrary, the writer did her best to create an illusion of reality of this recording. Again, a fictional situation appears to be an element designed to make the story more reliable. One may of course argue whether historical reportages should apply such created elements. The will to make the whole message more attractive seems to be the argument in favour of such a solution, especially because the arranged scenes, introduced by the reporter, do not distort the historical truth. Their role is based solely on making the utterance more realistic. However, such a stylistic measure is not compliant with the guidelines of the Polish school of reportage. The producers cross the borders of the genre perceived as radio documentary and take on the characteristics of radio drama.

Characters This kind of artistic creation in works focused on contemporary issues may seem surprising. However, fictional characters appear in such reportages as well. In most cases they are interwoven into the narration. They do not constitute a separate element of theatrical styling. Writers usually try to introduce them furtively, again creating an illusion of authenticity. Obviously, the narration itself makes it explicit that they cannot be treated as real, for example a child describing its own premature birth or a suicide victim who talks to his girlfriend after his death. Besides, in this case we may observe a fictional character in a fictional situation. However, the unreality of such situations makes it obvious for the listener that they are just an element of creation. The sole fact of introducing fictional characters into the reportage seems to defy its documentary values. The history of the reportage has seen various works with extended fictional sequences. Egon Erwin Kisch's reportage *Die Himmelfahrt der Galgentoni* (The Assumption of Galgentoni) is probably among the most famous of them. The reporter merged two elements here, fact and fiction, into one, attractive whole. Apart from an authentic character, (a Prague prostitute,) he introduced a fictional figure of the young protagonist's ghost. Such an artistic measure enabled his work to enter the canon of classic world reportages. This way, the pre-war Prague journalist gave birth to a new genre of literary reportage. However, in the case of a sound reportage, the situation looks quite different. In the past works of the Polish school of reportage, a narrator was the only acceptable fictional character, an omniscient presence, marking the flow of time, indicating a change of place or providing facts unnoted by the reporter. The narrator's presence was invisible to the protagonists. Introducing a fictional character is something different. Such a person becomes one of the story's protagonists. Fictional characters become the primary figures of the reportage which, in accordance with common assumptions about the definition of the genre, should merely report reality.

Documents Apart from fictional characters, the authors often introduce fictional documents to their reportages. Whether it is just a flashy method of making the recording more interesting or a form of deception is debatable. Some historical reportages, focused for example on the arrests in communist Poland, frequently present fictional reports of interrogations. In most cases, quoting of these 'documents' is accompanied by the sound of a typewriter, which constitutes an acoustic proof of credibility. We may also find quotations from diaries that have never been written. They were created for the purpose of the reportage only. For example: a terminally ill child in a vegetative state writes a diary that he later reads in front of a microphone. In such situations, the listeners may feel lost. It may be difficult for them to tell the real from the fictitious. They may be unable to appropriately distinguish between the real and created elements. A reportage that is meant to depict reality should be based only on authentic and verified documents. Meanwhile, fictional elements are introduced. Additionally, through the means of production, the fiction appears here in the guise of truthfulness. The listener is misled. Such a stylistic measure may be explained by the urge to make the programme more attractive, but it is contrary to common assumptions about the genre.

Extended narrative sequences Narration was written specially for the purpose of the reportage. Very often it takes the role of theatrical stage directions. Unfortunately, sometimes it is also used to rescue the situation and hide some imperfections and shortcomings of the journalist's work. Narration presents the things that the author could not paint with sounds. This way, the listener receives a description of situations, emotional states or a literary introduction to the story. What we have here is the creation of literary texts for the purpose of the reportage. Until recently, this 'privilege' was reserved only for radio drama. Before 2000, the unwritten 'golden rule' observed by radio reportage makers was based on their 'intentional absence' from the finished piece. The reporter's voice should not be heard in the recording. Everything, time, space, the protagonists' emotional states, should be described with sounds. The recording and its structure should be discernible enough to allow the listener to recognise the time and space of the story and to seamlessly read the context of the events being presented. The appearance of the reporter's voice asking a question was treated as a technical mistake, while the extended narrative sequence, additionally read by the journalist, was perceived as an attempt to cover a lack of source materials and inadequate sound recording. Only actuality, recorded in the field during the process of gathering materials, was considered proper material for a reportage. Any comments recorded in the studio were considered a mistake. Today, this situation has changed radically. The reporters use studio microphones to create a story and enrich it with sound pictures. Currently, hearing the voice of the journalist, an explanation of the context and even descriptions of the protagonists' emotional states are not surprising, nor disconcerting. In the time of the so called Polish school of reportage, until the end of the last century, the recorded voices needed to describe feelings and emotions for themselves, and sometimes they were even required to actually display them through sobs, laughter or agitation, for example. The reporter's primary role was to conduct the conversation in such a manner as to excavate these emotional states and record them. This demanded lots of tact and compassion, as well as perfect reporting skills. These were the foundations of the art of reportage. Simultaneously, it was a factor used to differentiate press reports from radio reportages. The first applied mainly a descriptive narration, the latter was focused more on personal reports. In contemporary sound reportages, this distinction has become blurred. The extended narrative sequences resemble press reports. There is not much room left for the aural imagination of the listener. Sound sensibility is not needed to understand these fragments. The listener receives a literary, dramatised description of the events, interpreted by a reporter.

Conclusions

In conclusion, therefore, we should consider whether the contemporary radio reportage may still be perceived as a documentary. Will this noticeable transformation into an artistic work lead to the death of radio non-fiction literature? We should also notice the change of the journalists' role – reporters cease to act like recorders of events and start to create stories. They turn into creative producers, while radio reportages dangerously teeter on the edge of radio theatre. They start to resemble acoustic movies, in which the presented events are only based on facts. So, radio reportage has changed. More often than not, it has taken on elements of audio production that used to be characteristic only of radio dramas. Today, no one worries about the introduction of fictional characters or documents, while fictitious scenes are merged with authentic recordings. We may attempt to analyse the reportage, by dividing it into particular elements and calculating their timing. What may be disturbing, though, is the fact that the fictional elements start to outweigh actuality in terms of duration. Can we still define the reportage as a report on a reality, or is it a fictional creation, built in accordance with the imagination and artistic assumptions of its author? Maybe the inclination of academic researchers to order and classify genres should be considered a mistake. As reality, especially such a dynamic one as a media reality, shows, the theory does not follow the practice. The convergence we now observe at the level of genres makes it difficult to arbitrarily tell the difference - documentary audio drama, artistic reportage or documentary programme. Even the proportion of the fictional elements introduced to the actual narration is very distorted and ceases to be helpful in genre differentiation.

As a Polish researcher of radio art, Elżbieta Pleszkun-Olejniczakowa noted that such a connection of creative and authentic elements is nothing new, but she warned us that:

'The boundary is very blurred and every time it depends on an arbitrary and subjective decision of the classifier. If we agree on the addition... allow this precedent, we make the boundary between radio drama adaptation and documentary programme "discretionary" and immeasurable' (2001). This blurring of the boundaries between various genres is surprising and puzzling for the practitioners as well. Katarzyna Michalak, one of the most notable Polish reportage producers, noted in a radio broadcast of Anna Lisiecka, *Radiowy dokument literacki w Europie* (Radio literary documentary in Europe): 'The border between drama and literary documentary starts to disappear. Radio drama starts to speak the language of the documentary, while documentary makers more often display their sensitiveness, the author's "myself"'. Answering the question at the beginning of this chapter, the changes undergone by the genre may already be firmly considered as fixed, and even though they are not approved by the journalists faithful to the Polish school of reportage, we are certain that these developments cannot be stopped. Most reporters of the older generation with whom I have spoken agree that contemporary reportages, produced with techniques and elements borrowed from radio drama, no longer fulfill the requirements of the genre. They introduce elements of creativity into a genre that was assumed to be reliable and closely linked to reality. However, there is also a large group of reporters who have changed their approach towards reportage. They began winning awards in international competitions. Their task is to tell a story. In order to make it more interesting, reliable or complete, they use fictional documents, situations and characters, they extend their narrative sequences and even use the production methods characteristic of radio drama. They try to disguise 'the naked truth' as 'artistic fiction', therefore increasing the attractiveness of their message.

What is the likely result of such change? Of course, the blurring of the boundary between particular genres. We will need to make changes in terminology and modify the definition, or, in accordance with the spirit of convergence, abandon the genre classification completely. We need to come to terms with the inevitable unification of the radio drama, feature and reportage. Surely, we all remember the story about Orson Welles' *The War of the Worlds*. It was a well-produced radio play, intended to create an illusion of reality. We all know what happened – the broadcast caused panic on the streets. Today, in the case of the radio reportage genre, a reversal of this situation can be observed. The sound record of reality is produced in the most unreal way, so the final effect is illusive and theatrical. Reality begins to copy fiction.

References

Bachura, J (2013) 'Feature – the marriage of fact and fiction', in Stachyra, G (ed), *Radio, community, challenges, aesthetics,* Lublin: Maria Skłodowska-Curie University.

Białek, M (2010) *Polski reportaż radiowy. Wybrane zagadnienia* (Polish radio reportage. Selected issues), Poznań-Opole: Wydawnictwo Naukowe Scriptorium.

Górak-Czerska, B & Jędrzejewski, S (eds) (1996) *70 lat Polskiego Radia* (70 years of Polish broadcasting), Warsaw: Polskie Radio S A, TENTEN.

Klimczak, K (2011) *Reportaże radiowe o krzywdzie I cierpieniu* (Radio reportages on harm and suffering), Łódź: Primum Verbum.

Pleszkun-Olejniczakowa, E, Bachura, J & Pawlik, A (eds) (2001) *Dwa teatry* (Two theatres), Toruń: Wydawnictwo Adam Marszałek.

Skrzypek, J (ed) (1999) *Popularna encyklopedia mass mediów* (Popular encyclopedia of mass media), Poznań.

Stachyra, G (ed) (2013), *Radio, community, challenges, aesthetics,* Lublin: Maria Skłodowska-Curie University Press.

Wolny-Zmorzyński, K, Kaliszewski, A, Furman, W (2006) *Gatunki dziennikarskie* (Journalistic genres), Warsaw: Wydawnictwa Akademickie i Profesjonalne.

Selected radio reportages:

Czyżewska-Jacquemet, A (2010) *Ostatni lot* (The Last Flight), Polskie Radio Lublin.

Fredo-Boniecka, D, (2009) *Preclowa dolina* (Pretzel Valley), Studio Reportażu i Dokumentu Polskiego Radia.

Gruszyńska-Ruman, P (2009) *WINna nieWINna* (GUILTy not GUILTy), Studio Reportażu i Dokumentu Polskiego Radia.

Krysowata, J (2003) *Osieroceni* (The Orphaned), Polskie Radio Wrocław.

Melion, K, (2004) *Nikifor, jaki był* (Nikifor, As He Was), Studio Reportażu i Dokumentu Polskiego Radia.

Michalak, K, (2003) *Eden za wąską rzeką* (Eden Behind a Narrow River), Polskie Radio Lublin.

Michalak, K, Hałasa, D (2009) *Modlitwa zapomnianej* (The Prayer of the Forgotten), Polskie Radio Lublin.

Piłatowska, I (2009) *Dogonić życie* (To Catch Up With Life), Studio Reportażu i Dokumentu Polskiego Radia.

Skawińska, M (2009) *Libacja* (Libation), Studio Reportażu i Dokumentu Polskiego Radia.

Słobodzian, M (2010) *Jestem niewidzialny* (I am Invisible), Polskie Radio PIK w Bydgoszczy.

Walentyn, Ż, (2009), *Przeklęci* (The Cursed), Polskie Radio PIK w Bydgoszczy.

Żerwe, M Mairowitz, D (2010) *Ludziom i zwierzętom* (To People And Animals), Polskie Radio Gdańsk.

Chapter 22

What is over is (not) over: Radio as an artist and its audience in Poland

Elżbieta Pleszkun-Olejniczakowa

Abstract

This chapter derives from my research into Polish radio and focuses on artistic radio studies. I am particularly interested in radio drama and artistic radio reportage, (or features,) from the perspective of social communication. Reportage was not fully developed between 1925 and 1939 due to technological deficiencies, but reached its full potential after World War II. There is a dualism in my approach to reportage, for it is common to make reportage as a form of journalism without its being considered as art. However, radio drama has often been created within an artistic paradigm, yet differentiation of the intellectual level of the audience was important too. Although there have been changes in this area, the impact of the audience is still valid.

From 1925 to 1939 the number of radio listeners in Poland rapidly increased due to cheaper receivers becoming available and a growing interest in listening to the radio, such as in community centres, schools and factories. Even uneducated listeners bought receivers, so the 'participation gap', in terms of access to receiving equipment, became virtually non-existent. Radio reception has changed considerably since the medium was born, the main reasons being technological progress and intellectual growth of the audience. Hence, I treat them as a cultural subgroup. The chapter examines a number of radio productions, in the context of changes in technology and communication, comparing the past with the present in order to emphasise the role of artistic radio in the context of cultural change.

Keywords: radio drama, reportage, technology, art, Poland

Introduction

When asked about radio, an average Pole's first thought would be for music, news, and entertainment; and, indeed, commercial radio stations these days seem to totally justify this view. Numerous works have been written in this field; my students at the Lodz school of radio have been or are tackling the problem in their PhD research, written usually from a relatively or even completely new perspective. Although music, news and entertainment are dominant in commercial radio stations, there still survives a different kind of radio, one fulfilling the role of an artist, offering the listener creative productions peculiar to radio drama. That is, radio productions which attain the status of a work of art: reportage approaching or reaching the status of the 'feature' programme, popularised in parts of Western Europe. In Poland it is still common to produce reportage as a form of intervention, a journalistic reaction to various events of today which do not aspire to reach the level of a work of art; rather, they belong to the sphere of journalism. I realise that my approach to radio reportage may imply a somewhat ontological dualism, because it stands somewhere between art and craft, artistic creation and journalism. However, I cannot think of a different and perhaps more convincing and relevant delimitation.

Artistic radio

In my research into Polish radio, over the last 25 years, I have been particularly interested in the role of artistic radio, which includes all kinds of radio drama series representing various subdivisions, (such as the family saga or the mini series,) as well as radio reportage, which began to obtain a work-of-art status halfway through the twentieth century and which already existed from 1925 to 1939 as a distinct genre, without its current meaning. The very term 'radio reportage' was used at that time quite frequently both in the press and on air, yet the awareness of what the genre represented was still in its making. Therefore the statement made by Jan Emil Skiwski that 'the term "reportage" is more and more commonly present, even abiding on air, yet its sense is often misrepresented' seems totally justified (Skiwski 1935: 9). Inspired by Regis Debray's invention of the term *mediology* – as quite distinct from the term 'media studies' – I decided to venture into the possibility of creating a subdivision of what could be termed 'general radio studies', namely '*artistic* radio studies'. I believe Debray is right in suggesting that the first thing that would come to our minds when asked about the scope of media studies would be the very subject of the domain, rather than its 'point of view... [as] every [academic] discipline sketches on the same anthropological foundation... the chosen figure - a new profile - that will become its reference point' (Debray 2010: 3-4). My objective within the domain of artistic radio studies is to follow radio productions from the moment of their broadcast to their ultimate effect, confronting them on the way with technological changes, looking at the conditions of their gradual proliferation, and tracing, as long as it is possible in the case of this medium, the scope of cultural impact within their reach. Unlike some of my Polish colleagues, my research interests are solely focused on Polish radio, including phenomena ranging from the appearance of artistic radio within the paradigm of art and literature to the contemporary interfusion of egalitarianism as it relates to *ex definitione* elite art.

Of course, both communication and art contribute to the process of what we could call 'imparting', marked by a certain historical horizon. In order, however, for that imparting to function, there must be media - that is a proper means of transfer or physical artefacts. Thus included here is an important material aspect, one disregarded by researchers for a long time until Walter Benjamin referred to it. What is significant is that to Benjamin 'culture is not... "a triumph of spirit over matter", but the opposite: it is a progressive triumph of matter over human subjectivity' (Bielik-Robson 2006: 262-3). Some scholars today still 'question the creative character of interactivity; they believe that a dialogue with a machine cannot contribute to anything artistic' (Hopfinger 2005: 21). Radio has always been heavily dependent on technological development, although it is also worth mentioning that it is that civilisational development that led in the previous century to the questioning of the 'sacred' status of art, that is to its deprivation of the formerly fundamental feature of autotelism (Marshall 2004: 166-7). There are other, no less attractive, works of audio art that contribute - although it is difficult to tell to what extent - to the process of shaping of, if not autotelic, then certainly instrumental values of art; and it is achieved by the very fact of their appearance, as well as by the fact of their inevitable interpretation of already existing texts, including also falsifications of those interpretations. Of course culture, according to Ralf Konersmann, is 'a notion... of widely diffused semantics and a complex structure' (2009: 97). I perceive it as something that effectively broadens our horizons and allows us – by the fact of converging with our life experience – to see the world in a different, deeper light, put order into our sensations, and at times also comprehend what has been unreachable for us before. In short: 'art offers us a better sense of direction both in the world and in our own existence' (Anzenbacher 2005: 37).

Until recently, everything that had the mark of high class was created in a very attractive environment of the epoch-friendly art paradigm, a tendency that can be particularly well seen in the interwar period. However, the contemporary frontiers of circulation of total or fragmentary pieces of art belonging to social communication or art tend to be more and more vague and the cooperation brings newer and newer results (Hopfinger 2010: 59-61). Thirty years ago Umberto Eco stated in his typical witty manner that 'the new (but also old) generation, tired of politics, wants to hear again the "true words"; that is how High Culture became triumphant again' (1996: 210). John Storey, when pointing to stereotypical images of mass culture, refers to 'fan culture', where 'groups of hysterical girls and women shout in the presence of celebrities'. This type of culture, as he indicates, differs from the dominant, official culture not only by the 'object of admiration...', but also by the 'methods of appreciation... Popular audiences are said to display their pleasure to emotional excess, whereas the audience for dominant culture is always able to maintain respectable aesthetic distance' (Storey 2003: 216-17). While we must keep in mind the differences existing among media, it appears that this idea could also be applied to the manners in which particular audiences choose and listen to radio broadcasts.

Although the title 'What is over is (not) over' is designed to deal – within the framework of this chapter - with artistic radio, the term could easily be extended in its application to the entire medium. As we know, radio has not ceased to exist, in spite of the fact that other attractive media, like television, or, later, the internet, have made their way onto the stage. The fear of one medium eliminating another, being at least as old as media, was also the experience of former times, which can be exemplified by the words of the popular Polish writer Zenon 'Miriam' Przesmycki who lamented in 1927 that 'the radio will kill the book'. Well, it has not; in fact, quite the contrary - it has not only become its patient and faithful propagator, but also, partially, distributor. This opportunity was noticed only eight years later by Melchior Wańkowicz, known later as the father of Polish reportage, who wrote: 'a writer can write a book that nobody will read... Between the moment of production and that of consumption there always exists... a gap of uncertainty called distribution. Radio allows us to close that gap to its absolute minimum: all that is required is to start using the loudspeaker' (Wańkowicz 1935: 85).

He failed, however, to indicate an important condition: just like we cannot force anybody to read, he/she cannot force anybody to listen, although we will often find ourselves in a situation of coercion, unable to do anything about the radio being broadcast in stores or on buses. Currently, of course, it has become so common that it can, indeed, be annoying. Yet there is evidence that even as early as in the interwar period the problem of that quasi-coercion was already existent. That early case should not, however, be taken unconditionally, because, unlike modern times where the problem concerns virtually anyone, in the interwar period it was usually performed with workers: they had a break, during which they were encouraged via the radio to fill that time by participating in exercises led by the speaker. The phenomenon of obligatory listening to the radio in factories or schools could not be evaluated with criteria fitting our times. The very fact of expanding radio listening in factories and schools was a difficult and expensive task for a society that had been in the process of lifting itself up from an economic downturn and geographical nonexistence for almost 150 years. It should be emphasised that the cost of the operation was covered usually, (totally or partially,) by owners in the case of factories and local governments in the case of schools. Listening to the radio should also be associated with another important phenomenon: self-imposed Sunday visits of entire families to local, radio-equipped community centres. What made radio programmes particularly attractive to the listeners, as sources show, was the effort on the side of the producers to suit the content to the intellectual capacities and interests of the audience.

Between the wars

It is true that in the interwar period common views on those who constituted the audiences of artistic radio broadcasting changed; sometimes this can be observed even in the case of the same individuals, whose opinions shifted depending on their current perspective and the time of evaluation. A good example of this trend is Witold Hulewicz, who, as the manager of the literary division of the local radio station in Vilnius, stated in 1929 that: 'a man of work in a great city, and moreover a man who can afford not to deny himself at least basic cultural attractions, does not listen to the radio' (Hulewicz 1929: 192). When the same man, however, became the manager of the literary division of a major radio station in Warsaw seven years later, his views changed considerably: 'We believe that the listener should be at times in awe, at other times touched, then again outraged... And it is good if radio drama as it evolves seems to some hard and to others touching. Otherwise we would not be able to come to terms with the audience of such varied tastes and on such different intellectual levels' (Hulewicz 1936: 6-7). Forty years later, Zdzisław Nardelli, the then executive manager of the Polish radio theatre, was surprisingly close to Marynowski's conclusion in his own assessment of the situation. He confirmed that: 'the potential impact of a radio drama depends on the interest of the listeners. The versatility of repertoire... should be (thus) guided by the versatility of the audience, whose tastes... and perception capacities must never be undermined' (1973: 528).

In 1939 Polish radio reached the level of a million registered receivers, which, taking into account the fact that every receiver served at least one family, and that there were many unregistered radio sets owned by people unwilling to pay the radio tax, amounted to a considerable, (for the times,) number of listeners. Those beginnings of mass reception must seem very modest, especially when compared to the mass culture of the first phase, which, in turn, in itself seems very modest in comparison to the number of listeners in the 1990s, due to the impact of the internet. Manuel Castels, referring to the crisis and conflicts characteristic of the first decade of the current century, wrote: 'At the end of the second thousand years of our era numerous vital... transformations took place simultaneously, and they gave rise to a new form of society... the society of the network' (2011: 9). Indeed, the internet and the computer are signs of our times. Although, as Jay David Bolter stated, 'computers do no work on their own' (2005: 357), it is owing to internet sites that we can talk about a new textuality today. Bachura added this: 'These sites have a heterogenous structure, because they combine audio transmission... with written text, photography, or video' (2012: 63). It is, however, worth considering the question posed by Lev Manovich, who asked: 'to what extent (do) new media continue older forms... such as stylistic conventions of strategies used by traditional media' (2006: 65). Living in this world and it being a 'cultural prison' (Burszta 2008), we keep playing various 'cultural games'. However, 'the principles of these games,' as Geert Hofstede argued, '...do not undergo a process of some deep change. The rules underlying the questions... of how to be successful, fail, or belong to a particular group, are still binding' (2007: 72). Burszta also emphasised the fact that 'culture as an intention-thought reality, written into various practical spheres of one's activity, is matched by a set of practices, in which he/she participates as a member of a particular cultural group' (2008: 160).

Therefore I believe that it is quasi-anthropological research that constitutes the most promising direction of progress for us – having been broadened to embrace various artistic forms, and recognising culture as not only a way of life, but also as, for example, cultural practices. Among the most ennobling cultural practices there have always been literature reading; I believe, however, that the practice of listening to artistic radio in the interwar period can also be included in that list, although one will easily find both supporters and adversaries of this concept. As Zygmunt Kisielewski showed, at the end of that period the primary distrust of, (and incapability of evaluating,) radio among scholars and art critics, was soon replaced by their vivid fascination in that new mass-medium. Among those who wrote letters to the radio were not only uneducated listeners, but also members of the intelligentsia and faithful theatre goers (Pleszkun-Olejniczakowa 2000: 349-351). Therefore we might be entitled to formulate a thesis that artistic radio listeners constitute a specific cultural (sub)group, marked, of course, by shifting in time preferences, just like the very culture, and also shifting in its nature. From a social psychological and, even more so, a sociological perspective this concept seems virtually undefendable. It lacks the hierarchy of status and prestige, as well as the traditional dichotomy of WE-YOU. However, according to Paweł Boski there still remain 'wide horizons… of dimensions and cultural symbols, deliberately ignored by social psychology. Particularly, [this] psychology… does not deal with such notions as cultural differentiation within one's own group… as well as [not recognising] markers of social belonging based… on a common style of cogniscence, either axiological or aesthetic' (2010: 490). Aspects of that belonging, not based on similar features characteristic of the cognition process, aesthetic fellowship or integration in the area of values, are, in the case of artistic radio listeners, quite easily discerned.

Let us remember that at the beginning of the twentieth century different cultural groups were considerably more distant from each other than today, and even though at the time the radio was introduced the situation was changing, the change should be seen as minor. In the interwar period there were many illiterate people in Poland, and few, initially expensive, radio receivers. Therefore, it should be emphasised that the state made sincere efforts to make the radio available to the poor, such as workers and farmers. Furthermore, as Stefan Żółkiewski stated, radio 'was at first perceived among peasants and blue collar workers as a luxury, yet… it soon made its way to community centres'. However, in order to encourage the less wealthy classes of society to potentially purchase a radio receiver, it was necessary to take steps to develop in them a need to listen to the radio, and then make it possible for them to buy a radio set for the lowest possible price. It should be perceived as a remarkable success that Poland did manage to swiftly implement a program of radio receiver production and make them available to people who could pay in low instalments. It was even more efficient than in Germany, which became known for its success in this field. This success would not have been possible without direct involvement in the process of the board of Polski Radio, and especially the executive manager, Zygmunt Chamiec.

Therefore it was possible, virtually from the very beginning of radio in Poland, to avoid the trap, as Henry Jenkins described it much later, of a 'participation gap'. That gap indicates not only an unequal distribution of goods, (the radio receivers,) but also differences among listeners in their capacity to take full advantage of the culture. Therefore the fact that from the beginning of the reborn state of Poland the radio reached virtually everyone, obtains a new meaning. In the face of high levels of illiteracy in Poland, the possibility of listening to the radio constituted an invaluable opportunity to educate, especially because the people listened not only to music, guides, or news – from which they would often start their adventure with the radio – but also to radio drama. Radio drama in the interwar period was often authored by writers who were also famous outside the radio world. Moreover, there were numerous productions based on fragments of works belonging to the cultural canon, which, in turn, allowed those least educated to get acquainted with the main characters, plot and general atmosphere of those distinct pieces of literature. All this gave people an opportunity to get familiar with at least the basic 'cultural particles' of the time. Thus the fact of being a listener to radio drama in the interwar period had a considerable impact on one's social and cultural status. Radio has always been considered a medium for the lonely. Edgar Morin even states that 'consumption of goods [including also those of a cultural nature] becomes, at the same time, auto-consumption of one's personal life' (2005: 65). Yet, it is not impossible for the radio to evoke in the listener a need for a group experience, which, however, happens usually only in specific situations. These situations generally do not include broadcasting of artistic events, although there is one noted exception to this principle: in the interwar period radio premieres of some shows were widely advertised, as was, for example, the case with Stanisław Wyspiański's *Wesele* (1936), which he announced both in the press and by means of personal invitations handed to certain individuals. The experience of joint reception of attractive mediated events is not infrequent today. Umberto Eco described, for example, important football matches as events gathering listeners and viewers around a single radio receiver, adding: 'These new masses come also because of the social nature of the event, that is… to spend some time together' (1996: 211). Phenomena of this kind are, however, relatively rare in the case of programmes we might describe as artistic radio.

Significant productions

It was, of course, a matter of utmost importance to create the right programme lineup. In total 2,522 radio drama pieces were broadcast in that time (Pleszkun-Olejniczakowa 2000), 76 per cent of them were based on Polish texts, which is similar to the current situation. Adaptations constituted a large majority (85 per cent) of all performances. Bachura-Wojtasik, although she appreciates literature as a source of 'ideas', rightfully claimed that: 'A broadcast should be treated as a peculiar piece of art, produced by means of mass-media' (2012: 10). When asked about the textual foundation of a radio drama, Waldemar Modestowicz, a contemporary director of the Polish radio theatre, stated that 'it must be "good' literature", but immediately added that 'the script should be characterised by radio-orientetedness, that is, capable of convincing the potential listener that the presented story… can only sound totally true in radio space' (Bachura-Wojtasik 2012: 345-61). The autonomy of the genre, although with due respect to the script, is also emphasised by another noted contemporary director, Andrzej Piszczatowski. When asked about the sovereignty of radio drama, he contended that it is 'absolute autonomy.' I will mention, at this point, the fact that some pieces of – to keep the traditional term – original radio drama find themselves in a peculiar ontological situation when on air. The most frequently met 'radio family saga is a variant of a radio series, where a family constitute the main characters… Their history… is presented in a long-term perspective and in keeping with the continuity of the plot which, in turn, takes into consideration the socio-political background. … It is a continuation series, which means that… it could have an almost infinite number of episodes' (Pawlik 2012: 280). Such series, which used to be called radio novels in the past, are still broadcast today. Their forerunner was a series entitled *Dni Powszednich Państwa Kowalskich* (The Everyday of the Blows), based on texts by Maria Kuncewiczowa, a distinguished inter-war writer. This series appears to be the first of its kind in Europe and perhaps even in the world (Zaworska 1983: 164-5).

Artistic radio reportage should, undoubtedly, be also included in the body of artistic radio. It is debatable, however, whether the productions from the interwar period could be termed artistic radio reportage. That is, whether they are in harmony with how artistic reportage is defined today (Pleszkun-Olejniczakowa 2004: 115-123). To cite an example, Marian Grzegorczyk clearly confused transmission ('reportage photography') with a literary broadcast (1936: 11) and Mieczysław Nałęcz-Dobrowolski refered to Melchior Wańkowicz's *Na tropach Smętka* (On the track of Smętek), a volume with reportage miscellanea, as 'one of the greatest cycles of radio reportage I have ever heard' (Nałęcz-Dobrowolski 1935: 9). The fact that genuine artistic reportage was almost not produced in the inter-war period appears to have resulted mainly from the technical shortages of the era. From the beginning out of the two genres it was definitely radio drama that had a better chance to develop and assume its role on radio, since the process of its recording was considerably easier; the giant reels of steel tape, called 'still' in Polish, although highly impractical, were still immensely desirable for selected radio stations. A more modern type of lateral recording was employed in the case of Berliner discs, although they became widely available only in the middle of the 1930s. Nevertherless, in 1937 a vigorous debate whether to choose 'still' or the disc, took place in the periodical *Antena*. In spite of the theoretical chance to record and archive various events, almost all of the brittle ebonite discs vanished during World War II. Today we only have one surviving radio drama, *Most* (Bridge) by Ignacy Fik, or, to be precise, a twenty-minute-long recording of its three parts. Nevertheless, in the interwar period radio drama was in a considerably better situation than radio reportage, because usually it did not necessitate leaving the studio, apart from, perhaps, the need to record natural background sounds - the so-called 'acoustic kitchen'. Today such sound effects are available through obtaining the sound archive of the BBC. It is all the more worthwhile noticing that the need to employ 'acoustic ornaments, and auditory space effects capable of affecting the listeners' imagination,' was perceived as important from virtually the very beginning of radio.

As an example of those amusing natural background recordings, let me quote the following: 'For example in the case of *Don Quixote* it was necessary to record the sounds of a donkey as well as of a duel. That was not a particularly rewarding type of task; the recording took one hour, the effect… four burps… the duel scene was recorded for three hours… A whole company of soldiers had to be employed to produce a sufficient number of exclamations, plus two horse riders and two more soldiers with big pot lids. The moment the riders passed each other, the two soldiers banged the lids, which on the recording gave the effect of a lance hitting an armour' (Pawliszak 1937: 6). Contemporary authors usually take advantage of a ready-made sound library, although occasionally some radio drama is recorded on location. Sound engineers are also able to produce extraordinary sound effects for the sake of a particular radio drama or reportage (Pawlik 2011: 434-43). During an interview with Bachura-Wojtasik, Andrzej Brzoska, a distinguished Polish sound engineer, contended that 'not every coin will sound like a coin on the radio, not every step will sound like a step, and when recording wind… one always has to be somewhat creative'. Let us add at this point that Bachura-Wojtasik is the first scholar to have analysed the sphere of sound production for radio drama in such a precise and versatile way, which is particularly well seen in the part of her work devoted to its semiotics (2012: 125-62). Equally valuable are Kinga Klimczak's insights into the sound sphere of a contemporary radio reportage (2011: 80-107). We must remember that radio, like television, let alone the internet and all other new media, is and has always been dependent on the progress of technology. As digitisation has even infiltrated radio production by revolutionising the processes of recording and editing, it is hard for us to imagine what really could have given pleasure to the listeners of the prewar era.

The first production truck was acquired by Polski Radio in the middle of the 1930s, which, according to Klimczak, had a milestone impact due to its contribution to enhancing recording and archiving possibilities. However, once on location, due to the level of equipment the vehicle could have only been used for recording; the recording was then replayed on air, becoming thus a 'retransmission' (2011: 62). Yet it was the introduction of mobile tape recorders and microphones as late as in the middle of the last century that made the existence of radio reportage, in the modern sense of the term, possible. She added: 'Two boundaries were crossed at that time: spacial and technological' (2011: 63). '[By] operating without image' the reportage was finally able to extract 'the true value of live speech... and on the other hand [it became visible that] its primary substance consisted of genuinely authentic speech' (2011: 247). A wave of international success in that field which came after the war, started by Witold Zadrowski with his prize at the Prix Italia 1966 for his reportage entitled *Śmierć słonia* (The Death of an Elephant), acknowledged the high artistic potential of Polish reportage. We became a reportage stronghold. Polish radio drama was also recognized and awarded on the international level. The first person to be honoured (1959) was Zbigniew Kopalko, the script author and director of *Neffru*, a radio opera. He was highly valued in Polish radio circles as early as in the inter-war era. The first proper radio drama to receive an award was *Z głębokości wód* (From the Depths of Waters), based on the script by Andrzej Mularczyk and directed by Henryk Rozen, which received the Prix Italia in Peruggia (1989). Let us add that the representatives of Poland, just like they did in the interwar period, occupy today important positions in the EBU, are members of RFPG, and young reportage producers participate in sessions of the EBU Master School.

Perceptions

The first critics and scholars who preoccupied themselves with artistic radio paid special attention to an aspect which can still be seen today, but whose role is considerably less relevant, or which we would, perhaps, term marginal; yet to those men it was one of the most prevailing factors of the medium: the educational role of radio. To mention but a few of them, Michał Lachowicz wrote: 'Although we might not be aware of this, in... the short period of its existence radio's contribution to the field of artistic life has been remarkable... It is owing to the loudspeaker that many people have begun to take interest in art. Many a name... or a literary term... has become known to people only by means of radio' (1939: 7). No more than three years after the launch of Polski radio, Zenon Kosidowski - a scholar and distinguished radio expert of the inter-war era – recommended in his book that radio should be a 'combination of artistic values, educational inclinations, and entertainment as well as of diligence and talent of the radio stage arranger' (1928: 28). Of course, the requirements and tastes of the radio audience evolved with time. We can say that today some of the most popular types of radio drama are dramatised radio documentaries, which apparently results from the increasing popularity of non-fiction and especially historical literature. To a certain extent one can also see ontic interdisciplinary changes between the two genres, although, I believe, both artistic radio reportage and radio drama still retain their generic autonomy.

Janusz Kukuła - the current director of the Polish Radio Theatre – also discerns changes in the more general radio framework as well as in the very fabric of radio drama, yet he declines to define them due to their lability (Bachura & Pawlik 2011: 202-16). It is worth adding, I believe, that ever since Kukuła took the position, (he is now in his second term of office,) the style of language used in radio drama has always been high, as far from colloquialisms and vulgarisms as possible. Krzysztof Zalewski – Kukuła's predecessor at the Polish radio theatre (2007-8) - in an attempt 'to get closer to the theatre of life' allowed for a slightly more colloquial language not devoid of some vulgarisms. Yet, the producers at TOK FM went even further and this is the only commercial radio station in Poland which, owing to the efforts of Mikołaj Lizut, produced its own radio drama for a sustained period.

The level of radio listeners' perception has undoubtedly changed considerably over the last 80 years. In the early period of Polish Radio its power influence and attractiveness depended largely on the simultaneity of an event and its transmission. Consider, for example, the famous case of panic caused by the radio broadcasting of *The War of the Worlds* in 1938, an episode of a series of radio drama produced in the United States for CBS. This potential simultaneity is what turned out to be particularly attractive about the radio to Zofia Nałkowska, a distinguished Polish writer and author of novels and a number of scripts for radio drama. She wrote: 'A concert… recitation by an artist; all this, uninterrupted, has its flow as if by the very fact of a microphone hanging under the ceiling of the hall... A radio connection… multiplies the event number-wise for the sake of the recipients, upholding, at the same time, its simultaneousness and identity' (1935: 6). Of course, that 'uninterrupted reception', and, even more so, that 'identity' in its semiotic sense, were merely a wish. It is clear that the level of reception, (by comparison with today,) was highly limited. It was so, on the one hand, due to the level of technology available at that time, and, on the other, to a relatively low level of radio-listening culture, as well as the fact that audio signifiers were still evolving, and so they were virtually unknown. I believe that what determines the reception of artistic radio broadcasts is, to use Dell Hathaway Hymes's term, communicative competence, transformed by the influence of new media, technological progress and globalisation, and thus enabling the discovery and use of codes predominant in radio. Presently most scholars take the stance that 'media convey those ideologies to which the recipient refers by means of codes created in his or her social circumstance, and dependent on the received educational and psychological tendencies predominant at that time' (Eco 1996: 164). This problem is closely connected to the question of communication, and concerns the intentions of both the sender and the receiver (Kurcz 2000: 130-46).

Zdzisław Marynowicz, Hulewicz's predecessor and the manager of the literary division of the theatre of imagination in Warsaw, (who also gave it its name,) wrote in 1933 the following words: 'the theatre of imagination must take into account the fact that among those who listen to the radio there are people of very different backgrounds… and cultural status, thus the repertoire should be selected with great versatility in mind' (Marynowski 1932: 3). The reception of a work of art, including one that is audiovisual, confirms Roman Jakobson's thesis that there are at least two codes - the encoding and the decoding – that are involved in the process of communication (Jakobson 1970: 335-351). If the artist and the recipient use two different codes, entropy is imminent. Listener will first tend to use familiar canons, but when this is not sufficient during the process of reception, the code of the author becomes deformed and is mixed with the other codes stored by the recipient, so that the final result – a hybrid - combines what is important with what is incidental, creating a wholeness of frequently random nature.

Conclusion

The perception level of an artistic audio text depends also, although only to a certain extent, on one's axiological horizons, and our value system is heavily conditioned, in turn, by our emotions. Artistic radio, (especially reportage, although it quite often does not constitute the ontological foundation of the work,) even listened to in the 'contaminated' atmosphere of a large, modern city, is still considerably more inspiring for the imagination than watching television. Surely it is works of high emotional load, (like reportage,) that are particularly well suited to the radio, because they help us to shape and preserve our ethical choices, allowing us, in turn, to reach a syntonic unity with the hero of the story. It is so because art, including audio productions, 'is not,' as Natalie Heinich claims, 'a naturally given fact, but a phenomenon constructed... on the practical level' (2010: 67). Thus as one can see, there exist close ties between technology, art and communication, which, when viewed from a historical perspective and through a comparison of past and present experience, call for a dynamic perception of artistic radio, a perception based on the recognition of the processes of both continuity and change within culture. It is so, I believe, because the question underlying the ontological and epistemological senses of those changes, be it in the interwar period or in the contemporary era of universal digitisation, is, in fact, a question about the true nature of processes responsible for aestheticisation of reality. This should not surprise us, because, as Lorenc holds, the cultural process is 'attended by both new technologies and new aspects of art' (2006: 254).

References

Anzenbacher, A (2005) *Wprowadzenie do filozofii*, Kraków: Unum.

Bachura- Wojtasik, J (2012) *Odsłony wyobraźni. Współczesne słuchowisko radiowe*, Toruń: Wydawnictwo Adam Marszałek.

Bachura, J & Pawlik, A (2011) 'Współczesne słuchowisko na tle przemian technologicznych i kultury konwergencji', in Pleszkun-Olejniczakowa, E, Bachura, J & Pawlik, A (eds), *Dwa Teatry. Studia z zakresu teorii i interpretacji sztuki słuchowiskowej*, Toruń: Wydawnictwo Adam Marszałek.

Bielik-Robson, A (2006) 'Gnostyk w wielkim mieście: Walter Benjamin i kultura. materialna', in Rosińska, Z & Michalik, J (eds), *Co to jest filozofia kultury*, Warszawa: Wydawnictwo Uniwersytetu Warszawskiego.

Bolter, J (2005) 'Komputer: maszyna i narzędzie', in Hopfinger, M (ed), *Nowe media w komunikacji społecznej w XX wieku*, Warszawa: Oficyna Naukowa.

Boski, P (2010) *Kulturowe ramy zachowań społecznych. Podręcznik psychologii międzykulturowej*, Warszawa: Wydawnictwo Naukowe PWN.

Burszta, W (2008) *Świat jako więzienie kultury. Pomyślenia*, Warszawa: Państwowy Instytut Wydawniczy.

Castells, M (2011) *Społeczeństwo sieci*, Warszawa: Wydawnictwo Naukowe PWN.

Debray, R (2010) *Wprowadzenie do mediologii*, Warszawa: Oficyna Naukowa.

Eco, U (1996) *Semiologia życia codziennego*, Warszawa: Wydawnictwo Czytelnik.

Eco, E (2009) *Teoria semiotyki*, Kraków: Wydawnictwo Uniwersytetu Jagiellońskiego.

Fiske, J (2010) *Zrozumieć kulturę popularną*, Kraków: Wydawnictwo Uniwersytetu Jagiellońskiego.

Grzegorczyk, M (1936) 'Słowo', *Antena,* volume 28.

Heinich, N (2010) *Socjologia sztuki*, Warszawa: Oficyna Naukowa.

Hofstede, G (2007) *Kultury i organizacje. Zaprogramowanie umysłu*, Warszawa: Polskie Wydaw, Ekonomiczne.

Hopfinger, M (2005) *Nowe media w komunikacji społecznej w XX wieku*, Warszawa: Oficyna Naukowa.

Hopfinger, M (2010) *Literatura i media po 1989*, Warszawa: Oficyna Naukowa.

Hulewicz, W (1929) 'Z zagadnień "sztuki słuchowej"', *Pamiętnik Warszawski,* issue II.

Hulewicz, W (1936) 'Odpowiedź na pytanie "dlaczego"?', *Pion,* volume 17.

Jenkins, H (2007) *Kultura konwergencji. Zderzenie starych i nowych mediów*, Warszawa: Wydawnictwa Akademickie i Profesjonalne.

Jakobson, R (1970) '[O wierszu i składni Majakowskiego]', title added by the editors, in Mayenowa, M, Renata, S, Zygmunt (eds), *Rosyjska szkoła stylistyki,* Warszawa: Państwowy Instytut Wydawniczy.

Klimczak, K (2011) *Reportaże radiowe o krzywdzie i cierpieniu*, Łódź: Wydawnictwo Primum Verbum.

Konersmann, R (2009) *Filozofia kultury. Wprowadzenie*, Warszawa: Oficyna Naukowa.

Kosidowski, Z (1928) *Artystyczne słuchowiska radiowe*, Poznań: Fiszer i Majewski Księgarnia Uniwersytecka.

Kurcz, I (2000) *Psychologia języka i komunikacji. Wykłady z psychologii*, Warszawa: Scholar.

Lachowicz, M (1939) 'O teatrze radiowym', *Pion,* volume 12.

Levinson, P (2010) *Nowe nowe media*, Kraków: Wydawnictwo WAM.

Lorenc, I (2006) 'Filozofia kultury estetyka. Przesuwanie granic', in Rosińska, Z & Michalik, J (eds), *Co to jest filozofia kultury?,* Warszawa: Wydawnictwo Uniwersytetu Warszawskiego.

Manovich, L (2006) *Język nowych mediów*, Warszawa: Wydawnictwa Akademickie i Profesjonalne.

Marshall, G (2004) 'Kultura popularna', in Marshall, G (ed), *Słownik socjologii i nauk społecznych*, Warszawa: Wydawnictwo Naukowe PWN.

Marynowski, Z (1932) 'XI muza', *Radio,* volume 18.

Morin, E (2005) 'Masowy odbiorca', in Hopfinger, M (ed), *Nowe media w komunikacji społecznej w XX wieku*, Warszawa: Oficyna Naukowa.

Nałęcz-Dobrowolski, M (1935) 'Krytykujemy', *Antena,* volume 52.

Nałkowska, Z (1935) *Moje pierwsze słuchowisko*, *Pion* 1935, volume 38.

Nardelli, Z (1973) 'Sztuka autonomiczna. Zapiski reżysera', *Pamiętnik Teatralny*, issue 3/4.

Pawlik, A (2011), 'Struktura adaptacyjna w słuchowisku adaptacyjnym. Na materiale >Ostatniej taśmy Krappa< według Samuela Becketta', in Pleszkun-Olejniczakowa, E, Bachura, J & Pawlik, A (eds), *Dwa Teatry. Studia z zakresu teorii i interpretacji sztuki słuchowiskowe*j, Toruń: Wydawnictwo Adam Marszałek.

Pawliszak, P (1937) 'Jak powstaje słuchowisko radiowe', *Antena,* volume 16.

Pawlik, A (2012) *Teatr radiowy i jego gatunki*, PhD Thesis.

Pleszkun-Olejniczakowa, E (2000) *Słuchowiska Polskiego Radia w okresie piętnastolecia 1925-1939*, Łódź: Wydawnictwo Biblioteka.

Pleszkun-Olejniczakowa, E (2004) 'O reportażu radiowym', in Stępnik, K & Piechota, M (eds), *Reportaż w dwudziestoleciu międzywojennym*, Lublin: Wydawnictwo Uniwersytetu Marii Curie-Skłodowskiej.

Pleszkun-Olejniczakowa, E (2012) >*Muzy rzadko się do radia przyznają< Szkice o słuchowiskach i reportażach radiowych*, Łódź: Wydawnictwo Primum Verbum.

Przesmycki, Z (1927) 'Przyszłość radia', *Radio*, volume 10.

Zaworska, H (ed) (1983) *Rozmowy z Maria Kuncewiczową,* Warszawa: Wydawnictwo Czytelnik.

Skiwski, J (1935) 'Krytykujemy', *Antena,* volume 41.

Storey, J (2003) *Studia kulturowe i badania kultury popularnej. Teorie i metody*, Kraków: Wydawnictwo Uniwersytetu Jagiellońskiego.

Wańkowicz, M (1935) 'głos dyskusyjny', in Hulewicz, Witold (ed), *Teatr Wyobraźni*, Warszawa: Wydawnictwa Radia i Telewizji.

Żółkiewski, S (1973) *Kultura literacka 1918–1932*, Wrocław: Zakład Narodowy im. Ossolińskich.

Chapter 23

Radio series in Poland: Characteristics, forms and trends

Aleksandra Pawlik

Abstract

The central focus of this chapter is radio series, a genre at the crossroads of high art and popular culture. Firstly, it considers the distinction between radio series and the older, more popular genre of artistic radio entertainment – the radio drama. Attention is drawn to the fact that Polish academic discourse seems to ignore the notion of 'radio series', as theoreticians and radio practitioners tend to use the imprecise and currently meaningless term 'radio novel'. The beginnings of radio series in Poland are traced back to the productions broadcast between the World Wars. The chapter then discusses the significance of radio series for various radio stations, taking into account the three major sectors of the radio market broken down according to the form of ownership (public radio, commercial radio and social radio, including religious and academic radio stations). Following the examination of the meaning of radio series for each of these sectors, the chapter attempts to characterise the two most popular types of radio series, namely the radio family saga, (represented by the oldest radio series which are still being broadcast: *Matysiakowie* and *W Jezioranach*,) and the mini-series, represented by a few new productions of Polski Radio.This analysis pays much attention to two phenomena in particular: the manner in which the poetics of the radio family saga are governed by the classical rule of the three unities, (of action, time and place,) and the highly individualised features of particular mini-series.

Keywords: radio drama, radio series, radio novel, Poland

Introduction: the different sectors of the Polish radio industry

To the Polish audience the word 'series' most commonly brings to mind associations with popular television soap operas, which are unceasingly attractive to the mass television audience. In contrast, serial productions on the radio are a rarely discussed phenomenon. This article will perhaps shed some light on the reasons for which this form of entertainment deserves particular attention, as it not only constitutes a distinct radio genre, but also plays an important role as the predecessor of the television series. From the point of view of ownership, radio in Poland can be divided into three sectors: public, commercial and social radio stations. The development of this tripartite structure has largely been the result of the manner of financing of particular radio stations, although legal regulations and technologies used by broadcasters have also contributed to this division (Beliczyński 2010: 20). Each of these types of radio broadcasting is focused on a different set of goals to be achieved in the contemporary media market.

Public radio is responsible for a social mission, the provision of wide public access to radio programming, the inclusion of productions and programmes targeted at minorities in their programming schedule, the promotion of national identity and culture and, perhaps most importantly, the obligatory inclusion of texts of high culture in their programming. This last goal is achieved by the provision of high quality programmes devoted to literature and culture in general, as well as continued development in the field of radio drama, with a particular focus on the broadcasting of radio plays and readings of literary texts by professional actors. To a certain extent this mission is also supported by the continuous presence of the oldest, traditional series in the stations' programming. Examples of such programmes include *Matysiakowie*, currently broadcast on Saturdays at 13:10, and *W Jezioranach*, aired at the same time on Sundays. One purpose of creating the radio novel *Motel w pół drogi* (2006-8) was educational and it focused on how to start a business in Poland (Bachura 2012: 98-116). Responsibility for the shape and continuity of culture is one of the most important and challenging tasks which public radio stations currently have to face. In the words of Stanisław Jedrzejewski, 'public broadcasters are now more and more often forced to face the usually veiled necessity to reconcile their social mission with successful operation alongside commercial media, with whom they have to compete for the large, perhaps even mass, audience' (2010: 35-6). The significant decrease in the number of listeners which public radio stations have been facing since the early 1990s makes mission-oriented broadcasters increasingly interested in following strategies aimed at finding new listeners, including mass audiences. The introduction of new serial productions in programming seems to be a good way to meet these new demands while remaining in compliance with the 'missionary' nature of public radio.

Producers of radio series attempt to match public radio's mission by incorporating and referring to only those texts of popular culture which have earned wide critical acclaim. Three contemporary productions - *Ręczna robota*, written by Ryszard Ćwierlej and directed by Janusz Kukuła (2011), *Każdy żyje, jak umie, czyli Skąd się wzięli 'Sami swoi'* by Andrzej Mularczyk and also directed by Janusz Kukuła (2011), and *Studenci Trzeciego Wieku: Czterdzieści lat minęło jak jeden dzień* by Jerzy Gruza and Krzysztof Teodor Toeplitz, and directed by Jerzy Gruza (2012) – are direct references to popular and acclaimed genres and texts: the crime story, the film *Sami Swoi*, and the television series *Czterdziestolatek*, respectively. References to popular cultural texts may also satisfy the need of the listeners to establish closer relations with the characters and to continue to follow their stories. Moreover, they also perform a marketing function, as the images of popular characters and references to well-known stories are a good way to yield the widest possible audience for the series.

Series broadcast by Polski Radio are normally more sophisticated in artistic terms than their television counterparts. They are performed by the most renowned professional actors and endowed with well-designed soundtracks which employ radio's aesthetic capacities. Unique and groundbreaking artistic solutions are also often attempted for this type of production. One result of this creative and artistically valuable attitude towards radio series is the latest production by Polish Radio 3, aired between 24 and 28 June 2013. In cooperation with the Teatr Nowy theatre in Warsaw and the Malta Festival initiative in Poznan, Radio 3 broadcast a continuation of its series entitled *Miejska Powieść Odcinkowa*, comprising five episodes with each one written by a different author. The assumed urban nature of this venture was supposed to be reflected by the fact that each episode of this specific 'novel' was written in a different Polish city. The episodes were written by, (in the order of broadcast,) Sylwia Chutnik, Tomasz Man, Małgorzata Sikorska-Miszczuk, Krzysztof Bizio and Bartosz Żurawiecki, and read out on air by the actors of Teatr Nowy in Warsaw. Another attempt by public radio to compete with commercial radio stations is the introduction of series broadcast on weekdays, (whereas previously, radio series were aired only at weekends). Short episodes – no longer than a few minutes – are designed to increase the dynamics of the radio experience and bring it closer to the standards of commercial radio stations. Moreover, daily broadcasting of episodes matches the strip programming strategy widely employed by formatted radio stations (Stachyra 2008: 59). All of these factors are aimed at increasing listeners' loyalty and attachment to the station, and result in the audience tuning in for new episodes at times which are normally characterised by low ratings for public radio. Thus, by introducing new series into their programming, public radio stations gain their own equivalents of popular commercial programmes, embrace the aesthetics of private radio, (mainly by adopting a more dynamic pace,) and follow the strategies typical of formatted radio stations targeted at closely defined audiences.

Commercial radio is oriented towards generating profit. Owners of commercial radio stations attempt to address their message to the widest audience possible and to reach maximum ratings in order to safeguard for themselves the continuous interest of advertisers, and thus generate profit. For their programming such stations are guided by the rule of the lowest common denominator, which means they select topics and programmes which should provide interesting messages for the widest and most diverse group of listeners (Steciąg 2006: 98-108). Such a strategy implies the lowering of the quality of the content of their broadcasts, in both linguistic and musical terms. Taking into account the strong competition which characterises the radio market, radio formatting seems to be an interesting alternative business model for station owners (Jędrzejewski 2003: 147-51), as specialised radio content allows them to attract defined groups of listeners by satisfying the specific needs and expectations of such audiences. Formatting is a means by which a radio station can create its own unique profile while continuing to follow its business goals by attracting large groups of listeners. Radio formats may be music or talk-oriented, or can comprise a variety of radio genres. In order to attract a large audience which meets the criteria defined by the radio format, commercial radio stations currently broadcast various types of series. The use and selection of series, however, is governed and dictated by commercial rather than artistic principles. Radio series broadcast by commercial stations are usually novels, read on air in episodes; however, apart from radio adaptations of renowned literary works, commercial radio stations often broadcast texts written at their request, many authored by journalists employed by the stations. Performances of such texts are normally characterised by a rather poor sound quality: read out by a single actor or voice actor, usually known for his or her television appearances, and devoid of any musical background or sound effects. Episodes of such series are short, dynamic, and often humorous in nature – uses of parody, pastiche and satire are common.

RMF FM is the commercial radio station which employs the genre of the radio novel most often nowadays. The station broadcast a series of satirical, politically-involved novels, written at its request, and clearly referring to the current social and political situation in Poland. All nine radio novels aired by RMF FM, (*Ostatni Transfer, Zbić Zenona Zmyłera, Towarzysze Oni, Kot Aleksandra, Trzeci Bliźniak, Łabędzi Śpiew Gąsiora, W Imię Ojca, Trzy Dni Gąsiora, Co Gryzie Malkolma Pluska*,) were authored by a writer known only under the pen name Klara Weritas, and became quite popular among listeners. A noteworthy example of an original series written specially for the radio is the novel entitled *Stara, Nowa Baśń*, replete with archaic terms and expressions and styled as a raconteurish dialogue between Marcin Ziobro and Tomasz Olbratowski, RMF FM's journalists. Another case of a recently popular radio novel is *Facet To Świnia*, a comedy series in the form of an internet blog whose female author exposes and mocks the vices and defects of men. Authors of radio novels for RMF FM often employ intertextual references to television productions. In the summer of 2010 the station introduced its listeners to a humorous documentary series about animal life, narrated by the popular television presenter Krystyna Czubówna. According to Paulina Czarnek, an interesting example of a television-inspired radio series is *Dom Nad Wysypiskiem* (later known as *Dym Nad Wysypiskiem*), narrated by the popular voice actor Tomasz Knapik. The series, broadcast on RMF FM in the morning, evoked the television soap opera genre and included repeated references to popular television series such as *Klan* and *M jak Miłość* (2012: 210-11). The very title of the series paraphrases the title of Małgorzata Kalicińska's first novel, *Dom Nad Rozlewiskiem*, whose extreme popularity with readers resulted in the production of a television series based on the book. A similar radio series, broadcast three years earlier than *Dom Nad Wysypiskiem* was *A jak Amor*, a parody of Venezuelan telenovellas, or soap operas, popular among a wide group of Polish viewers.

Commercial radio stations seem to view the 'missionary' obligation of public radio as a limitation to the forms and themes which can be broadcast by the latter. In contrast to public radio stations, private radio owners strive for their competitive advantage by resorting to content which is not only popular but also sensational, controversial, and often shocking. This strategy is best exemplified by the commercial stations' fondness for broadcasting literary works which are generally recognised as controversial and of little critical acclaim. In 2012 Radio Zet – the second largest commercial radio station in Poland – broadcast a radio adaptation of the shocking, overtly erotic and internationally bestselling novel *Fifty Shades of Grey*, read out on air by the popular young Polish actress Małgorzata Socha.

Social radio in Poland is represented by either religious or student radio stations. Their offer is characterised by the dominance of talk over music-oriented programming, including numerous valuable and original programmes on specialised themes. Religious radio stations generally focus on educational and personal development programmes. Popular radio series aimed at undemanding listeners are absent from their programming, which instead employs the series format for the broadcasting of artistically valuable literary works performed by professional actors. The station VOX FM has broadcast adaptations of literary works divided into radio episodes for the past two years. Their selection of texts has so far included *Zalotnice i Wiedźmy*, authored by Joanna Miszczuk and performed by Joanna Koroniewska, (an actress best known for her performances in television series,) *Kamienica Przy Kruczej* by Maria Ulatowska and performed by Anna Seniuk, and *Jak Oddech* written by Małgorzata Warda and narrated by Anna Cieślak.

Student and academic radio stations, on the other hand, tend to include radio series in their programming. One of the earliest examples of this genre's presence on student radio was a series broadcast in 2008 by Akademickie Radio Index, whose production was financially supported by the European Regional Development Fund. The series was aimed at shaping entrepreneurial attitudes among college and university students in Poland. The adventures of the protagonist, (named eL eRPeO, after the phonetic rendering of the Polish acronym for the Lubuski regional operational programme for 2007-13), instructed listeners on how to obtain and best use financial resources from the fund. The series director played with various artistic conventions, weaving elements of thriller, comedy and action genres into the story. The student-oriented radio station which employs the radio series genre most actively is perhaps the Poznan-based Radio Afera. In 2011 the station launched a project titled *Bagaż Podręczny* (www.bagazpodreczny.pl), a series whose two seasons comprised a total of twelve, one-hour long episodes and was heavily marked by social and political commentary. The characters appearing in the series present new perspectives on the problem of social exclusion. The second series of the project, broadcast in 2012, focused on issues of homo- and heterosexuality by taking a stand against stereotypes and by exposing the mechanisms of discrimination in unexpected, sometimes even subversive ways. Also in 2012, the online radio station Akademickie Radio UL, associated with the University of Łódź, broadcast over a dozen episodes of a comedy series entitled *Baza Byk*, following the personal lives and job-seeking of a group of students of Łódź-based universities.

Student radio series are composed of short episodes written on an ongoing basis. The plot developments and endings of such series are usually not planned or designed beforehand, and the adaptations are performed by students of various departments, with little or no experience in acting. Sound effects and background music are kept very simple and normally employed only to additionally illustrate the dialogues. Such series satisfy the students' need of artistic expression and development, allow them to bring their own ideas and creations to life, help them learn about the art of script writing, and increase their knowledge about the theatre of the imagination. The themes and storylines of student radio series are often surprisingly original and unique; however, their dramatic construction and sound quality usually tend to be less than perfect.

The radio series as a genre

The overview provided above of the presence of radio series in the programming of various radio stations in Poland can serve as an introduction to a more detailed description of the genre. However, before discussing the particular characteristics of radio series, a remark should be made about the relatively sparse presence of the genre in academic discourse and the resulting confusion of radio series with another genre, that of radio drama. As with radio drama, which is the oldest existing form of radio theatre (Pleszkun-Olejniczakowa 2000), the radio series is a form of radio broadcasting which employs lines delivered by actors in conjunction with radio-specific means of expression, such as sound effects, music and silence. The difference between radio series and radio drama lies primarily in the fact that the former features a simplified sound background and a reduced dramatic construction, both aspects being devoid of metaphorical or symbolic meanings. Sound effects in the radio series are normally limited to the illustration of simple domestic activities performed by the characters; silence is usually used in dialogue between particular characters and is endowed only with the most conventional meanings, (most often it is employed to express surprise, confusion or puzzlement,) and music is generally absent from the genre. As regards dramatic construction, the short episode duration of usually no longer than ten minutes requires a simplified plot and fosters standardised dramatic tropes. Another feature which characterises radio series is their normally episodic structure, where particular episodes constitute separate dramatic units which, nevertheless, together form a coherent storyline, (adventures of the same characters,) and a logical composition.

The term 'radio series' is generally absent from academic discourse. The phrase most commonly employed by radio theorists and practitioners continues to be 'radio novel'. The use of this term in relation to the radio series genre used to be accurate in the early days of radio, when it used to be closely tied with literature – indeed, the immediate predecessor of the radio novel was the literary text, in particular the types of novels which had been published in the press in instalments since around the 1850s. The term 'radio novel' highlights the genre's affiliation with literature and suggests that the programme which is thus being described is either a radio adaptation of a literary form, namely a novel (Głowiński 2000: 423), or a radio form whose genre characteristics are similar to those of a literary novel. This, however, is only true today for those radio forms which are erroneously classified as radio series and broadcast by commercial radio stations; such forms – including novels performed on air in episodes, adaptations of literary texts, or original scripts written particularly for radio use – should actually be referred to as radio novels. Contemporary radio series, (radio soaps or 'radio novellas',) are usually broadcast by public and academic radio stations and lack the close ties with literary characteristics of the radio novel. They are characterised by their own genre-specific features typical of radio rather than literary aesthetics. Therefore, the use of the term 'radio novel' in relation to radio series becomes not only unreasonable but also confusing, as it incorrectly suggests an affiliation between radio series and literary work, and thus undermines the currently dominant academic assumption of the autonomy of radio art.

According to Sadowska in Poland the radio novel, (and the radio series which followed,) was created as a result of the 'necessity to find the most flexible literary form which could present educational content related to all areas of everyday life – hitherto included only in casual radio conversations – in a new and attractive form, as well as increase the quality of radio shows in general' (1972: 88). The radio novel was intended to reach its didactic goals through an attractive form of delivery: episodes coherently connected into a single storyline and replete with dialogue – which many listeners found particularly appealing. The first Polish radio novel was *Dni Powszednie Państwa Kowalskich*, authored by Maria Kuncewiczowa (Pleszkun-Olejniczakowa 1989: 197). As the period between the World Wars was a time of intense searching for new artistic forms, Polish radio produced a significant number of radio novels during that era. These included *Anielcia i Życie* by Helena Boguszewska, *Pięć Dialogów o Zmierzchu* by Maria Kuncewiczowa and *Cyklon* by Aniela Gruszecka (Bardijewska 2001: 162). Post World War II implementations of the genre included *Uliczka Klasztorna*, written by Anna Kowalska and broadcast from 1948, *Buntownicy* and *Paweł i Agnieszka* by Krystyna Salaburska, and *Milionerzy* by Stanisława Fleszarowa-Muskat. These later productions, however, were significantly less popular than the radio novels broadcast in the interwar period. The genre's revival took place in the mid-1950s, when Polish radio began broadcasting two popular sagas: *Matysiakowie* and *W Jezioranach*.

Radio family sagas

A close analysis of radio productions characteristic of particular sectors of the media market implies the dominance of two defined types of radio series, namely the family saga and the mini-series. Each of these sub-genres presents a peculiar modification of a set of characteristics representative of radio series. The primary characteristic of the radio family saga is the presence of a collective protagonist: a multigenerational family whose adventures are normally presented against a broader historical and social background. This type of radio series features a range of strongly individualised characters, including family members, relatives, friends and neighbours. The main characters usually share a common system of beliefs and values, according to which all life goals and activities are subordinated to the supreme value of family wellbeing. The number of characters increases as the plot develops, and sometimes the storyline comprises several generations of the same family. The radio family saga is based on the principle of continuation, which means that it is not oriented towards any specific, planned ending and the number of episodes may, in theory, be infinite (Uszyński 2004: 65). The family saga genre is represented in Polish radio by the two oldest running radio novellas, or soap operas broadcast by public radio stations, namely *Matysiakowie* (broadcast since 15 August 1956) and *W Jezioranach* (since 29 May 1960). In classifying both series as family sagas I follow the line of thought expressed by Alicja Kisielewska in her exhaustive study of television sagas. In her words, '*Matysiakowie* and *W Jezioranach* can be said to represent model radio novels. However, it should be noted that such 'stills of life' on the radio are created not only with words – which are means of literary expression – but also with voice, acting techniques and other radio tropes. Therefore, perhaps the category "radio family saga" should be used to describe productions of that type. I believe this phrase to be a more fitting signifier for this specific genre, which represents long-running histories of Polish families, thus resembling literary family sagas, but also employs specifically radio-oriented means of expression, which makes it a radio family series rather than a novel *per se*' (2009: 88).

Initially, the radio saga *Matysiakowie* followed the daily lives of characters from a working class background. The lives of Józef and Helena Matysiak revolved around their attempts to cope with everyday challenges such as financial shortcomings, raising their children or reconciling conflicts between family members and neighbours (Toeplitz 1970: 121-24). Today, the main protagonists of *Matysiakowie* – children of the original characters, their own families and more distant relatives – represent a more intellectual milieu. The story is set in a tenement house on Dobra street, where Gienek and his wife Dorota live in an apartment inherited from Gienek's parents, (the original Matysiak couple,) while two neighbouring apartments are inhabited by two other couples: Kasia and Tomek and Stach and Wisia. Each of the three couples now has children and grandchildren. Gienek and Dorota are the parents of the adolescent Justyna, while his older brother is the father of Kasia, who lives with her husband and has a child of her own. The saga follows the daily adventures of typical residents of the Powiśle neighborhood in Warsaw and reveals their concerns relating to their work and family life, and the difficult decisions and challenges of the twenty-first century. What is noteworthy is the fact that, currently, *Matysiakowie* is primarily the story of the family; in the face of the ongoing social and economic changes which are taking place in Poland, this presentation may be read as a rather idealised model of a unified, closely bonded family. Whenever the families meet at one of the apartments, the listener is presented with friendly conversations between two or three family members discussing either the current social and political situation or their personal problems. Since September 2009 the saga has been directed by Waldemar Modestowicz; the script is currently authored by Dżennet Połtorzycka-Stampf'l and Janusz Dziewiątkowski.

W Jezioranach was first broadcast by Polski Radio in 1960 and followed the story of the Jabłoński family – a clan of quite educated people of a peasant and rural background whose lives revolve around small daily events. The choices made and actions taken by the characters were designed to set an example for the listeners; thus, an important aspect of the saga was its close connection to the realities of rural life and adoption of the values commonly shared by rural communities in Poland (Dudowa 1971: 7). Nevertheless, the rural background of the Jabłoński family does not prevent them from embracing technological and social progress – on the contrary, they are eager to learn and improve their family wellbeing in a responsible and planned manner. Currently, the plot of the saga focuses on a family composed of three generations and residing on a country farm known as Trojaki. Even though the grandchildren of Stefan and Aniela Jabłoński live in different parts of Poland, (some of them in the vicinity of the family village, others in cities,) the family home, situated in the eponymous village of Jeziorany, remains the central point of family traditions. Thus, although the number of main characters in the saga has increased significantly over the past two decades, and the Jabłoński family members' close relations with neighbours have resulted in the creation of an expanded family in the village, the Trojaki estate continues to symbolise the continuity and endurance of the family and the cultivation of longstanding and valuable traditions. At the same time, the Jabłoński farm may be read as a stereotypical vision of Polish rural culture: the family's unity is preserved by the social and cultural activities of the characters, such as the loud reading of letters in front of other family members, regular visits to the cemetery and the care of the graves of deceased relatives, (which also indicates strong bonds between particular generations,) family ceremonies such as festive celebrations of name days, and casual, friendly visits. Rituals related to Catholic holidays and events such as All Saints' Day, Christmas or Easter are performed with particular celebration and consideration. The continuation and preservation of family unity is traditionally the obligation of all family members, including more distant relatives.

Radio family sagas can be distinguished by their dramatic construction, inspired by classical models. The most significant feature of this genre is its close compliance with the classical rule of the three unities: of time, place and action. The unity of time means that the real duration time of an episode perfectly matches the time of events presented in this episode. Each episode invites the listeners into the house or apartment of one of the families and registers the events which take place exactly as the audience listens to the episode. The series thus becomes a chance for the listener to 'eavesdrop' on a Warsaw-based family (*Matysiakowie*) or residents of a fictional settlement in the Lubelskie region (*W Jezioranach*). This resemblance to live coverage is, of course, a mere conventional imitation, as the episodes are always prerecorded several days in advance. Radio family sagas take place exclusively in the present and employ the effect of 'virtual nowness', which gives the listener the impression of being a participant in the ongoing events (Helman & Pitrus 2008: 87). Moreover, this effect of nowness allows for the inclusion of social and cultural background and commentary into the series. The rule of the unity of place, until recently almost invariably employed by the family saga, defines the space of the world inhabited by the characters. Traditionally, all events presented in the series took place in one and the same space, namely the apartment or house of the protagonist family. For *Matysiakowie* this was initially the setting of Helena and Józef's room, later replaced by the apartment of Gienek and Elżbieta, and – following the breakdown of their marriage – by the apartment of Gienek and Dorota. However, the introduction of Janusz Dziewiątkowski to the series' script-writing team generated several brand new ideas; for the past several years the saga's protagonists have moved freely within the limits of the tenement on Dobra Street. Sometimes, the events take place in a small cafe run by the Matysiak family or – as has been the case most recently – in apartments belonging to distant relatives of the family and located in various parts of Warsaw. Today, the unity of place in the Polish radio saga means that each episode only features those fragments of the fictional world which the characters could physically reach within the time of the episode's duration.

The action in family saga is defined by the characters – most of the events are related to communal behaviours such as meetings, family rituals, leisure time activities and various forms of fostering family life. Creators of family sagas simplify the storylines of episodes in order to make sure that the listeners will recognise and understand the plot and follow the main thread of each episode. Episodes are normally composed of three threads, including one overriding thread which is the source of the most significant event of the episode. Over the course of the many decades of their being broadcast, radio sagas have to employ new and original threads, although always related to typical family problems, daily life situations and interpersonal relationships.

What is worth mentioning is the fact that the storyline of the radio family saga is always dominated by the static conversational form. One might think that, in the absence of dynamic events, there would not be enough material to craft an interesting plot. The dialogue itself, however, performs numerous functions: it creates the storyline, reveals the characters' features and attributes, introduces social and political background to the story, and exposes the characters' beliefs and interests. In other words the storyline of the series is not based on particular events as much as on the characters' opinions and statements about them. Each character can make a statement about the reality which surrounds them, take a stand, express a point of view, or share some knowledge on the subject under discussion. Radio family sagas create the impression of the characters' lives being registered objectively and live, as they speak into the microphone. This effect of nowness is achieved by the employment of documentary aesthetics and the realist mode of representation. The quintessential quality of radio broadcasting, which is the ability to capture and render all the sounds of our reality, is the basic tool for the achievement of this sense of realism, which has become both one of the most recognisable features of the radio saga and a factor which attracts the audience.

The realist mode of representation employed by the radio saga dictates a particular form of acting performance. The character's utterances are styled to resemble colloquial, spoken language, characterised by repetition, the use of clichés, syntactical errors, (the syntax of sentences is less strict than in the case of the written language,) and mispronounced words. Grandiose phrasing or extravagant expression are completely absent from the radio saga. What is more, the realism principle results in the intentional departure from the rules of correct voice production which would be expected from professional actors. Thus, the errors and mistakes in the actors' delivery of their lines usually remain uncorrected, as long as they sound like errors and mistakes which would normally be made by people in everyday conversations. This technique contributes to the genre's sense of authenticity and makes the fictional world seem more 'real.' Moreover, this principle of authenticity strongly affects casting decisions for the series. For example, the character of Kasia Piekarska in *Matysiakowie* – one of the listeners' favorite characters – has for many years been played by Agnieszka Migalska, who is not a professional actress, but nevertheless has voice acted as Kasia since the character's birth. Her lack of professional acting training thus becomes an asset, as it contributes to the realist mode of representation.

Mini-series

Another form of radio series which has become particularly popular in recent years is the so-called mini-series. Mini-series are composed of a set number of short, (several minutes long,) episodes usually broadcast on weekday afternoons by public radio stations and, less popularly, academic stations. In his study of television forms Jerzy Uszyński observed that the mini-series can be characterised by a closed dramatic structure on the level of the entire series, not particular episodes. The mini-series is composed of a limited number of episodes, which means that the threads of the storyline must continue from one episode to the next and be directed towards a designed ending, where the problems presented in the series are finally resolved' (2004: 68). As the plot of the series progresses, the characters become more experienced and the listeners receive an increasing volume of information about the protagonists, whose psychological profiles are gradually revealed. As the characters' stories are shaped by particular events in their lives, an important factor is the listeners' awareness and understanding of the cause-and-effect patterns for the events and the character's motivations. Not unlike their television counterparts, radio mini-series, (which are especially popular among commercial radio stations,) tend to be spectacular productions involving contributions from exceptional script-writers, directors and actors. Normally, a series of this type becomes the highlight of a station's programming, repeatedly recommended and advertised on air.

The mini-series genre became popular on Polish radio in 2011, when three productions of this type were broadcast at short intervals: *Ręczna robota*, authored by Ryszard Ćwierlej and directed by Janusz Kukuła, *Każdy żyje, jak umie, czyli Skąd się wzięli 'Sami swoi'* by Andrzej Mularczyk and also directed by Janusz Kukuła, and *Studenci Trzeciego Wieku: Czterdzieści lat minęło jak jeden dzień* by Jerzy Gruza and Krzysztof Teodor Toeplitz, directed by Jerzy Gruza. In terms of its dominant themes and subjects, the mini-series is not precisely defined. Apart from the common features listed above, particular productions of this type are highly individualised and refer to themes that are characteristic of various genres. Thus, the following analysis of the mini-series genre will be based on a reading of one single production, namely *Studenci Trzeciego Wieku...* Comprising 26 episodes and first broadcast on 25 October 2011, *Studenci Trzeciego Wieku...* was inspired by a popular television series from the 1970s entitled *Czterdziestolatek*. The creators of the series intended not only to reach back to the themes and stories from the original series, but also to employ the same team of script-writers who authored the television production. The new mini- series was thus written, directed and performed by the same people who had worked on the original series: Jerzy Gruza, Krzysztof Teodor Toeplitz, Anna Seniuk and Andrzej Kopiczyński.

Czterdziestolatek went down in the history of Polish television as one of the most popular series, and was a brilliantly comical representation of prosperous Poland (Stachówna 1994: 192). The authors of the radio continuation of the adventures of the Karwowski family successfully employed the tropes and conventions of the original series. They not only presented the power mechanisms of contemporary Poland in a humorous way, but also included some commentary and suggestions for social change in their story. While the original series was set in the absurd reality of the People's Republic of Poland, its contemporary counterpart exposes the nonsensical aspects of Poland today. The protagonists of *Studenci Trzeciego Wieku...* seem to be well predisposed to comment critically upon our contemporary reality. Stefan and Madzia Karwowski are now in their seventies and bear the scars of the previous era. On the other hand, they are trying hard to catch up with the dynamically developing modern world: they live on the 25th floor of a luxurious apartment building fitted with a swimming pool, sauna and gym. The Karwowski couple are both physically and intellectually active, as they have enrolled in classes at the University of the Third Age. Stark contrasts between the realities of the twenty-first century and their experiences from the socialist era bring about a series of humorous situations which reveal the protagonists' poor adjustment to modernity. For example, while trying to learn a hymn in Latin they find the words incomprehensible and finally decide to just learn it by heart, without understanding the meaning. They also criticise the contemporary tendency of Polish people to replace Polish words with their English counterparts. Through such protagonists – representing the convergence tradition and modernity – the series creators are able to adopt a specific perspective on reality. The world in the series is seen through the eyes of elderly people who are not hostile towards modernity, but instead try to understand it in relation to their experiences from the past.

The comedy in *Studenci Trzeciego Wieku...* is, to a certain extent, still based on the 'exposure of the institutional aspect of daily reality... and its absurd and surreal manifestations' (Mioduszewska 2006: 156). However, the institutional aspect in the series is presented alongside social and cultural factors, which are also shown in a distorting mirror. The building of the University of the Third Age has no elevator because, according to the doorman's explanation, it is a listed historical site. Queues are as long as in the socialist era, but today people wait in them to enroll for classes rather than buy food. The first episode of the series provides an example of a relevant social commentary, with a scene where a crowd of elderly people are waiting in line in the university hallway, while Magda Karwowska and her husband arrive at the last moment and sign their names in the two last free slots for university candidates. Many people in the waiting crowd are outraged, as they had thought they would be accepted to the university because of the medals they had been awarded in the People's Republic of Poland, but were rejected. The medals are now meaningless, and the recruitment committee is unrelentingly observant of the rules – the order of applications is absolutely decisive. The authors of the story thus reveal how the ruthless rules of the free market are surprisingly similar to the mechanisms which governed the People's Republic of Poland forty years ago.

The structural elements of the series also deserve discussion. Most episodes are characterised by a single main thread, introduced and resolved within one episode, thus constituting complete and individualised plot units. In episode five, for example, Stefan sees in a newspaper a photograph of a Czech model in her late forties. While he raves about the young looks of the woman, Madzia explains to him that the picture has definitely been airbrushed. The theme of the model recurs at the very end of the episode, when Stefan learns from his fellow university students that the airbrushed photographs of the same model under different names often appear in all sorts of press, including adult magazines in particular. Apart from the closed dramatic construction of each episode, the recurrence of motifs from previous episodes is also a characteristic structural device of the series. A case in point is the motif of Mrs. Jola's therapeutic methods: in episode 15, the therapy resulted in the smashing of Madzia's salad bowl; in episode 24, Madzia recalls this event and resents her husband's lack of any reaction to that loss. Finally, many of the episodes end with a punch line or significant statement uttered by one of the characters. For example, at the very end of episode 10 Stefan sums up the strange noises coming from Mrs. Jola's apartment by delivering the following line: 'Fine well, our neighbour is silencing Mr. Attorney with some music.'

Prospects for future development

The radio series is the second, (after the radio play,) most artistically-refined genre of radio art in Poland. The characteristic high quality of this genre can be attributed to the role of public radio, which pioneered the broadcasting of radio series in Poland and spawned its two sub-genres, the radio family saga and the mini-series. So, what about possible directions for the genre's development in the future? The radio series has been present in radio programming for several decades but this long tradition of its presence on air does not translate into a quantity of academic interest in the genre. The use of the serial form is a strategy eagerly employed by radio broadcasters, although the radio novel has recently become significantly more popular than radio series. These factors seem to indicate that the further development, or even the very existence of, radio series might be at risk. Public radio stations continue to be those which broadcast the broadest range of radio series, which may be dictated by public radio's 'missionary' nature and its obligation to foster artistically valuable forms. Nevertheless, in recent years public broadcasters have also displayed a tendency to favour the radio novel over the radio series. While the latter requires an original script, the former can be adapted for the radio merely by abridging the original text. Moreover, recording a several-minute long episode takes no longer than one hour, including editing. The radio novel is thus a quickly produced and relatively cheap form, and is therefore favoured by Polish radio theatre, an institution financed exclusively from small, irregular listener subscriptions.

Commercial radio stations do not broadcast radio series as such, and normally use the term to describe radio novels instead. Serial radio novels are mainly a form of entertainment, and the broadcasters usually tend to spend a larger part of their budget on employing a popular actor instead of providing high quality artistic radio values. Commercial radio stations doubtlessly contribute to the development of the contemporary radio novel by promoting their own adaptations of literary and quasi-literary texts; but nevertheless, their main focus is on popular entertainment and on catering to the expectations of the audience with attractive, sometimes even shocking subject matter. It can reasonably be assumed that the radio novel, read out by actors in episodes, is a form which will continue to develop in Polish radio, as this form of radio entertainment is not only relatively quickly and easily produced and attractive to the mass audience, but it also helps to create in the listeners' minds an association between particular radio stations and the names of popular television and film actors.

Academic radio stations attempt to cultivate the radio series genre by developing their own independent productions and acting performances. Creators of student-oriented series experiment with the means of expression offered by radio with a view to discovering interesting and unexpected artistic effects. Although their actions are both valuable and interesting, their unprofessional nature does not guarantee the development, or even continued existence, of the genre. One invaluable and effective way to preserve the radio series genre would be the continuation of its broadcasting by public radio, whose responsibility over the past several decades has been precisely to maintain the high artistic profile of radio art.

References

Bachura, J (2012) *Odsłony wyobraźni. Współczesne słuchowisko radiowe*, Toruń: Wydawnictwo Adam Marszałek.

Bardijewska, S (2001) *Nagie słowo. Rzecz o słuchowisku*, Warszawa: Dom Wydawniczy 'Elipsa'.

Beliczyński, J (2010) 'Rozwój radia w Polsce latach 1989-2009', in Wolny-Zmorzyński, K, Furman, W, Nierenberg, B & Marszałek-Kawa, J (eds), *Radio i gazety. Transformacja polskich mediów regionalnych po 1989 roku*, Toruń: Wydawnictwo Adam Marszałek.

Czarnek, P (2012) 'Współczesne formy rozrywki w polskim radiu komercyjnym', in Gierula, M & Szostok, P (eds), *Konwergencja mediów masowych i jej skutki dla współczesnego dziennikarstwa*, Katowice: Wydawnictwo Uniwersytetu Śląskiego.

Dudowa, H (1971) 'Powieść nasza powszednia', *Współczesność*, issue 1.

Głowiński, M (2000) 'Powieść radiowa', in Sławiński, J (ed), *Słownik terminów literackich*, Warszawa: Ossolineum.

Helman, A & Pitrus, A (2008) *Podstawy wiedzy o filmie*, Gdańsk: Gdańskie Wydawnictwo Oświatowe.

Jędrzejewski, S (2010) *Radiofonia publiczna w Europie w erze cyfrowej*, Kraków: Universitas.

Jędrzejewski, S (2003) *Radio w komunikacji społecznej. Rola i tendencje rozwojowe*, Warszawa: Profi-Press.

Kisielewska, A (2009) *Polskie tele-sagi – mitologie rodzinności*, Kraków: Wydawnictwo Rabid.

Mioduszewska, Z (2006) 'Społeczna architektura blokowisk', *Kwartalnik Filmowy*, issue 56.

Pleszkun-Olejniczakowa, E (1989) 'Literatura w Polskim Radiu w okresie międzywojennym', *Prace Polonistyczne*, volume 45.

Pleszkun-Olejniczakowa, E (2000) *Sluchowiska Polskiego Radia w okresie piętnastolecia 1925-1939*, Łódź: Wydawnictwo Biblioteka.

Sadowska, A (1972) 'Matysiakowie, czyli o powieści radiowej', *Dialog*, issue 7.

Stachyra, G (2008) *Gatunki audycji w radiu sformatowanym*, Lublin: Wydawnictwo Uniwersytetu Marii Curie-Skłodowskiej.

Stachówna, G (1994) 'Film telewizyjny', in Zajiček, E (ed), *Encyklopedia kultury polskiej XX wieku. Film. Kinematografia*, Warszawa: Instytut Kultury. Komitet Kinematografii.

Steciąg, M (2006) *Informacja, wywiad, felieton: sposób istnienia tradycyjnych gatunków w radiu komercyjnym*, Zielona Góra: Oficyna Wydawnicza Uniwersytetu Zielonogórskiego.

Toeplitz, K, (1970) 'Historia wielkości i upadku Rodziny Matysiaków', in Topelitz, Krzysztof & Teodor, *Mieszkańcy masowej wyobraźni*, Warszawa: PIW.

Uszyński, J (2004) *Telewizyjny pejzaż genologiczny*, Warszawa: Biblioteka Zeszytów Telewizyjnych. www.bagazpodreczny.pl

Chapter 24

'Always on the air, always with you': Rádio Clube Português in 1963

Rogério Santos

Abstract

The slogan 'Always on the air, always with you' reflects the continuity of radio transmission during all 24 hours of the day from 1963 of Rádio Clube Português on its AM frequency. The radio station also launched separate and quite independent FM programming, with a new generation of producers and announcers. The slogan has provided the inspiration for this chapter, the principal objectives of which are to look at the great innovations of 1963, at the actions and careers of the principal agents, the announcers and producers, and their programmes, while also contextualising the changes that took place. As early as 1963, there was a separation of types of radio programming: the most popular Portuguese music programmes with two announcers, male and female, short-three minute newscasts every hour and a lot of advertising as the AM programming, with Anglo-American music and programmes sponsored by companies on FM. Throughout the 1960s, Rádio Clube Português was the most important radio station in Portugal and its programming won large audiences of young people, to whom the programme *In Orbit* would become very special.

Keywords: producers, FM, Rádio Clube Português, Portugal

Introduction

At the beginning of 1960, moving the studios of Rádio Clube Português from Parede (Cascais) to Lisbon brought about a profound alteration to the station's life. The decision was made by Alberto Lima Bastos, one of the founders of the radio station. His rationale was that Lisbon was the country's business centre and Parede's urban growth, just over 20 kilometres from the capital, threatened the quality of transmissions[1]. At first the option didn't seem to be the right one: instead of a house, they went to a garage. But this garage, due to its configuration, enabled the installation of quality studios: six recording booths, a concert studio, a lecture booth, a newsreading booth, three voice booths and four recording studios.

This geographic change brought new people who became responsible for the station, such as Júlio Botelho Moniz. Representing the second generation, son of the founder Jorge Botelho Moniz, vice-president of the board in 1960 and commercial director at the general assembly of Rádio Clube Português in March 1963, he brought impetus to the transformation of the station into a business, and he was responsible for technological innovation and selling airtime to independent producers who sold on advertising time during their programmes. Fifty years ago, in August 1963, Rádio Clube Português became a surprise phenomenon due to the transformation that took place. It introduced continuous transmission 24 hours a day from its transmitter in Parede and the split in programming to begin separate FM and AM stations. A slogan was launched: 'Always on the air, always with you', reflecting the continuity of transmission. It is from the starting point of that slogan that this chapter has been developed, the main objective of which is to examine the great innovations of 1963, as well as the actions and careers of the principal agents, the announcers and producers, and their programmes, while also contextualising the changes at the radio station within some wider socio-political issues of 1960s Portugal.

Voices and programmes

Throughout the history of Portuguese radio many radio voices became known, such as Mary Guilhermina Sylvia Tarrant Rodrigues, who became a symbol of Rádio Clube Português for decades. The daughter of English parents, Mary, as she was popularly known, did almost everything that was possible to be done in a radio station, including programming. She started working in February 1936 and one of the programmes on which she collaborated as an announcer was APA, which we shall return to later in this chapter. Another female voice that resonated with listeners to Rádio Clube Português was that of Clarisse Guerra, the presenter of Tallismã. In 1961, one year before she became the presenter of this programme, Clarisse Guerra applied for a post as an announcer for SNI, (the propaganda service of the regime). In a letter, the director of PIDE, (the political police of the regime,) noted the following information: 'She offers no guarantees that she will cooperate in bringing about the higher ends of the State'[2]. Curiously, she was to become the voice of some of the first communiqués of the military movement that overthrew the regime of the Estado Novo in 1974.

Talismã, a programme by Armando Marques Ferreira and Gilberto Cotta, was first broadcast on 1 December 1952, leading the morning schedule from 07:00. A character created for this programme was Mr Messias, with the voice of Armando Grilo, who spoke every Sunday with an accent that was representative of a certain region of the country. In addition to Portuguese music, *Talismã* had a feature called 'Banco dos Réus' (In the Dock), with actors from the Teatro Nacional, and serials with only one performer, Manuela Reis, who was responsible for the many voices in the stories. According to Armando Marques Ferreira (1915-1995), regarding the programme *Talismã*:

> 'I was in Brazil in Rádio Cultura de São Paulo. I was there for about two years. I asked for my resignation from Emissora [Nacional, in Lisbon] just to come to Rádio Cultura de São Paulo, which invited me. At Rádio Cultura, I was responsible for the noon programme called *Talismã*. The programme was born in Brazil. Later on, when I made *Talismã* here with Gilberto Cotta, I used a title that I had invented and that I had made in Brazil. In fact, I had made it at Rádio Peninsular, when I was still here at Emissora [Nacional] in 1950. Over two months I made a programme on Saturdays at noon called *Talismã*... In Brazil I learned a lot, since this type of relaxed radio programming that I brought to Portugal, such as *Talismã*, which was a big success, and the system of direct dialogue with the presenters, had not yet been done in Portugal. I can proudly say that I was a pioneer'[3].

Another programme that at the time was a big hit of Rádio Clube Português was *Onda do Optimismo* (08:30-10:00), a Sonarte production. Fernando Conde, one of the producers, said:

> 'Artur [Agostinho] brought the records, the tapes, and we made a great programme. It was a big hit. Afterwards, due to Emissora's exclusivity, Artur Agostinho was no longer allowed to speak at the microphone... Meanwhile, we had moved to other studios, which had a certain rigour in technical and quality terms. It was already recorded. For a long time there was a team with [Fernando] Pessa, Etelvina [Lopes de Almeida], Henrique Mendes, and afterwards came Maria Adalgisa, who was a novelty as an announcer, since she was mainly a famous operetta singer. She had a beautiful voice and read very well'[4].

Francisco Igrejas Caeiro's participation in the programming of Rádio Clube Português should also be mentioned here. In 1951, at the end of the Portugal bicycle tour, its organisers invited Igrejas Caeiro to organise shows in the municipalities where each stage of the tour ended. It was the beginning of *Os Companheiros da Alegria*, which became famous for its dialogues between Zequinha and Lélé, with Vasco Santana and Irene Velez, written by Aníbal Nazaré and Nelson de Barros. Caeiro said:

> 'The Portugal tour lasted three weeks. I structured everything for a month, contacted the artists. I went to France to get a 10-seat station wagon: "I buy it and sell it at the end of the month". We made shows at the end of each stage. The reels came by motorcycle or by train and were sent back to Rádio Clube Português on the following day. I brought in new contests. There was *À Procura de Uma Estrela* (In Search of a Star) in each show. During each performance we chose someone to go to the final. The final was in Vila do Conde'[5].

Later on, the programme *Os Companheiros da Alegria* regularly went on tour throughout the country. It was suspended in 1954 when Igrejas Caeiro took a favourable political stance regarding the Indian Union, which had occupied in that country two enclaves Portugal regarded as its own. Even before that, in 1948, Francisco Igrejas Caeiro had been expelled from Emissora Nacional for participating in Norton de Matos' electoral campaign for president of the Republic, as a candidate for the opposition. This man, who was from the theatre, and also a show organiser and an announcer, had to reorganise his professional life, producing radio soap operas and programmes such as *O Casal Caeiro Conversa com o Companheiro Ouvinte Acerca de Literatura* (The Caeiro Couple Talks With the Listener About Literature), *O Casal Caeiro Dá-lhe Uma Ajuda* (The Caeiro Couple Helps You) and *Perfil do Artista* (Profile of the Artist). This last show interviewed 300 people from the arts and the literary field, especially those linked to the political opposition, showing great courage and political backbone, a show that created great upheaval and was eventually forbidden[6].

On the other hand, transmissions of football matches were becoming very popular. Those were the years of Artur Agostinho at Emissora Nacional and of the Produções Lança Moreira at Rádio Clube Português and the small local stations in Lisbon and Oporto. For several years there was a conflict between the football clubs and Emissora Nacional, since the former were afraid of losing spectators if the matches were to be broadcast live on radio. Thus, a recording was made on disc, and was later transmitted at 18:00, when the match ended[7]. Sonarte for Rádio Renascença and Produções Lança Moreira for Rádio Clube Português started to make live and simultaneous transmissions from two or more grounds. Lança Moreira introduced the running commentaries on the matches with two announcers, sports commentaries during intermissions and also advertising. However, we were still far from the dynamism of the Brazilian transmissions, with metaphors and humorous language, which marked the second half of the 1970s and the following years.

Evening programmes: the role of António Miguel (*Meia-Noite*, *Sintonia 63*)

Early every morning Rádio Clube Português went off the air between 03:00 and 06:00. It was thought that there were no listeners during that time. But society was changing: some activities continued throughout the night, such as in hospitals, bakeries, some industries with continuous activity, taxi services and lorries, security, ports and airports. Many people who worked night shifts had the radio to keep them company. One of the measures that was immediately taken under Júlio Botelho Moniz's management was to fill that period of time, so that there would be a continuous transmission. His idea was for a new programme from 03:00 until 06:00 to begin on 24 August 1963, a Saturday. As announced by the newspaper *O Século* on that same day, 'As of today, Rádio Clube Português will start broadcasting without interruption, through its medium and short wave transmitters, from Parede, which is something unique in our country and very unusual abroad'. The inclusion of a news service at 04:45 was another sign of the dynamism of this station. News broadcast at that time was effectively a preview of the themes to be tackled during the subsequent daytime transmissions. António Miguel e Fernando Curado Ribeiro structured the programme in order to have the booth with an open door, so that the telephone would be heard, creating the impression of an active audience, although of course the concept of interactivity, now very familiar to us because of the internet, was still very far away. In a conversation with the author, António Miguel recalled:

'I said to [Júlio] Botelho Moniz: "Hey boss, it looks like they [Emissora Nacional] are going to close". "Then we close today". "It can't be today. Just wait because this needs some time for adjustments. Maybe tomorrow". And that's how it was. From one day to the next, all the transmitters are informed, for this involves some engineering. And the next day we were transmitting something called *Sintonia 63*. That was in 1963. That is, suddenly the station completed the 24-hour cycle. "But what shall we name it, what shall we not name it?" Curado Ribeiro and I "what shall we name it?" "*Sintonia 63*"[8].

Producers and announcers tried new models of radio broadcasting, such as record requests, which resulted, right from the first few days, in many letters and telephone calls supporting the programme, with 25,000 telephone calls in the first year. Matos Maia (1995: 282) considered that this would perhaps be the only programme in which the telephone operators on 682075, the number used to request a record, give general information and make appeals, were the real stars, rather than the presenters. The goals and values of *Sintonia 63* (1963-7) were the same as those promoted in the evening programme until 03:00, the *Meia-Noite* (1959-67). António Miguel had been one of the directors and producers of this last programme, together with Armando Marques Ferreira. At first, the programme *Meia-Noite* ran until 02:00, and later until 03:00, going on to receive an award, the Oscar of the Press, in 1962, for both producers (Maia 1995: 293). Rádio Clube Português positioned itself to face competition from the popular programme *23ª Hora*, on Rádio Renascença, which had begun in 1959. On special days, such as Christmas or Carnival, the *Meia-Noite* would broadcast until seven o'clock. *Sintonia 63* would definitely occupy the time slot that was still available.

The programming on FM

In addition to the continuous transmission on medium wave in the Lisbon area, Rádio Clube Português committed itself to FM, which of course had a better sound quality. On the other hand, it separated this programming from medium wave, accepting young producers and presenters for its programmes - a new generation. The appearance of separate FM programming gave rise to technical discussions on radio transmission and to the introduction of new aesthetics. FM radio would privilege music to the detriment of the announcers' dialogues. At the same time, Portuguese, Latino and South American music was giving way to music from the Anglo-American world. Joel Nelson, Fernando Curado Ribeiro, Produções Lança Moreira, Paulo Fernando, José Nascimento, Teixeira Mota and Duarte Ferreira were all names from the radio world who were invited by Júlio Botelho Moniz to start the FM transmission for Rádio Clube Português[9]. The FM programming changed quite a lot in subsequent years, but it is worth revisiting the first schedule of the beginning of August 1963. Fernando Curado Ribeiro from 08:00 to 10:00, *Estúdio 9* produced by António Miguel and Paulo Fernando with the collaboration of Edite Maria and Manuel Seleiro from 10:00 to 11:00, Produções Lança Moreira from 11:00 to 13:00, a programme by Ribas Martins and Fernando Santos from 13:00 to 15:15, *RPO* (Rádio Press Office) from 15:15 to 17:30 and *Alta Fidelidade* by Duarte Ferreira from 24:00 until 01:00. There were other programmes, such as *Música sem Fronteiras* (Music Without Frontiers) playing Portuguese versions of international hits, *Momento para os Jovens* (Music for Youth) featuring new releases, and *Ritmo da Semana* (Rhythm of the Week).

The FM transmission of Rádio Clube Português was still an intention in search of affirmation, as could be inferred from an interview with Júlio Botelho Moniz, the station's commercial manager, who recommended a network of twelve transmitters all over the country, with the possibility of opt-outs to serve the needs of several regions, making local advertising possible. He seemed to anticipate the flux and decentralisation of local radio stations in the 1980s. Clearly, the luxury of having its own FM transmission was made possible by the money earned from the medium wave service[10]. One of the main producers of the programme *Em Órbita* (In Orbit) and one of the managers of the station, Jorge Gil, later said: 'When FM started, at the beginning we didn't pay anything to Rádio Clube Português... FM was considered a useless extension'[11]. A few years later the station started to charge fees for airtime, allowing producers to set up profitable arrangements during that time. *Em Órbita*, which started on 1 April 1965, won the international prize Onda 67, given by the Catalonian magazine with that same name. Jorge Gil, once told the group responsible for this programme: 'you are always in orbit...'[11] This was at the time of the Sputnik launch. Pedro Albergaria, another producer of the programme, agreed, saying:

> 'What was the programme going to do? Just play records? Did we have to write scripts? I believe we slowly got the formula... Álvaro Jorge, the former manager of Rádio Clube Português, chose the name. He came up with this *Em Órbita*. And, well, at that time, it was really in fashion. Every day, there were things that seemed exciting and new, even more so when something went into orbit. On 1 April 1965, with its opening tune... the only instrumental [The Kinks] recorded [*Revenge*][12].

Joel Nelson, one of the pioneers of FM at Rádio Clube Português, who later became famous for his productions of *Espaço 3P*, which clocked up many transmission hours, created the programme *Boa Noite em FM* (Good Evening on FM), the signature tune of which was an instrumental Portuguese tune, *Boa Noite Lisboa* (Good Evening Lisbon). With this programme, Joel Nelson had a clear goal:

> '[To spark the] interest of the listeners in radio through music. I always thought and still think that FM is eminently for musical transmission. And that was even more so at the time because there was great a differentiation from medium waves... In our understanding, they should touch on topics of general interest, there was cinema, there was music. And, thus, we were present at festivals[13].

APA, news programmes and Luís Filipe Costa

APA (Agência de Publicidade Artística) was an important Portuguese advertising agency following the end of World War 2. Its owner, José Fernando Leitão, initially with Mário Rodrigues Rocha, produced radio programmes and variety shows. Thus the programme *Passatempos APA* came into being, three times a week, either transmitted live or recorded for the Rádio Clube Português medium wave service (1946-58). For a time the programme even had a twenty-four piece orchestra, with two side pianos, conducted by Fernando de Carvalho[14]. Well-known presenters presented the programme, as well as comedy sketches, some of them humourous[15]. APA was in competition with programmes such as *Os Companheiros da Alegria*. Firmino Antunes recalled the 1950s:

'There was an artist who had a great impact on that advertising agency, on *Passatempos APA*. He was Odyr Odillon, a Brazilian artist who made the audience sing – and he was the one who made the money. But the audience didn't mind. He stayed for three consecutive years at *Passatempos APA*. We started with *Passatempos* on Mondays and Fridays. The programme became so successful that it was extended to Mondays, Wednesdays and Fridays. The programmes were not transmitted live, they were recorded by Rádio Clube Português and, quite often, it happened [that] we were transmitting the programme [and] transmitting to the audience'[16].

Here we detect the transition from live transmission to recordings and the importance of exclusive singers, Odyr Odillon, Max, Rui de Mascarenhas, who were then known as radio artists, since they were bound to the programmes of each station. Some of those singers came from the Centro de Preparação de Artistas da Rádio, (a centre for the preparation of radio performers run by Emissora Nacional, created in 1947 and reactivated in 1954), but they were also popularised by the producers of variety shows, (as the light music shows were then called,) a phenomenon that lasted until the middle of the following decade, when television started to win bigger audiences, especially with the Song Festival, which had already started in the 1950s.

APA created an aesthetic and a specific language during the sports afternoons. Domingos Lança Moreira, an APA contributor and author of *Suplemento Desportivo*, would become the main independent producer of radio sports events, with voice, reports and interviews, creating an enterprise with his own name. Luís Filipe Costa, whose professional activity began with the APA programmes, recalled:

'Private radio was some kind of ink that sold hours. Its auto-production was basically based on the presentation of records for half an hour, one hour. Sometimes there was a programme, but that was very rare. [The stations] lived off fees, they charged by the hour, from 10:00 to 11:00, an advertising agency, the so-called producer, who had the freedom to do whatever he wanted, including the advertising he was able to get. Such advertising was, however, more or less kept within some time limits... Afterwards the programme usually consisted of talk between a man and a woman, two presenters'[17].

In 1959, Luís Filipe Costa switched from APA to news broadcasting at Rádio Clube Português, during the move of the station's studios to Lisbon. Through his commitment he earned the nickname of *homem-notícia* (news-man). The praise came in regularly, given the fact that the news didn't simply follow the information that poured into the newsroom on the telexes, but also information transmitted by news agencies such as France Presse and foreign broadcasters. The news bulletins were composed of short, related stories, creating a narrative as if they were advertising spots or documentary films. According to António Miguel, this system of short news bulletins grew out of the requirements of the programme *Meia-Noite*. Since bossa nova, the new Brazilian musical genre, was just making its appearance, this news broadcast at 00:45 came to be known by that name.

Advertising and independent producers

Advertising is essential for some radio stations. Although not referring to Rádio Clube Português, the rates that were in force in 1961 were around 500 escudos per day for fifteen-minute programmes, such as that produced and written by Mário Lisboa, *Cavalgada do Ritmo*, for Rádio Graça[18]. Of that amount, Mário Lisboa would get 220 escudos, for he would obtain the advertising. 500 escudos was the average monthly salary for a radio announcer, which was then a highly paid profession. This was still the time of programmes with just one advertiser or with several in a very short time-frame, which was not popular with many listeners. Therefore, Júlio Botelho Moniz took a critical look at some producers, as he recalled when interviewed:

> 'I believed that... the best solution was the entire production of the station and the sale of time slots to producers. With competition, the tendency would bring improvements. In the particular case of Rádio Clube Português, that has been the system and only the extraordinary demand for time had led us to abdicate, partly, from that process. This, in fact, only benefited independent producers'[19].

The ideal, he added, would be to reduce the percentage of advertising, to improve the commercial production, which would then improve programmes and, thus, the price of the advertisement would then increase and provide the producers with a higher income. If, on the side of radio stations there was a recognition that processes would have to be reviewed, on the side of advertisers small changes were taking place. During the 1950s it was normal for an enterprise to exclusively sponsor a programme, with the production of scripts of some literary worth; however, at the beginning of the 1960s, with the advent of international advertising agencies, the recurrent spot became predominant, and it was then possible for several brands to advertise in just one programme, especially the longer ones, which lasted one and a half or two hours.

The issue between independent producers and station owners was an old one. It was the former who paid for transmissions on medium wave. Rádio Clube Português could not dispense with that and might not have intended to change everything, for that would mean having to create programmes and get advertising themselves and take on more full-time employees. The defence of renting transmission slots meant the existence of a great variety of producers with new ideas, renewing schedules, attracting new listeners and, thus, new advertising. There was a permanent oscillation between independent production and station production, with a third option, that of announcers-producers. That is, they had a link with the station, with a base salary for that activity, and they could exploit time slots, getting their own advertising and paying a rent to the station. Confusions could arise if, when interrupting the programme, the announcer would announce a news broadcast in collaboration with sponsor of that programme. Rádio Clube Português, using its Oporto transmitter, tried a fourth option: most of the programming was their own, and they rented only a few time slots[20], as with FM.

Wider contexts

During this period, Portugal was under a dictatorial regime. Rádio Clube Português came into being in 1931 and its management, especially its founder, Jorge Botelho Moniz, always followed very closely the regime's guidelines. The colonial war, which had started in 1961 on three African fronts, was in a deadlock or was leaning towards Portugal's defeat. The heads of the dictatorship didn't accept the situation and had conducted an internal propaganda campaign, in which the enemy was the countries of the Soviet bloc, which encouraged and supported the African 'terrorists'. In 1963, the imprisonment of some members of the Communist Party, such as Blanqui Teixeira, was a great victory for the political regime, which was amplified by the newspapers. On the other hand, the effort placed on internal propaganda was quite evident: Salazar made several speeches and there were demonstrations of support for his policies, with enterprises encouraging their workers to participate in such endeavours. Américo Tomás, the president of the Republic, paid a visit to Angola, which was highly praised by the newspapers, showing large crowds welcoming him. Newspapers and the media in general were under heavy censorship. Just as in other radio stations, Rádio Clube Português had its own censor, appointed by the regime, but there was a good relationship between them, which was recorded in the minutes of the general-assembly of the station, praising lieutenant-colonel José Raposo Pessoa, the delegate from the Government appointed to Rádio Clube Português, for the trust he placed in all acts of management.

Conclusions

How did the station innovate? I have some suggestions, which are still working hypotheses. The announcers and producers had to keep records of musical repertoires and negotiated with sources of advertising funding. That made them become trend setters, especially on FM and with their evening programmes on medium wave. The programmes with more impact worked as the drivers of the whole programming. Aside from the internal factors, such as the increase in transmission hours and greater competition among professionals within stations and between stations, there were also external factors, such as competition with television and the mass phenomenon of a change in musical tastes from Portuguese and Latin European music to Anglo-American music. This last trend was called by some people 'denationalisation of music'.

Endnotes

[1] Interview with Jorge Botelho Moniz, by Luís Garlito, 6 February 1995, RTP Archive, AHD 2646.

[2] Minute of 7 September 1961 from the direction of PIDE to SNI (PT/TT/SNI-DSC/A/4/1, SNI, Censorship, Box 465).

[3] Interview with Armando Marques Ferreira, by Luís Garlito, on 5 September 1991, RTP Archive, AHD 12028.

[4] Interview with Fernando Conde, by Luís Garlito, on 29 January 1992, RTP Archive, AHD 14792.

[5] Interview with Francisco Igrejas Caeiro (and Irene Velez), by Luís Garlito and Cristina Paula Carvalho, on 24 April 1991, RTP Archive, AHD 11872.

[6] Interview with Francisco Igrejas Caeiro (and Irene Velez), by Luís Garlito and Cristina Paula Carvalho, on 24 April 1991, RTP Archive, AHD 11872.

[7] Interview with Fernando Conde, by Luís Garlito, on 29 January 1992, RTP Archive, AHD 14792.

[8] Interview given by António Miguel to the author, 2 November 2011.

[9] Interview with Joel Nelson, by Luís Garlito, on 23 April 1996, RTP Archive, AHD 2844.

[10] Interview with Jorge Botelho Moniz, by Luís Garlito, on 6 February 1995, RTP Archive, AHD 2646.

[11] Interview given by Jorge Gil to the author, 17 January 2012.

[12] Interview with Pedro Albergaria, by Luís Garlito, on 1 June 1995, RTP Archive AHD 14946.

[13] Interview with Joel Nelson, by Luís Garlito, on 23 April 1996, RTP Archive, AHD 2844.

[14] Interview with Firmino Antunes, by Luís Garlito, on 28 April 1992, RTP Archive, AHD 14778.

[15] Interview given by Luís Filipe Costa to the author, 27 January 2012.

[16] Interview with Firmino Antunes, by Luís Garlito, on 28 April 1992, RTP Archive, AHD 14778.

[17] Interview given by Luís Filipe Costa to the author, 27 January 2012.

[18] Letter from Mário Graça to SNI, 13 February 1962 (PT/TT/SNI-DSC/A/4/1, SNI, Censorship, Box 465).

[19] *Rádio e Televisão*, 13 April 1963.

[20] Interview given by Rui Melo to the author, 25 June 2012.

Reference

Maia, M (1995) *Telefonia*, Lisbon: Círculo de Leitores.

Author biographies

Irati Agirreazkuenaga was awarded a PhD in journalism and radio communication by the University of the Basque Country in 2013. She is currently a postdoctoral researcher at the Department of Media and Communications of the London School of Economics and Political Science, where she is developing a research project entitled 'Political participation and ordinary people in public media: Building participatory citizenship?' In 2011 and 2014 she completed visiting fellowships at the University of Glasgow Centre for Cultural Policy Research, investigating minority languages in the media, public broadcasting companies, convergence processes in media newsrooms, political participation and citizenship. Her publications include 'The role of the media in empowering minority identities' in *Media, Culture & Society*.

Karolina Albińska is a PhD candidate at the University of Łódź, Poland, researching hybrid radio genres. She is a graduate of the university's department of journalism and social communication, with an MA in English Philology from AHE where she majored in translation. A member of the Łódź school of radio studies and the society of radio art fans, Radiofania, her scientific interests lie in the fields of social communication in the environment of media convergence, namely radio visualisation, as well as the historical development of such genres as radio drama and radio breakfast shows. She has authored more than thirty academic articles.

Joanna Bachura-Wojtasik is a doctor of humanities and an assistant professor in the department of journalism and social communication at the University of Łódź in Poland. She is the author of *Odsłony wyobraźni. Współczesne słuchowisko radiowe* (Scenes of Imagination: A Contemporary Radio Play) published in Poland in 2012 and the co-author (with Elżbieta Pleszkun-Olejniczakowa and Aleksandra Pawlik, of *Dwa teatry: Studia z zakresu teorii i interpretacji sztuki słuchowiskowej* (Two Theatres: Research in the Theory and Interpretation of the Art of the Radio Play) published in Poland in 2011. Her research interests are radio, especially artistic radio genres, and contemporary culture, its transformation, properties and functions.

Richard Berry is Senior Lecturer in Radio at the University of Sunderland, who currently also manages the university's community radio station, Spark FM, for which he also researched and wrote the licence application to the regulator, Ofcom. He is a graduate of the University of Humberside, (now the University of Lincoln,) and the University of London. He previously worked in local radio news and further education before joining the University of Sunderland in 1997, where he now teaches undergraduate and postgraduate radio production and broadcasting. Since 2004 he has been researching and teaching on the impacts of new technologies in radio, specifically in the areas of digital radio, podcasting and visualised radio.

Monika Białek is an assistant professor at the cultural studies institute of the University of Gdansk in Poland. Her work is focused on media communication, and radio broadcasting in particular. She is professionally associated with Polski Radio, where she previously worked as a reporter. Monika is the author of several publications about different artistic forms of radio features. She published a book entitled *Polish Radio Features: Selected Issues*, in which, as the first scholar in Poland to do so, she presented a taxonomy and typology of the radio feature and analysed its structural properties and use of the characteristics of radio as a means of expression.

María Blanco has a PhD in communication from UPSA, Spain, and obtained the qualification of *distinction cum laude* and a PhD extraordinary award from the Pontifical University of Salamanca. Her research focuses on new media, such as podcasting, and linguistic analysis, which was the subject matter of her doctoral thesis.

Tiziano Bonini was elected a vice-chair of the ECREA Radio Research Section in November 2014. He was awarded a PhD in media, communication and the public sphere from the University of Siena in 2008, and is a lecturer in media studies at the IULM University of Milan. He has published extensively on radio and new media, and he co-edited the book *Radio Audiences and Participation in the Age of the Network Society* (Routledge, 2015). His current research interests are the intersection between radio, the internet and social media, digital ethnography, public service media, production studies, freelance work in the creative industries and issues around digital free labour. Since 2005 he has also worked as a freelance radio producer, winning the special mention at the swiss public radio documentary awards.

Paulina Czarnek is a research and teaching assistant at the department of journalism and social communication at the University of Łódź, Poland. In her academic research, as well as in her doctoral dissertation, she concentrates on the types of entertainment offered by Polish commercial radio stations. A member of the Łódź radio school, she is a board member of the Radiofania association. She is also the author of 24 academic papers, the editor of the book *Entertainment in Media*, published in 2012 and the author of numerous articles in the university magazine *Kronika UŁ*.

Urszula Doliwa has a PhD and is an assistant professor and the vice director of the institute of journalism and social communication at the University of Warmia and Mazury, Poland. She is author of the book *Radio studenckie w Polsce* (Student Radio in Poland). Nowadays her research interests focus on community media, non-commercial radio and local radio stations. She is a secretary of the Community Media Forum Europe and a member of the Editorial Board of the Polish journal *Media-Kultura-Komunikacja Społeczna* (Media-Culture-Social Communication).

Esther Dorn-Fellermann has been a research assistant at the Deutsche Welle academy in Bonn, Germany since April 2014. Her field is media development in the department of studies and evaluation. Her PhD thesis focused on community radio stations in South Africa and their contribution to civil society. She initially studied political science, media studies and European anthropology at the Friedrich-Wilhelms University in Bonn, Germany and worked as a research assistant for the department of media studies there. Her special research interests are audio media, journalism cultures, democratisation processes and media systems.

Eva María Ferreras Rodríguez gained her first degree in advertising and public relations at Complutense University, Madrid, in 1999, then another in journalism at the Carlos III University, Madrid, in 2002, and then a PhD in journalism from the University of the Basque Country in 2010. Her research is focused on digital journalism, social networks, and on the impact of new ways of communication.

Susana Herrera Damas has a PhD from the Carlos III University, Madrid, a bachelor degree in audiovisual communication (1998) and one in sociology (2004). She also has a PhD in audiovisual communication from the University of Navarra (2002). A full professor at the Carlos III University, Madrid, she teaches radio journalism there and she is researching into ways in which mainstream media might best embrace social media to improve the quality of journalism. She has been a visiting professor at the Universities of Ottawa (Canada) and Texas (United States).

Stanisław Jedrzejewski is a professor in the department of social science at Kozminski University, Poland, as well as a former member and vice-chairman of the European Broadcasting Union Radio Committee, (1995-2007). He was a board member of the public radio broadcaster Polski Radio (1994-98), the programme director of Polski Radio (1990-93) and the controller of Polski Radio 1 (2003-5). A former member of the Polish national broadcasting council, he was also the chairman of the supervisory board of public radio in Poland (2011-2014). He worked at the communication and society research centre at the University of Minho, Braga, Portugal (2009-11) and he is the author of several studies, articles and reports on radio and new media.

Evangelia Karathanasopoulou studied classical music in Athens, and then came to the United Kingdom to study radio. She gained a First Class (Hons) BA in Media Production: Television and Radio at the University of Sunderland and an MA in Radio at Goldsmiths College, University of London. She has worked as a radio producer and presenter in Greece and the United Kingdom. She gained her PhD at the University of Sunderland, researching radio theory and issues around the radio voice and intimacy. She is now Associate Lecturer in Audio Production at Bournemouth University, UK.

Olatz Larrea is an assistant researcher and lecturer in the communication department at Pompeu Fabra University (Barcelona). She has an MSc in social communication from the Pompeu Fabra University, and she is a visiting researcher in The Voice Neurocognition Laboratory at Glasgow University, UK. Currently teaching public speaking courses to undergraduate students, she is a published author of papers and book chapters about radio, audio, voice perception and communication.

Ainara *Larrondo* is a senior lecturer at the University of the Basque Country, where she lectures in online news writing, media convergence and journalism genres, as well as on masters programmes in multimedia communication and communication research. In 2012 she was a visiting researcher at the Centre for Cultural Policy Research of the University of Glasgow, where she investigated newsroom convergence, later publishing findings in *Media, Culture & Society* and *Journalism Studies*. She has participated in several national and international research groups and she is author and co-author of such books as *The Impact of the Internet on the Mass Media in the Basque Country*, *Genres in Journalistic Newswriting: Context, Theory and Practice*, *Journalistic Design on the Internet* and *Shaping the News Online: Comparative Research on International Quality Media*.

Lluís Mas has a PhD in audiovisual communication and advertising with honours from the Universidad Autónoma de Barcelona, Spain. He is a visiting professor in the communication department of Universidad Pompeu Fabra in Barcelona, Spain. He is a lecturer in audio advertising production. His current research focuses on the impact of audio elements and forms of nonverbal communication, especially voice and prosody, on information processing in the media.

Koldo Meso has a PhD in journalism and he is a senior lecturer in the subject at the faculty of social and communication sciences of the University of the Basque Country, where he teaches subjects related to media models and online journalism. He was formerly the director of the digital journalism course of the Asmoz Fundation, organised by the Basque studies society and one of the two departments of journalism at the University of the Basque Country faculty of communication. His main research fields are new technologies and cyberjournalism.

Madalena Oliveira was elected chair of the ECREA Radio Research Section in November 2014. She is an assistant professor at the institute of social sciences at the University of Minho, Portugal, where she is the coordinator of a masters programme in communication sciences and vice-chair of the communication and society research centre. Her PhD was on metajournalism, but since 2010 she has been working mainly in the field of radio studies. She is the principal investigator of the project NET Station: Shaping radio for web environment, funded by the Portuguese foundation for science and technology. She is general secretary of Sopcom, the Portuguese association of communication sciences, within which she also coordinates the radio and audio group.

Simon Order is a senior lecturer in the School of Arts at Murdoch University in Western Australia. His specialist teaching areas include radio studies, radio production, sound production and music technology. Simon has been actively involved in the delivery and development of sound and radio curricula for further and tertiary education since 1993. His research interests currently focus on the value of community radio and mobile music technology. Simon is a believer in the power of audio for unlocking the creative potential within students. He continues his professional practice as a composer and producer of electronic music.

Aleksandra Pawlik has taught journalism and cultural studies since 2008, currently at the department of journalism and social communication at the University of Łódź, Poland. Her research interests include radio theory, in particular radio art, and art in mass media. The author of more than a dozen academic articles as well as international post-conference publications in Belarus, Czech Republic and Russia, she co-authored *Dwa Teatry: Studia z zakresu teorii i interpretacji słuchowiska radiowego* (Two Theatres: Studies in Theory and Interpretation of Radio Drama) (Torun, 2011). Her doctoral dissertation focused on the typology of radio drama, with a special focus on the genres of radio plays and radio series.

Carmen Peñafiel Saiz gained her PhD in journalism from the University of the Basque Country in 1992, later serving as a member of the university senate, the governing council, and then the board of directors. Previously she worked at Cadena SER, Radio Popular de Bilbao and Radio Euskadi-EITB, in management, news, and cultural and entertainment programmes. She is currently researching into communication and health. A founding member of the International Radio Research Network (IREN) and a member of the scientific committee of the francophone radio research group, GRER, she is on the scientific council of TELOS (Telefónica Foundation) and she has been the coordinator of the digital and cultural communication section of the Asociación Española de la Investigación en Comunicación (AE-IC).

Elżbieta Pleszkun-Olejniczakowa is professor and chair of the department of journalism and social communication at the University of Łódź, Poland, having set up and run the first Polish school of radio studies there. Her academic interests are focused mainly on artistic radio, namely radio drama and artistic radio reportage, a genre which is very similar to the western radio feature. Her recent research is usually presented in a wide interdisciplinary context, including, among others, anthropology, cultural sociology, social psychology, media studies and socio-cultural communication. She has authored almost seventy publications, including four books.

Ana Isabel Reis gained her PhD at the University of Minho, Portugal, and is professor of journalism at the department of journalism and communication sciences at the University of Porto, where she teaches radio journalism, comparative journalism, and specialised journalism. A researcher at the communication sciences and technologies research center CETAC.MEDIA and at the cyberjournalism observatory ObCiber, she coordinates the online academic journal *JPN*, published by students of communication sciences at the University of Porto. She was radio journalist for 18 years.

José Luis Requejo Alemán gained his bachelor degree in journalism in 1997 and his PhD in public communication in 2001 at the Universidad de Navarra. He is a full professor at the Carlos III University, Madrid, where he teaches communication theory and research methods in journalism. He has been a Visiting Professor at the University of Texas (United States) and at the Södertörns högskola in Sweden. At present he is researching new funding models for non-profit making investigative journalism.

Emma Rodero has a MA in journalism and a PhD in communication. She lectures at Pompeu Fabra University in Barcelona, Spain, but she is currently in the United States as a Marie Curie Research Fellow at the Institute for Communication Research of Indiana University and the Speech Processing and Auditory Perception Lab at the University of California, Los Angeles. With a MA in cognition and communication from the Autonomous University, Spain, and in voice pathologies from Alcala de Henares University, she is also a PhD candidate in psychology and an author of around forty scientific papers or book chapters about communication, audio and speech.

Rogério Santos gained his PhD in communication sciences in 2002, becoming associate professor and coordinator of the scientific area of communication sciences at the Catholic University of Portugal (2006-13). He has taught communication theory, media history, sociology of media and journalism studies. He published the journal *Media XXI* (2003-2005) and was head of CESOP, the Centre for Studies and Opinion Polls (2010-2012). His most recent books include writing *Do jornalismo aos media: Estudos sobre a realidade portuguesa* (From Journalism to the Media: Studies on the Portuguese Reality) (2010) and editing *Os dias dos media - uma análise de estruturas organizativas* (The Days of Media - an Analysis of Organisational Structures) (2012).

Toni Sellas is associate lecturer in the philology and communication department at the Universitat de Girona having gained a PhD in communication sciences at the Universitat Internacional de Catalunya. His main research areas include cultural industries, public relations, new media technologies and social media. As a result, he has published articles in such journals as *The Radio Journal, Communication & Society* and *El profesional de la información*. He also contributed to the European Broadcasting Union report *Why it Works*. Before joining the academy, he worked for a decade at several radio stations in Catalonia such as Catalunya Ràdio, Ona Catalana and RAC1.

Grażyna Stachyra was re-elected a vice-chair of the ECREA Radio Research Section in November 2014. She is an assistant professor with a PhD in media communication from the Maria Curie-Skłodowska University in Lublin, Poland. The author of numerous books and papers on radio communication, previously she gained long-term experience as a radio journalist, becoming the Vice Chair of Radio Centrum in Lublin, head of the news department and a consultant on speech programming. She also worked actively as a NGO coach and advisor. Her main research areas are new forms of radio genres, anthropological contexts of radio communication, aesthetics of modern radio and the convergence process in contemporary radio.

Guy Starkey is Professor of Radio and Journalism at the Centre for Research in Media and Cultural Studies of the University of Sunderland, United Kingdom, where he was Associate Dean (Media) (2007-8) and Head of the Department of Media (2008-10). He was Chair of the Radio Research Section of ECREA (2008-14), and a member of the ECREA Executive Board (2013-14). A former radio producer and presenter who broadcasts daily on internet radio, his academic publications include *Local Radio, Going Global* (Palgrave Macmillan, 2015), *Radio in Context*, second edition (Palgrave Macmillan, 2014), *Radio Journalism* (with Professor Andrew Crisell, Sage, 2009) and *Balance and Bias in Journalism: Representation, Regulation and Democracy* (Palgrave Macmillan, 2007).

Miroslawa Wielopolska-Szymura is an assistant professor at the institute of political science and journalism at the University of Silesia, Poland. Her PhD thesis concerned the formation of cultural policy in Poland in the years 1989-2000. Her research interests are focused on public media, especially radio, but also radio more generally. She is also interested in intercultural communication and the social and cultural impact of the media. She served as spokesperson for the University of Silesia and she was also a journalist. Currently a member of the audit committee of the The Polish Communication Association (PCA), she is also the editor of books and the author of articles on media and journalism.